ESSENTIAL
SHAREPOINT® 2010

ESSENTIAL
SHAREPOINT® 2010

OVERVIEW, GOVERNANCE, AND PLANNING

Scott Jamison
Susan Hanley
Mauro Cardarelli

With Contributions from

Chris Bortlik and Donal Conlon

✦Addison-Wesley

Upper Saddle River, NJ • Boston • Indianapolis • San Francisco
New York • Toronto • Montreal • London • Munich • Paris • Madrid
Capetown • Sydney • Tokyo • Singapore • Mexico City

Many of the designations used by manufacturers and sellers to distinguish their products are claimed as trademarks. Where those designations appear in this book, and the publisher was aware of a trademark claim, the designations have been printed with initial capital letters or in all capitals.

The authors and publisher have taken care in the preparation of this book, but make no expressed or implied warranty of any kind and assume no responsibility for errors or omissions. No liability is assumed for incidental or consequential damages in connection with or arising out of the use of the information or programs contained herein.

The publisher offers excellent discounts on this book when ordered in quantity for bulk purchases or special sales, which may include electronic versions and/or custom covers and content particular to your business, training goals, marketing focus, and branding interests. For more information, please contact:

U.S. Corporate and Government Sales
(800) 382-3419
corpsales@pearsontechgroup.com

For sales outside the United States, please contact:

International Sales
international@pearson.com

Visit us on the Web: informit.com/aw

Library of Congress Cataloging-in-Publication Data

Jamison, Scott.
  Essential SharePoint 2010 : overview, governance, and planning / Scott
Jamison, Susan Hanley, Mauro Cardarelli.
      p.   cm.
  Includes index.
  ISBN 978-0-321-70075-9 (pbk. : alk. paper)
  1. Intranets (Computer networks) 2. Microsoft SharePoint (Electronic resource)
I. Hanley, Susan, 1956- II. Cardarelli, Mauro. III. Title.
  TK5105.875.I6J352 2010
  004.6'82—dc22

                                                    2010014024

Pearson Education, Inc.
Rights and Contracts Department
501 Boylston Street, Suite 900
Boston, MA 02116
Fax: (617) 671-3447

ISBN-13: 978-0-321-70075-9
ISBN-10:   0-321-70075-9

Text printed in the United States on recycled paper at Edwards Brothers in Ann Arbor, Michigan.
Third printing, September 2011

To my close friends and family, who supported me tremendously during the writing of this book.

—Scott

To my youngest son, Corey, and my husband, Bruce, who had many dinners and many weekends to fend for themselves while I worked on writing this book. And to my older children, Brian and Jamie, who reminded Corey that I can't really cook anyway.

—Susan

CONTENTS

Foreword xix
Preface xxi
Acknowledgments xxv
About the Authors xxvii
About the Contributors xxix

PART I   PLANNING **1**

Chapter 1   Getting Started **3**

Reader's Guide 4
Planning a Successful SharePoint Solution Strategy 5
    Key Stakeholders 7
    Business Objectives 9
    Measuring Success 15
Key Points 19

Chapter 2   Introduction to the SharePoint 2010 Platform **21**

Microsoft's Collaboration Evolution 23
    Exchange as a Collaboration Platform 23
    Office Server Extensions and SharePoint Team Services 24
    SharePoint Portal Server 2001 24
    Windows SharePoint Services 2.0 25
    SharePoint Portal Server 2003 25
    Windows SharePoint Services 3.0 25
    Microsoft Office SharePoint Server 2007 26
Current Versions of SharePoint Products and Technologies 26
    Microsoft SharePoint Foundation 2010 26
    Microsoft SharePoint Server 2010 27

Microsoft SharePoint Server 2010 and Office 2010 27
   Operating System Services:
     Windows Server 2008 SP2 (64-bit) 28
   Database Services: Microsoft SQL Server 28
   Workflow Services: Windows Workflow Foundation 29
   Web Page Services: ASP.NET 29
   Collaboration Services 29
   Portal 29
   Enterprise Content Management (ECM) 30
   Search 30
   Social Computing (Communities) 30
   Business Intelligence (Insights) 30
   Composite Applications (Composites) 30
SharePoint 2010: What's New? 32
Comparing SharePoint Foundation to Microsoft SharePoint
   Server 2010 34
SharePoint: The File Share Killer 35
   File Storage Is Not Dead 38
SharePoint: The Access and Excel Killer 45
   Walkthrough 46
Key Points 57

Chapter 3   **SharePoint 2010: Architecture Fundamentals** **61**

Functional Overview 61
   Operating System 62
   Database Services 62
   SharePoint Foundation 2010 62
   Application Features 63
   Service Applications 64
SharePoint Fundamentals 65
   Sites and Site Collections 66
   Site Templates 74
SharePoint Lists, Libraries, and Items 78
Pages 80
Navigation 81
   Adding Service Applications to the Mix 83
   Putting It All Together 84
Understanding SharePoint Administration 84
   Central Administration 85

Site Collection Settings 86
Site Settings 87
Physical Deployment Options 89
Single-server Deployment 90
Two-server Deployment 90
Three-server Deployment 91
Four-server Deployment 91
Five-server Deployment 91
N-server Deployment 91
Key Points 94

Chapter 4   Planning for Governance **97**
Why Is Governance Planning So Important? 97
How Do I Create a Governance Plan? 100
What Is in the Governance Plan? 100
Vision Statement 102
Roles and Responsibilities 103
Guiding Principles 106
Policies and Standards 112
Key Points 121

Chapter 5   Planning Your Information Architecture **123**
Getting Started 125
Site Architecture 129
Page Architecture 135
Metadata Architecture 138
Content Types 142
Columns 146
Managed Metadata 152
Maintaining Your Information Architecture 161
Key Points 161

Chapter 6   Making Enterprise Content Management Work:
Documents and Records **163**
Getting Started with ECM 164
What's New for ECM in SharePoint 2010? 165
Document IDs 165
Document Sets 165

Managed Metadata 166
Content Type Syndication 166
Content Organizer 166
In-place Records Management 167
Document Management 167
Document Libraries 167
Item-level Security 168
Versioning Settings 168
Document Sets 175
Document IDs 178
Managed Metadata 180
Workflow 182
Document Information Panel 184
Document Center 185
Records Management 186
Record Declaration 186
Auditing 189
Information Management Policies 190
Walkthrough: Configuring Enterprise
Document and Records Management 192
Key Points 199

Chapter 7   Getting Social: Leveraging Community Features 201

Getting Started: Developing a Strategy for
SharePoint Community Features 202
Clearly Identify the Business Problem 203
Identify Use Cases 205
Be Prepared to Respond to Barriers 205
Define Your Governance Plan 209
Define a "Do-able" Pilot Project 216
Prepare a Launch and Communications Plan 216
Social Networking: Engaging People 217
User Profile 217
Status Updates and Activity Feeds 219
Organization Browser 219
Content 221
Memberships 222

Social Data: Enhancing Value with User Contributed Content 223
    Tags and Notes 224
    Ratings 227
Social Sites: Providing a Structure for Collaborative
  Conversations 230
    Blogs 230
    Wikis 232
Key Points 237

Chapter 8   **Planning Your Security Model** **239**

Overview of SharePoint Security Elements 240
    Securable Objects 240
    People and Groups 244
    Permissions 249
Defining and Documenting SharePoint Security 252
    Step 1: List and Describe Where Unique Security
    Is Required 253
    Step 2: List and Describe Who Needs Access 257
    Step 3: List and Describe the Permission Levels 257
    Step 4: Define and Create the SharePoint Security
      Groups You Need 257
    Step 5: Apply Security Permissions 260
Maintaining Your Security Model 263
    Checking Permissions Assigned to a Group 263
    Displaying Permission Levels on an Object 264
    Troubleshooting 266
Key Points 268

Chapter 9   **Getting Ready to Launch: Planning for**
                 Training and Communications **271**

Training 272
    Audience 273
    Timing 274
    Approach 277
Communications 282
Key Points 289

PART II   **OPTIMIZING** **291**

Chapter 10   **Making Search Work: Content, People, Data** **293**

Search as a Business Capability 293
Using Search 294
   Keywords 296
   Property Filters 296
   Prefix Matching 297
   Inclusions and Exclusions 297
   Boolean Expressions 297
   Numeric Values 297
   URL Searches 298
   Alerts 298
   Using Advanced Search 298
   Searching from Within Office 299
How SharePoint Search Works 300
   The User Experience 300
   Index and Query Components 302
Analyzing and Designing Search 303
   Business Analysis 304
   Creating a Business Requirements Document 304
   Creating a Design Document 305
   Planning 307
Configuring Search 312
   Configuration Overview 312
   Adding and Configuring Content Sources 313
   Federated Locations 315
   Authoritative Pages and Demoted Sites 316
   Metadata Properties 316
   Search Scopes 317
   Search User Interface 318
   Keywords and Best Bets 318
Monitoring and Enhancing Search 319
SharePoint 2010 Search: What's New? Limitations?
Flavors? 319
   SharePoint Server 2010 Search Limitations 320
   What Flavor of SharePoint 2010 Search Is Right for You? 320
Key Points 322

Chapter 11 **Making Business Processes Work:**
Workflow and Forms **325**

Getting Started with Workflow 325
Workflow Terminology 327
Templates, Associations, and Instances 327
Using the Provided Workflows 328
Associating a Workflow with a List 330
Testing Your Workflow 331
Starting the Workflow from the Item Workflow Page 332
Starting the Workflow from Office 2010 Client 335
Checking the Workflow Status 335
Creating Custom Workflows with SharePoint Designer 2010 338
Introducing SharePoint Designer (for Workflow Development) 340
Workflow Types 341
Workflow Association Options 343
Workflow Actions 343
Creating a Simple Workflow 343
Testing Our Workflow 351
Designing Workflows with Visio 2010 354
Designing a Visio Workflow 355
Importing the Workflow into SharePoint Designer 357
Using InfoPath 2010 to Create Electronic Forms 360
Introduction to InfoPath 361
Creating an InfoPath Form 362
Publish the Form to a SharePoint Library 366
Testing the Published InfoPath Form 367
InfoPath Forms Services 369
Key Points 371

Chapter 12 **Putting Your Site on the Web** **373**

Why SharePoint for Internet-facing Web Sites? 374
Web Content Management: The Basics 375
Web Publishing 101: Publishing Sites 377
Content Deployment: Key Terms and Architecture 380
What Has Improved in SharePoint 2010
Web Content Management? 382
Richer User Experience 383

Additional Features 385
    Content Organizer 386
    Managed Metadata 387
    User Ratings 388
    Web Reporting and Analytics 389
    Social Networking 389
Customizing the User Experience (UX) 389
    Working with Master Pages 390
    Working with Page Layouts 392
    Media Field Control 394
Putting It All Together: A WCM Strategy 395
Key Points 397

Chapter 13   Making Business Intelligence Work 399

Getting Started with Business Intelligence 400
    Reports 400
    Charts 402
    Dashboards 402
    Scorecards 403
    Key Performance Indicators (KPIs) 404
Which Presentation Tool Is Right for You? 405
Excel Services 406
    Getting Started with Excel Services 408
    How Does Excel Services Work? 408
    What's New in Excel Services with SharePoint 2010? 410
PerformancePoint Services 411
    How Does PerformancePoint Services Work? 412
    Why Use PerformancePoint Services? 412
    What's New with PerformancePoint Services in
    SharePoint 2010? 413
Visio Services 414
    Why Use Visio Services? 415
Putting It All Together 415
Key Points 417

**Chapter 14   Composite Applications with
                   Business Connectivity Services 419**

What Is a Composite Application? 420
Introducing Business Connectivity Services 420

BCS Components 421
    External Content Types 421
Types of BCS Solutions 422
Getting Started with BCS 423
    Creating an External Content Type 424
    Creating an External List in SharePoint 427
    Adding Custom Actions to an External Data List 430
Using an External Data column 432
Building a Composite Application 432
Key Points 436

Chapter 15   Office 2010 Client Applications **439**

What's New in Office 2010? 440
Office Client Applications That Connect with SharePoint 2010 441
SharePoint Workspace: Taking a SharePoint Site Offline 444
Documents and Data Caching 450
    Documents 450
    Other Considerations: Synchronization of Office
        Document Changes and Branch Cache 453
    Data 454
    Recommendations 457
Backstage 457
Other Clients: Office Web Applications and Office
    Mobile Applications 459
    Office Web Applications 461
    Office Mobile Applications 462
Key Points 462

**Chapter 16   Planning for Disaster Recovery:
                Backing Up and Restoring** **465**

Disaster Recovery Planning 466
    Creating a Disaster Recovery (DR) Operations Document 466
Backup and Restore Options 467
    Central Administration Backup and Restore Tool 468
    Command-line Backup Tools 479
    Two-level Recycle Bin 480
    SQL Server Backup 483
What's Not Covered in a SharePoint Backup 484
Key Points 486

PART III   MIGRATING **487**

Chapter 17   Planning Your Move from SharePoint 2007 to 2010 . . **489**

You're Ready to Deploy SharePoint 2010: Now What? 489
Planning Your Upgrade 490
   Governance 492
   SharePoint–Driven Business Processes 492
   Electronic Forms and Document Workflow 493
   Preparing for Social Computing 495
   Working with SharePoint Content Offline 496
   Getting Your Timing Right: When Should You Upgrade? 497
   Fixing Your SharePoint Structure 500
   Addressing New Features in SharePoint 2010 500
   User Comfort, Skill Level, and Training 501
   SharePoint 2007 Customizations 502
Upgrade and Migration Options 502
   In-place Upgrade 504
   Content Database Migration 504
   Rebuild: Create a Separate Farm and Selectively
   Migrate Content 505
What Plan Is Best for You? 505
Upgrade Considerations 507
   Additional Considerations 509
Key Points 511

Appendix A   SharePoint User Tasks **513**

1. Create a New Team Site or Workspace 514
2. Create a List or Document Library 516
3. Apply Security to a Site or Workspace 518
4. Apply Security to Lists or Document Libraries 519
5. Create a View 521
6. Add Web Parts to a Page 523
7. Add Files to a Document Library 525
   Using the SharePoint Web UI to Add Files to SharePoint 525
   Using Windows Explorer to Add Files to SharePoint 526
8. Save a File from Office to SharePoint 527
9. Add Metadata and Standardized Document Templates
   to a Document Library for Better Content Tagging 529

10. Recover a Document from the Recycle Bin 531
11. Building and Contributing to a Blog 532
12. Build a Wiki 534
13. Expose List Data as an RSS Feed 535
14. Sign In as a Different User 536
15. Enhance a Site's Navigation 537
16. Work with a Document Offline 539
17. Document Routing 540
18. Filter and Target List Content Using an Audience 543
19. Find Content by Using Search 544
20. Manage "My" Information 544
21. Create a List of Key Performance Indicators 546
22. Make Use of Business Data 547
    Searching External Data 547
    Using External Data as Metadata in a Document Library 549
    Showing External Data in a Web Part 550
23. Publish an Excel Workbook for Web Rendering 550
24. Publish an InfoPath Form for Web Rendering 552
Key Points 552
    Tasks That Require SharePoint Foundation (at Minimum) 552
    Tasks That Require SharePoint 2010 Standard (at Minimum) 553
    Tasks That Require SharePoint 2010 Enterprise 553

Index **555**

FOREWORD

Remembering back to the late nineties, I can still recall when we decided to start building a product code-named Tahoe. For those of you who don't keep up on our code names here at Microsoft, Tahoe was the code name for SharePoint Portal Server 2001. At the time, I was in the Exchange Server group, which supplied the underlying storage technology to the Tahoe team. Many folks, including myself, were nervous about how customers and partners would accept the new technology, especially given that it provided portal, enterprise search, and document management functionality, of which two of the three were completely new categories offered in Microsoft software.

Fast forward to 2010, and we're just about to release the latest version of SharePoint: SharePoint Server 2010. Three years of development went into this release. We've enhanced all the categories in the product, acquired and integrated FAST search technologies, and introduced the cloud version of SharePoint—SharePoint Online.

The product has sold over 100 million licenses and broke $1 billion in the past nine years, making it one of the fastest-growing server products in Microsoft's history; tens of thousands of companies depend on SharePoint technologies every day to achieve business goals. Much of the success of SharePoint has to be attributed to the early adopters who saw the vision we were painting in the 2001 release and volunteered to help shape and mold that vision and the product over time.

One of those early adopters is Scott Jamison. I first met Scott 12 years ago when he was doing consulting work and I was on the Exchange Server team. Scott was a pro at developing Microsoft Office applications that connected to the new set of server technologies Microsoft was introducing. He believed in the collaboration vision in which Microsoft was investing, and he saw the potential offered by that vision to help his customers increase their business productivity. In fact, Scott worked with the original WSS (which back then was the Web Storage System), which was the underlying platform technology for SharePoint Portal Server 2001.

Any reader of this book will benefit from the history, teachings, and best practices that Scott has internalized over his many years working with Microsoft technologies. Scott has also tapped the experienced minds of Mauro Cardarelli, Susan Hanley, Chris Bortlik, and Donal Conlon, who are Microsoft and industry experts and work with customers every day to solve business issues through software. This book will become a mainstay in your SharePoint library. You will find yourself reaching for it whenever you run into a difficult situation or need extra guidance on how to use the new SharePoint product set. As I was reading this book, I was happy to see the breadth of coverage of the new functionality in SharePoint with no sacrifice of depth and expertise.

When you are done reading this book, you will have a better under-standing of SharePoint, SharePoint Online, and how both can help you achieve new levels of personal and business productivity. I guarantee that you will have earmarked many pages where you learned new skills or ideas that sparked your interest for follow-up. Enjoy the book, and enjoy the product. Both are labors of love.

—Tom Rizzo
Senior Director, SharePoint Product Management
Redmond, Washington
March 2010

PREFACE

Collaboration. Portals. Social computing. Knowledge management. Governance. Search. Document management.

These are terms that are thrown around when talking about Microsoft SharePoint Server 2010. But what do they really mean?

Most books are designed to address the "how" behind SharePoint, from either an administrative perspective or a programming perspective. This book complements the typical SharePoint book with some of the "what" and "why" of SharePoint, provides insight into targeting needs with collaboration technologies, and helps you understand how those needs might be addressed using SharePoint.

What Is This Book About?

The Information Worker is central to Microsoft's strategy to bring productive computing to the enterprise and beyond. Navigating the various client and server products can be confusing and daunting. This book will help you navigate these waters, providing direction and understanding. Specifically, this is a book about Microsoft's SharePoint platform, with a particular focus on four commonly requested topics: a business-focused overview, defining proper strategy, governance and end-user rollout, and a business-focused discussion on how to apply SharePoint's key features. This book was written because collaboration, knowledge and content management, and Web accessibility are three of the most sought-after features in a corporate software solution. The key product that is the basis for most Microsoft-based solutions in this area is SharePoint Server 2010. Because of this functionality, SharePoint is perhaps one of the most important server products that runs on Windows Server. If you want to deploy SharePoint in your enterprise or upgrade from previous versions, or if you need a concise introduction to collaboration solutions with SharePoint, you're starting in the right place. This book provides a great user-level guide to Microsoft's latest version of SharePoint, along with usage strategies and some insight into the technologies involved. This book is intended to be a tutorial as well as a handy reference.

What You Will Learn from This Book

To implement a collaborative system effectively, you'll likely need to consider a number of key questions:

- Do I need a portal or collaboration strategy? If so, how do I create one?
- What should my governance plan look like?
- How do users perform the top activities that they'll need to do?
- What do I need to consider when I upgrade from previous versions of SharePoint?
- Where are documents stored currently? Where should documents live?
- How do users collaborate today?
- What kind of hardware do I need? How do I deploy the product properly?
- How does the Web fit into my collaboration needs? What about Office and smart client applications? How about SharePoint Workspace, InfoPath, and Microsoft Access?
- Will I share information outside of my organization? Should I?

Who Should Read This Book

If you're a developer, you probably already own a SharePoint programming book or SharePoint API guide (or are looking for one). This is not a book about SharePoint programming; however, developers will find this book useful when building solutions (in conjunction with an API guide) because there are business considerations that are critically important to every SharePoint-based solution.

If you're a project manager, consultant, or business analyst, you'll find that this book helps with all of the intangibles of a SharePoint rollout. For example, "What roles should exist to support SharePoint?" or "What should my governance/offline/search/business data strategy be for

SharePoint?" This book also introduces you to some key technical concepts and provides simple walkthroughs of the key features that many businesses need to leverage.

How This Book Is Organized

This book is organized into three key parts:

- Part I, "Planning," helps you determine what kinds of business needs are addressed by SharePoint and how you should think about SharePoint-based solutions within your organization. It's also a great introduction to the SharePoint feature set and architecture.
- Part II, "Optimizing," helps you implement SharePoint to its fullest potential.
- Part III, "Migrating," helps you determine your plan for upgrading from previous versions of SharePoint.

Appendix A provides a list of the top SharePoint user tasks.

Key Points

At each chapter's conclusion is a section called "Key Points," which summarizes the key facts, best practices, and other topics that were covered in the chapter.

Thank You

Thank you for reading this book. Our goal was to write the most concise yet useful business-centric guide to Microsoft SharePoint Server 2010. Enjoy!

ACKNOWLEDGMENTS

First, I'd like to thank Addison-Wesley for giving me another opportunity to write a book, with special thanks to Joan Murray, Olivia Basegio, Julie Nahil, Carolyn Albee, and the rest of the Pearson team for shaping the book into something great.

This book could not have come to fruition without the expertise of Susan Hanley. Her experience and perspective are invaluable to projects like this; every project team should be lucky enough to have her. She provided useful insight, fantastic writing, and real-world expertise to make this a high-quality book.

Thanks to Mauro Cardarelli, who once again lent his deep knowledge of SharePoint to another edition of the book.

I'd also like to thank our team of early reviewers, including Andy Kawa, Arpan Shah, Shelley Norton, Ken Heft, and Ryan Sockalosky who all provided insightful feedback and corrections. I'd like to thank Tom Rizzo for answering numerous questions, lending his team when needed, and writing the Foreword for the book (again!).

I'd also like to acknowledge Chris Bortlik, Donal Conlon, and Nicholas Bisciotti who were instrumental in contributing useful insight and writing to the book.

Special thanks to Joel Oleson for letting us again use his blog posting on file shares versus SharePoint for file storage.

Finally, I'd like to extend a deep and sincere thanks to my family, friends, and customers, and the fantastic team at Jornata who all supported me while writing the book.

—Scott Jamison
Boston, MA
June 2010

ABOUT THE AUTHORS

Scott Jamison is a world-renowned expert on knowledge worker technologies and collaborative solutions, and is an experienced leader with almost 20 years directing managers and technology professionals to deliver a wide range of business solutions for customers. Scott is a strong strategic thinker, technologist, and operational manager. Scott is currently Managing Partner and CEO of Jornata (www.jornata.com), a SharePoint and Microsoft Online Services consulting and training firm.

Prior to joining Jornata, Scott was Director of Enterprise Architecture at Microsoft and has held numerous leadership positions, including a senior management position leading a Microsoft-focused consulting team at Dell. Scott has worked with Microsoft teams on local, regional, and international levels for years, often participating as an advisor to the Microsoft product teams. Scott is a recognized thought leader and published author with several books, dozens of magazine articles, and regular speaking engagements at events around the globe.

Scott received his MS in computer science from Boston University, with post-graduate work at Bentley's McCallum Graduate School of Business. Scott is a SharePoint Certified Master.

Susan Hanley, president of Susan Hanley LLC, is an expert in the design, development, and implementation of successful portal solutions, with a focus on information architecture, user adoption, governance, and business value metrics. She is an internationally recognized expert in knowledge management and writes a blog on SharePoint and Collaboration for Network World Magazine that can be found at http://www.network world.com/community/sharepoint. Prior to establishing her own consulting practice, Sue spent 18 years as a consultant at American Management Systems where she led AMS's knowledge management program. During this time, she was recognized by *Consultants News* as one of the key "knowledge leaders" at major consulting firms. Sue left AMS to lead the Portals, Collaboration, and Content Management consulting practice for Plural, which was acquired by Dell in 2003. In this role, she was responsible for a team that developed hundreds of solutions based on the Microsoft SharePoint platform and participated as a member of Microsoft's Partner Advisory Council for Portals and Collaboration. In 2005, she established Susan Hanley LLC (www.susanhanley.com), a consulting practice dedicated to helping clients achieve high-impact business outcomes with portals and collaboration solutions. Her clients include some of the largest global deployments of SharePoint.

Sue has an MBA from the Smith School of Business at the University of Maryland at College Park and a BA in psychology from Johns Hopkins University.

Mauro Cardarelli is a SharePoint evangelist and has been active in the SharePoint community since its inception in 2001. He has 20 years of experience designing and building technology solutions for customers representing a wide range of industry verticals. His deep knowledge of the Microsoft platform and recognized expertise in the areas of knowledge management and business intelligence make him a popular technology expert.

ABOUT THE CONTRIBUTORS

Chris Bortlik, a SharePoint technology specialist at Microsoft, works with Enterprise customers and partners in the Northeast in a presales technical role. Chris speaks frequently at Microsoft events, including the SharePoint Conference. He also publishes a blog on TechNet at http://blogs.technet .com/cbortlik. Prior to joining Microsoft in 2008, Chris was a Microsoft customer for 14 years, working in technical IT architect, development, and management roles—primarily leading .NET- and SharePoint-related projects. Chris lives in Woburn, Massachusetts, with his wife Marisa and their two daughters, Kayla and Jessica.

Donal Conlon, senior consultant at Jornata, is a technology expert with 15 years in the IT industry, working primarily on Microsoft and IBM technologies. The majority of his career has been spent providing collaboration solutions on many platforms with a focus on Microsoft SharePoint. Donal has held leadership positions at several companies in his career and currently works as a senior consultant at Jornata, delivering solutions on SharePoint 2007 and 2010. Donal holds an engineering degree from University of Ireland, Galway.

PLANNING

CHAPTER 1

GETTING STARTED

In March 2008, Microsoft Chairman Bill Gates kicked off the Microsoft SharePoint Conference. He told the sold-out crowd that "There is an incredible demand today for solutions that help businesses to harness the power of a global work force and tackle the challenges that come with the explosive growth of digital information. The spectacular growth of SharePoint is the result of the great combination of collaboration and information management capabilities it delivers. I believe that the success we've seen so far is just the beginning for SharePoint." (Microsoft Corporation, 2008)

Microsoft SharePoint Server 2010 (SharePoint 2010) is the next version of the SharePoint family to which Gates alluded in his talk in early 2008. Much like the "digital natives" who have grown up with digital technology and are now entering the workforce, SharePoint 2010 can be characterized by the simple phrase "we are not alone." The new SharePoint is far more "social" than the generations that preceded it. SharePoint 2010 relies not only on the structured design provided by the solution architect, but as much or more on the collective contributions of the user community. From ranking content they like to collaboratively creating content to "tagging" content with their own taxonomy, users have the opportunity to improve an organization's ability to deliver and share knowledge and best practices. Some features in SharePoint 2010 will be new to users of previous versions, but "digital natives" will feel right at home with the platform because of its similarities to the "social web," which encourages users to actively participate rather than simply read static content. SharePoint 2010 recognizes the global nature of information and enterprises, making it easier to support multiple languages, on multiple browsers, and on multiple platforms, such as handheld devices. The new world of SharePoint is both "flat" and "social," and this book is designed to help you navigate this new world.

This chapter contains the following key sections:

- Readers Guide
- Planning a Successful SharePoint Solution Strategy

Reader's Guide

This book is not targeted to any one specific role. If you are a developer, this book is the ideal companion to your SharePoint 2010 API guide and/or development books. It explains SharePoint best practices and helps you understand your organization's business needs and how they might be addressed using this powerful solution platform. No developer should use SharePoint without first understanding the important people and business considerations to every SharePoint-based solution. Likewise, for IT Pros and SharePoint administrators, the key to being successful with your SharePoint implementation is to first understand the big picture. If you are a project manager, consultant, or business analyst, you'll find that this book helps with the intangibles of a SharePoint rollout. For example, "What roles should exist to support SharePoint?" or "How can I best take advantage of the new social media features of SharePoint?"

While we hope that all readers read the book cover-to-cover, each chapter of this book can be read independently. The first section of the book is designed to help you think about planning your SharePoint project—the overall strategy for the solution you will build, the elements and features you will use, the organization of your information, your governance plan, your security model, and how you will launch the solution when development is complete. The second section describes how to optimize your solution, describing strategies for search, forms and workflow, deploying your solution as a public-facing Web site, leveraging business intelligence capabilities, and building solutions that combine information from multiple sources including other Office 2010 products. This section also includes a summary of strategies for planning for disaster recovery. The final section of the book is specifically for readers who have existing solutions built on SharePoint 2007 and talks about alternative migration strategies for moving your solution to the new 2010 version.

Microsoft describes SharePoint 2010 as "The Business Collaboration Platform for the Enterprise and the Web" and breaks SharePoint down into six key feature areas. We discuss each of these areas throughout the book.

- **Sites**. The core capability to facilitate the creation and management of Web pages sites that contain, display, and aggregate content. Information about sites is described in many places in the book, but to get started, please review Chapters 2, "Introduction to SharePoint 2010 Platform" and 3, "SharePoint 2010: Architecture Fundamentals."

- **Communities**. The ability to interact with (and solicit feedback from) other users through social tools. Communities are discussed in Chapter 7, "Getting Social: Leveraging Community Features."
- **Content**. Enterprise content management (document, records, Web, rich media). Content management is a broad topic that is discussed in Chapter 5, "Planning Your Information Architecture," as well as Chapter 6, "Making Enterprise Content Management Work: Documents and Records."
- **Search**. The ability to find information and people across SharePoint and other sources. Chapter 10, "Making Search Work: Content, People, Data," provides advice about planning the use of search in your SharePoint solution.
- **Insights**. Business intelligence tools. Chapter 13, "Making Business Intelligence Work," discusses this topic at length.
- **Composites**. The ability to create applications rapidly (mashups, composite applications, and so on). Developing composites is discussed in Chapter 14, "Composite Applications with Business Connectivity Services."

This first chapter provides a critical foundation for understanding your SharePoint-based solution objectives and a foundation for the rest of the book. So put away Visual Studio and SharePoint Designer for a moment. Take a deep breath and a step back. Start thinking about why your organization needs SharePoint and how you know you'll be successful after your solution is deployed. Software is expensive to purchase and integrate. If you want to build a successful solution, you need a carefully defined plan.

Planning a Successful SharePoint Solution Strategy

Despite all the new features and powerful features, SharePoint is a platform for developing solutions such as portals, intranets, and extranets that solve business problems. It's up to you to ensure that you configure your platform optimally—in a way that will deliver the most value to your organization. One of the most powerful lessons learned from SharePoint 2007 deployments is that truly successful solutions have a significant end-user focus—from design to training to persistent communications. The new features available in SharePoint 2010 bring even more power and control to end users, making it even more important to *carefully consider your collaboration strategy before installing any software.*

SharePoint provides a convenient and often personalized way for your employees to find the information and tools they need to be more productive. However, as great SharePoint is, it comes with a unique challenge: You often have to convince users to give it a try! In many cases, the use of a solution based on SharePoint cannot be mandated in the same way that the use of a new accounting or payroll system can be mandated (for example, to process an invoice or generate paychecks). Employees have other options for accomplishing many of the tasks SharePoint enables, even if some of these options are "suboptimal." For example, SharePoint may provide a convenient summary of financial information about a project that might also be available by looking at existing reports generated by the financial system. SharePoint may be more convenient and efficient but not necessarily *required* to surface the project financial information. SharePoint may also include "subportals" or online collaborative team spaces where users can efficiently share documents to minimize e-mail traffic and ensure that everyone on the team always has the latest versions of documents. Still, users may e-mail documents back and forth to collaborate, resulting in a disorganized collection of documents and correspondence that is not reusable by other team members. These are some of the many reasons why it is so critically important to have a clearly articulated business strategy for your new SharePoint portal or collaboration solution. Practical experience indicates that technology has only a small impact on the success of SharePoint solutions; organizational and political (process and people) strategies have a much greater impact, and as a result, a comprehensive SharePoint strategy is vital for success.

There are a number of key elements to consider in your SharePoint strategy. We discuss the first three in this chapter and focus on the remaining topics in subsequent chapters of the book.

- Who are the key stakeholders? This might include the CIO, the chief knowledge officer (CKO), or key business leaders in areas such as corporate communications, marketing, and human resources, among others.

- What are the critical business objectives for the key stakeholders? (In other words, what keeps these executives awake at night?) How can the SharePoint solution address these key business objectives?
- How will the organization as a whole measure the business success of the SharePoint initiative? In other words, which key business goals does the SharePoint solution address? Remember, portals are not successful just because they are free of software defects. Successful portals must be designed to have an impact on key business objectives.
- What processes do you need to have in place to ensure that all of the SharePoint users are aware of and accept their roles and responsibilities with regard to the SharePoint solution? This topic is discussed in Chapter 4, "Planning for Governance."
- How will you plan for both the design and ongoing maintenance of the content in SharePoint? Accurate and relevant content is the foundation of your SharePoint solution. Your strategy needs to include a plan to ensure that content remains relevant over time. This topic is also discussed in Chapter 4.
- What type of roll-out strategy should you pursue? What types of communications and training do you need to provide for users? Your roll-out strategy needs to prepare both users and content for the new SharePoint solution. The strategy needs to include a communications plan to make sure that users are aware of and, ideally, eagerly anticipate the business value of the new SharePoint solution. In addition, the strategy needs to include a plan for launching the new solution and training users. These topics are discussed in Chapter 9, "Getting Ready to Launch: Planning for Training and Communications."

Key Stakeholders

In many organizations, the information technology (IT) group is separated both physically and "emotionally" from the organizations they are designed to serve. Because the success of SharePoint solutions is critically dependent on business user adoption, it is imperative that business stakeholders take an active role in portal design and governance planning and that IT staff fully understand how the solution they build addresses business needs. One way to ensure that your SharePoint project will fail is to have

IT build the solution without engaging a broad spectrum of potential users. In the past, portal and collaboration projects were primarily driven by IT organizations. Many of these early initiatives failed to gain acceptance by users because they were essentially IT-only projects—driven by IT with limited user input. Today, more and more portal and collaboration projects are driven (and funded) by business users, though they are clearly dependent on IT. Many intranet projects are sponsored by the corporate department responsible for internal communications. One or more business units may fund and drive an external or customer portal initiative. As a result, it is critically important for IT to work with the sponsoring business unit as well as all key stakeholders to ensure that the inevitable decision trade-offs that will be made during the SharePoint design and development are made in favor of the business stakeholders as often as possible. SharePoint provides an important opportunity for IT and business owners to collaborate. IT managers who fail to take advantage of this opportunity put their projects and potentially their careers at risk.

Who should your key stakeholders include? Clearly, the executive for the sponsoring organization is an important key stakeholder. This individual will likely be your project sponsor. For intranet portals, this is often the director of marketing or internal communications but should also include the director of knowledge management or CKO if your organization has someone in that role. This will ensure that your intranet is not just about communications, but will also effectively enable your collaboration strategy. For extranet portals, this may be a key executive in an operational business unit. Your stakeholders should also include representatives from your major organizational units, both internal and customer-facing. When you look to identify stakeholders, recognize that there are different types of stakeholders, all of whom should be included in the development of your strategy and ongoing governance model. Many of these stakeholders will also be included in your requirements definition process. Business executives should be included in the stakeholder community to provide overall direction and validate that the SharePoint deployment is critical to achieving business objectives. IT managers should be included to ensure that the solution meets IT standards for operations and development. Content providers (internal departments like Human Resources, Finance and Accounting, Legal, and so on) should be included given that the portal will become a critical communications vehicle. End users ("rank and file") should be included to ensure that the SharePoint solution rollout addresses more than just executive objectives and concerns. Remember that while the executive sponsor may have the "grand vision" for the solution, the solution end users are critical to the ultimate success. End users need the solution to be easy to use in the context of their work and need to be able to see "What's in it for me?" For example, the key stakeholders for a portal project to support a university should include administrators, faculty, and students. In addition, if the portal is externally facing, the "customer" community might be represented by examining the perspective of applicants or prospective students. Keep in mind that if you choose to enable the social computing functionality available in SharePoint 2010 (refer to Chapter 7 for more information), everyone in the organization has the potential to become a producer rather than just a consumer of information. These features provide a rich and engaging opportunity to improve content relevance and "findability." However, they make understanding your organizational culture and user community even more important than ever before. In fact, in the new world of SharePoint 2010, there may no longer be a true "end user."

After you've identified your key stakeholders, it's important to engage them in the process of defining business objectives for the SharePoint rollout.

Take Action

Be inclusive rather than exclusive as you identify key stakeholders. It's important to gather as much business user support for your solution as possible.

Be sure to include end users in your key stakeholders. At the end of the day, these are the people who will help make your solution successful (or not).

In addition to traditional department or business executives, try to include employees who may not have the title but who are influential in the business. These people tend to have broad networks across the enterprise and can help drive your success because many people trust them.

Business Objectives

In successful SharePoint implementations, IT and business owners carefully frame the SharePoint project with clearly defined business goals and objectives that are used to guide the decisions that need to be made during the solution design and ongoing operations. More often than not, the key issues influencing the success of a SharePoint solution are organizational and political. Technical issues rarely derail a SharePoint project. As a result, it's particularly important to document why you are building the SharePoint solution in the first place and to ensure that all key stakeholders agree on the objectives.

The first business objectives that should be considered as part of your SharePoint strategy are the overall business objectives for your organization, such as improving profit margins, increasing revenues, cutting costs, improving customer or partner relationships, and so on. Your goal should be to tie the specific objectives for the SharePoint rollout to one or more strategic objectives of the corporation. Doing so enables you to ensure that your SharePoint project stays "front and center" in the organizational agenda and minimizes the risk of becoming "number 11" on the organizational top 10 priority list. In other words, you want to avoid becoming the project that gets done "in our spare time," pretty much ensuring that the SharePoint project is not a career-making experience for the people working on it.

In addition to these organization-specific business objectives, there is another set of common business drivers that cause companies to implement SharePoint. Some or all of the following business objectives will probably resonate for your organization. If you can tie these specific objectives to your overall enterprise strategic objectives, you will be in even better shape to ensure the right amount of attention and focus is directed to your project.

- Provide an organized "one-stop shop" for information by making it easier to find authoritative information.
- Provide easier and timelier access to the information employees need to get their work done.
- Provide more effective mechanisms to move work between business entities, such as self-service for customers or partners or enabling outsourcing by providing business partners to a collaboration environment or business data on an extranet.
- Improve the ability to share and exchange information across the organization by providing an electronic publishing method that is easy for users to leverage and assures "one version of the truth" for shared documents.
- Improve the ability to find and leverage expertise.

- Improve organizational learning by providing easier access to critical information and organizational memory.
- Maximize the reuse of best practices across the enterprise, enabling the organization to replicate successful business practices in all geographies.
- Improve the "time to talent," the speed with which new employees become productive.
- Reduce training costs for enterprise applications by providing a consistent user interface to all applications.
- Improve time to market for proposals and contracts by providing easier access to reusable assets.
- Improve project execution by providing an opportunity for work teams to collaborate and to electronically store project information in fully searchable, organized team sites.
- Improve customer service by providing direct access to the information customers need.

It is critically important to document business objectives at the start of your SharePoint initiative and to keep these objectives at the top of your mind as you design and build your solution. Use the business objectives to guide your decisions about which features should go in each release of the solution. Ask portal owners/stakeholders to prioritize their business objectives so that you understand how to make trade-offs between alternative design approaches. Users often have a very difficult time articulating requirements for SharePoint solutions. This is because it is virtually impossible to envision how the solution will help solve business problems until users see the solution with "real" data. When users do express requirements, they may express their requirements in very specific ways, which could require a significant amount of custom coding. However, if you understand the objectives or outcomes users are trying to achieve, you may be able to accomplish the objective using "out-of-the-box" or minimally customized functionality. To accomplish this, you will need to have SharePoint experts, both Power Users and developers, know what you can and can't do easily. You really can't gather user requirements for SharePoint solutions like you do for a traditional software development project. Instead, solicit and try to understand business objectives. You can then, as an IT design team, *derive* requirements based on the business objectives and outcomes. When a user learns that a requirement will cost $250K to implement, the requirement is often no longer "required." Therefore, it's important to ensure that you understand the strategic objectives for the company, the business objectives for SharePoint in general, and the specific outcome objectives for each aspect of the implementation.

> ### Take Action
> Identify three or four main features that will produce the most business impact and do them exceptionally well.
>
> Articulate, well in advance of launch, the long-term vision associated with your solution and how the first delivery sets the stage.
>
> Set clear and reasonable expectations for all business users—encourage users to focus on the business outcomes they want to achieve. In your "requirements (objectives) gathering" meetings, try to proactively explain how you can accomplish the business outcomes using SharePoint out-of-the-box features so that you can get a feel for whether this will be acceptable to the user. Use phrases such as "This is how we might accomplish what you are asking for in SharePoint ... " Your goal is to rapidly deploy a first release of your solution so that your stakeholders can see the solution "in action" with their content. You will probably find that it is only when users "meet SharePoint" with their own content that they can start to envision additional functionality that will add value to the business.

For each possible business objective, there are numerous SharePoint features you can implement to help enable that objective. Table 1-1 presents a chart of some of the features of SharePoint 2010 that you can leverage to explicitly accomplish your business objectives. Use this table with great caution, however. Just because a feature can *help* achieve a business objective doesn't mean it *will*. People achieve business objectives, not software. While well-designed software solutions can *enable* people to achieve business objectives, simply implementing the features in this table will not guarantee that you will achieve the desired business objectives.

Table 1-1 Mapping of SharePoint Features to General Business Objectives

Business Objective	Enabling Feature or Functionality
Provide an organized "one-stop shop" for information by making it easier to find authoritative information	Search and Search Results Refinement Business Connectivity Services (integration with Line of Business Systems) Metadata
Provide easier and timelier access to the information employees need to get their work done	Search Alerts News Metadata Bookmarks Activity Feeds and Status Updates Social Tags and Ratings Blogs Wikis RSS Feeds
Provide more effective mechanisms to move work between business entities, such as self-service for customers or partners or enabling outsourcing by providing business partners a collaboration environment or business data on an extranet	Extranets Business Connectivity Services (integration with Line of Business Systems) Rich Security Model that users can administer
Improve the ability to share and exchange information across the organization by providing an electronic publishing method that is easy for users to leverage and assures "one version of the truth" for shared documents	Document Versioning Records Retention Document Sets Unique Document IDs
Improve the ability to find and leverage expertise	People and Expertise Search My Sites Activity Feeds and Status Updates Blogs and Wikis
Improve organizational learning by providing easier access to critical information and organizational memory	Search and Search Results Refinement People and Expertise Search Document Repositories with Metadata (both user and organizationally defined) Blogs and Wikis

(continues)

Table 1-1 Mapping of SharePoint Features to General Business Objectives *(continued)*

Business Objective	Enabling Feature or Functionality
Maximize the reuse of best practices across the enterprise, enabling the organization to replicate successful business practices in all geographies	Site Templates Search and Search Results Refinement People and Expertise Search Document Repositories with Metadata (both user- and organizationally defined) Blogs and Wikis
Improve the "time to talent," the speed with which new employees become productive	Search and Search Results Refinement People and Expertise Search
Reduce training costs for enterprise applications by providing a consistent user interface to all applications	Search and Search Results Refinement Business Connectivity Services (integration with Line of Business Systems) Site Templates Third-Party Solutions designed for integrating with SharePoint (Many application vendors now provide SharePoint integration (typically Web Parts) for their products.)
Improve time to market for proposals and contracts by providing easier access to reusable assets	Search and Search Results Refinement People and Expertise Search Document Repositories with Metadata (both user- and organizationally defined)
Improve project execution by providing an opportunity for work teams to collaborate and to electronically store project information in fully searchable, organized team sites	Team Sites Document Repositories with Metadata (both user and organizationally defined) Announcements and Events (Team Calendar) Rich Security Model that users can administer
Improve customer service by providing direct access to the information customers need	Extranets Mobile Access Business Connectivity Services (integration with Line of Business Systems) Rich Security Model that users can administer Web Content Management

Measuring Success

Even if you have carefully defined and documented your business objectives and engaged all levels of stakeholders in the solution definition and strategy process, the time will come when you will need to assess the value of your organization's SharePoint investment. This process may have already started as part of the justification to build out the SharePoint environment. Once the SharePoint investment has been approved, however, a metrics program should be established so that you can demonstrate that the solution meets the business objectives. The metrics program should include more than simply capturing usage statistics, though usage statistics are one important proxy measurement for SharePoint value. A good metrics program includes both qualitative and quantitative measures that tie the SharePoint solution as directly as possible to business success. The metrics program also needs to start with established baselines for all measures. Portals and collaboration tools have started to become a more common part of IT infrastructure—sometimes even considered a basic application like e-mail. However, despite increasingly wide acceptance, SharePoint solution builders should be keenly aware of the likelihood that management will want to understand how SharePoint is delivering against expectations. Having a metrics program in place provides an opportunity to monitor the solution deployment to ensure that usage is optimized. It also provides a basis for justifying enhancements in the future.

If you worked with your key stakeholders to understand and document business objectives, then you've already accomplished the first important part of your metrics program. The next key step is to identify a potential set of qualitative and quantitative measures that can be used to identify whether and how your solution addresses these objectives. Qualitative metrics can be "discovered" from user feedback during quality assurance testing and initial training and on an ongoing basis. Seek out "stories" or anecdotes where users can describe how using the portal and/or collaboration tools (finding a person with an unknown skill, rapidly accessing previously difficult-to-find information, and so on) helped contribute to increased revenue or profitability, increased client satisfaction, or other metrics that are already reflected in the key performance measures for the organization. The following sidebar provides an anecdote describing the value of a knowledge management portal for a consulting firm. Note that

Table 1-2 Suggested SharePoint Metrics

Objective	Possible Measure	Capture Frequency	Issues and Challenges	Target
Maximize the reuse of best practices across the enterprise, enabling the organization to replicate successful business practices in all geographies.	*Quantitative:* Number of downloads of best practice or reusable assets *Qualitative:* Usage anecdotes where users can describe in quantitative terms how a SharePoint asset that they reused contributed to business objectives	Monthly	Frequent downloads are a proxy for content value, indicating that the content is delivering value to users. Gathering anecdotes is a labor-intensive process and may require some creativity to obtain. You may want to consider a success story contest (with prizes) to get SharePoint users to share high quality success stories.	Look for an upward trend in the number of downloads for new content or new portals. Look for steady state activity in more mature environments. Targets should be set based on the maturity of the solution and the strategic importance of the content. Targets for success stories might be based on total "value" represented in the stories collected and/or based on the number of stories documented.
Improve time to market for proposals and contracts.	*Quantitative:* Average proposal or contract development time	Ideally, captured for each proposal or contract and then compiled (averages) on a semiannual or annual basis	This measure will be easiest to capture if it is already a key performance measure for the enterprise.	Trend downward from baseline. Target might also be a specific percentage of time reduction.
Reduce training costs for enterprise applications.	*Quantitative:* Total training costs for enterprise applications	Annual	Some organizations justify their SharePoint investment solely on the reduction in training costs. The assumption is that most users are not "power users" of enterprise applications. Instead of investing in full training programs for these users, you only need to train them in the use of the portal, not each enterprise application.	Percentage or absolute reduction in training expenses for enterprise applications.
Provide an organized "one-stop shop" for information for SharePoint users	*Qualitative:* Usage anecdotes where users can describe in quantitative terms how using SharePoint has	Monthly	Gathering anecdotes is a labor-intensive process and may require some creativity to obtain. Consider using the built-in SharePoint survey capability to identify users	Targets for success stories might be based on total "value" represented in the stories collected or based on the number of stories documented.

Objective	Possible Measure	Capture Frequency	Issues and Challenges	Target
that helps users reduce information overload.	improved their productivity.		with a story to tell. It is probably not realistic to assume that users will be able to write down their stories in a way that will be useful to your metrics program. Instead, think about a "journalistic approach": get users to identify that they have a story to tell and then assign your "roving reporter" to capture and document the story. Be sure to define a place to store and classify your stories for subsequent reuse.	

while the story is an example of a qualitative measure, it is a good one because it includes a quantitative value estimate that is defined by the "actor" in the story. With a quantitative "punch line," this story provides a much clearer demonstration of value than it would have if no "bottom line" were presented. You should try to ensure that all of your anecdotal evidence of value includes a realistic value estimate, ideally provided by the "narrator" of the story.

Sample Qualitative Measure: Portal Success Story/Anecdote

I joined the organization on March 16 without previous experience. After one week of training, I joined a project team.

After one day of training on the project, I was assigned a task to learn a particular technology that was new to everyone on the team. I was given a bunch of books and told that I had three days to learn how to create a project plan using this technology.

In my first week of training, I remembered learning that I could use the company intranet to search for people with expertise in a particular topic. I did a query based on my assigned topic and found four people with relevant expertise. I sent an e-mail to each of them asking for their help. One of them sent me a link to a document on the portal containing exactly what I wanted. *Instead of three days, my task was completed in half a day.*

Quantitative metrics can often be obtained from usage analysis reports, and while these metrics may not be a direct measure of value, certain measures can be used as a proxy for value. Table 1-2 (see page 16) suggests some possible quantitative and qualitative metrics associated with several of the business objectives described earlier.

Your organization will most likely have a preferred format for documenting metrics. This might be a balanced scorecard, documented key performance indicators, or a simple "report card." Your goal will be to ensure that you are capturing metrics that, as best as possible, directly relate SharePoint's value to the business. In addition, you want to make it very easy for users to provide feedback. Keep in mind that you also want to be sure that you are not spending more time counting metrics than you are doing real work, so look for measures that are both meaningful to the organization and practical to obtain.

Take Action

Do not underestimate the importance of a metrics plan. Even if your solution is fully funded for the first release, you will very likely need to be able to show meaningful business impact to get funding for "release 2 and beyond."

Remember that business executives will respond most favorably to your metrics when you can combine both quantitative measures with real-world stories that describe how the solution added value to the business.

Look to leverage key performance indicators that your organization already measures so that you can look at your solution's impact on the important indicators of success in your organization.

Key Points

Getting started with SharePoint 2010 means thinking about your strategy first. Remember:

- Portal and collaboration software can be expensive to purchase and integrate. If you want to build a successful solution, you need a carefully defined strategy.
- Identify and engage key stakeholders. Make sure they are involved as core members of your project team.
- Ensure that the SharePoint solution has a clear connection to business goals and objectives.
- Develop a method to identify and quantify pragmatic, tangible benefits for the solution. Do not underestimate the importance of a metrics plan.
- High-impact collaboration involves culture changes blended with the right technology. It is a small part technology and a large part business process change.
- Software does not achieve business objectives—people do. Just because a feature can help achieve a business objective doesn't mean it will. Incorporate an effective training and communications strategy to ensure user adoption.
- Not all content needs to be stored in SharePoint, but all business-critical data should be *accessible* through your portal.
- SharePoint 2010 provides a single platform for intranet, extranet, and Internet solutions. This allows you to extend your messaging to employees, clients, partners, prospects, and general observers—the entire extended enterprise, including the Web.

CHAPTER 2

INTRODUCTION TO THE SHAREPOINT 2010 PLATFORM

In Chapter 1, we looked at some essential factors in planning your enterprise portal and collaboration strategy. A platform that supports this strategy will need to enable tasks that users will undertake on a regular basis, including creating documents, sharing information, managing content, communicating in real time, and making business decisions.

All of these tasks are supported by SharePoint 2010 and Office 2010. The products all work well individually, and together they form a comprehensive collaboration, communication, and knowledge management platform. This chapter provides an overview of this collection of technologies, the corresponding architecture, and what is new about this version of the SharePoint Products and Technologies. The platform includes core technologies such as the Office 2010 client, SharePoint Foundation 2010 (formerly known as Windows SharePoint Services), SharePoint Server 2010, Exchange Server 2010, and Office Communications Server 2010. Figure 2-1 and Figure 2-2 highlight the core products and technologies in the overall Microsoft communications and collaboration platform. The chapter contains the following key sections:

- Microsoft's Collaboration Evolution
- Current Versions of SharePoint Products and Technologies
- Microsoft SharePoint Server 2010 and Office 2010
- SharePoint 2010: What's New?
- Comparing SharePoint Foundation to Microsoft SharePoint Server 2010
- SharePoint: The File Share Killer
- SharePoint: The Access and Excel Killer

Project Server 2010
SharePoint Server 2010
SharePoint Foundation 2010
Exchange Server 2010
• Email
• PIM Data
• Voice Mail
Office Communications Server 2010
• Presence
• Instant Messaging
• Video
Windows Server 2008

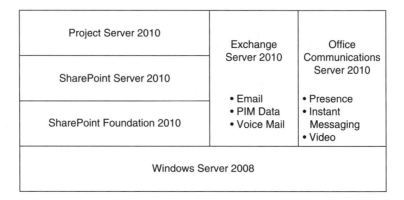

Figure 2-1 The server products that make up Microsoft's information worker platform include capabilities to enable portals, collaboration, social computing, enterprise content management, e-mail, real-time communication, and other key features

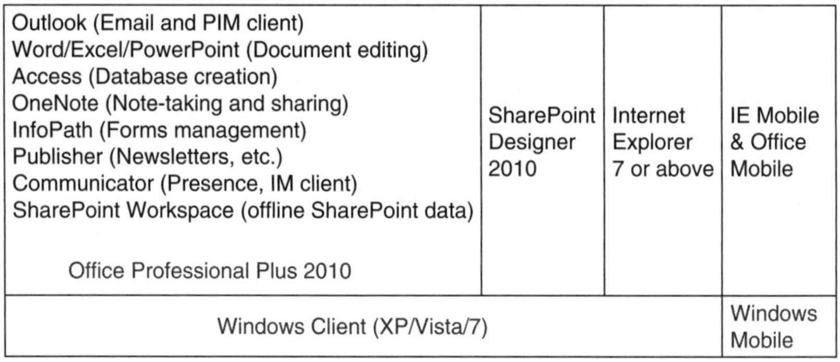

Outlook (Email and PIM client)
Word/Excel/PowerPoint (Document editing)
Access (Database creation)
OneNote (Note-taking and sharing)
InfoPath (Forms management)
Publisher (Newsletters, etc.)
Communicator (Presence, IM client)
SharePoint Workspace (offline SharePoint data)
Office Professional Plus 2010
SharePoint Designer 2010
Internet Explorer 7 or above
IE Mobile & Office Mobile
Windows Client (XP/Vista/7)
Windows Mobile

Figure 2-2 The Microsoft client-side information worker components can be purchased separately or as a suite: Office 2010

Microsoft SharePoint Foundation 2010 is the fourth generation of Microsoft's core collaboration platform. SharePoint Foundation provides the core engine, toolset, and runtime that enables both end users and IT professionals to create collaborative workspaces and Web sites. Microsoft SharePoint Server 2010 is built on top of SharePoint Foundation and provides a large number of additional features, including aggregation, targeting, enterprise search, social computing, and content management functionality along with business intelligence and line-of-business data integration. The next section shows how all of the pieces (including client products like SharePoint Workspace and Office communicator, as well as related products like Exchange Server) fit together in a typical environment. It also provides a little of the history behind the evolution of SharePoint products.

Microsoft's Collaboration Evolution

The world of Microsoft collaboration really started with Outlook 97 and Exchange 5.5, when public folders represented the extent of collaboration technology at Microsoft. At that time, Lotus Notes was the de facto enterprise collaboration product.

Exchange as a Collaboration Platform

When Microsoft Exchange 2000 Server was released, Microsoft positioned Exchange and its Web Store (the Exchange database plus some schema and Web-enablement features) as a collaboration server that would compete with, among other things, Lotus Notes. Exchange 2000 also provided a real-time communication piece that could provide instant messaging within an organization. The strategy seemed to make sense—use Exchange as the core asynchronous messaging, synchronous messaging, and collaboration platform. Build it, and they will come.

Unfortunately, they never came. Using Exchange as the core collaboration platform never took off (mainly due to the fact that applications had to be run directly on the server, a situation that didn't sit well with Exchange administrators). It became clear to Microsoft that messaging was a mission-critical application and letting application developers build on top of Exchange was not going to be a popular option among Exchange administrators. Microsoft repositioned Exchange as a pure messaging server. Microsoft also carved the real-time communication option out of Exchange 2000 and created a new product, Live Communications Server (LCS), keeping Exchange firmly planted in the e-mail and Personal Information Management (PIM) camp.

Office Server Extensions and SharePoint Team Services

Microsoft was addressing real-time collaboration with LCS, but they still had a gap in the provision of technology for groups that wanted to collaborate in a team environment. To meet this need, Microsoft leveraged some existing technology originating with the FrontPage group and evolved it into SharePoint Team Services. Technology-wise, SharePoint has its roots in Front Page Server extensions, which became Office Server Extensions, then SharePoint Team Services, and finally Windows SharePoint Services. Based on FrontPage Server Extensions (a technology that enabled Web developers to save Web pages directly to the server over HTTP), Office 2000 included a server-side feature that provided list functionality called Office Server Extensions. This led to the next revision of the Web-based team collaboration concept in 2001—SharePoint Team Services (STS). STS was included with FrontPage 2002 and OfficeXP Developer.

Note   You might notice that certain files in the SharePoint installation folders contain OWS or STS in them. These are artifacts from previous versions of SharePoint that stand for *Office Web Server* and *SharePoint Team Services*, respectively. You may also wonder what VTI stands for (as in VTI_BIN)—it's Vermeer Technologies, Inc., which was acquired by Microsoft. Vermeer Technologies was the original developer of FrontPage.

SharePoint Portal Server 2001

The collaboration platform was moved out of Exchange 2000, but Microsoft was determined to use the Web Store database technology. At this point, Microsoft realized that there were three key collaboration/portal needs: real-time collaboration, ad-hoc team collaboration, and an enterprise portal framework. SPS 2001 took a number of existing concepts and integrated them in one product: search (which came from Index Server), workflow (which evolved from Exchange 5.5 workflow concepts), document management (which was based on the Web Store), and a customizable Web portal (which evolved from the Digital Dashboard 3.0). The idea of a combined set of portal technologies was good; the implementation was, in hindsight, bad. SPS 2001 wasn't based on the same technology as SharePoint Team Services (which provided the team collaboration solution). Worse yet, you couldn't even install them on the same machine. SPS 2003 fixed this using a better architecture, mostly based on WSS 2.0, and better integration.

Windows SharePoint Services 2.0

The next revision of the Web-based team collaboration concept emerged as Windows SharePoint Services 2.0. Microsoft decided to include the platform with Windows Server 2003, rather than Office 2003. However, Office and WSS provided key integration points that made them each better when used with the other. The concepts from SharePoint Team Services were brought forward with an emphasis on a scalable and consistent architecture.

SharePoint Portal Server 2003

SPS 2003 was based on WSS 2.0 and provided search, portal, and aggregation features. Microsoft took a big leap forward, basing SPS on WSS (instead of being a completely separate product). However, in the end it was still two teams, two architectures, and two different user experiences. Microsoft also realized that WSS belonged as a core part of the operating system—which had a huge impact in terms of development focus and install base. Most customers bought SPS 2003 to implement a simple Intranet and to search across WSS 2.0 team sites.

Windows SharePoint Services 3.0

Microsoft took key feedback from customers, which included the following core mandates:

- *Do* continue to provide core Web, management, and collaboration features in the WSS platform.
- *Do* add incremental improvements (like a Recycle Bin and workflow) that will enhance the experience and usability of the product.
- *Don't* change the core architecture to the point where migration will be next to impossible.

Microsoft has done an impressive job evolving the SharePoint platform in a way that accomplishes those objectives.

Microsoft Office SharePoint Server 2007

MOSS 2007 was a true superset of WSS 3.0 and provides search, portal, and aggregation features, along with business data, Excel Services, and Web-based forms. And in this release, the WSS and MOSS technologies are completely integrated from the management to the UI to the end-user features to the programming APIs. Another key addition in this release was the inclusion of Web Content Management functionality, formerly found in a separate product, the Content Management Server. MOSS 2007 allowed organizations to create highly stylized pages and gave them a foundation for running not only their intranets and extranets, but also their public facing Internet sites, on top of the SharePoint platform.

Current Versions of SharePoint Products and Technologies

There are three primary versions of SharePoint in the 2010 timeframe: Microsoft SharePoint Foundation 2010 (which replaces WSS 3.0), Microsoft SharePoint Server 2010 Standard, and Microsoft SharePoint Server 2010 Enterprise. Microsoft SharePoint Server 2010 Standard includes the features of SharePoint Foundation 2010, and Microsoft SharePoint Server 2010 Enterprise includes the features of SharePoint Foundation 2010 and Microsoft SharePoint Server 2010 Standard. In this way, each version is a complete superset of the one it builds upon.

Microsoft SharePoint Foundation 2010

With the 2010 release of SharePoint technologies, Microsoft has evolved both the core platform as well as development options through products such as SharePoint Designer 2010 and Visual Studio 2010.

SharePoint Foundation 2010 is freely available as a component of Windows Server 2008. SharePoint Foundation 2010 provides core collaboration services, with templates for team sites, workspaces, blogs, and wikis. SharePoint Foundation 2010 is based on ASP.NET 2.0 and requires .NET Framework 3.5.

Microsoft SharePoint Server 2010

Like MOSS 2007, Microsoft SharePoint Server 2010 is a superset of SharePoint Foundation 2010 and provides additional application features on top of the core SharePoint platform. The next section describes the changes to Microsoft SharePoint Server 2010.

Microsoft SharePoint Server 2010 is the next version of Microsoft Office SharePoint Server 2007 (MOSS). SharePoint Server 2010 comes in two distinct licensed versions: Standard and Enterprise. SharePoint Server 2010 Standard builds on top of SharePoint Foundation to provide portal, enterprise search, social computing, and enterprise content management features. SharePoint Server 2010 Enterprise builds on top of SharePoint Server 2010 Standard to include services such as InfoPath forms services, Excel Services, Visio Services, Word Services, Access Services, and Performance Point Services.

Microsoft SharePoint Server 2010 is also licensed in an Internet mode called Microsoft SharePoint Server 2010 for Internet Sites, with both a standard and enterprise version. This licensing mechanism is targeted at Internet-facing SharePoint installations (that is, public Web sites and extranet sites).

In addition to the traditionally licensed versions of SharePoint 2010, Microsoft provides a cloud-based offering called SharePoint Online, which can be found at http://www.microsoft.com/online/sharepoint-online.mspx.

Microsoft SharePoint Server 2010 and Office 2010

Microsoft's goal is to provide consistent collaboration functionality in an architecturally sound manner. One of the core principles that contribute to this is the reuse of common services. The Windows Server operating system provides core Web server and workflow services (via .NET 3.5 SP1). The .NET Framework provides the Web Part Framework and Web concepts like master pages. SQL Server provides database services. SharePoint Foundation provides core information services such as security, management, and a site provisioning engine. The rest of the SharePoint 2010 server components build on top of the core SharePoint Foundation platform to provide additional features. Figure 2-3 shows the many components, built on top of a succession of platform services that comprise the overall architecture. In the rest of this section, we explore each component in more detail.

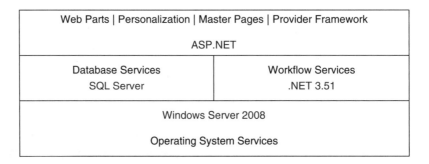

Figure 2-3 The SharePoint 2010 technologies provide a wide array of capabilities, built upon Windows Server and .NET, and are delivered in three tiers: SharePoint Foundation 2010, Microsoft SharePoint Server 2010 Standard, and Microsoft SharePoint Server 2010 Enterprise

Operating System Services: Windows Server 2008 SP2 (64-bit)

Windows Server provides base operating system services, such as the NTFS file system, the Internet Information Server Web server, and provides application server features such as messaging queuing and component management services. *The collaboration platform technologies discussed in this book only run on Windows Server 2008 SP2 (64-bit) and above and are not supported on other operating systems such as Linux or Solaris.* They are, however, accessible via a Web browser from clients on these systems.

Database Services: Microsoft SQL Server

Both SharePoint Foundation 2010 and Microsoft SharePoint Server 2010 require the use of a database server for storage of configuration information, metadata, and file storage. SharePoint 2010 requires the use of either Microsoft SQL Server 2005 SP3 (64-bit edition) or SQL Server 2008 SP1

(64-bit edition). For very small workgroup deployments, SharePoint will run using the SQL Server Express database included with SharePoint Foundation. *SharePoint 2010 is not supported on non-Microsoft databases such as MySQL and Oracle.*

Workflow Services: Windows Workflow Foundation

SharePoint 2010 supports workflow by building on top of the Windows Workflow Foundation (the .NET 3.51 SP1 version). There are essentially three native ways to create workflows: use the out-of-box workflows (which ship via templates in Microsoft SharePoint Server 2010), create a workflow using SharePoint Designer 2010 or Visio 2010, or create a workflow in Visual Studio 2010 (for more complex workflows). We cover the use and creation of workflows in Chapter 11, "Making Business Processes Work: Workflow and Forms."

Web Page Services: ASP.NET

Core Web functionality in SharePoint 2010 is provided by the .NET Framework, specifically in the ASP.NET toolset. The Web Part Framework is included in ASP.NET, enabling developers to create Web Parts that work in ASP.NET Web sites, SharePoint Foundation sites, and Microsoft SharePoint Server 2010 sites. (It is important to note, however, that ASP.NET Web Parts are not exactly the same as SharePoint 2010 Web Parts.) In addition, ASP.NET and SharePoint 2010 share some key features such as master pages, which makes user interface (UI) customization much easier.

Collaboration Services

SharePoint Foundation provides a core set of services for developing collaborative workspaces. We focus on SharePoint Foundation as both a platform for the other SharePoint Server 2010 features as well as a rich collaborative technology in its own right.

Portal

Microsoft SharePoint Server 2010 provides a core set of services for developing sites that enable users to view aggregated lists of content, links, and other information. With SharePoint Sever 2010, enterprises can manage their intranets, extranets, and Internet sites with the same platform. Features such as audience targeting enable content administrators to direct Web Parts and other content to dynamic groups of users.

Enterprise Content Management (ECM)

Microsoft SharePoint Server 2010 provides content management features that enable organizations to develop and manage HTML-rich Web sites. SharePoint Server 2010 provides Approval, Policy, Rights Management, Retention, Multilingual, and Web Publishing features. Content is content is content; it doesn't matter whether you serve content up as HTML or a Word Document anymore. Enterprise content management is discussed more in both Chapter 6, "Making Enterprise Content Management Work: Documents and Records" and Chapter 12, "Putting Your Site on the Web."

Search

SharePoint 2010 provides a number of key features, including searching against disparate content sources, people search, and business data search. For more information on search, see Chapter 10, "Making Search Work: Content, People, Data."

Social Computing (Communities)

Microsoft SharePoint Server 2010 provides features that enable users to provide social feedback on content, including tagging, ratings, and comments. SharePoint Server 2010 also provides a number of people-centric features such as a profile store and personalized sites. My Sites, as these are called, were introduced in SharePoint Portal Server 2003 and provide a site for users to call their own. Through the social computing features in SharePoint Server 2010, businesses can create an experience akin to Facebook or LinkedIn for their end users. We discuss social computing in Chapter 7, "Getting Social: Leveraging Community Features."

Business Intelligence (Insights)

Microsoft SharePoint Server 2010 brings business intelligence (BI) features to the mainstream. Excel Server Calculations, PerformancePoint Services, KPIs, Dashboards, Report Center, and SQL Reporting Services all provide business intelligence via the SharePoint 2010 platform. We cover the BI features in Chapter 13, "Making Business Intelligence Work."

Composite Applications (Composites)

Collaboration is useful and becomes compelling when integrated with real business data. Being able to create rich applications quickly that combine information in SharePoint with information from other sources (such as a database, LOB application, or the Web), is compelling. We cover how to quickly create dynamic applications ("mashups" and "composites") in Chapter 14, "Composite Applications with Business Connectivity Services."

Table 2-1 shows the respective technologies that make up Microsoft's overall information worker platform. This book's focus is Microsoft SharePoint Server 2010.

Table 2-1 Microsoft's Information Worker Products

Technology	Description
SharePoint Foundation 2010	SharePoint Foundation is the core Web-based team workspace and site tool. SharePoint Foundation is licensed free with Windows Server 2008 Server, available as a download from the Microsoft Windows Server site.
Microsoft SharePoint Server 2010 Standard	Microsoft SharePoint Server 2010 builds on top of SharePoint Foundation to provide additional functionality along with aggregation, search, social, content management features, and most of the Business Connectivity Services (BCS).
Microsoft SharePoint Server 2010 Enterprise	Microsoft SharePoint Server 2010 Enterprise builds on SharePoint Server 2010 Standard to provide additional features such as InfoPath Web forms, Visio, Access, and Word Services, and business intelligence (BI).
Office Communicator (Client)	Office Communicator is the core real-time messaging client.
Office Communications Server	Office Communications Server is the server-side component that enables real-time communications features, such as instant messaging, presence, and real-time meetings.
Microsoft BizTalk Server 2008	BizTalk provides core integration functions and ships with an adapter for SharePoint.
Exchange Server 2010	Designed to run on the 64-bit version of Microsoft Windows Server 2008, Exchange Server 2010 is Microsoft's mail server product.
Office 2010	Office 2010 provides e-mail integration, offline content synchronization, Excel publishing, and other features that integrate with SharePoint 2010.

SharePoint 2010: What's New?

The previous version of SharePoint was a breakthrough version of Microsoft's core collaboration platform. Microsoft's plan for SharePoint 2010 was to build upon the far-reaching success of SharePoint 2007. Specifically, the architectural goals for SharePoint Foundation 2010 include

- Scalability
- Performance
- Security
- Support for a large number of deployment scenarios (intranet, extranet, and Internet)
- Core out-of-the-box features
- Easier administration and health monitoring
- Claims-based authentication
- Better upgrade scenarios
- Easier-to-deploy solutions

One of the key tenets of the SharePoint 2010 release was to build upon the success of previous versions while preserving the items that made SharePoint 2007 a success. Thus, the SharePoint team kept the core architecture the same while adding a number of new features. Table 2-2 lists some of the new features in SharePoint 2010.

Table 2-2 SharePoint 2010: What's New?

Feature	Description
UI and Navigation	<ul><li>Office-like ribbon user interface</li><li>Better Web editing (sites are a collection of pages)</li><li>Out-of-box MUI (Multi-User Interface)</li><li>Better audience targeting</li><li>Additional WCAG 2.0 compliance</li><li>Office Web Applications (licensed with Office 2010)</li><li>Silverlight support</li><li>AJAX support</li></ul>
Core Collaboration	<ul><li>Enhanced site templates</li><li>Offline access via SharePoint Workspace 2010</li><li>Enterprise wikis</li></ul>
Social Computing	<ul><li>Enhanced blogs and wikis</li></ul>

Feature	Description
	■ Enhanced My Sites (status updates and social activity feeds) ■ Knowledge mining ■ Social tagging, bookmarking, ratings, and comments ■ WYSIWYG wiki editing ■ Wikis for mobile clients ■ Enhanced blogging: user and team blogs
Search	■ Improved search user experience ■ Improved people and expert search ■ Nickname search ■ Social behavior search ■ FAST Search for SharePoint 2010
Enterprise Content Management	■ Managed metadata ■ Unique Document IDs ■ Document sets ■ Advanced routing ■ In-place records management ■ Enhanced Web content management ■ Rich media management (audio, video)
Business Intelligence	■ Enhanced Excel Services ■ PerformancePoint Services ■ Visio Services ■ Chart Web Parts and status indicators
Composite Application Support	■ Read/Write data connections via Business Connectivity Services ■ Access Services ■ Excel Services ■ Improved application support via SharePoint Designer 2010 ■ Sandboxed solutions
IT Pro Improvements	■ Easier upgrade ■ Visual upgrade ■ Service applications instead of SSPs ■ Powershell support ■ Multi tenancy
Developer Improvements	■ Enhanced APIs ■ Visual Studio 2010 project templates ■ Improved interoperability via REST, WSRP, Client Object Model ■ Sandboxed solutions

Comparing SharePoint Foundation to Microsoft SharePoint Server 2010

SharePoint Foundation 2010 is a collection of services for Microsoft Windows Server 2008 that you can use to share information, collaborate with other users on documents, and create lists and Web part pages. You can also use SharePoint Foundation as a development platform to create collaboration applications and information-sharing applications, as discussed in the next section.

Microsoft SharePoint Server 2010, a step up from SharePoint Foundation, is a scalable enterprise server that is built on top of SharePoint Foundation. You can use Microsoft SharePoint Server 2010 to aggregate SharePoint Foundation sites, other information, and applications in your organization. Because Microsoft SharePoint Server 2010 requires SharePoint Foundation, all features of SharePoint Foundation are available in Microsoft SharePoint Server 2010. In addition to the core features of SharePoint Foundation (core site-based services and collaboration site templates), Microsoft SharePoint Server 2010 Standard and Enterprise include the following features:

Microsoft SharePoint Server 2010 Standard

- **Portal**. Provides a way to create an Intranet portal, an extranet portal, and an Internet facing .com site on a single platform.
- **User Profiles**. Provides an extensible profile for each employee, the ability for users to search and find expertise within the company.
- **Social Computing**. Provides a way for users to socially tag, rate, and comment on content.
- **Audiences**. Provides a way to target content to groups of users based on rules.
- **Search**. Provides extensible search functionality across file shares, Web sites, Microsoft Exchange Public Folders, Lotus Notes, and SharePoint sites.
- **Records Management**. Provides document auditing, expiry, and other features that enable you to manage company records.
- **Web Content Management**. Provides functionality for business users to create and manage Web-based content (HTML) based on templates.

- **Business Connectivity Services (BCS)**. Provides a way to integrate line-of-business data into portal pages, team sites, document metadata, enterprise search, and employee profiles. (Note: most, but not all, of BCS is available in Standard edition.)
- **Word Services**. Provides the ability to publish and render Word 2010 documents on the server.

Microsoft SharePoint Server 2010 Enterprise

- **PerformancePoint Services**. Provides business intelligence capabilities, a report center template, and Key Performance Indicator (KPI) lists and Web Parts.
- **InfoPath Forms Services**. Provides the ability to publish, render, and consume InfoPath 2010 forms and Web controls via a Web browser.
- **Excel Services**. Provides the ability to publish and render Excel 2010 workbooks on the server; enables calculations and graphics rendering via a Web interface.
- **Access Services**. Provides the ability to publish and render Access 2010 databases on the server; enables the Access application to run within SharePoint via a Web interface.
- **Visio Services**. Provides the ability to publish and render Visio 2010 diagrams on the server.

Table 2-3 describes the feature set included with the core SharePoint 2010 products.

So with all of these features, what does SharePoint 2010 provide from a collaboration and solutions perspective? For many companies still using file shares for document sharing and Access databases (and Excel, for that matter) for tracking applications, it provides a perfect next step. Let's take a look at these two trends: using SharePoint as a file share replacement and as an Access database/Excel workbook replacement.

SharePoint: The File Share Killer

Microsoft salespeople often describe SharePoint as a great file share replacement. Customers frequently ask whether SharePoint will completely replace file shares. If you put SharePoint into place, should you disconnect your file shares for good? The answer is a resounding *No!*

Table 2-3 Comparing SharePoint Foundation 2010 to Microsoft SharePoint Server 2010 Standard and Microsoft SharePoint Server 2010 Enterprise

Business Need	SharePoint Foundation 2010	Microsoft SharePoint Server 2010 Standard	Microsoft SharePoint Server 2010 Enterprise	Microsoft SharePoint Server 2010 for Internet Sites
Collaboration using user-created team sites and workspaces	Yes	Yes	Yes	Yes
Browser-based end-user customization	Yes	Yes	Yes	Yes
E-mail-enabled discussion boards	Yes	Yes	Yes	Yes
Document management (check in/out, versions, Content Types)	Yes	Yes	Yes	Yes
Blogs and wikis	Yes	Yes	Yes	Yes
Local search (sites and subsites)	Yes	Yes	Yes	Yes
Custom lists, surveys, templates	Yes	Yes	Yes	Yes
RSS feeds on any list	Yes	Yes	Yes	Yes
Offline (synchronization with SharePoint Workspace 2010)	Yes	Yes	Yes	Yes
Integration with LOB data through Business Connectivity Services	Yes	Yes	Yes	Yes
Out-of-box workflow templates for approval and review		Yes	Yes	Yes
Enterprise search (docs, sites, people)		Yes	Yes	Yes
Records management (auditing, retention policy)		Yes	Yes	Yes
Centralized user profiles		Yes	Yes	Yes
Social tagging and feedback		Yes	Yes	Yes
Managed metadata services		Yes	Yes	Yes
Targeting content to rule-based groups (Audiences)		Yes	Yes	Yes
Create and maintaining news		Yes	Yes	Yes
Personal sites		Yes	Yes	Yes

Business Need	SharePoint Foundation 2010	Microsoft SharePoint Server 2010 Standard	Microsoft SharePoint Server 2010 Enterprise	Microsoft SharePoint Server 2010 for Internet Sites
Track team sites with metadata for searching and browsing (Site directory)		Yes	Yes	Yes
Web content management		Yes	Yes	Yes
Web-based InfoPath forms			Yes	Yes
KPI lists and Report Center			Yes	Yes
Excel Services			Yes	Yes
Access Services			Yes	Yes
Word Services		Yes	Yes	Yes
Visio Services			Yes	Yes
Licensing model	Windows Server License + Windows Server CAL or Windows External Connector	Windows Server License + Windows CAL + Microsoft SharePoint Server 2010 Server License + Microsoft SharePoint Server 2010 Standard CAL (or Core CAL Suite)	Windows Server License + Windows CAL + Microsoft SharePoint Server 2010 Server License + Microsoft SharePoint Server 2010 Standard CAL (or Core CAL Suite) + Microsoft SharePoint Server 2010 Enterprise CAL (or Enterprise CAL Suite)	Windows Server License + Windows External Connector + Microsoft SharePoint Server 2010 + for Internet Sites (No CALs)

First, SharePoint is designed for file *sharing*, while Windows file shares are good for file *storage*. Ask yourself whether the files in question have little collaborative value or are simply too large or costly to store in SharePoint. If any of these are true, a file share is probably a better place for these files.

File Storage Is Not Dead

Joel Oleson, a former product manager at Microsoft, describes why you still need file shares. This section is from Joel's blog (reprinted with permission):

> The file servers that end users are using by copying a word doc and sending a link to an associate or friend are on their way out. The U: drive or M: drive, or whatever it might be in your company for sharing your collaborative data, and the S: or N: drive, or whatever it might be for team file sharing, the days may be numbered. Team shares currently on long UNC paths (\\mystorage\users\joelo\docs\ and \\myshared\marketing\ collateral\) for sharing office or collaborative files ... there are more efficient ways of sharing those files making them easier to find, consume, and easier to use with contextual collaboration.
>
> Before the party breaks out and the monolithic servers look to move all their data into the SharePoint platform, let me try to hold these virtual horses. File Storage is *not* dead.
>
> There are many extremely useful scenarios for intelligent file storage. Let me first separate file storage from file sharing. The end user file sharing of collaborative files is a great scenario for the SharePoint platform whether it happens to be SharePoint Foundation 2010 or Microsoft SharePoint Server 2010. Let me break down

Table: Simplified Comparison of File Server File Features and SharePoint Server File Features

Windows 2003 R2 File Share	SharePoint Server Document Center
ACL-based file security and effective permissions (AD only)	Authorization based item security with user picker, supporting AD, LDAP, and .NET-pluggable providers

Windows 2003 R2 File Share	SharePoint Server Document Center
	Opt-in e-mail based access request
Windows auditing	Security and policy based auditing, expiration and pivot reports
Shadow copy user restore (not configured by default)	User restore with recycle bin Second-stage Site Collection recycle bin (default)
Distributed file system replication (not recommended with two way editing)	One-way content publishing paths and jobs including quick deploy
WAN throttling	# Threads throttling and scheduling
RDC (Remote Differential Compression)	Multi farm shared services (not over WAN)
	E-mail enabled (requires configuration)
	Check-in/check-out w/ forced check-out
Snapshotted versions (not changed based versions)	Version history/major/minor versions
File-level rights management	File and document library rights management integration policies
Sorting (grouping in Vista), workflow engine (requires customization)	Filtering, grouping, workflow (out of the box), Content Types
File service resource manager for quotas or third party	Site collection quotas, built in usage reporting, storage manager
NTFS compression, EFS and My Documents redirection (client dependencies)	Database encryption with third party, backup compression with third party
Nontransactional; no rollback without shadow copies	SQL Server transaction logs

(continues)

the some top features of document libraries and document centers vs. an intelligent Windows Server 2008 file server.

After that glowing file-level analysis, there are some other things to look at. In SharePoint technologies with transaction-level logging and storage in relational databases, there is overhead associated. As a result, file storage in most cases will be cheaper than storage in SharePoint or SQL databases in general. When evaluating the service for your end users, try to understand the value to the business.

There are some scenarios that are clearly better served by Windows Server file services. This is why you will likely still have file servers in your company.

File Server Scenarios

Product Distribution (Product packages like Office)—by default Windows file servers have a great mechanism for transferring large packages. SharePoint lists work well with files under 50MB and can be used up to 2GB, with configuration. When you roll out Office 2007 to your end users it will most likely not be stored in SharePoint doc libraries for example, but the page or list for communication and link to install it from might be.

SMS distribution point (desktop patches and hot fixes)—for hot fixes, patches, application distribution such as add/remove program distribution points are much better served directly from a DFS Distributed File Services file share. With optimization for your WAN leveraging the DFSR (replication) technologies packages can be distributed and optimally updated across the wire. This same DFSR technology does not work well in a multi master scenario where multiple users are working on the same files due to lack of ability for scheduling or remote locking.

NT Backups, Backup Servers and Desktop Backups (backups)—Many corporations that use "My Documents folder redirection" with group policies may wonder if a backup of their desktops or redirection to a SharePoint site is a good scenario. This is an untested scenario. Creating mapped drives to the Web folder location of your "my site" may work for some users, but it is not recommended to create policies for your corporation. With disk-based backups file storage is going to continue to be a commodity inside a corporation.

Corporations that desire to migrate this scenario from file servers can choose to force users to keep their master documents in their "my site" with offline in Outlook 2007 or Groove 2007. If you can get users to store their important or business critical personal files on their SharePoint "my site", the arduous desktop backup task may not be as necessary (depending on the scenario/corporation).

Database Storage—(.mdb, .ldf, ndf, .pst, .ost)—SharePoint lists are incredible ways of capturing data or displaying information from your information workers. These flat structures can be extended now with lookup columns simulating a simplified relational storage. At this stage relational databases should not be considered to be stored in SharePoint lists, but via the Business Data Catalog, data can be displayed or indexed or leveraged for column validation or as lookups. Databases such as SQL databases themselves are not good candidates for storage in a document library. Files that require locking or that have transaction logs would be more appropriate for storage on the file system. If your data needs triggers or stored procedures you may look at the workflows and events as mechanisms for this, but it is not supported to create triggers or stored procedures inside the SharePoint databases. Access databases in Access 2007 have a number of ways that they can both be published to SharePoint lists, consume lists, and display reports. In these new Access 2007 scenarios you will need to determine what the best scenario for the storage is. Access 2003 databases should not be stored in SharePoint document libraries where multiple users need to edit the access database simultaneously.

Large Audio/Video and Streaming Media and other large archive read-only media such as DVDs, CDs storage (.iso, .wmv, .ram, .vhd)—Media can easily be linked to/from a SharePoint site, but often the storage is simply more costly. Unless the audio is contextual with the collaboration or workspace or is under 50 MB, you may consider leveraging Windows Media Server for streaming the content, which will have a better experience for your end users and be more manageable for those trying to distribute the media. VPCs could fall into this scenario very easily. If you have a 5GB VPC you are trying to share with a group, a temporary location on a file server is going to be cheaper and efficient. Inside your company you may decide to increase the default upload file size from 50MB to 100MB, or maybe if you collaborate on large files you could increase this up to a

(continues)

maximum of 2GB. Most companies have found that 50MB or 100MB has encouraged users to use the platform appropriately.

Developer Source Control—Although versions and version history and check out are common terms for developers working on projects, the SharePoint platform is not the best use for source control. Likely a source control application like Visual Source Safe, Source Depot, or other third parties, would be best. The storage may be a database or sit on the file system. Solutions can be packaged and stored and distributed if they are small and common within a team. Visual Studio Team System has its own source control tools but, it also uses WSS for collaboration for specs, tasks and document storage.

Batch, Command Scripts, Executables (.exe, .vbs, .cmd, .bat)—By default most scripts and executables are blocked in SharePoint. This is for your own protection. You may find that most of these file types are blocked in e-mail by default as well. This is to slow down the distribution of virus-prone files. It is recommended to install an antivirus product such as Forefront for SharePoint for WSS 3.0 and MOSS 2007 or Antigen for WSS 2.0 and SPS 2003. With the feature of "blocked file types" you can decide what to do with these files. Based on how they are executed via the Web UI or via Web folders many executables with other dependencies may not work. For this reason, you may want to package any small applications or simply block them from being added to the SharePoint lists.

Application Server ... Client Application Storage Linked Files and File Dependencies (.lnk, .lck)—A lot of this scenario has to do with client applications and how they interact with the file type. The protocols are very different and behave differently. They both have their pros and cons. For example, some AutoCAD drawings that may have dependencies in other files that expect a path over SMB and not HTTP or relative will break and not properly render. You may notice when loading a Visio with a template that some template dependencies may not load (this is not very common). As well, Excel files that link cells between spreadsheets may expect a specific file path that is not there and the link will not load properly. In the Excel example, there are now new Excel 2007 publishing scenarios that enable calculations, spreadsheets, and charts to render on the server. If you have multiple data in multiple spreadsheets that is business critical you may consider moving this and storing it in a data warehouse and creating queries, using analysis services and surfacing those in Excel Services on SharePoint Server. Another example of dependencies is the lock files which require an .lck when in use. Editing these files may experience problems or simply not lock when editing. I recommend using the check out, then downloading the file and uploading and check in for users of files that require a lock. Most of these scenarios will end up as FAQs rather than blocked file types.

Archives and Dumps (.arj, .rar, .zip, .dmp, .bak)—Since file storage is cheap and plentiful, and your SharePoint platform storage is the premium, you can make some decisions about what type of storage is leveraged for database dumps. Obviously copies of production databases can easily and cost efficiently be dumped to disk. Disk-based backups are becoming more and more common for backing up your application servers. Being able to do a point-in-time backup and recovery very quickly from disk is important for keeping short business continuance SLAs. Tape vs. disk is the next question. Offline vs. near line vs. online is pushing near line to nonexistence and with business-critical data the offline is getting pushed further and further out and eliminated in some cases by remote failover. Your SLAs will drive the disaster recovery, business continuance … distance, failover and offline storage strategy.

Exception: For most archives it is cheapest for online storage to be on file storage, but for resources that need to be quickly searched and indexed a SharePoint server will provide more accessibility for a cost. For example, your legal team wants to create Exchange journaling for e-mails that have a legal retention placed on them. With Exchange 2007 and managed folders the e-mails can be archived to a list which can be used to search for e-mails with this requirement. As well, with records management scenarios the SharePoint lists themselves may need to be archived, but still be accessible. These online archives can be done on cheaper disks with less frequent backup requirements or even 97% SLA since they need only be used very infrequently.

Small zips as well can be an efficient way to store a small package on SharePoint, and many end users know how to deal with them with built-in compression utilities in recent desktop OSs.

(continues)

Disk Space and Cost Considerations

I have mentioned cost a few times; consider RAID 5 volumes for your SharePoint Data drives and RAID 0+1 for transaction logs when comparing the systems. Although SharePoint server storage is SQL server, the disk I/O for the content databases is extremely low compared to Exchange drives, for example, with the exception of the search database. Many enterprises are now using RAID 5 for their content databases. The backup methods and differences between the SQL backups and the File server backups do have cost implications as well as associated software costs.

So Who Wins—File Shares or SharePoint?

Collaborative file shares can be replaced with SharePoint deployments. Product distribution and database storage will continue to persist as valid scenarios. End users will need training to understand where to save their files. With most file sharing scenarios for the most common file sizes SharePoint lists will be the Microsoft-recommended way of sending files inside the corporation, and with collaborative SharePoint site extranet deployments, it's the way to share with partners. Most nontechnical end user scenarios such as the most common HR, Sales, and Marketing teams can say goodbye to using file shares for file sharing. Some groups and divisions like IT SMS/Product Distribution, Data Warehousing (SQL), Media, and Development groups won't be saying goodbye to file servers in Windows 2003 and in code name "Longhorn" with key scenarios leveraging cheap NTFS file storage.

Analyzing your current file servers by server or share or folder may allow you to group them by purpose. Here are some examples of common classifications: Collaborative File Sharing, Historical Archive, Media Server, Dump/Desktop Backup, Source Control Servers/Databases, Personal Storage, Product Distribution, and Application Servers.

As you can see, there are a number of valid reasons for having both file shares and SharePoint document libraries in your organization. In fact, you may decide to keep existing collaborative content on your file shares and simply use SharePoint 2010's search technology to enable users to search for existing documents (rather than migrating those documents to SharePoint).

So the file share question is answered … but what about Access databases and Excel workbooks? Are those dead?

SharePoint: The Access and Excel Killer

Overheard at an organization near you:

Business User (to IT Department): We need an application to track donations to our upcoming fundraising campaign.

IT Department: What are the requirements?

Business User: We need to track donors, contributions, project tasks, documents, and approvals; search on items; and provide reports to management.

IT Department: We can build it in four months.

Business User: (Gasp)

IT Department: If you can secure additional funding, we can do it in two.

Business User: Never mind. I'll create an Access database and throw it on a file share.

IT Department: (Gasp)

The problem with this fairly common scenario is that now there's yet another database out there that's probably not backed up properly, cannot support Web-based access, and is virtually unknown and unsupported by IT. This is another reason why IT departments are putting SharePoint in place—to support requests by the business for collaboration and tracking applications.

> **Q: What's the world's most widely used database application?**
>
> **A: Microsoft Excel.**

In addition to its great collaboration features, SharePoint 2010 can be very effective as a platform to create information-sharing and tracking applications. Let's look at an example of the business need described by the business user—one that can be addressed in a matter of minutes without code. Previously, this type of solution would take months for a development team to build from scratch.

Let's say that one of the business units within your organization needs to track donations that are being raised for a campaign of some sort. There is a team of fundraisers that needs to track contributions, project managers who need to plan various fundraising events, and management personnel who need to see an updated status of progress. Let's say that the team tracks donors in a spreadsheet that gets e-mailed around. However, items like actual contributions made by whom, event planning documents, and other items are not tracked in an organized manner.

During discovery, some of the requirements that come to light are as follows:

- The need to track the following entities:
  - Donors (contacts)
  - Contributions (associated with donors)
  - Project tasks (for planning fundraising events)
  - Team announcements (with RSS feeds)
  - Documents (including version tracking, community tagging, ratings, and comments)
- A workflow-based approval process
- Highly scalable, Web-based access
- Item-level security
- Search
- Threshold reporting and visual indicators for management

While this type of application could be written as a custom Web application, it would likely take several weeks (or possibly even several months) of custom development. Let's see what a no-code method of creating the solution in SharePoint 2010 would look like. It's as simple as creating a new site, importing the existing spreadsheet, and configuring some new elements.

Walkthrough

The following steps illustrate how to build a collaborative application in SharePoint Server 2010. To get a peek at the application in its final form, check out Figure 2-15 on page 59, which shows the completed collaborative application—created in less than an hour. We assume that you've got at least a test environment set up that you can play with, or maybe you already have a production environment; either way, you will need site creation permissions to perform these actions.

Note   If you keep getting prompted for a username and password when using your SharePoint site, make sure that the root URL (say, http://intranet.company .com) is added to your local Intranet zone within your browser.

Step 1: Create a new, blank site by navigating to the home site.

1. Click Site Actions → New Site.
2. Add title, description, URL name, and select the Blank Site template (see Figure 2-4).
3. Select the option to use unique permissions.
4. Click Create.
5. The wizard offers to create three new SharePoint groups; add the appropriate users to the groups (see Figure 2-5).
6. Click OK.
7. When prompted to Set Up Groups for this Site, accept the defaults and click OK.

The result is a blank SharePoint team site (see Figure 2-6).

Step 2: Create a new SharePoint list based on an existing spreadsheet full of contacts (donors). You can download a sample spreadsheet at www. jornata.com/books.

1. Click Site actions → More Options … (see Figure 2-7).
2. Under Custom Lists, select Import Spreadsheet (Note: If you've installed Silverlight, you'll find Import Spreadsheet under Blank & Custom—then click Create).
3. Name the list **Donors** and then click Browse to select an Excel file that contains the list of contacts.
4. Click Import.
5. SharePoint opens the Excel sheet. Select the range of values and click Import.
6. The list is created using the schema from the Excel file (see Figure 2-8).

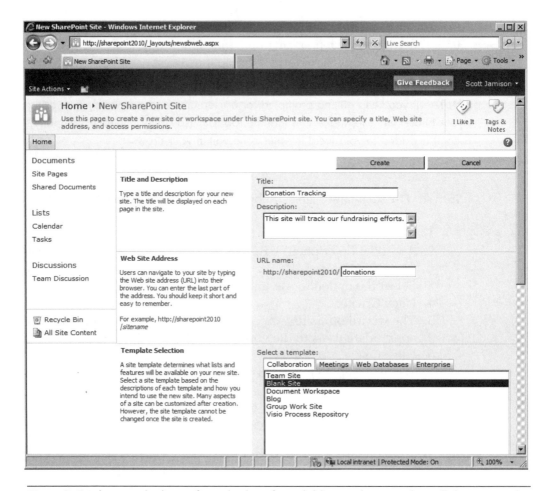

Figure 2-4 Selecting Blank Site from the list of available templates on the collaboration tab will provision a site with no predefined lists

Step 3: Create a list to track donations made by donors in our contact list.

1. Click Site Actions → More Options ...
2. Under Blank & Custom, select Custom List.
3. Name it **Donations** and click Create.
4. In the Ribbon UI, click List Settings to configure the list.
5. Under the Columns heading, click Title, change its name to **Donation** (you cannot delete this column because it provides the link to the item), and click OK.
6. Under the Columns heading, click Create Column, name the new column **Donation Method**, making it a Choice field. Replace the

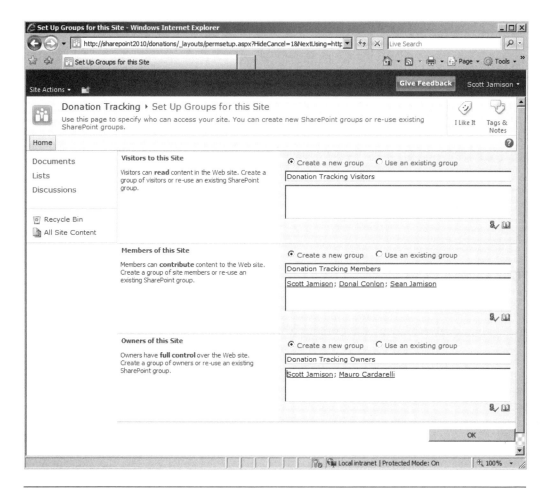

Figure 2-5 SharePoint's new site create wizard will automatically create groups

default choices (Enter Choice #1, and so on), with Cash, Stock and Clothing. Click OK.

7. Click Create Column and name the new column **Donor**. This time, select the Lookup column. Select the Donors list, FullName column. This associates a donation with a donor. Two new features in SharePoint 2010 enable you to enforce unique values and to enforce relationship linking behavior. Let's skip those for now. Click OK.

8. Click Create Column and name the new column **Amount**, designating it as a Currency field. Click OK.

Figure 2-6 After the blank site has been provisioned, you can add lists, Web Parts, and additional items to the site

Step 4: Create a document library with a workflow approval process.

1. Click Site Actions → New Document Library.
2. Name the library **Documents** and enable Document Version History.
3. Click Create.
4. Click Library Settings in the Library Tools Library tab in the Ribbon UI.
5. Under the Permissions and Management column, Click Workflow Settings.
6. Select the Approval—SharePoint 2010 Workflow. This is one of the out-of-the-box workflows that ship with Microsoft SharePoint Server 2010 (and is not available with SharePoint Foundation).
7. Call it **Fundraising Document Approval**.
8. Change the Start Option, Start this workflow when a new item is created (see Figure 2-9 on page 53).
9. On page 2, add one or more approvers (either a group or an individual).
10. Give each person two days to approve (see Figure 2-10 on page 54).
11. Click Save to save the workflow.

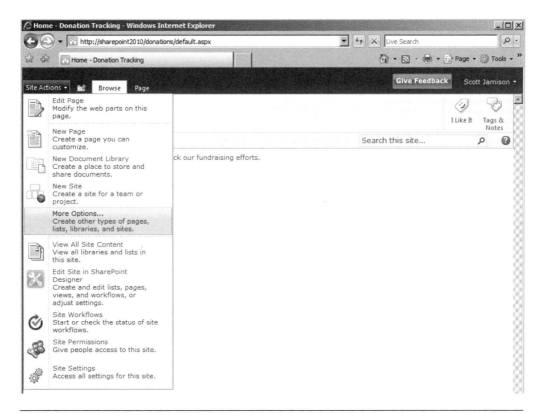

Figure 2-7 To create a new list within the SharePoint site, click More Options ... from the Site Actions menu

Step 5: Create a project task list.

1. Click Site Actions → More Options ...
2. Under Tracking, select Project Tasks, which enables you to track tasks and view Gantt Charts.
3. Name the list **Event Planning Tasks** and click Create.

Step 6: Create an announcements list.

1. Click Site Actions → More Options ...
2. Under Content & Data, select Announcements
3. Name the list **Announcements** and click Create.

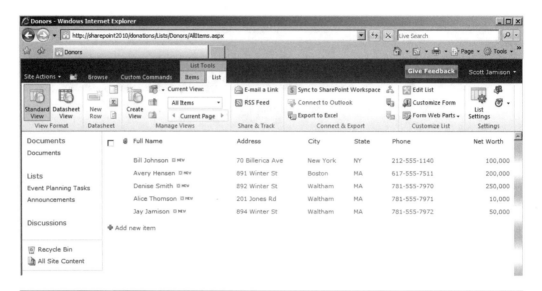

Figure 2-8 Creating a custom list by importing an Excel file is a quick first step in turning a spreadsheet into a full-fledged collaborative application. Note the ribbon UI, which enables the user to switch between managing the items in the list or the list itself.

Step 7: If you are using Microsoft SharePoint Server 2010 Enterprise, you can add some icon-based status indicators for threshold reporting (for management).

1. Click Site Actions → More Options ...
2. Select the Status List type.
3. Name the list **Goals** and click Create.
4. Add an item to track progress toward the fundraising goal. Let's assume we need to raise $10,000.
   a. Click New → SharePoint List based Status Indicator
   b. Name the item Fundraising Goal.
   c. Select the Donations list as your data source by clicking the icon next to List URL (see Figure 2-11 on page 55).
   d. Use Calculation using all list items in the view.
   e. Use the Sum of the Amount field, using indicator values of 10000 for the goal and 7500 as the warning threshold (see Figure 2-12 on page 56).
   f. Click OK.

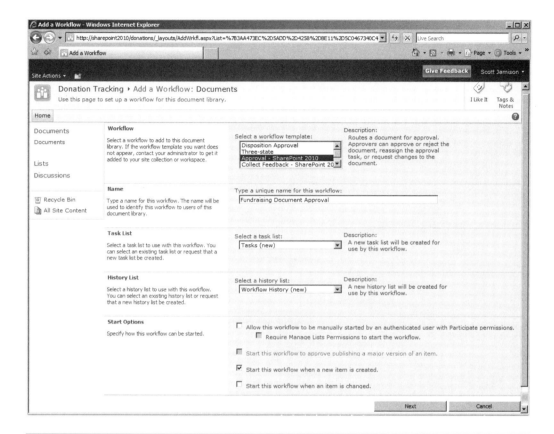

Figure 2-9 SharePoint supports workflow processes through out-of-the-box workflows or custom workflows. The out-of-box templates in SharePoint Server 2010 enable multistage workflow scenarios.

Note   If the list type option you are looking for does not appear as a choice, you may need to enable Microsoft SharePoint Server 2010 features on the site. To do so, click Site Actions → Site Settings. Under Site Actions, click Manage Site Features. Click Enable for both the Microsoft SharePoint Server 2010 Standard Site Features and the Microsoft SharePoint Server 2010 Enterprise Site Features. You can also enable features at the Site Collection level, which will typically cascade down to the subsites. You will need administrative permissions to enable site and Site Collection features.

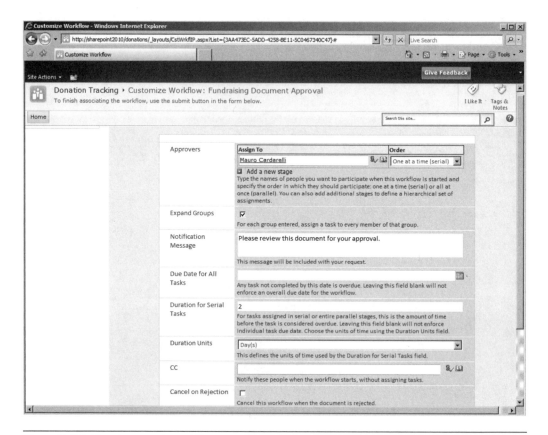

Figure 2-10 The Approval workflow enables a business user to configure a set of approval steps through a Web-based wizard interface

5. Next, let's add an item to track event planning tasks.
   a. Click New → SharePoint List based Status Indicator.
   b. Name: Event Planning.
   c. Point to the Event Planning Tasks list.
   d. Use Percentage of list items in the view where the % complete field is equal to 1 (which means True or 100%).
6. Set your Status Icon Rules so that Green = 80 (%) and Yellow = 60 (%).

Step 8: Add all of your Web Parts onto your site home page. Navigate back to the home page of your Donation Tracking site by clicking the site name in the breadcrumbs at the top of your page.

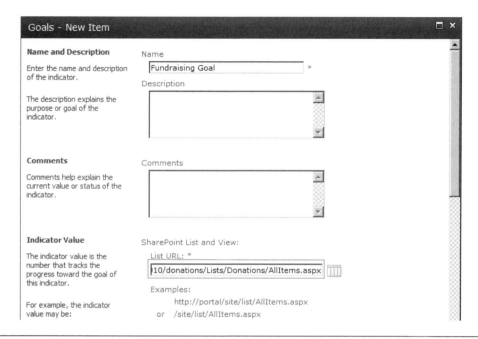

Figure 2-11 A Status list item (formerly known as a KPI list) enables you to define target data sources, which include other SharePoint lists

1. Click Site Actions → Edit Page.
2. In the Left Web Part zone, click Add a Web Part.
3. One at a time, add the list-based Web Parts except for the Goals list, which we will add in a moment (see Figure 2-13 on page 57).
4. In the Right Web Part zone, click Add a Web Part, this time selecting the Status List Web Part under the Business Data section of the Web Part gallery (see Figure 2-14 on page 58). Click Add.
5. In the Right Web Part zone, click the Edit Web Part menu option for the Status List Web Part.
6. Using the options pane, select the Goals list as the Indicator List. Click OK at the bottom of the options pane.
7. Click Stop Editing in the Ribbon UI to return to end-user mode.

Note When you click Edit Page, you are changing the page for all users. To edit the page for you only (a personalized view of the page), use the Personalize This Page option under the Welcome <username> in the top-right corner of the site.

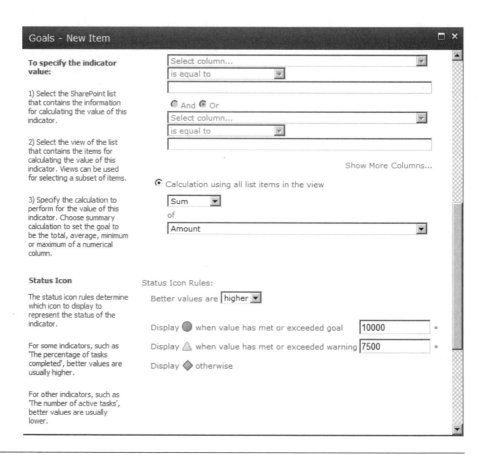

Figure 2-12 Status icon rules let you define threshold levels for your status indicator

Step 9: To complete your application, arrange your Web Parts so that the site looks good. In addition, you'll want to add some data.

1. Click Site Actions → Edit Page (or click Edit Page in the Ribbon).
2. Drag and drop your Web Parts to locations on the page that meet your liking. You'll also want to create custom views and then have the Web Part use those custom views.
3. Click Stop Editing in the Ribbon UI to return to the site.
4. Start adding data to the site. See Figure 2-15 on page 59 for an example of our new collaborative site.

This solution enables the tracking of data, file storage with metadata, a portal-centric interface, and search capabilities. All in under an hour! This

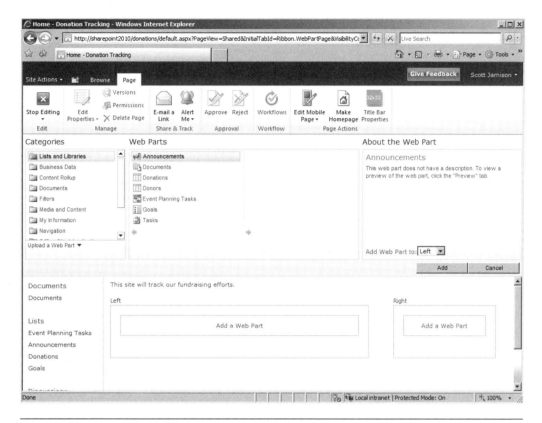

Figure 2-13 You can add the site's list-based Web Parts one at a time by selecting them from the site's Web Part gallery and clicking Add. (You can no longer add several Web Parts at once.)

is the power of a collaboration platform that enables business users, not developers, to create solutions based on a set of ready-to-assemble tools and features.

Key Points

We've covered a lot of information in this chapter—everything from the SharePoint 2010 family of products to what to do with your file shares to a sample collaborative SharePoint 2010 application. We hope that you're starting to get a feel for the functionality of SharePoint and the types of business issues it can help address.

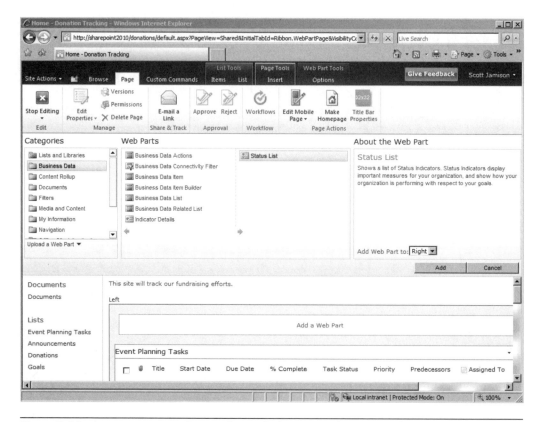

Figure 2-14 The Status List Web Part (formerly known as the Key Performance Indicators Web Part) enables you to configure how your indicators look—you can use check marks, traffic lights, and other visual elements

- Microsoft's family of communication and collaboration products, which includes the Office client applications, Microsoft SharePoint Server 2010, Office Communications Server, and Exchange Server 2010, comprises the foundation for Microsoft's Information Worker strategy.
- SharePoint Foundation 2010 provides a number of feature and developer enhancements over WSS 3.0 but keeps the fundamental architecture intact.
- SharePoint Foundation is based on ASP.NET and .NET 3.51 SP1.
- SharePoint Foundation provides a set of collaborative functionality, including Web page support, collaboration, document management, and a team workspace platform.

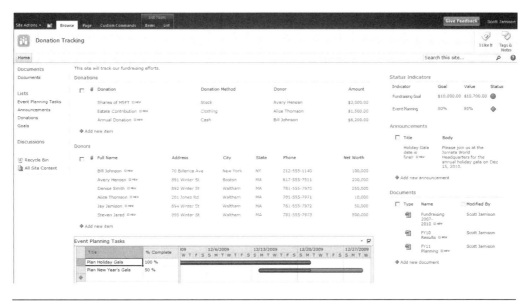

Figure 2-15 In less than an hour and with no code, SharePoint 2010 enables a business user to create a collaborative application, complete with related list data, documents, workflow, search, project tasks, RSS enabled announcements, and real-time reporting through visual indicators

- Microsoft SharePoint Server 2010 provides additional features on top of the SharePoint Foundation, including enterprise content management, social computing, search, business process management, and business intelligence.
- SharePoint Foundation 2010 and Microsoft SharePoint Server 2010 each require the 64-bit versions of Windows Server 2008 SP2 and Microsoft SQL Server (either 2005 SP3 or 2008 SP1) to run.
- Unlike previous versions, SharePoint 2010 supports claims-based authentication.
- SharePoint 2010 is a great place to build collaborative-style tracking applications with little to no code.

In the next chapter, we conclude our introduction by covering the architecture fundamentals of SharePoint 2010. The chapter is more technical than the rest but is very useful as the basis for understanding how to organize your Site Collections, sites, and pages within SharePoint.

CHAPTER 3

SharePoint 2010: Architecture Fundamentals

Whether you're a business user, manager, architect, developer, or IT pro, you'll want to understand the fundamental structure and core terminology of SharePoint 2010, given it will influence many choices you make, such as internal business ownership and total hardware costs. After reading this chapter, you'll understand the difference between sites and Site Collections, the difference between sites and pages, what service applications are, and why you may need as many as twenty servers or as few as one. Key sections of this chapter include

- Functional Overview
- SharePoint Fundamentals
- SharePoint Lists, Libraries, and Items
- Pages
- Navigation
- Understanding SharePoint Administration
- Physical Deployment Options

Functional Overview

Let's first review the key components of Microsoft SharePoint Server 2010, including the operating system, database services, SharePoint Foundation, SharePoint applications, and SharePoint application services. It is important to understand which functionality is provided by which component and how these components relate to each other.

Operating System

Microsoft SharePoint Server 2010 is built on top of SharePoint Foundation, which, in turn, is built on top of the technologies and services provided by Microsoft Windows Server 2008. The core platform services use the Microsoft .NET 3.51 Framework. This combination of Windows and .NET provides SharePoint with the following technologies:

- Internet Information Services 7.0 (for hosting Web applications)
- ASP.NET 2.x and above master pages, content pages (Web Part pages), Web Parts, personalization, membership, and navigation
- Workflow Foundation (part of .NET 3.51)

Database Services

Microsoft SQL Server (either SQL 2005 SP3 or SQL 2008 SP1) is the relational database used for storing all content, data, and configuration information used by Microsoft SharePoint Server 2010. And yes, that means that all content (including large documents) is stored in the database and not as files in the file system. Other relational databases, such as Oracle or MySQL, do not work and are not supported. If a separate database is not specified during installation, a specialized version of SQL Server 2008 Express is installed locally. The SharePoint-specific version of SQL Server 2008 Express has a database limit of 4GB and cannot be managed directly by SQL Enterprise Manager. For this reason, most organizations install SharePoint 2010 in a farm configuration and specify a separate SQL Server machine for the database server.

Note   Several third-party vendors provide options for storing documents on a file system instead of in the SQL Server database.

SharePoint Foundation 2010

SharePoint Foundation builds on the operating system and database services to add additional features, such as team sites and collaboration features. Specifically, SharePoint Foundation provides the following platform capabilities:

- **Storage**. Through content databases, which are literally SQL databases managed by SharePoint to accommodate the pages, data, and documents stored in the various portals, team sites, and workspaces
- **Management**. Administration pages with deep configuration options
- **Deployment**. Web farms, physical servers, roles
- **Site Model**. Web application, Site Collection, sites
- **Extensibility**. Features, Web Parts, templates

SharePoint Foundation provides more than just these core technology services. Microsoft decided to make SharePoint Foundation a powerful application out-of-the-box and thus provide the core collaboration features for Microsoft SharePoint Server 2010. These are:

- Document collaboration, including check-in/out and versions
- Wikis and blogs
- RSS support
- Project task management (lightweight functionality, which should not be confused with Microsoft Project Server 2010, which is built on top of and requires Microsoft SharePoint Server 2010 Enterprise Edition)
- Contacts, calendars, and tasks
- E-mail integration
- Integration with Office client applications

Application Features

Architecturally, Microsoft SharePoint Server 2010 consists of a common set of application features that support a number of areas:

- **Portal**. Templates, people, audience targeting
- **Search**. Search center, cross-site search
- **Content management**. Authoring, publishing, records management

- **Business process**. Forms server, line-of-business (LOB) integration
- **Business intelligence**. Status Indicator lists, report center template
- **Composite applications**. Mashups, agile applications

Each of these is built upon the platform services and collaboration components of SharePoint Foundation and the application services components of Microsoft SharePoint Server 2010.

Service Applications

Service applications provide the features that are used by multiple applications in Microsoft SharePoint Server 2010. What does that mean? Let's use an example—user profiles. You may want to use the user profile feature, which provides an out-of-the-box employee directory, including basic information (including name and phone number, for example), along with some custom properties and a photograph. You also may want to create several different portals within your organization—for example, an Internet presence, an employee intranet site, and a collaboration portal for self-service team site use. You wouldn't want to create and manage three separate profile databases. In this case, the user profile service can be shared across the various portals. Specifically, the following features are provided as service applications in Microsoft SharePoint Server 2010:

- User Profile Store
- Audiences
- Search Services
- Usage Reporting and Web Analytics
- Excel Services
- Word Services
- Access Services
- PowerPoint Services
- Visio Services
- PerformancePoint Services
- Social Tagging
- Managed Metadata Services
- Business Connectivity Services

- Notification Service for Generating Alerts
- Single Sign-on Services

So what exactly do service applications support? They are the middle-tier feature that supports SharePoint Site Collections by providing either processing or data support (or both).

SharePoint Fundamentals

There are fundamental concepts in SharePoint that are key to truly understanding the platform. Every portal, team site, workspace, Internet page, and extranet site is based upon these building blocks:

- **Web applications**. In IIS, a Web application is comprised of an Internet Information Services (IIS) site with a unique application pool. While not a technically perfect definition, you can think of a Web application as a URL like http://my.intranet.com or http://sharepoint.intranet.com.
- **Sites**. A site consists of a data repository, visual elements, administration, and almost every other core element of the functionality and experience for the user. Visually, a site is represented as one or more Web pages, lists, and Web Parts.
- **Site Collections**. A Site Collection consists of a top-level site and its subsites. It is a logical unit for administration: There are settings that can only be configured at the Site Collection level (in other words, at the top-level site). Each Web application can host many Site Collections.
- **Lists**. A list is a data repository that can hold columns of data and/or documents. The objects stored in a list are called items. Visually, a list is represented by views or a Web Part. It is analogous to a database table or Excel worksheet.
- **Items**. Items are the fundamental data objects that are stored within a list. An example of an item might be a contact, a task, or a document. Items are analogous to rows within a database.
- **Site templates**. A template defines what the site will look like, what lists comprise the site initially, how publishing will work on the site, and a number of other settings. It enables a site to be created via

self-service using a precreated definition. You can think of a site as a cookie (that you eat) and a template as the cookie cutter.

- **Service applications**. Each service application provides a set of capabilities to one or more Web applications.

Sites and Site Collections

Sites are the cornerstone of SharePoint's infrastructure, which allow individuals or teams to store, share, and alter structured and unstructured content in a single environment. Sites also enable organizations to quickly share information across organizations as well—for example, a regular communication with suppliers, partners, or customers.

Sites are not a new concept to SharePoint users. WSS 3.0 and Office SharePoint Server 2007 both had site templates to support a number of business scenarios, including virtual teams, custom applications, and aggregation portals. SharePoint 2010 has extended the use of sites by introducing added features and functionality to enhance the experience for site members.

For those not familiar with the previous version of SharePoint, sites are containers that allow you to store lists and libraries of information. These lists and libraries can store documents, lists of data, and other information. Think of a site almost like a file share combined with a database, but with lots of additional features such as a Web-based user interface (UI). The content that you store may include documents, hyperlinks, customized lists, contacts, and lots of other types of information. The value of a site is measured at three levels:

- **Individual**. An individual can leverage a team site as a single repository for all team-related material. It is the place to go to get up to speed if the individual joins the team mid-project, and it is the one place to go to add or access the content generated by the team. An individual can be a contributor to all, some, or none of the content. Security associated with the site, from the page down to the content group (or Web Part), is managed by the Site Administrator.
- **Team**. Teams can leverage a team site as a means of sharing without using e-mail or other methods. Document libraries have version control to monitor changes as well as check-in/check-out to ensure there is always only one active version of a document. Geographically dispersed teams don't have to struggle with how to share their work.

■ **Organization**. All members of an organization can leverage the information within a team site by allowing direct access to all exposed team content. Because sites are template-driven, organizations can ensure that all project or product sites are organized in the same manner; thus giving users a consistent look and feel and a quicker path to finding relevant content.

In SharePoint Foundation 2010 and SharePoint Server 2010, everything starts with a site. To explore the concepts of SharePoint, let's start with a simple example comprised of a single Web server and its logical elements (see Figure 3-1). At the highest level, you have a physical server running Internet Information Server (IIS). Within IIS, you have a Web application, which maps to a URL (such as http://myportal), a port (such as 80), and an IP address (such as 192.168.1.4). Once a Web application is extended with SharePoint functionality, one or more top-level sites can be created. Each top-level site can contain one or more child sites. The collection of sites that includes a top-level site and all of its decedents

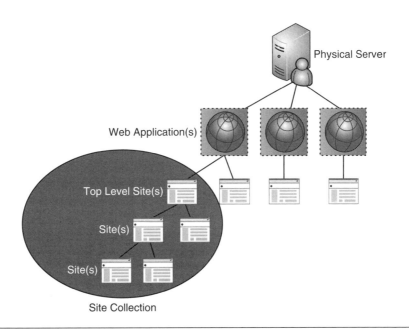

Figure 3-1 In SharePoint, a top-level site and its descendants are collectively referred to as a Site Collection

down to the leaf site(s) is called a *Site Collection*. This is important, given that much of SharePoint administration (quotas, backup and restore, permissions, Web Part access, and so on) is based on the Site Collection concept.

After you determine which sites your solution requires, the next step is to plan how these sites and portals are implemented across Site Collections. A Site Collection is a hierarchical set of sites that can be managed together. Sites within a Site Collection have common features, such as shared permissions, galleries for templates, Content Types, and Web Parts, and they often share a common navigation. All sites in a Site Collection are stored together in the same SQL database. A portal site is often implemented as a Site Collection with the top-level Web site as the home page of the portal.

In general, we recommend that you put each of the following types of sites in separate Site Collections right from the start. This will help you manage Site Collections and content databases better in the long run.

- Intranet portal sites
- Extranet sites
- Team sites related to a portal site or Internet site
- My Sites (by default, each my site is a Site Collection)
- Internet sites (staging)
- Internet sites (production)
- Lines of business within a conglomerate
- Document Center sites
- Records Center sites

So for example, if you were to deploy a company intranet, a corporate Internet-facing site, and a records management repository, you'd want to create three Site Collections from the beginning. This enables you to manage the Site Collections individually, provide separate content databases, and more easily accommodate growth over time.

The downside of multiple Site Collections is that there are some features that do not work *across* Site Collections. This is important because a large deployment of SharePoint will dictate multiple Site Collections. The following features do not work across Site Collections:

- **Content Types**. How common documents, forms, and other content is normalized in your organization. (Note: In SharePoint 2010 there is the notion of Enterprise Content Types that can be syndicated across Site Collections.)

- **Content by Query Web Part**. This Web Part aggregates information from across sites but does not work across Site Collections.
- **Workflow**. When you deploy workflow, it is only accessible within the Site Collection it is deployed in.
- **Information management and retention policies**. Records management policies are set at the Site Collection level, forcing organizations to deploy the same policy multiple times for large enterprises.
- **Quotas**. You should absolutely define quotas so that users are used to limited storage from day one; also configured at the Site Collection level, which means that you will need to configure quotas separately at each top-level site.

Let's say you decided to create two Site Collections for project workspaces: one Site Collection for IT and one Site Collection for finance. Due to the Site Collection limitations just described, if you wanted consistent document metadata properties on a particular document type, you'd have to deploy the Content Type twice—once for each Site Collection.

So far, all of this is true for both SharePoint Foundation 2010 and SharePoint Server 2010 deployments. When you install SharePoint Server 2010 over and above SharePoint Foundation 2010, several additional capabilities are added to all sites—additional Web Parts, additional templates, and more features, some enabled by service applications.

There are several ways to create new sites. You may want users to ask IT to create sites on their behalf. Or, you may want to let users create their own top-level sites directly. Either way, you'll want to configure self-service site creation in Central Administration appropriately. Simply go to Application Management → Configure Self-Service Site Creation and select either On or Off (see Figure 3-2).

For users to create top-level sites, they need to go to http://your-Web-application/_layouts/scsignup.aspx (see Figure 3-3). This page works in both SharePoint Foundation 2010 and SharePoint Server 2010, enabling users to create top-level sites and only works for users if you've enabled self-service site creation.

Note   For those of you familiar with SharePoint 2007's site directory template, this template is hidden in SharePoint Server 2010.

As a user, if you have Silverlight installed, you'll get a fancier menu than if you don't. With Silverlight installed, you see a section for template selection that contains multiple categories: Blank & Custom, Collaboration,

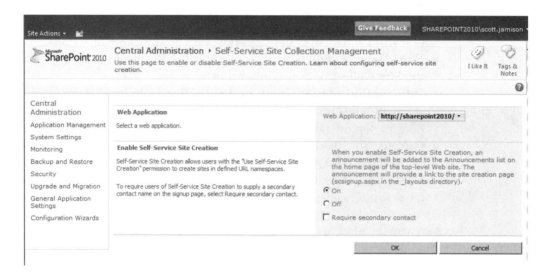

Figure 3-2 Enable Self-Service Site Creation from Central Administration if you want users to create new top-level sites directly

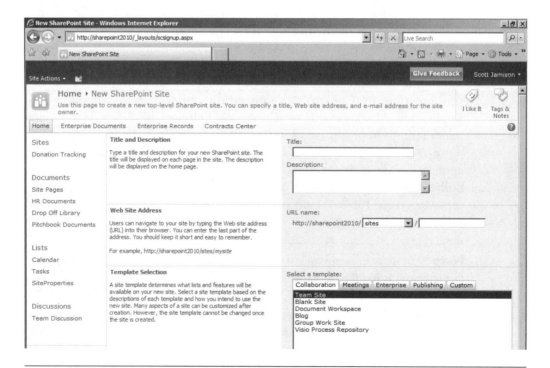

Figure 3-3 Users can create new top-level sites directly via the site creation page

Content & Data, Search, Tracking, and Web Databases. The most popular group is the list of Collaboration templates. The last item in the list is Team Site, while most of the others are Workspaces. Team sites and workspaces are very similar, with the concept that team sites are long-lived and used by teams, while workspaces are shorter-lived and geared toward a specific work task. But in the end they are pretty much the same because they are based on the same underlying site definition. Figure 3-4 shows the site creation page, where you can simply supply a site title and URL name to complete the creation process. By selecting More Options, you can add a description, set a specific security permissions model, and specify navigation options (see Figure 3-5).

Note SharePoint sites may not include the following characters:
\ / : * ? " < > | # { } % & <TAB>.
The following characters cannot be used in the naming of files to be uploaded to SharePoint:
" # % & * : < > ? \ { } | ~ _
SharePoint file names cannot exceed 128 characters in length.

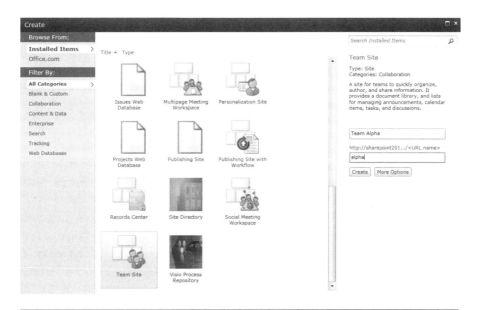

Figure 3-4 SharePoint 2010 enables you to select from a number of new site templates via a Silverlight-based menu

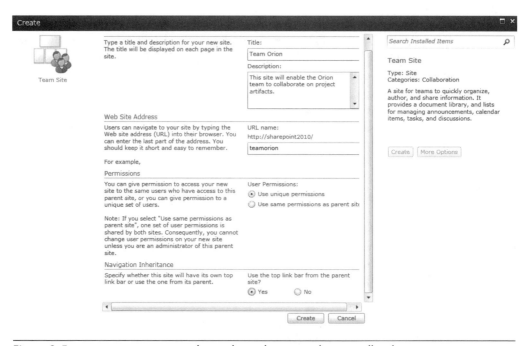

Figure 3-5 To create a site, provide a title and URL, and optionally, description, security, and navigation information

Figure 3-6 shows the newly created team site. By default, the site contains no underlying data within its lists and libraries and hosts a few default Web Parts on the home page. If the site inherited security from the parent (this is the default), the list of site users matches the parent, and the site creator is the Site Administrator and the only person who can access the site.

Sites vs. Pages   What's the difference between a site and a page? A *site* is a SharePoint container that holds lists, libraries, permissions, and some settings. A *page*, on the other hand, represents a single item (a Web page, actually) that enables a user to see one or more visual elements such as a collection of Web Parts. For example, a site may contain a document library and a discussion list. A page, on the other hand, is a single .aspx file (such as default.aspx or home.aspx) that lives within the site, typically in the pages library, which lets you visually see the information from the lists within the site. For each site, you can create as many pages as you'd like (although many sites just have one page).

Figure 3-6 A site contains lists and libraries that hold the site's information, combined with pages that contain Web Parts that enable you to display information to users. The default starting page is called either home.aspx or default.aspx.

To add additional users to the site, use the Site Actions context menu and select Site Settings. The first Column is Users and Permissions. Click Users and Groups to add more members.

Let's look at how the default presentation of a team site is organized. The left-side navigation gives users quick access to specific lists (things like document libraries, custom lists, and calendars). The main body of the page contains Web Part zones (or placeholders for Web Parts). Additional Web Parts can be added by using the context menu associated with Site Actions and selecting Edit Page. Note that you will need specific permissions on the site to do so. Figure 3-7 shows a team site in Edit mode. There are boxes around Web Parts that allow for drag and drop into other Web Part zones. You can also choose a Web Part by selecting Insert → Web Part from the ribbon, which allows you to introduce a new Web Part from the Web Part gallery.

A team site is an effective way to organize content and people around a specific objective. The value is measured not just during the life cycle of the site, but for some time after as other virtual teams can leverage the information captured in the environment to better accomplish their goals.

Figure 3-7 If you have permissions, clicking Site Actions → Edit Page enables you to make changes to the shared version of the page, which means everyone will see your changes. The Insert tab on the ribbon lets you add Web Parts, links, images, and videos to your page.

If additional containers of information below existing sites are needed, users can create *subsites* (or sites that are contained within a parent site) by choosing Site Actions → New Site. This will create a site hierarchy.

Site Templates

Because a site is simply a Web Part page with some administration and some lists to back it up, how do you get a different look and behavior for each site in SharePoint? Templates. Templates are collection of lists, Web Part pages, and Web Parts that are packaged together to define a starting point for your site. Because everything is a SharePoint Foundation 2010 site in SharePoint, the template defines the look and behavior of the page(s). Table 3-1 lists the out-of-the-box templates in SharePoint Server 2010. In addition to the out-of-the-box templates, you can make an unlimited number of custom templates available to users. Templates are your building blocks, allowing you to quickly create complex solutions that include custom branding and functionality.

Table 3-1 The Out-of-the-Box Templates in SharePoint Foundation 2010 and Microsoft SharePoint Server 2010

Category	Name	Best Suited For ...	SharePoint Server Only?
Collaboration	Team Site	Team collaboration	
Collaboration	Blank Site	Custom collaboration applications	
Collaboration	Document Workspace	Actively working on documents	
Collaboration	Wiki Site	Adding, editing, and linking Web pages	
Collaboration	Blog	Posting information in chorological order; others can comment	
Collaboration	Internet Presence Web Site	An Internet-facing corporate Web site with several various pages like publishing and search (Site Collection level)	Y
Collaboration	My Site Host	A site used for hosting My Sites (Site Collection level)	Y
Collaboration	Records Repository	Storing documents that should not be modified after being added	Y
Collaboration	News Home template	Creating and managing new articles	Y
Collaboration	Publishing and Team Collaboration Site	Publishing Web content along with team collaboration	Y
Collaboration	Publishing Site	Publishing Web content (like an intranet or Internet site)	Y
Meetings	Basic Meeting Workspace	Tracking meeting data	
Meetings	Blank Meeting Workspace	Tracking meetings	
Meetings	Decision Meeting	Tracking meetings that lead to a decision	

(continues)

Table 3-1 The Out-of-the-Box Templates in SharePoint Foundation 2010 and Microsoft SharePoint Server 2010 (*continued*)

Category	Name	Best Suited For ...	SharePoint Server Only?
Meetings	Social Meeting Workspace	Planning social events	
Meetings	Multipage Meeting Workspace	Tracking meeting data	
Enterprise	Document Center	Centrally managing documents (active, broadly published items)	Y
Enterprise	Records Center	Centrally managing records (corporate 'sealed' items)	Y
Enterprise	Personalization Site	Hosting a My Site page for a user	Y
Enterprise	Report Center	Managing reports and BI information	Y
Enterprise	Search Center	Hosting a central search page	Y
Publishing	Publishing Site	A blank site for quickly publishing HTML Web pages	Y
Publishing	Publishing Site with Workflow	A site for publishing Web pages on a schedule by using approval workflows	Y
Publishing	Corporate Intranet Site	Creating an intranet site with News, Sites Directory, and Search (Site Collection level)	Y

If you've made customizations to a site, you can save those customizations as a *site template*. This enables you to create new sites in the future based on your customization. To save a site template, simply click Site Actions → Site Settings and then select Save Site as Template (see Figure 3-8). You are then prompted for a name for the file, a title, description, and whether you want to save the content (the items or documents in the lists). Figure 3-9 shows the Save as Template page. Saving the content is useful for when you want a new site to contain some "starter" content, such as a deliverable document, some scheduled tasks, or workflows. Note that content cannot exceed 10MB and permissions are not saved with the template.

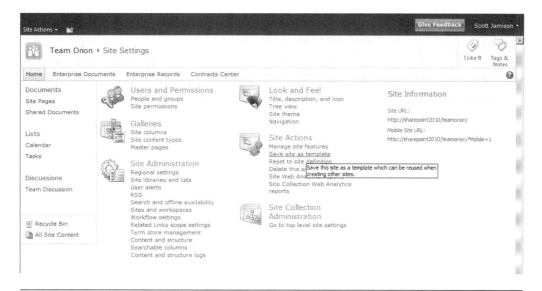

Figure 3-8 Choosing "Save site as template" enables you to save the site (the lists, libraries, and Web Part pages) as a reusable template that can be used for the creation of future sites

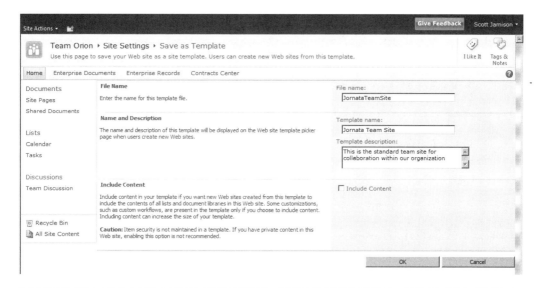

Figure 3-9 When saving a site template, specify whether you want to include content. Including content is useful for priming your new site with starter content.

Site templates are stored in the User Solutions Gallery, which is at http://<site URL>/_catalogs/solutions (see Figure 3-10). To use a site template, simply create a new site; your custom template appears in the custom section.

Sandbox solutions, a new feature in SharePoint 2010, are also stored and tracked in the User Solutions Gallery. For more about sandbox solutions, see http://msdn.microsoft.com/en-us/magazine/ee335711.aspx.

SharePoint Lists, Libraries, and Items

Once you have a site, you can populate a site with lists and libraries. You can think of lists and libraries as analogous to tables in a database. Each list (or library) can hold many *items*. To create a list, select Site Actions → More Options. You can sort the categories by either Library or Lists. Table 3-1 shows the lists and libraries that you can create with SharePoint. In addition, you can create *views*, which enable you to create custom ways to look at the items within a list or library, providing customized sorting and filtering options. We highly recommend creating custom filtered views for your lists because this provides a better user experience for users while reducing the load on SharePoint.

Figure 3-10 The User Solutions Gallery enables you to track user solutions, which include site templates and sandbox solutions

SharePoint 2010 introduces a resource governor that notifies a user if the system is trying to display a view with too many items (typically >5,000). This is to prevent a common problem in SharePoint 2007 whereby a list with a large number of items could slow the server down (or worse yet, crash the server completely).

If you've customized any lists or libraries, you can save them as templates (much in the same way you can save a site template). To save a list or library as a template, click Library Settings from the ribbon and then select Save <library/list> as Template. Give the template a filename, template name, description, and select whether to save content. List and library templates are stored in the List Template Gallery, which is located at http://<your_site_name>/_catalogs/lt/Forms/AllItems.aspx (see Figure 3-11).

To use a list or library template, simply create a new list or library; your custom template will appear in the custom section.

Figure 3-11 The List Template Gallery enables you to provide list and library templates for users

Pages

As mentioned earlier, pages are items that are stored within a site that enable a user to view information. There are two main types of pages: content pages and Web Part pages. *Content pages* are useful for when users will want to directly edit the content on the page itself. These pages can contain text, images, and other content. *Web Part pages* are typically used to aggregate information from other sources, whether those sources are lists, libraries, or data pulled from databases or the Web.

Every site contains a library called Site Pages, which is where new pages are stored. To create a new page, simply click Site Actions → More Options. Next click Page under the Filter By menu (Figure 3-12).

Use pages when you want to display information within a site, but don't create a new site unless you need to; you're better off simply creating more pages within your existing site.

Make sure your users are educated on the difference between sites and pages. It might seem obvious, but many users are confused by this.

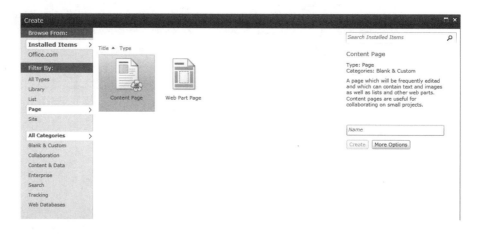

Figure 3-12 The Create Page option enables you to create either a content page (which is good for direct editing), or a Web Part page (which is better for aggregating information stored in other places)

Navigation

SharePoint 2010 has added a number of new user interface elements, most noticeably the ribbon. This section covers the ins and outs of the new interface.

The Navigate Up icon, which is the small yellow folder with the green up arrow on the top of the page, provides a hierarchical view of the site, enabling a user to navigate directly to the site of his or her choice (see Figure 3-13). This button can be a handy way to quickly jump to another page in the hierarchy and exists mainly due to the ribbon obscuring the breadcrumb, depending on which tab the user has open.

Tip Within your sites, rename the titles from the default, Home, to something more descriptive. This results in a much better navigation experience for users.

Figure 3-13 The Navigate Up button shows the user a view of the site hierarchy, enabling direct navigation

Next to the Navigate Up button is the Edit button, which is the small icon that turns the page into Edit mode. Next to that is the Browse tab, which shows the site breadcrumb. Finally, the Page tab lets the user check the page out, edit properties about the page, e-mail a link, and set page permissions (Figure 3-14).

In terms of menu-based navigation, there are two primary types: global navigation and current navigation. Global navigation is shown at the top of the page and shows the top-level sites, while current navigation shows elements within the current site (see Figure 3-15). You can change navigation elements via the Navigation link within the site's Site Settings page.

Figure 3-14 The Page tab shows the user options for modifying attributes for the current page

Figure 3-15 Navigation within a site includes Global Navigation, shown at the top of the page, and Current Navigation, shown along the left side of the page. Both types of navigation are defined within the site's master page and can be modified within Site Settings.

Adding Service Applications to the Mix

If you want to add additional functionality to your sites, you can make use of service applications, which can provide things like user profiles, enterprise search, and business connectivity services (among many other eatures). In MOSS 2007, services were grouped together within a Shared Services Provider (SSP). In Microsoft SharePoint Server 2010, this is no longer the case. Instead, service applications are hosted within SharePoint Foundation 2010 and no longer have to be grouped within an SSP. This makes the configuration of service offerings much more flexible (and much more prone to spaghetti architecture). Single services can be configured independently from one another. In addition, third-party software vendors can add services to the platform.

Figure 3-16 shows Central Administration has its own, dedicated site. Figure 3-17 shows how service applications are organized in SharePoint 2010 (and how they compare to SharePoint 2007).

Note SharePoint Server 2010 does not support service applications over a WAN. This factor can impact design and deployment in large organizations.

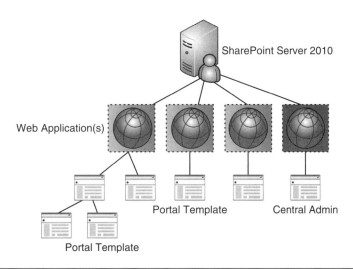

Figure 3-16 Central Administration has its own site

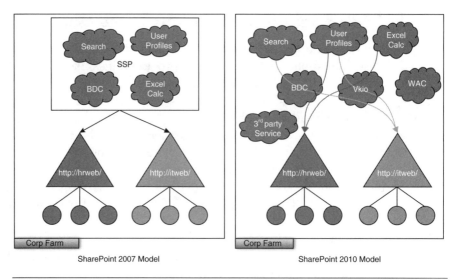

Figure 3-17 Gone are Shared Service Providers (SSPs). You can create multiple service application instances if your environment needs them—for example, if you need to keep searches between your business units separate.

Putting It All Together

To illustrate how sites, templates, and service applications work together, consider this: A *portal* is constructed simply by using a SharePoint Foundation 2010 site (after all, everything is a site), plus a portal template (for example, the Enterprise Publishing Site template), plus some service applications. This gets you a portal.

Sites, templates, and services are important to understand, given that how you configure your portal and team sites largely depend on that understanding. Another consideration is who in your organization will administer various parts of your SharePoint environment. The next section covers how SharePoint administration is segmented and why it matters.

Understanding SharePoint Administration

Administration in SharePoint is a set of Web pages that allow both IT pros and business users to configure settings and add new content. In general, administration is broken out by role and grouped by type of task.

There are fundamentally three tiers to SharePoint administration: Central Administration, (which is where all global SharePoint settings are configured), Site Collection administration (with unique settings for each Site Collection), and site-level administration (with unique settings for each site).

Central Administration

There is one Central Administration per farm; it includes settings like topology, security, and application services. For an overview of what the Central Administration site looks like, see Figure 3-18.

Who? IT Administrators

What? Used for things such as adding a new physical server to the farm or configuring service settings

Where? Farm level

How many? One per farm

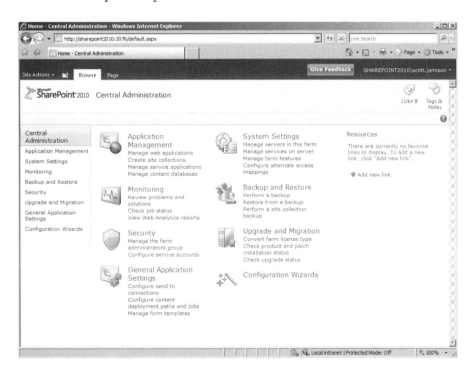

Figure 3-18 The home page of SharePoint Central Administration provides you with the core tasks you'll need to undertake to get your farm working properly

There is no longer an Operations tab in SharePoint 2010. The main page is broken into eight sections, each of which contains links to pages that help you manage your server or server farm, such as changing the server farm topology, specifying which services are running on each server, and changing settings that affect multiple servers or applications. For example, the System Settings section enables you to manage servers in the farm (see Figure 3-19).

Finally, the Application Management page contains links to pages that help you configure settings for Web applications and Site Collections that are on the farm (see Figure 3-20). Within Application Management is also a section called Service Applications, where service applications are now config-ured (see Figure 3-21). This section includes administration of user profiles, My Sites, search, usage reporting, audiences, Excel Services, business connectivity services, and the other service applications.

Site Collection Settings

Administration for a specific Site Collection.

Who? Business user or IT (Site Collection owner)

Where? Every Site Collection

Figure 3-19 The System Settings section of SharePoint Central Administration provides physical and logical configuration settings for your farm

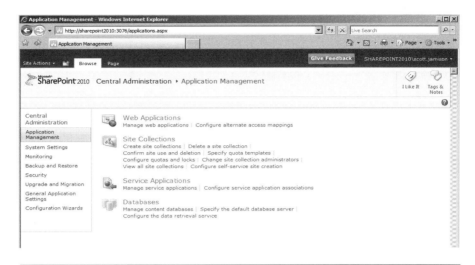

Figure 3-20 The Application Management section of SharePoint Central Administration provides ways to configure your core application components, such as Web application settings and Site Collection settings

Site Settings

Administration for a specific site.

> **Who?** Business user or IT (site owner)
>
> **What?** Used for things such as site configuration, creating new lists, adding users to the site, storage, and site hierarchy
>
> **Where?** Every site
>
> **How many?** One admin page per site with an extra Column for Site Collection settings for top-level sites

The primary usage of the site settings page(s) is to provide a UI where business users can manage their sites. This includes the site-specific permissions, the look and feel of the site, and miscellaneous site settings (Figure 3-22). We recommend that business users who will be administering a site get adequate training on the Site Settings pages.

As you have seen, the various SharePoint 2010 configuration and administration settings require multiple administrators. You should carefully plan and designate which users should administer which pieces of the SharePoint administration puzzle.

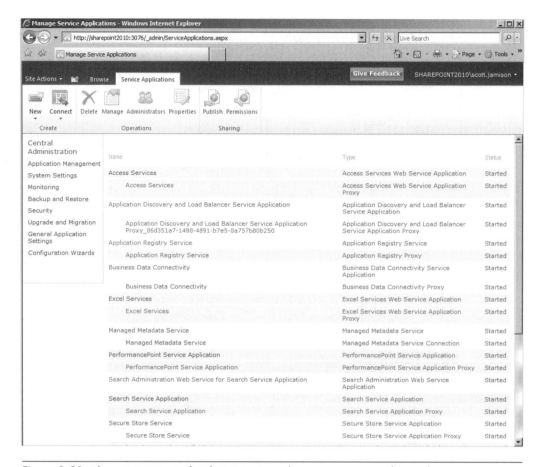

Figure 3-21 SharePoint Central Administration also gets you to a place where you can administer service applications. This replaces the separate SSP administration site in MOSS 2007.

In addition to these administration options, another major consideration for your SharePoint deployment is physical deployment. Specifically, this means, "How many servers do I need to deploy?" The next section helps you think through this question by helping you understand your options.

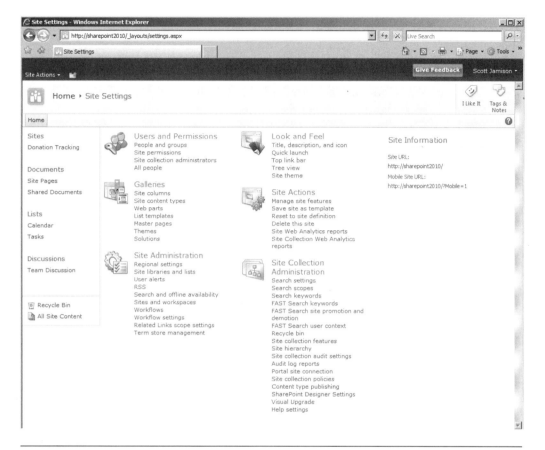

Figure 3-22 The administration page on a site lets a user (typically the site owner) configure site-specific items, such as site-level permissions, the lists and libraries stored within the site, and the look and feel of the site

Physical Deployment Options

When considering deployment options for SharePoint, you are really considering your *topology*. In other words, you are determining how many servers you will deploy in your SharePoint farm and what roles they will play. In SharePoint Server 2010, how you deploy SharePoint is very flexible.

In SharePoint Server 2010, servers have one of three roles:

- **Web front end (WFE)**. The SharePoint bits with just Web rendering enabled.
- **Application server**. May include Indexing, Search, Excel Calculations, Project Server, and other features.
- **Database server**. No SharePoint-specific software is installed (only SQL Server).

Therefore, you have an unlimited number of physical configurations to use when rolling out SharePoint, and in this section, we present several common deployment scenarios. Your environment will have special requirements around server roles, authentication, DMZ, application services, among other needs.

Here are some configurations you may want to consider—they are by no means the only way, but the most common:

Single-server Deployment

A single server hosts all three roles (WFE, application server, and database server) on a single machine. This is good for very small deployments because it's fast and easy. The major downsides include scalability issues (there is no room to grow except for expanding things like memory and processor) and availability issues (if the server goes down, SharePoint is down). From a logical perspective, all SharePoint objects are located on this server (content sites, service applications, Central Administration, and databases).

Note   Choose your deployment topology carefully. There is no direct upgrade from a stand-alone installation to a farm installation.

Two-server Deployment

In a two-server scenario, one of the servers hosts the WFE and the application server, while the second hosts the SQL Server database. This provides a way to manage the database separately but adds complexity without adding scalability or availability. This step adds a second tier to the deployment. In most organizations, this is the smallest deployment that is recommended for anything other than a demonstration environment or very small group.

Three-server Deployment

By adding an additional server to the two-server deployment that acts as an additional WFE/application server, you gain scalability (by being able to service more requests) and availability (by load-balancing requests, so that if one server goes down, the system stays up and running on the other machine). The single point of failure is now the SQL machine.

Four-server Deployment

By adding a machine to the database role and upgrading the SQL Server machine to a full cluster, we can achieve availability on both tiers of the environment. This is the smallest highly available environment, meaning that there are no single points of failure. Note that clustering is not a simple upgrade but rather a reinstall where you must move databases.

Five-server Deployment

The next step that you should consider is to start breaking out the application services for additional performance. For example, the indexing process is very CPU-intensive and should often be put onto its own server. In a five-server deployment, the fifth server would host just an application server, primarily serving as an indexing machine. This creates a three-tier environment, with a new application server tier being added.

N-server Deployment

The beauty of the scale-out process is that you can continue adding servers at each of the tiers, depending on the needs of the business. Do you need to serve more Web pages per second? Add more WFEs. Need to dedicate processor time to calculating Excel sheets? Add some more application servers specifically dedicated to Excel Services. You get the idea. Let's say you decide that ten production machines make sense. You may then want to deploy a separate Internet farm in the DMZ and an intranet farm behind the firewall. In addition, you may want staging and testing machines so that you can adequately test new features and Web Parts. This could bring your server count to 20 servers or more.

In the next section, we provide three specific examples: departmental, corporate intranet, and Internet-facing deployments, which are the most common examples of specific SharePoint usage models.

Departmental

A departmental solution is typically for collaboration but may include a team portal and will often consist of a single SharePoint server and a database (see Figure 3-23). Sometimes a department will run a local database on the same server. However, savvy departments should deploy a second SharePoint server for availability.

Corporate Intranet

A corporate intranet—serving anywhere from hundreds, up to tens of thousands of employees—will start to incorporate dedicated application servers (see Figure 3-24). All servers are deployed within the company firewall.

Internet (Web Content Management)

A corporate Internet presence gets a bit more complicated, considering you not only want to have enough Web servers to serve a large number of external users, but you also want an internal cluster for authoring purposes.

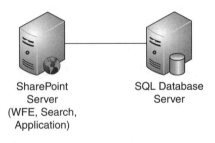

SharePoint
Server
(WFE, Search,
Application)

SQL Database
Server

Figure 3-23 A departmental solution is often deployed as a single SharePoint server with a database

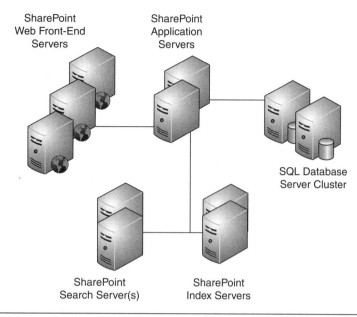

Figure 3-24 Corporate intranet farms typically consist of multiple WFEs, dedicated application servers, and dedicated search and index servers

SharePoint then deploys all content changes from the authoring cluster to your production cluster in a one-way manner. Figure 3-25 shows an example of a SharePoint deployment in a publishing environment.

When considering the question, "How do I know how many servers I will need?" the short answer for deployment is this: Carefully consider your usage plan (collaboration, portal, Web content management, and so on), uptime needs, number of users, application processing demands, geographic dispersion, and budget when determining your deployment architecture.

For more information about SharePoint 2010 capacity planning, refer to http://technet.microsoft.com/en-us/library/cc789337%28office.14%29.aspx.

For a step-by-step guide for installing SharePoint Server 2010 in a farm configuration, go to http://technet.microsoft.com/en-us/library/cc303424%28office.14%29.aspx.

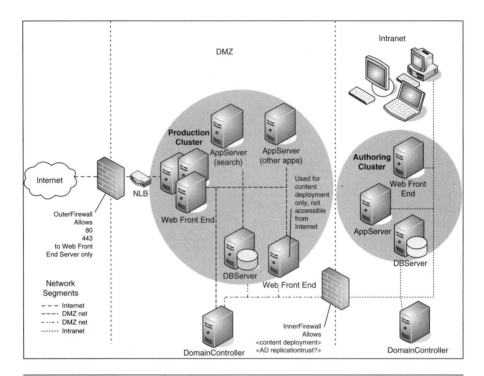

Figure 3-25 For your Internet presence, you'll want to include servers outside your corporate firewall (for Internet user access) as well as servers inside the firewall (for employee access)

Key Points

Remember:

- In SharePoint Foundation 2010 and SharePoint Server 2010, everything starts at the Web application level, which contains zero or more Site Collections.
- A Site Collection is a hierarchical collection of zero or more sites that can be managed together. All sites in a Site Collection are stored together in the same content database. Some features do not work across Site Collections, so it's important to plan how to use them.
- Sites contain zero or more lists.

- Lists are the containers in SharePoint that enable you to store items.
- "Web application" is something that SharePoint manages and maps to between one and five IIS Web sites.
- Shared Service Providers (SSPs) no longer exist. Service applications are individually managed from within Central Administration. A service application still provides shared services to one or more Web applications.
  - Both SharePoint Foundation 2010 and SharePoint Server 2010 support shared services via service applications.
  - A portal is a SharePoint Foundation 2010 site plus a SharePoint Server 2010 template plus a collection of service applications.
- There are no specific topologies that have to be adhered to (small farm, medium farm, large farm). In SharePoint Server 2010, servers have one of three roles:
  - Web front end (WFE)
  - Application server
  - Database server

CHAPTER 4

PLANNING FOR GOVERNANCE

The *governance plan* describes how your SharePoint environment will be managed. It describes the roles, responsibilities, and rules applied to both the back end (hardware, farm, application, database configuration, and maintenance) and the front end (information architecture, taxonomy, and user experience). Effective governance planning is critical for the ongoing success of your SharePoint solution. In the previous edition of this book, we embedded the discussion of governance in the chapter on strategy. In this edition, we give governance a well-deserved chapter of its own but focus primarily on front-end governance because this is the topic that is, quite frankly, hardest to get right. A good governance plan is "necessary but not sufficient" to ensure success, so be advised: A governance plan alone will not guarantee the success of your solution. You still have to ensure that the governance plan is *applied*. However, not having a governance plan or having a plan that is either impractical or unrealistic is a clear recipe for disaster. This chapter contains the following key sections:

- Why Is Governance Planning So Important?
- How Do I Create a Governance Plan?
- What Is in the Governance Plan?

Why Is Governance Planning So Important?

A portal or collaboration solution is only as good as the value of its underlying content. A strong governance plan is essential to ensure that a solution delivers worthwhile content to its users in an effective way. Moreover, governance planning is especially important for SharePoint solutions because SharePoint is designed to empower end users who are typically not Information Technology (IT) or content management experts and may not be aware of best practices that will not only improve usability but also save them a lot of time and energy when creating and deploying new sites.

A governance plan establishes the processes and roles required to

- Avoid solution, team site, and content "sprawl" (that is, unmanaged sites and content that is not periodically reviewed for accuracy and relevance) by defining a content and site review process.
- Ensure that content quality is maintained for the life of the solution by implementing content quality management policies.
- Provide a consistently high-quality user experience by defining guidelines for site and content designers.
- Establish clear decision-making authority and escalation procedures so policy violations are dealt with and conflicts are resolved on a timely basis.
- Ensure that the solution strategy is aligned with business objectives so that it continuously delivers business value.
- Ensure that content is retained in compliance with record retention guidelines.

Adoption of a new SharePoint solution often involves a dramatic change in user behavior—specifically, greater integration of technology into day-to-day work and increased collaboration. In more traditional IT solution deployments, the solution business logic changes relatively infrequently. In a SharePoint solution, both the back-end database and business logic change frequently and often significantly. Moreover, the business, market, and technology are guaranteed to change during the lifetime of the solution. This implies that business stakeholders must be continuously engaged given that SharePoint's ability to meet user needs is critically dependent on areas such as data quality, content relevance and currency, and frequent updates, all of which are business user responsibilities.

What new aspects of governance do you need to consider for SharePoint 2010?

- Governance planning is even more important in SharePoint 2010 because the increased emphasis and availability of social computing features means there are more types of content to govern.
- SharePoint 2010 offers users a far more participatory role in the solution information architecture through the use of "social data" such as tags, bookmarks, and ratings. Users need to understand and internalize the value proposition for leveraging these features. Solution designers will likely need to provide both guidance and encouragement for their use.

Refer to Chapter 7, "Getting Social: Leveraging Community Features," for additional governance guidance regarding the use of SharePoint 2010's social computing features.

- SharePoint 2010 introduces new capabilities for sharing metadata across multiple Site Collections and even server farms, which require planning and control to leverage. An additional new role is required to manage and maintain the dictionary of shared metadata.
- SharePoint 2010 includes new and more user-friendly records management capabilities, including the ability to declare a record "in place." (Refer to Chapter 6, "Making Enterprise Content Management Work: Documents and Records," for a description of the new records management capabilities in SharePoint 2010.) While many organizations had records management plans and policies for their MOSS 2007 implementations, enforcing and acting on these plans was not consistent. The new records management capabilities introduce an opportunity to create and enforce your records management plan.
- SharePoint 2010 offers many more opportunities for users to customize their sites with easy-to-apply themes, SharePoint Designer, and the opportunity to create "sandbox solutions." Your governance plan now needs to include decisions regarding how, where, and when to allow configuration using these expanded capabilities.

You should prepare a governance plan prior to the launch of your solution,[1] but do not think of it as being "done" at any one point in time. Your governance plan is a living, breathing document—make time in your project plan to revisit the plan as you learn more about how users are using the solution and capture feedback from their experiences. As your SharePoint environment evolves, revisit your governance plan to adapt to changing needs. You may find that you need greater oversight to ensure conformance. You may also find that you need less oversight to encourage more creative application of core features.

---

1. Note that throughout this chapter we use the word "solution" to refer to the business problem you are using SharePoint to solve. The solution includes the hardware and software platform, of course, but it also includes the people and business processes that are critical to a successful outcome. The solution itself might be an enterprise portal, a departmental collaboration site, a partner extranet, or any one of the many business activities you can enable with SharePoint.

Communicating the substance of the governance plan is a core component of launch planning and the ongoing management of your SharePoint environment. It is especially important to ensure that page and site owners understand and commit to the content management responsibilities included in the roles and responsibilities section of your governance plan. Integrate relevant elements of your governance plan into the training and ongoing support you provide for site and content owners.

How Do I Create a Governance Plan?

If you are documenting your governance plan for the first time, you will probably find it most effective to put together a small team to help define the key "framing" decisions for governance and then divide up the work to document the details among the team members. The team should clearly include representatives from IT who are responsible for overall IT system use policies, but you will also want to include representatives from the team responsible for system maintenance within IT and outside of IT, people who can represent the interests of those responsible for training, human resources, corporate communications, and if this role exists, people responsible for knowledge management in the organization.

Use the vision statement your SharePoint project sponsors and stakeholders established as a foundation for your governance plan. Identify the basic governance principles at a high level before beginning to draft the actual governance plan. Meet with team members who have the appropriate expertise to draft sections addressing how the various aspects of your environment will be managed. Review each major component of your plan with sponsors, stakeholders and core team members to ensure you are in agreement about the major components of the plan: vision, guiding principles, roles and responsibilities, and key policy decisions.

What Is in the Governance Plan?

An effective governance plan provides a *framework* for design standards, information architecture, service-level agreements, infrastructure maintenance, and your overall measurement plan. It is intended to summarize and tie together, not *replace*, the documents that describe these activities in detail. Referencing this related content rather than embedding it in the governance plan will keep the plan from becoming unnecessarily bloated and unmanageable.

In addition, the governance plan should reference all of your existing IT policies for topics such as the appropriate use of technology resources, confidentiality of content, and records retention. As you begin to deploy more and more "Web 2.0" functionality into your environment, new IT policies will emerge that will impact SharePoint governance. Again, your plan doesn't need to *include* these emerging policies, but should reference them where appropriate.

The governance plan is a business document, its primary audience being the business (content) owners of your SharePoint sites and the users who produce and consume the content on those sites. Because all users can effectively produce content in SharePoint via social tags and ratings (if you allow these in your solution), everyone in the organization needs to be familiar with the governance plan.

The formal governance plan document includes several critical elements, each of which is discussed in more detail in the remainder of this chapter:

- Vision statement
- Roles and responsibilities
- Guiding principles
- Policies and standards

In addition to these elements, your plan will likely also include a section that references procedures for common tasks such as requesting a new site, requesting a new shared Content Type or attribute, requesting a new site template, and so on. Publish these procedures so site owners can easily find and follow the processes you define. These tasks typically vary from one organization to the next, so we're not going to address them explicitly in this chapter other than to remind you that you need to provide guidance in this area.

As you think about creating your governance plan, consider how users will consume and internalize the content in your plan. There is a great quote from Blaise Pascal that is often misattributed to Mark Twain (and others). In the original French, the quote reads "Je n'ai fait celle-ci plus longue parceque je n'ai pas eu le loisir de la faire plus courte." Loosely translated: "If I had more time, I would have written a shorter letter."

Think about this quote as you are working on your governance plan because it's very easy for these documents to get very, very long. The longer they are, the more difficult it is for users to digest them. Putting in the extra time needed to make sure your plan is as concise as possible will make it easier for your users to understand and follow the rules.

As you create your governance plan, think about how you might create companion material to go with the plan—a "cheat sheet" of your most important guiding principles, a laminated card or magnet with your vision statement, individual brief job descriptions for each core role, a records retention "ad campaign," or supplements to the governance plan (shorter letters) that will help users remember and internalize this important content.

Vision Statement

A vision statement describes, at a high level, what you want to achieve with SharePoint, essentially describing how the solution delivers value to the enterprise and to each individual employee. A clear vision statement provides critical guidance to the inevitable decision trade-offs you will need to make in thinking about your governance plan. The vision statement is typically written when the project to create the solution is initiated and may be refined as the project matures.

Here are two examples of vision statements:

- "The portal enables the creation, management, and sharing of document assets in a business-driven environment for collaboration, classification, and access across all of the company. Through its workflow capabilities and application development foundation, it will support the organization's information management needs and provide a business process framework for all business units."
- "SharePoint provides a holistic view of organizational assets that simplifies employee interaction with our enterprise business systems and helps improve collaboration within the company and with our suppliers, partners, and customers, thus improving employee productivity and employee and customer satisfaction."

Once you have set forth your vision statement, the next step is to gather your core project team together to think about the principles that will guide the creation of your governance plan.

Roles and Responsibilities

Roles and responsibilities describe how each employee as an individual or as a member of a particular role or group is responsible for ensuring success of the solution. Documenting roles and responsibilities is a critical aspect of the governance plan, which defines who has authority to mediate conflicting requirements and make overall branding and policy decisions. Some of the policy decisions that will frame your governance plan and form the basis of the specifics of your roles and responsibilities definition include deciding the following:

- Who is responsible for technical management of the environment, including hardware and software implementation, configuration, and maintenance? Who can install new Web Parts, features, or other code enhancements?
- Who is allowed or who will be responsible for setting up new sites? If this responsibility is controlled by the IT department, then it is likely that IT will have to negotiate a service-level agreement (SLA) for site set-up responsiveness with the business stakeholders. If this responsibility is delegated, users will need training to ensure that they follow acceptable conventions for naming, storage, and so on.
- Who has access to each page/site? Who can grant access to each?
- How much responsibility for page/site design will you delegate to page owners? Can users modify Web Parts (Web-based data and UI components) on pages that they "own" in team sites? Can they modify Web Parts on pages that are part of the corporate intranet publishing solution?
- Will some Web Parts be "fixed" on the page, or will page owners be allowed to customize all of the content on their pages?
- Who is responsible for managing metadata? Who can set up or request new Content Types or Site Columns? How much central control do you want to have over the values in Site Columns? (Content Types and Site Columns allow you to specify elements in your taxonomy. These SharePoint features are discussed in detail in Chapter 3, "SharePoint 2010: Architecture Fundamentals.")
- If the governance plan says that page and site owners are responsible for content management, are you prepared to decommission pages where no one in the organization will step up to page ownership responsibilities?

There are several key roles to consider. In smaller organizations, many roles may be fulfilled by a single individual. Table 4-1 and Table 4-2 present lists of typical roles and responsibilities in successful solutions. You will likely need to adapt both the responsibilities and even the terms you use to describe each role for your organization, but these lists give you a good place to start.

Table 4-1 Overall Roles for the Solution

Role	Key Responsibilities
Executive Sponsor	Serves as the executive level "champion" for the solution. The primary responsibility of the Executive Sponsor is strategic, positioning the solution as a critical mechanism for achieving business value and helping to communicate the value of the solution to the management levels of the organization.
Governance Board/ Steering Committee	Serves as a governance body with ultimate responsibility for meeting the goals of the solution. This Board is typically comprised of representatives of each of the major businesses represented in the solution, including corporate communications, HR, and IT.
Business Owner	Manages the overall design and functionality integrity of the solution from a business perspective. The Business Owner does not have to be an IT expert but his job function typically includes responsibility for internal communications.
Solution Administrator (Technology)	Manages the overall design and functionality integrity of the solution from a technology perspective. Works in partnership with the Business Owner.
Technology Support Team	Ensures the technical integrity of the solution. Makes regular backups of the solution and its content. Also usually sets up and maintains the security model, at least the components in the Active Directory. Develops new Web Parts and provides support to Site Sponsors/Owners seeking enhancements to their pages or new uses of the solution.

Role	Key Responsibilities
Metadata Steering Committee/Content Steward	While some large organizations may already have an individual or group serving in this role, SharePoint 2010's enterprise content capabilities require an overall metadata management plan and an individual or team responsible for maintaining the "metadata dictionary" over the life of the solution.
SharePoint "Coach" or Center of Excellence	Provides coaching and design consulting to new users who have Full Control design privileges to ensure that best practices are followed and that the appropriate SharePoint features are applied in individual sites or Site Collections. In many organizations, a particular SharePoint feature becomes the defacto solution for any business problem—a "hammer in search of a nail." For example, you don't want to see users creating wiki sites when what they really need is a custom list. If you will be delegating site design capabilities to users who have limited solution design experience (which pretty much means every organization), having experienced site design "coaches" available to help users get started can ensure that you end up with a solution that actually gets used. One successful organization implemented "drop-in" office hours where new site owners could come and spend an hour or two with an experienced solution architect to ensure that they got appropriate guidance (in addition to formal training). Several others have established in-house consulting services to help new site owners get started. In many cases, the first hour or two of consulting is "free," and services beyond that require a charge code.
"Power Users" Community of Practice	Supports the successful deployment of SharePoint in the organization by sharing best practices and lessons learned in a Community of Practice team site. Members serve as SharePoint advocates and change agents.

Table 4-2 Roles for Each Site or Site Collection

Role	Key Responsibilities
Site Sponsor/Owner	Serves as the centralized, primary role for ensuring that content for a particular page/site is properly collected, reviewed, published, and maintained over time. The Site Sponsor is an expert in the content that is showcased on the site or page and will likely need to learn about SharePoint, but his or her primary expertise is business-focused. The Site Sponsor/Owner may designate a Site Steward/Contact who will provide the primary day-to-day interface between their business and the users of the page or site.
Site Steward/Contact	Manages the site day-to-day by executing the functions required to ensure that the content on the site or page is accurate and relevant, including records retention codes. Monitors site security to ensure that the security model for the site matches the goals of the Business Owner and Site Sponsor/Owner and support Users of the site by serving as the primary identified contact point for the site. Acts as the Content Steward for the sites for which they are responsible.
Site Designer	In an environment where site design is delegated to business users, the Site Designer creates and maintains the site (or Site Collection) design. Follows design best practices and guiding principles to ensure that even sites with limited access are optimized for end-user value. Defines and executes the security plan for the site.
Users	Uses the solution to access and share information. Users may have different access permissions in different areas of the solution, sometimes acting as a Contributor (content producer) and other times acting as a Visitor (content consumer).

Guiding Principles

Guiding principles define organizational preferences supporting the vision. These critical statements reflect best practices that all users and site designers must understand and internalize to ensure the success of your solution. It is very likely that your organization will share many of the same guiding principles that we've seen in successful SharePoint deployments.

Use the examples shown in Table 4-3 to help define a starter set of guiding principles for your solution. Think about how you might create some supplemental reference material to help users internalize these principles— or consider adding a "principle of the day" to the home page of your solution. If users have a good understanding of the guiding principles, you have a reasonable shot at getting them to follow your governance guidelines.

Table 4-3 Examples of Guiding Principles

Governance Guiding Principle	Implication	Remember ...
General Principles Policies are tied to the scope and intention of the site. Governance policies will be more flexible for sites with more limited access than they will for sites that are shared with a broad audience.	The different audiences for sites allow you to adapt the governance model according to business needs. While some policies will be enforced across the entire organization, others may be determined by each site owner. This means that there may be some content that will not be as structured or searchable compared to other content that will be consistently "managed."	*One size does not fit all. Yes, we've got rules, but we're smart enough to know when it's appropriate to deviate from a standard in order to achieve a business objective more effectively.*
Even though SharePoint may be a new vehicle for collaboration, SharePoint content is governed by all general policies pertaining to the use of IT resources, including privacy, copyright, records retention, confidentiality, document security, and so on.	Content ownership, security, management, and contribution privileges are distributed across the entire organization, including users who may not have had content contribution, security, or records management privileges in the past. All content contributors need to be aware of organization policies for business-appropriate use of IT resources.	*Existing rules still apply— would you want your mother/ boss/customer/ client to see this picture? Should your mother/ boss/customer/ client be able to see this content?*

(continues)

Table 4-3 Examples of Guiding Principles *(continued)*

Governance Guiding Principle	Implication	Remember ...
Security Principles Overall firm security policies about who can see what content still apply and govern the portal. Role-based security will govern access control and permissions on each area of the portal (intranet and extranet).	Users need to think about where content is published to ensure that confidential content is only shared on sites with limited access. Users may have different permissions on different areas of the portal, which has an implication for both governance and training. While most users may not have content contribution privileges for tightly governed intranet pages, every user has Full Control privileges on his or her My Site.	*Publish to meet the "need to know" standards for your organization: No more, no less!* *You may not have the same permissions on every page of the portal.*
Site Design Principles Provide a consistent user experience—users should be able to consistently find key information on any collaboration site and search for the content they need.	All sites will also follow a consistent baseline design template to ensure consistency and usability across collaboration sites.	*Hey—it's not about you, it's about the user!*
Design to minimize training requirements for end users—use the best (and simplest) feature for each business objective.	Any user with site design privileges will be encouraged to participate in training to ensure that they use the most appropriate Web Parts and lists for each task.	*Just because you can, doesn't mean you should. You don't really need to try every new feature!*
Ensure that "findability" governs design decisions— optimize metadata and site configuration to	In situations where design trade-offs must be considered (more metadata versus less, information above or below "the fold," duplicating links in multiple	*Avoid building the roach motel— where content "checks in" but it never "checks out."*

Governance Guiding Principle	Implication	Remember ...
provide the best value for the end-user audience, not just the content contributor.	places), decisions should be made to make it easier for end users rather than content contributors. "Findability" means designing sites so that important information is easily visible and that navigational cues are used to help users easily find key information. It also means using metadata to improve accuracy of search results. Both the "browse" and "search" experience for users will guide design decisions in initial site development and modification over time.	
Site designers must understand the objectives of the recommended site design standards and make changes only when they can be justified with a valid business need.	Even though site designers may have permissions that allow them to make changes to site templates and other "controlled" site areas, they agree not to arbitrarily make changes to the basic site templates based on personal preference. Suggestions for changes to the standard site templates should be elevated to the Governance/Steering Committee.	*It's all about Spiderman: "With great power comes great responsibility." Use your powers wisely.*
All sites/pages must have a clearly identified content "owner."	Users need to know who to contact if information on a page or site is out of date or inaccurate.	*Make it obvious who owns the content on all pages and sites.*

(continues)

Table 4-3 Examples of Guiding Principles *(continued)*

Governance Guiding Principle	Implication	Remember ...
Content Principles		
All content is posted in just one place. Users who need access to content should create links to the document ID* for the document to access the content from its "authoritative" location.	This means that the official version of a document is posted once by the content owner (which may be a department, not necessarily an individual). For the reader's convenience, users may create a link to the official copy of a document from anywhere in SharePoint but should not post a "convenience copy." Users should not post copies of documents to their personal hard drives or My Sites if they exist elsewhere in the solution.	*Post one copy of a document.*
Edit in place—don't delete documents to create new versions.	Version control will be enabled in document libraries where prior versions need to be retained during document creation or editing. If prior versions need to be retained permanently for legal purposes, "old" versions of documents should be stored in an archive location or library. Documents will be edited in place rather than deleted and re-added so that document links created by other users will not break.	*Someone may be linking to your documents. Update, don't delete!*

*Document ID is a new feature in SharePoint 2010. The document ID is a unique identifier (a static URL) for the document that remains associated with the document even if it is moved to another location.

Governance Guiding Principle	Implication	Remember ...
Site Sponsors/ Owners are accountable, but everyone owns the responsibility for content management.	All content posted to a site shared by more than a small team will be governed by a content management process that ensures content is accurate, relevant, and current. Site Sponsors/Owners are responsible and accountable for content quality and currency and archiving old content on a timely basis, but site users are responsible for making Site Sponsors/Owners aware of content that needs updating.	*We're all responsible for content management.*
Links instead of e-mail attachments.	Users should send links to content whenever possible rather than e-mail attachments.	*No more e-mail attachments!*
Copyrighted material will not be added to the portal without the proper licensing or approval.	Copyright violations can be very costly. This is probably one of the most frequently ignored principles on corporate intranets and one that your corporate librarian (if your organization still has one) is going to be particularly concerned about.	*Don't publish what we don't own.*

It is especially important to remember the "one size does not fit all" guiding principle when it comes to governance. Use Figure 4-1 to help plan both the principles and communications around your governance plan.

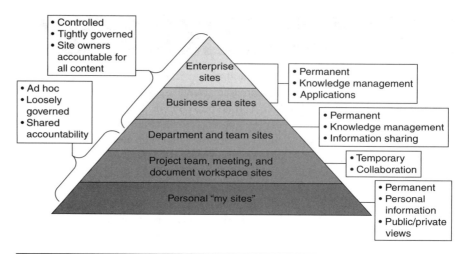

Figure 4-1 Governance based on the scope of a site

Policies and Standards

Policies define rules for SharePoint use; standards describe best practices. From a governance perspective, policies are usually driven by statutory, regulatory, or organizational requirements. Users are expected to meet policies without deviation. If your organization is subject to regulatory oversight, be sure you can actually enforce your policies because a failure to do so may target you as being noncompliant. Standards are usually established to encourage consistent practices. Users may adopt some elements of the standard that work for them while not implementing others.

As applied to the topic of file names, a policy might state, "Do not include dates or version numbers in file names," while a standard might state "File names should be topical and descriptive." In another example, the policy might state "All SharePoint sites will have a primary and secondary contact responsible for the site and its content," and the standard might state, "The site contact is listed on the site home page and in the site directory."

Each organization will have its own set of policies and standards. General topics should include content oversight, site design, branding and user experience, site management, back-end systems (hardware, software, and database management), and security. To ensure your content is relevant, do the following:

- Verify that your SharePoint polices and standards do not conflict with broader organizational polices.
- Publish policies and standards where users can easily find and follow them. Some policies may need to be published to "all readers," while others may need to be secured to protect the integrity of the application.
- Regularly review and revise policies and standards to keep them aligned to organizational needs.

The next sections describe some specific examples of policies and standards that you might want to consider for your organization. This is not an exhaustive list but includes some reusable ideas to consider.

Content Policies and Standards

Consider the following example content policies and standards, each of which is discussed in more detail in this section:

- Posting content to existing pages or sites
- Posting content to the home page
- Content auditing and review
- Records retention

Posting Content to Existing Pages or Sites   You will definitely need a policy or standard to ensure that the "one copy of a document" guiding principle is enabled. Take a look at the Content Contribution and Ownership sidebar that follows for a good policy to guide users regarding only posting content that they "own." In addition, consider creating policies for these other content topics:

- **Content posting cycle**. Create a policy to remind users to delete content from its original source or collaboration environment when it is "published" to the official SharePoint repository (or use automated content disposition policies to make sure this happens routinely).
- **Content editing**. Because content contributors on one site might have a link to content on a site they don't own, it is important to have a standard reminding users to "edit documents in place" so that links do not break.

■ **Content formats and names**. Decide whether you need policies for where certain types of content are stored in your solution and whether or not you need file naming standards. Consider a policy for defining what types of content belong in your SharePoint solution and what types of content belong in other locations. Given the rich search capabilities in SharePoint, it is not always necessary to define strict standards for file names other than to encourage users to choose names that will help someone else identify the file contents.

■ **Content containing links**. Clearly define who is accountable for making sure that links in content or on a site are not "broken."

Sample Policy: Content Contribution and Ownership

Site Sponsors are accountable for ensuring that the content posted on their pages is accurate and relevant and complies with records retention policies.

Only post content on a collaboration site or in My Site that you "own." Ownership means that the document is or was created by someone in your department, and your department is committed to maintaining the content for its entire life cycle. If a document is not owned by your department, but access to the document is needed on your site, ask the owner to post it and then create a link to it on your site.

Do not post content that you do not own the legal right to post electronically, including .pdfs or scanned images of journal articles or other documents from sources to which your organization does not have online publishing rights. A link may be created to this content on the content owner's Web site.

Posting Content to the Home Page   You will definitely want to consider creating a specific policy for posting content to the home page of your portal solution. Most content on the home page should be carefully controlled, especially for your intranet. After all, you get one chance to make a first impression, and your home page is where users get that impression! On an enterprise intranet, the home page can become a battle for "real estate" among several business units, usually Corporate Communications or Marketing and Human Resources. Even if your "solution" is a project team site, you will need to carefully consider how information is presented on the home page of the site and who is allowed to create and place content in this critical location. Some organizations solve the battle for home page real estate by assigning areas of the page ("neighborhoods") to specific departments. Others assign primary ownership to one specific department (often the department responsible for internal communications) but use the Portal Governance Board or Steering Committee to provide oversight and escalation if there are disagreements about content.

Content Auditing and Review   Consider a policy to define the frequency and type of review that you will have on each type of content or site. All content posted to enterprise-wide sites should be governed by a content management process that ensures content is accurate, relevant, and current, but even private team sites should have a content management strategy. For most sites, the maximum content review cycle should be no more than 12 months from the date content is posted. Confirm that your review cycles conform to any regulatory or statutory requirements.

Records Retention   Be sure you define clear policies regarding how your records retention policies will be implemented in your solution and the responsibilities content owners have to identify content as records and associate the appropriate record retention code to a given content item.

Design Policies and Standards

Consider creating policies and standards for each of the following design elements:

- Creating new subsites
- Page layout and organization
- Content Types and metadata
- Content-specific guidelines/policies
- Security
- Branding

Creating New Subsites   If individual "end-user" site owners will have permissions that enable them to create their own information architectures for sites under their control, it is important to provide some guidance to help them understand best practices for creating nodes in an information hierarchy. For example

- **Content ownership**. If a particular business group is the primary owner of all of the content to be posted on the page or site, creating a separate subsite ("node") for that business group probably makes sense.
- **Security**. If a significant group of content is highly sensitive, create a separate subsite, workspace, or node to more easily control the security settings for that content.
- **Database administration**. If there is a need to backup, restore, or otherwise manage content in a single group, having a unique subsite or page for that content will make these processes easier to manage.
- **Navigation**. Minimize the levels of nesting in the information architecture. It is a good practice to keep the number of levels in the hierarchy to no more than three so that users do not have to continuously "click through" to get to critical content. If a new node in the architecture is not needed for any of the other reasons just outlined, don't create it.

Page Layout and Organization   Nothing makes a site more confusing than a random collection of disorganized Web Parts cluttering a page. Anyone with page design permissions needs to remember the guiding principle about focusing on the end user, but these page designers should also be familiar with general design usability best practices. Usability guru Jakob Nielsen publishes a bi-weekly newsletter with excellent advice, best practices, and tips for Web page designers. You can sign up to get your copy directly in your e-mail inbox at http://www.useit.com/ alertbox. Some of the recommended best practices for page design include

- **Consistency**. Establish a standard design for all pages of each site to ensure that users can navigate without getting surprised by changing page layouts.
- **Speed**. Make sure that users can get important information as quickly as possible.
- **Scrolling**. Does the page layout require that users scroll up or down or left to right to find important information? Design a page to fit your organization's standard screen size and then make sure that

users do not have to scroll to find the most important information or Web Parts on the page. Scrolling should never be tolerated for critical information.

■ **Important content in the upper left**. Put the most important content toward the top-left part of the page. This is where readers will "land" visually when they get to the page. If the most important information is in this location, chances are better for capturing the user's attention than if the information is buried somewhere else on the page.

Content Types and Metadata   A Content Type is a collection of settings that define a particular type of information, such as a project plan or financial report, and can be defined for the entire enterprise, for an entire Site Collection, or it can be defined "locally" for a specific page or site. Site Columns are the "properties" of a particular type of content. Columns are part of the attributes or properties of a Content Type. Site Columns can also be defined across the entire solution or for an individual site or Site Collection. Content Types and Site Columns are both types of "metadata" in SharePoint 2010. The values for many Site Columns (metadata) are specific to specific sites. Best practices and concepts for defining a good metadata structure are presented in Chapter 5, "Planning Your Information Architecture." Your governance plan needs to include your standards and policies for the Content Types and Site Columns used in your solution as well as policies for how users can request the creation of a new enterprise Content Type or Site Column.

Social Tags and Ratings   Social feedback, content added by users as tags and ratings, is new in SharePoint 2010. These capabilities allow users to participate and interact with your SharePoint solution and improve content "findability" by allowing individuals to supplement formal classification with additional tags they find personally meaningful. Social tags refer to metadata that users add to content to help define what it is, what it includes, or what it does. Your governance policies should include guidelines for how you want users to participate in social tagging and provide guidance and examples of meaningful tags for your organization. You should also make sure that users understand that social tagging uses the Search Index to provide security trimming on content that is stored in SharePoint, which means that users will be able to tag confidential documents, but those tags are not visible to anyone who doesn't have read access to the document.

If you choose to activate the Ratings feature in SharePoint 2010, users will have the option to "rate" documents (and pages) on a scale of 0 to 5 stars. Your governance plan should document how you intend to use ratings in your organization—for example, are you asking users to rate whether they think the content is well-written or whether or not they think it is useful? An October 2009 article in the *Wall Street Journal*[2] cited a statistic that states when consumers write online reviews of products, they tend to leave positive ratings: The average rating for items online is 4.3 stars out of 5. If you want to have meaningful ratings on content in your organization, you will need to define your expectations and make it clear to users how ratings will be used. Obviously, if all the ratings are positive, it's going to be hard to find value. Some organizations try to identify stellar examples as best practices, but this is a very difficult process to sustain over time without dedicated resources. Allowing users to rate content as they see fit may help identify potential best practices, but you need to be careful about assuming that low-rated content is necessarily "bad."

Content-specific Guidelines/Policies   High-impact collaboration solutions ensure that content is easily accessible by end users. This means that the content is not just "findable," but that it is structured and written to be consumed online. Assuming that your content contributors are good writers to begin with, they may not be familiar with best practices for writing for the Web. It's helpful to provide some standards and policies for specific SharePoint lists and libraries. Following are several examples of standards, policies, and best practices you may wish to consider for your solution.

- **Blogs and wikis**. End users should be aware of what your organization considers appropriate for posting social content to personal sites such as blogs and wikis. While in some organizations, blogging about your hobbies is acceptable; in others, it's not. Be very thoughtful about how you define governance policies for social content because you need to be sure that you are not placing so many rules on your content that you will discourage content contributions. There is no single right answer for every organization. Chapter 7

---

2. Geoffrey Fowler and Joseph De Avila, "On the Internet, Everyone's a Critic but They're Not Very Critical." *Wall Street Journal*, October 5, 2009, available at http://online.wsj.com/article/SB125470172872063071.html.

includes some specific governance suggestions for social computing features that you should consider as part of your governance plan.

- **Announcements.** Overall, the tone of all text should be concise and helpful. For announcements, create a descriptive but succinct title. In the announcement text, put the important information first and write briefly, using no more than four to five sentences. Try to avoid using large fonts and avoid lots of white space in announcement text. Do not underline anything that isn't a hyperlink. Make the link text a concise description of the link so that it aids the reader in scanning:
  - **Bad**: <u>Click here</u> for the latest application form
  - **Better**: <u>Download the latest application form</u>
  - **Best**: Download the latest <u>application form</u>
- **Discussion boards**. Effective discussion boards must have someone who will serve as the discussion board moderator to ensure that questions are answered and that the discussion board adds value. In some organizations, you will need to consult with the Legal department to ensure that information about products, research, patients, data, regulated content, or legal issues are appropriate in online discussion boards.
- **Picture or video libraries**. Content posted to picture or video libraries should be business-related and appropriate for publication in the corporate environment. Be sure to obtain permission from any individual in a picture or video that will be posted to a site before it is uploaded. Also make sure that your organization owns the image or has obtained the proper licenses for its use.
- **Links**. In some cases, users and site designers will have the option to indicate whether or not a link should open up in a new window. In general, the following standards are recommended for links:
  - Links to documents or pages within the Site Collection: Do not open in a new window.
  - Links to documents or pages in another Site Collection: Open in a new window.
  - Links outside your intranet (to another application within the company or to an Internet site): Open in a new window.
- **Document libraries**. (For additional best practices for document libraries, please see Chapter 5.) Consider how documents will be used when you upload to SharePoint. Documents may be uploaded to SharePoint using almost any document format (Word, .pdf, Excel, PowerPoint, and so on). If you upload documents in their native formats, users will be able to download them and easily edit

them to create their own versions. Unless they have Contributor privileges to a library, they will not be able to post them back to the same sites. Documents that might be reused as an example for others should always be uploaded in their "native," editable formats. Documents that must be protected from editing or changing, even on a "private" copy, should be uploaded in a "protected" format or with passwords for editing. Consider the .pdf format for very large documents given that this format will reduce the file size and thus download time for others.

Security   Security considerations are one of the most important design elements for a SharePoint site. It is important to think about security during the design process because understanding how objects will need to be secured on the site will affect the site structure, page layout, and metadata design. Considering that in almost all SharePoint deployments, end users will have some capabilities to manage security for sites they control, it is critical to ensure that anyone with permissions to assign security understands how SharePoint security works.

SharePoint provides the capability to secure content down to the item level and provides multiple options for creating security groups. This is both a blessing (due to the flexibility it enables) and a curse (because it makes it very easy for users to create overly complex and virtually unmanageable security models). As a best practice, it is helpful to offer "security planning" consulting to users who are new to SharePoint because planning security can easily fall into the category we call "Don't try this at home."

We talk more about planning security in Chapter 8, "Planning Your Security Model." In your governance plan, you need to clearly articulate specific security policies and how they should be applied within SharePoint sites.

Branding   The Corporate Communications department (or its equivalent) in most organizations will typically define branding standards for your intranet and Internet presence. A key governance decision you need to think about is whether the corporate branding can be changed in a given SharePoint Site Collection. There may be valid business reasons to deviate from the corporate brand: For example, you may want an extranet collaboration site that is "co-branded" with your organization and a partner. Within an intranet solution, users may find it confusing and wonder "Where am I?" if the site branding changes from site to site, so you need to consider defining branding standards and policies with the site user in mind. Using some elements of color or brand variability in the site branding might help reinforce your security model. For example, you may want the site "brand" or theme to communicate the security model on the site—one theme or brand for enterprise-wide intranet sites and another theme or brand for secure team sites. This can help to provide visual cues to content contributors, reminding them when they post to a site with the "public" brand, the content can generally be seen by everyone in the organization.

Key Points

The key takeaways to remember from this chapter are to

- Establish a governance plan to ensure quality and relevance of content and ensure that all users understand their roles and responsibilities.
- Make sure that you have a Governance Board or Steering Committee with a strong advocate in the role of Executive Sponsor.
- Keep your governance model simple. Solutions need a strong governance model, but they don't need complicated models with lots of bureaucracy.
- Don't make the solution itself more complicated than it needs to be. Be careful about "over designing." Just because SharePoint has a cool feature doesn't mean that you need to deploy it—at least not right away.
- Ensure that all users with design or Full Control privileges have internalized your design guiding principles and that content contributors understand guiding principles related to content.
- Think about how you will ensure compliance with your governance plan over time, particularly for highly visible sites. You may want to carefully monitor and review some sites and only spot-check others.
- An effective governance plan doesn't have to constrain every move—it has to provide guidance to users to ensure that your solution remains effective and vibrant over time.

CHAPTER 5

PLANNING YOUR INFORMATION ARCHITECTURE

Information architecture (IA) is a strategy and plan for information delivery and access. It describes how information managed in SharePoint will be organized and how users will navigate through the environment. A library catalog is a classic example of information architecture. Content is assigned to one or more topic headings (for example, Fiction or Mystery) but also has additional properties, such as Author Name, Title, Publishing Date, and Publisher. Another example is an online music library that stores metadata such as Genre, Artist, Song, and Publisher. In an online catalog, content can be accessed or queried using any one, or often several, metadata values.

Your information architecture helps users find content in your SharePoint environment the way a library catalog helps you find information in a library.

- It supports browsing for information because it defines the overall structural organization of the solution and presents consistent navigational structures.
- It supports searching for information because it defines a content classification scheme that presents consistent labeling and enhances search engine accuracy.

Information architectures should be driven by purpose. A well-designed ontology (where information is stored) and taxonomy (what it is called) increases the likelihood that users will find what they are looking for with minimal clicks. An effective information architecture is a tool that will assist users in understanding and interacting with the solution.

Your information architecture helps users find information in any of three scenarios:

- I know it exists, and I know where it is.
- I know it exists, but I don't know where it is.
- I don't know if it exists.

Thus, the goal of your information architecture (IA) is "findability."

SharePoint buyers expect intuitive navigation out-of-the-box, but we often hear users complain, "It's not intuitive," when they talk about their organization's SharePoint solution. Most often, these users are not complaining about SharePoint as a platform; they are complaining about the way that their information architects have designed and implemented the sites they use. Investing in your information architecture helps:

- **Improve user adoption**. Well-organized content gets found, which helps users see the value of the solution and participate in the collaboration process.
- **Improve user satisfaction and productivity**. When users can find what they are looking for, they are more productive. A *Network World* article in 2007[1] mentioned two productivity statistics related to information "findability." The first references a research study reporting that as much as 10% of an organization's salary costs are wasted on ineffective searches. A big contributor to ineffective searches is a lack of metadata, a key element of your information architecture. The second statistic, from a different study, suggested that information workers spend between 9 to 10 hours per week looking for information, of which about 3.5 hours is wasted on searches that don't turn up the right information.
- **Reduce IT costs**. Good information architecture helps eliminate redundant content, thus reducing storage costs. Planning your information architecture may also help you identify redundant solutions (for example, two solutions for storing the same type of content), which can reduce both maintenance and support costs.
- **Reduce information overload**. Good information architecture also reduces information overload because it helps move the most

---

1. Jon Brodkin, *Network World*, 1/23/07 http://www.networkworld.com/news/2007/012307-wasted-searches.html. Accessed January 1, 2010.

relevant content to the top of search engine results, which means users can quickly get to the information they need.

- **Reduce compliance risks**. When users clearly understand how content is organized, they don't feel the need to store multiple "convenience" copies of the same document.

Your information architects need to understand how different audiences will navigate and search for information. The benefits of your SharePoint solution depend on how content is organized, labeled, and categorized. Thus, your information architecture is critical to your solution's success. The key sections contained in this chapter include

- Getting Started
- Site Architecture
- Page Architecture
- Metadata Architecture
- Maintaining Your Information Architecture

Getting Started

Your information architecture is especially important for your SharePoint 2010 solution because content in SharePoint is typically divided into multiple Site Collections for performance, storage, and management. A Site Collection administrator has access to the entire Site Collection and, for the most part, can create and manage content within it. With this type of distributed content and responsibility, as the number of Site Collections grows, you will be challenged to create and maintain your information architecture. In large organizations, the IT department typically delegates Site Collection administration and often Site Collection design to users who have a good understanding of the business but not information architecture best practices. The result: poorly designed sites and decreased information "findability." Therefore, it is especially important to ensure that all users to whom Site Collection administration or site design privileges have been extended have training in information architecture skills.

What's new in SharePoint 2010?

- SharePoint 2010 includes several features to make it much easier to design and maintain your information architecture centrally by adding the ability to distribute and control metadata across multiple Site Collections and across your entire farm. This makes if far easier to "enforce" information architecture best practices. However, it doesn't absolve you of the responsibility to train all of your Site Collection administrators and designers in information architecture best practices.

■ With these new capabilities in SharePoint 2010, you have new decisions to make about your information architecture governance, including deciding what architecture decisions can be delegated and at which levels: departments, teams, and projects.

Building your information architecture includes three key foundational elements:

■ Knowledge of the domain to be modeled
■ Content organization
■ First-hand understanding of the end user

The first key element of well-designed information architecture is knowledge of the domain to be modeled. Information architects must work with content owners to establish an effective and useful taxonomy, which describes the structure and classification of your content. Carefully and thoughtfully designing the optimal model for site organization and the structure and values for metadata is a very detailed process. As painful as the process might be, content owners must actively participate in detailed data and site design reviews because they have the best knowledge of the domain. (It often helps to have a lot of chocolate available when you are working on your detailed metadata and site design.)

The second key element is content organization—this involves a combination of data modeling and library science skills. Content needs to be organized so that users who are not experts in the content can find it. In other words, the content taxonomy should not assume that all users have an in-depth knowledge of the content or the domain. "Findability," the key goal of your information architecture, is significantly improved in SharePoint 2010 because in addition to the authoritative taxonomy content editors apply when they assign metadata to sites and documents, end users can add "social" metadata in the form of tags and notes (also called "folksonomy"), which provides additional information to help users find what they are looking for (see Chapter 7, "Getting Social: Leveraging

Community Features," for more information about social metadata and the metadata architecture discussion later in this chapter).

The third key element is a first-hand understanding of the end users. In general, when there are trade-offs to be made in information architecture, design for the "reader" of the content, not the person who contributes the content. For example, our experience has been that most people who are contributing content will have about 30–45 seconds of patience available for entering metadata. This means that you can probably include no more than about five contributor-entered fields in your design for most content. The exception (and the trade-off) comes in for content that you will publish for a discipline such as human resources, where the *job* of the contributor is to communicate everything they can about the content they are publishing. Entering more metadata (more than the recommended five or so fields) is generally not an issue for people contributing human resource content because the additional time spent entering metadata makes it significantly easier for end users to filter or search for content and ultimately saves time for the human resources team due to the reduction in phone calls asking for content that can be easily found with the additional classification.

In Chapter 1, "Getting Started," we talked about the process you should go through with your key stakeholders to understand both their objectives for the solution and how they use and create information. The questions about information creation and use form the basis of the information gathering activities that inform your information architecture. As a reminder, you will need the following general types of information to develop your information architecture:

- Who are the key users/stakeholders? Do they include only people inside the organization, or do they also include your clients or customers, partners, and vendors? Look at who uses content and why they need it. Why is the content relevant to the user? What is their desired outcome?
- Do your users include the entire organization or just selected departments or roles?
- Do geographical boundaries matter for your content access or storage?
- How do your stakeholders use and access the information they need today?
- Who creates content? What types of content do they create?

- Who reviews and edits content, and who might need to approve publication?
- What types of content needs to be identified as a record?
- How is information organized today? Take a look at your existing file shares, intranet, and collaboration sites. Do a comprehensive inventory and decide what can be deleted or archived.
- What information will be migrated to SharePoint? Is there any information that might be indexed "in place" or migrated to archival storage?
- How is content managed throughout the life cycle?
- How much content will be managed of each type?

Manually defining and documenting information architectures requires significant effort and cost, but some manual effort is usually required. A good information architect starts by examining existing structures—typically found in folder hierarchies, existing intranets, industry sources, or organizational charts—and uses these existing structures as a starting point to review proposed architectures with domain experts. The process will most certainly be iterative—starting down from the top as well as working up from the bottom. As an alternative or complement to a completely manual process, automated classification tools can suggest an information architecture by analyzing the content from a collection of documents. Some of the automatic classification engines include machine-learning algorithms that help the engines train themselves from example data. At best, automated classification systems can help get you started with building your information architecture. For the most part, building effective information architecture requires at least some manual effort.

In this chapter, we provide a general overview of three different levels of information architecture or taxonomy:

- **Site architecture**. The navigational structure of the solution. The site architecture is important because it defines how users will "browse" through the solution.
- **Page architecture**. The position of Web Parts on each page. The page architecture is important because consistency across similar pages helps users quickly find what they are looking for. In addition, placing the most important Web Parts in the most prominent and visible parts of the page ensures that users won't miss important information.

- **Metadata architecture**. The structure of the content within the solution (the attributes that you will use to classify and organize your content the way a librarian organizes content in a library). The metadata architecture is important because it helps improve the user experience when he or she is searching for information. The site architecture supports users who *browse*. The metadata architecture primarily supports users who *search*, but as you will see later, the metadata architecture also helps users browse for information in context because it allows you to add descriptive information about content that users can use to assess its value.

Each of these levels probably deserve a book of its own, so simply reading this chapter is not going to make you an expert information architect. Getting your information architecture right is not a one-time process—a good IA needs to evolve as your organization changes. Investing in expert support for your initial information architecture is well worth it. Look for an expert who will help transfer knowledge about IA best practices to your organization. You don't need someone to hang around for life, but you should consider engaging an expert, ideally someone with a background or degree in library science or information management, to help you get started and help your organization develop the skills needed to maintain and evolve your IA.

To improve adoption, we encourage usability testing of your site, page, and metadata architecture by representatives of key user areas and roles. Retest as your architecture evolves to ensure you will continue to have highly satisfied users when you deploy or alter your solution.

The following three sections discuss each of these topics in more detail.

Site Architecture

In a portal or content management system, an effective site architecture helps users navigate to content without having to search. Your site architecture also allows users to see documents and other components of the solution in context, which helps them assess whether a document or component is relevant for what they are trying to accomplish. Our experience indicates that users use a combination of hierarchical navigation and search when both are available. It is impossible to predict who will be a "browser" and who will be a "searcher" in practice. The challenge is that while creating an optimal site architecture for navigation and content organization is vitally important, you probably won't get it right until you get real users using the solution with real data. As you learn more about how users interact with your solution when you observe their behavior and gather feedback after deployment, you should evolve your site architecture to make your solution even more effective.

As you conduct interviews and workshops to develop an understanding of user objectives for the solution and how they use information to guide their work, think about how that information fits within the overall conceptual organization of the company. Think about how content can be separated into major groups, based on key business processes, major projects, key business roles, or organizational functions. Within each major classification, you may need to break each concept into subunits, depending on both the type of content, who will "own" the content, and how you believe people will use the content.

One technique you might use to plan your site architecture is to gather together three to five representative stakeholders to brainstorm key content areas. Write down the major content categories that users will expect to find on your site. Use the team members you have gathered for this purpose as well as the information you documented during the stakeholder interviews described in Chapter 1. If you don't have access to actual site users, you may have to imagine what users will find on your site. If this is the case, consider creating user "personas"[2] and approaching your site architecture design from the perspective of each persona. Use your stakeholder team and interview results to document major content areas on sticky notes and then group the sticky notes into related groups. These related groups will form the starting point for your site's main navigation. As you iterate through the site architecture process, you will want to take out duplicate items, combine similar items, and look for opportunities to create primary and secondary or subgroupings where appropriate.

One mistake made by novice information architects is organizing their site architecture based on the organization of their company. The company organization chart should *not* be the starting point for your site architecture. That doesn't mean you should ignore how your company is organized; it just means that you should use the organization chart to *inform* your site

---

2. Personas are fictional characters created to represent the different user of your solution. A user persona represents the goals and behavior of a real group of users. You use the persona to imagine the site design from that user's perspective, which helps you create a meaningful site architecture.

architecture, not to *guide* it. That said, there are some organizational units that are also functional units—for example, human resources and legal. It is perfectly fine to represent HR and legal in your site architecture because while these may, in fact, be represented on the organization chart as "departments," they are also each a function within a typical organization. The mistake designers often make is putting a business function like corporate communications "under" HR in the site architecture because the corporate communications department happens to report to the head of HR in their company (or when they put HR and legal under finance because these two business units report to the CFO). This structure might make sense temporarily, but if there is a reorganization and communications moves to another business group, the site architecture will no longer make sense. In addition, new employees who are not familiar with the company's organization structure will be far less likely to understand the site navigation if functions are aligned by organizational "ownership."

A well-designed site architecture can contribute to organizational goals and objectives. It should allow people to quickly find the information they need to do their jobs, effectively improving operational efficiency. It should also help people place the context of their work in the overall context of the organization, enabling them to gain an understanding of what is available on the solution as a whole, even if they primarily focus on their own particular space. It is important to provide meaningful labels to the elements of your site architecture. It is even more important to test your chosen labels with representative users to make sure that your nomenclature makes sense. Labels should be succinct—not more than three words each. Terms should be straightforward, consistent, and convey the desired tone for your solution. Try not to make up words for your navigation—use terms that users will understand. There is no single "right" way to organize the content in your site. However, there are some approaches that are frequently used in well-regarded solutions:

- Many public facing Internet sites and internally facing intranet sites group general information about the organization in a section called About Us or About [Company Name]. You can put information such as the mission and vision, directions, company history, and organization charts in this section. Because this is such a familiar concept, users will generally know what to expect in this category.
- Functional groupings can be based on "what we do," "who we serve" (both customer groups and industries), and what employees need to

do their jobs. Different organizations will have different terms for these groupings. For example: Our Customers, Our Clients, My Life and Career, My Role.

- Activity groupings are based on primary activities. This structure may work for a departmental in addition to an enterprise-level solution. For example, the following types of activities might form a basis of your site architecture:

    - **Project work**. Activities that are designed to produce a specific result during a finite period of time.
    - **Support work**. Ongoing services that maintain an existing process (such as application maintenance and support).
    - **Enabling work**. Initiatives such as career planning, a project management office, or portfolio tracking that help your organization deliver project or support activities.
    - **Customer work**. Activities related to engaging with partners, suppliers, and customers.
    - **Team work**. Activities related to administering a team such as managing vacation and travel schedules and conducting regular team meetings.
    - **Leadership work**. Information and activities for management personnel only such as performance management, budgeting, and sharing other confidential information.

- Duplicate groupings if content "belongs" in more than one collection. One of the biggest benefits of organizing information online is that the same content can be grouped logically in more than one location even if it "lives" physically in only one place. For example, you may organize your sites based on industry groups, but there may be a subgroup that could be classified in more than one industry. For example, imagine an information architecture for an executive search firm. The site that supports the CIO practice could appear under the "CxO" group and the Information Technology group, which would help users navigate to the practice page no matter where they are looking for it. However, be careful about overusing this capability and creating lots of "weak" categories because this will confuse your users who will wonder why the same topic appears in so many places.

In some organizations, the solution design team will define the major organizational groupings for the site architecture but leave the detailed architecture to content planning teams at the division or group level. This practice works effectively if experienced information architects are available to support the divisional teams and if some common architecture principles are defined at the enterprise level to ensure consistency in user experience across the solution and to ensure that the optimal SharePoint features are leveraged in the architecture design. As stated earlier, the key to success in a delegated model is to ensure that you empower all users with design permissions with information architecture skills and best practices. This means that you will need to define a training program to ensure that users get the knowledge they need to effectively define their information architecture. In addition to training, you should also consider providing expert coaching to new site designers until they feel proficient.

Before you implement your site architecture, it is important to review it with several stakeholders. While you may be tempted to immediately implement your proposed architecture in SharePoint, this is not a good idea. You should go through at least one round of "paper" site architecture documentation. There are several techniques that information architects use to document a site architecture, and several information architects we know like to use mind maps and a mind mapping tool such as MindManager (http://www.mindjet.com) to document a proposed site architecture. Others use Microsoft Office Visio or PowerPoint. The goal of your site architecture diagram is to show the relationship of the various elements of your proposed site navigational structure in a picture that allows you to review your proposal with your key stakeholders. The technique you use isn't nearly as important as the conversation that you need to have, so choose a diagramming technique that best facilitates your conversation. Figure 5-1 shows a simple site architecture diagram created with Microsoft Office Visio. This example shows some diagramming techniques that you might use to help facilitate your architecture conversation.

Your site architecture diagram should include the following:

- Hierarchical diagram showing each level ("node") and how the nodes are connected. Note that the example in Figure 5-1 suggests that you try to limit your nodes to no more than three levels deep. This is not a hard and fast rule, just a guideline. Don't use this rule to eliminate useful "landing" pages for major sections in your site. Category or landing pages help provide context when users land on subpages or subsites from search results.

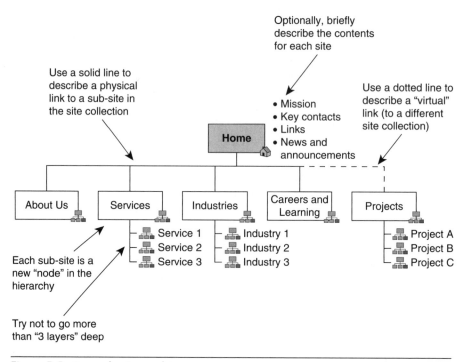

Figure 5-1 Example site architecture

- Labels for each subsite or page and, if possible, a general description of the content on the page.
- Plan for navigation (using tabs and/or other navigational links).

As you consider whether a particular topic, process, or function needs a separate "node" (page or site) in the site architecture, it is also helpful to consider several factors in overall site administration:

- **Content ownership**. If a particular business group is the primary owner of all of the content to be published on the page or site, creating a separate site ("node") for that business group probably makes sense.
- **Security**. If a significant group of content is highly sensitive, creating a separate node in the architecture allows you to more easily control the security settings for that content.
- **Database administration**. If you think that you might want to backup, restore, or otherwise manage content in a single group,

having a unique portal node for that content will make these processes easier to manage.

■ **Navigation**. Try to minimize the levels of nesting in your information architecture. It's a good practice to keep the number of levels in the hierarchy to no more than three so that users do not have to continuously "click through" to get to critical content. If you don't need to create a node in the architecture for any of the other reasons outlined here or your content group does not need a "landing page," don't create it.

Effective site architecture design is not a simple or quick process, even for small organizations or simple sites. If you invest the time to learn about your users' information needs, the result will be a site that is easy to learn and use.

Page Architecture

When you are satisfied with the overall site architecture for your solution, you will need to plan how to organize the content on each page. This should be done in an iterative process with content owners and domain experts. SharePoint 2010 provides dozens of possible templates that provide a great starting point based on common usage patterns for different types of pages and sites. Note that the discussion in this chapter applies primarily to end-user designed team sites, not the "managed" page templates that you will use for your "publishing" sites. Refer to Chapter 12, "Putting Your Site on the Web," for a discussion of how to control page layout using master pages.

One of our clients made this comment about investing a lot of time redesigning pages based on the Microsoft templates when we started her SharePoint design project: "Why should I spend time and money on designing page layouts to improve usability when Microsoft has already spent millions on this effort? Unless we have a really good reason to vary based on an expressed business objective, let's just start with what is provided out-of-the-box and focus on content." While the Microsoft solutions will give you a good place to start, do not assume that the out-of-the-box templates are the only solutions for your organization. At a minimum, you will want to replace the standard "Microsoft" images and logos in your team site templates with images that are relevant for your organization.

Even if you start with a template provided in SharePoint 2010, you still need to think about how users will use each site. Consider the following basic design principles when configuring your page architecture:

- **Consistency**. Provide a standard design template for all pages on the portal and take steps in your governance processes, which are described in Chapter 4, "Planning for Governance," to ensure that these design standards are followed. This ensures that users can navigate around the intranet without getting surprised by changing design standards. For example, if key contacts are always at the bottom of the page, users will know immediately how to contact someone when they need help or when they need to inform the site owner about inaccurate information. Consistency provides a very real benefit for your organization because you will not have to pay people to spend their time trying to figure out what the site or page owner is trying to say as they navigate through the solution. Users become familiar with the template so that they do not have to reorient themselves on various pages of the site.
- **Speed**. Make sure that users can get information as quickly as possible. This goes along with consistency but should inspire you to think about a few additional design principles. For example, does the information or placeholder you are adding improve the ability for users to quickly find what they are looking for or get in the way? Think about using "clickable" images to help users find content on your site. However, try to avoid images that move or bounce. Think about all the unnecessary "dancing elephants" you've seen on Web pages. As a general rule, images that spin or rotate detract from usability.
- **Scrolling**. Does the page layout require that users scroll up or down or left to right to find important information? Design your page to fit your organization's standard screen size and then make sure that users do not have to scroll to find the most important information or Web Parts on the page. Scrolling may be acceptable in your design standards, but scrolling should never be tolerated for critical information. Think about designing your page the way that news editors design a newspaper—the most important information should be "above the fold." As a best practice, avoid designing sites that require left-to-right scrolling for sites viewed using your organization's standard display size; up-and-down scrolling is generally okay.
- **Important content in the upper left**. Put your most important content toward the top-left part of the page. This is where readers

will "land" visually when they get to your page. If the most important information is in this location, you have a better chance at capturing your user's attention than if the information is buried somewhere else on the page. One mistake we see pretty often is that site designers will put "permanent" content in prime "real estate." You want to avoid this at all costs—put content that changes frequently in the places where users will be most likely to see it.

- **Images**. Use images to help create visual interest on your site and also to provide visual cues for key site content. You can easily create clickable images by inserting an image in a content editor Web Part and adding a hyperlink to the target content. However, be sure to size your images to work effectively in your screen real estate and use an appropriate resolution for the Web to minimize screen "paint time," especially for users who will access your site at slower speeds. When you select images for your site, be sure they are relevant and be sure that you own the right to publish them on your site.

We usually like to do at least one iteration of page architecture design (wire frames) before creating a prototype in SharePoint. There are several wire frame tools that you can use to help lay out the content on your site, including Visio. Microsoft Office Visio 2010 includes some wire framing templates, but in a clear opportunity for a third-party add-on, they do not include any "shapes" for SharePoint Web Parts. Balsamiq (http://www.balsamiq.com) is an inexpensive mockup tool for which users in its "community" have created some SharePoint elements (the SharePoint 2007 elements, which are reusable for SharePoint 2010, are at http://mockupstogo.net/prebuilt-sharepoint-elements). Figure 5-2 shows a simple page wire frame created using Balsamiq.

In general, plan to develop an initial page layout proposal when you are designing your site but consider offering stakeholders a second opportunity to reevaluate page layout design when you have completed the initial build and are ready for users to load content. This phase in the life cycle occurs after the initial build is complete and is essentially part of the user acceptance test. Because this is usually the first opportunity for users to interact with the solution using real data, we call this phase "Meet the Portal." You will get a chance to improve even your best ideas for page layout when users have a chance to see the solution with "real" data; the "Meet the Portal" opportunity is a great way to ensure that you have the optimal page architecture.

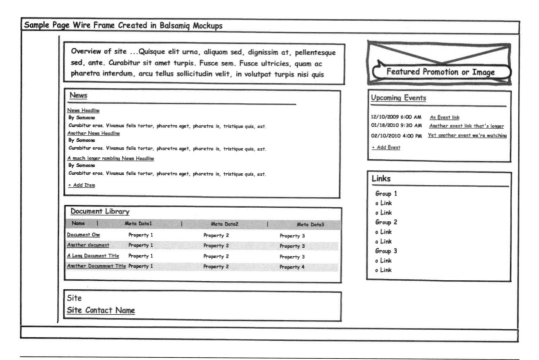

Figure 5-2 Sample page architecture created with Balsamiq

Metadata Architecture

Metadata (literally, data about data) defines the structure of the content within your SharePoint solution—the attributes that you will use to classify and organize your content the way a librarian organizes content in a library. Why do you need to think about metadata? Metadata makes it easier for users to find content; in other words, "findability" is the key rationale for metadata, just like the other elements of your information architecture. Metadata can also provide context for content, helping users quickly identify whether a document or other asset will be helpful—without having to examine the content of the document in detail. Metadata provides a far superior organizational framework for document classification than the dreaded "F-word" (folder), but please review the next sidebar, "Folders … They're Back," as you think about the best approach for your metadata architecture. SharePoint 2010 introduces new features that will significantly improve the way you can manage metadata in your organization, but the new features add complexity to the planning process.

For the most part, users think of metadata as attributes that are assigned to documents, but you can use metadata attributes to classify and organize any type of list content. The basic design principles are the same, no matter what type of content you are organizing, but we talk primarily about document metadata in this section.

There are three elements of SharePoint 2010 that you will use to design your metadata architecture: Content Types, Columns, and Managed Metadata.

- A *Content Type* is a collection of settings that define a particular type of information, such as a project plan or financial report. A Content Type can be defined at the portal level or at the site level and reused across multiple document libraries and sites. A new feature of SharePoint 2010 allows you to define Content Types across your entire SharePoint farm and share Content Types across multiple Site Collections, functionality that used to require third-party tools in earlier releases. A Content Type defines the attributes of a document, a list item, or a folder.
- *Columns* are the "properties" or attributes of a particular type of content. For example, the Columns of a document Content Type might include Name, Description, Author, Status (such as Draft or Final), or Region. Columns can be defined across the entire portal (Site Columns) or for an individual site or Site Collection and across your entire farm or one or more Site Collections. This is one of the most exciting features of SharePoint 2010 because sharing metadata across multiple Site Collections was not available out-of-the-box in earlier releases. Columns can also be defined inside a particular list (List Columns). The primary difference between Site Columns and List Columns is reusability. Site Columns can be reused on any lower-level site. List Columns are unique to the list or library in which they are created. As a best practice, you should define Columns at the site level unless they are only applicable within a single list or library.
- *Managed Metadata* is a new type of metadata for both Content Types and Columns. Managed Metadata is just that—metadata that is controlled and managed centrally.

You will need to plan how you will use these features across your entire solution as well as in individual sites, lists, and libraries. Metadata planning requires careful thought and a significant interest in details. However, a wonderful feature of SharePoint is that your metadata architecture can evolve and grow as your business and knowledge about users' needs changes. Your metadata architecture should be thoughtfully planned, but you do not have to agonize over every decision that you make. Put a stake in the ground, try it out, and continue to monitor your solution over time. Use the suggestions at the end of this chapter to ensure that your entire IA remains "alive."

In the remaining sections of this chapter, we discuss considerations for planning Content Types and Columns in more detail, followed by a discussion about planning Managed Metadata.

Folders . . . They're Back

One of the most challenging jobs for any information architect is convincing users about the benefit of organizing their documents with metadata rather than folders. Folders, the traditional organizational framework for documents in file shares (and file cabinets), have several problems:

- It takes lots of clicks to get to the content you are looking for.
- Folders are inflexible—you either put the same content in two different folders if it applies to more than one folder, which immediately creates version-control challenges, or you have to live with the structure you created and make sure all users understand how to correctly put documents "where they are supposed to go."
- Using folders to organize content assumes that you and your colleagues all have the same mental model for content organization.
- Folders don't let you easily sort, filter, and create ad hoc views of your content—folders assume you know today how you might want to see your content tomorrow.

Metadata is a better organizing principle for several reasons:

- It's easy to see what content is available in a library or list.
- Users can look at, sort, or filter content by any dimension that is useful to today—and use a different dimension tomorrow.
- Metadata improves the ability to serendipitously discover what is available in a content repository—it surfaces rather than buries content.

- With metadata, you have the option to use "group by" in views if you need to collect content of a similar type to create an organizing experience similar to folders but still have the flexibility to group your content along multiple dimensions.
- Metadata improves search engine results. Most search engines factor the content metadata into the algorithm that returns results. In essence, it provides bonus points that can boost the content's position or rank on a results page. In addition, some search engines can be customized to support searches on specific metadata elements.

Information architects and good SharePoint designers have spent many years trying to break users of the "folder habit." However, with SharePoint 2010, folders have an opportunity for a comeback because they are the vehicle through which "location-based" metadata is assigned. In SharePoint 2010, you can assign default metadata values to a folder using the Column default value settings feature in Library Settings (see Figure 5-3), and then all the documents that you create in or upload to that folder will "inherit" the metadata value associated with the folder automatically. Now that folders can actually provide a valuable "service," they may have a renewed place in your information

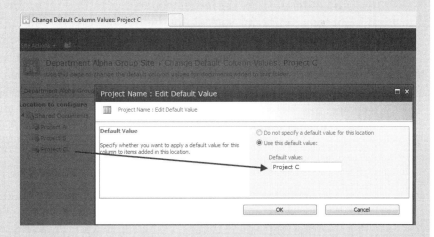

Figure 5-3 Setting the default value of a Column for a folder

architecture—especially if you create views that show your items without folders.

In addition, the new Content Organizer feature (described in Chapter 12) can be used to automatically "route" content to a specific location or folder in your site.

Does this mean that we are now recommending that you use folders to organize your content by default? Absolutely not. However, you now have additional *options* you can consider for your information architecture, depending on the type of repository you have and whether or not you want to take advantage of the new content management features in SharePoint 2010. See Chapter 6, "Making Enterprise Content Management Work: Documents and Records," for planning considerations associated with the SharePoint 2010 document routing and location-based metadata features.

Content Types

It is often difficult to find related information when you are searching through a large repository. For example, let's assume that you need to create a project plan for a new project and you know that there have been other projects similar to yours in the past. In a portal with many project team sites, it can be challenging to find all of the project plans. Content Types in SharePoint helps simplify this task. If you define "Project Plan" as a Content Type, you can then find all project plans in your portal easily with a single search. Content Types also let you associate specific Site Columns with different types of content. For example, you can associate an Effective Date with a Policy but not with other types of documents. If you share and manage the Policy Content Type across your entire farm, you can ensure that all Policy documents, created in any Site Collection, will have Effective Date as an attribute.

A Content Type contains these elements:

- **Metadata (Site Columns).** The attributes required by a Content Type are metadata about the content that can be used for categorization. You cannot define default values for Columns in a Content Type, just which properties or Columns are associated with the Content Type. The values for a particular metadata Column are defined for the Column, not the Content Type. If the values for a particular Column are unique to a Content Type, consider defining a separate, unique Column that is associated with a particular Content Type.

- **Document template**. Document templates can be used to create files with predefined styles and boilerplate content. You can assign one unique document template to each Content Type.
- **Custom "forms."** Specific New, Edit, and Display forms can be defined to use with a Content Type.
- **Workflows**. Some Content Types have a consistent process that can be assigned for approval. For example, all Status Reports may have to be routed to the project manager before they can be published on the portal. A workflow can be associated with a particular Content Type. Workflows can be triggered automatically based on a specific event or manually with a user's action.
- **Information management policies**. Your organization may have rules about how particular Content Types should be managed. This is particularly useful for records management. You can associate policies with a Content Type to manage characteristics such as retention period.

You can also associate workflows, properties, templates, and policies directly in a list or library. However, when you associate these items "locally," they are not reusable, even within a specific site.

Content Types are organized in a hierarchy that allows one Content Type to inherit characteristics from another Content Type in parent-child relationship. For example, while a memo is an "instance" of a document, if your organization wants users to leverage a standard template when creating a memo, you will want to create a new "Memo" Content Type as a child of the parent "Document" Content Type. The Memo Content Type can inherit all of the properties of the Document Content Type but can leverage a different template.

As a general rule, define Columns and Content Types at the highest possible level in your solution so that they are reusable and "manageable" across the entire solution. Depending on your role, you can define Content Types at the site, Site Collection, or enterprise level. Once you define a Content Type, it is available in that site and all subsites.

- If you want a Content Type to be available to a specific site (and its subsites), define it in the site Content Type Gallery.
- If you want a Content Type to be available to all sites in a Site Collection, define it in the Site Collection Content Type Gallery.

- If you want to create a Content Type to be used across your entire form or across multiple Site Collections (at the enterprise level), define a Site Collection to be a "Content Type hub." The Content Type created in the hub can then be associated with each Site Collection using the Managed Metadata service. Once an enterprise Content Type is published, it can't be changed within the local Site Collection.

As you might imagine, if you are going to define metadata at the enterprise level, you are potentially introducing the need for a new governance role— an enterprise data or content architect or metadata planning group. Someone (or some group) in the organization should be responsible for planning and managing enterprise-level Content Types and other shared (managed) metadata. This does not have to be someone in a full-time job (though it may be in large organizations), but the role will clearly need to be defined in someone's job description.

There is as much art as science required to determine what Content Types you need in your solution. Consider the following when you are planning Content Types for the enterprise, Site Collection, or individual site:

- Does this type of content have unique requirements based on the Content Type elements listed here?
- Should this Content Type be available across the entire enterprise or in one Site Collection or one site? For example, if your organization has implemented a records management policy, you may want to add a Records Retention Code to one or all enterprise document Content Types and make it a required field. This will ensure that users will assign a Records Retention Code to all documents.
- Would a user want to search for this type of content uniquely? For example, if you think that your users might want to be able to search for all forms in your portal, no matter who publishes the form, you will want to create a unique Content Type called Form. However, if personnel forms have a different template or workflow than accounting forms, you will want to create a "parent" Content Type called form and two "children" Content Types, perhaps called Form-Personnel or Form-Accounting.
- Many users find that having too many unique Content Types creates more confusion than value. Try to keep the number to less than 10 to 15 if you can. A smaller number of Content Types is probably better, especially for document repositories.

The Content Types that you define will be very specific to your organization; however, here are a few examples to consider in addition to those provided out-of-the-box. This list is not meant to be exhaustive, but it will give you a sample of some Content Types other organizations use:

- Article
- Brochure
- Case Study
- Form
- Job Description
- Lesson Learned
- Policy
- Project Plan
- Trip Report

Figure 5-4 shows a simple example of how Content Types can inherit metadata (Column) values from their parents.

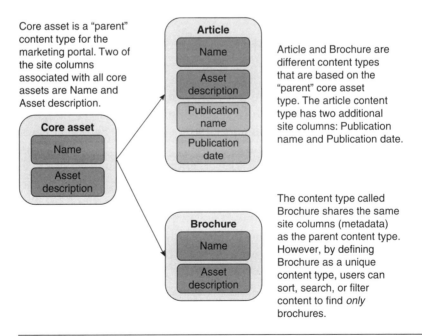

Figure 5-4 Content Types and Columns—working together to organize content and improve reuse

Columns

The specific authoritative fields or attributes that are used to "tag" each SharePoint item are called Columns. Columns allow you to keep metadata about an item consistent across libraries and lists and can be defined at the Site Collection or site level and can be inherited by "child" sites or defined locally in a library or list. Columns have a name and a type, such as

- Single line of text
- Multiple lines of text
- Choice (menu to choose from: drop-down, check box, radio button)
- Number
- Currency
- Date and Time
- Lookup (information already on this site)
- Yes/No (check box)
- Person or group
- Hyperlink or picture
- Calculated (calculation based on other Columns)
- External data
- Managed Metadata

The Managed Metadata type is new in SharePoint 2010. Managed Metadata allows you to share a hierarchical set of attribute values across your entire SharePoint infrastructure. Refer to the "Managed Metadata" section later in this chapter for additional information about this great new capability.

If you are not using Managed Metadata to share values for Columns, you should still consider creating all Columns as Site Columns at the top site in a Site Collection. Managing Columns centrally allows you to automatically propagate new values to any library or list that uses that Site Column. For example, if you maintain a list of offices centrally in a "global" (Site Collection level) Site Column called Office and you open a new office, you only have to update the list of offices in one place if Office is a Site Column at the top level of your Site Collection. You can also use Lookup Columns with reference lists supplying value choices. Of course, you may also want to manage Office as a Managed Metadata term if it makes sense to share these values across multiple Site Collections. Deciding the best structure for your metadata requires knowledge of the domain, as stated earlier, but it is also possible to evolve your metadata architecture over time.

Effectively planning your Content Types and Columns can make or break the effectiveness of your SharePoint solution. It's very frustrating to look at solutions in organizations that have been experimenting with SharePoint by essentially throwing the platform at users without providing any support for metadata architecture design. What typically happens is that users tend to use the same structures they are used to—folders—for organizing content rather than exploring the multiple ways of collecting and organizing content that are enabled by assigning just a few Columns and Content Types. While SharePoint supports the concept of folders in document libraries, folders can be a restrictive way of organizing content because a piece of content can only "live" in one folder. By contrast, the same document can be classified into multiple groups using Columns. For example, Columns allow you to group the documents in your document library by Authors (to associate a document that was written by Sue and Scott and then find all of the documents written or cowritten by Sue) or all of the documents for the West region or all of the documents written by Sue for the West region. Folders may have a new role to play in your information architecture in SharePoint 2010, but they are not necessarily the best organizing principle for your content (see the sidebar on folders earlier in this chapter).

Table 5-1 provides a list of metadata Column best practices to help guide you in the choices you need to make regarding metadata Column labels and values.

Table 5-1 Metadata Column Best Practices

Best Practice	Recommendation
Identify universal metadata applied to all content assets.	Many organizations require a Records Retention Code for all document (and some other content) assets. This is the most consistently applied "universal" metadata attribute we see in practice. Some organizations also find it helpful to require an "owner" and a revision date attribute for all documents. This helps identify the person responsible for the content (who may or may not be the "author") and determine content freshness.

(continues)

Table 5-1 Metadata Column Best Practices *(continued)*

Best Practice	Recommendation
Limit the number of required Columns in Content Types and lists.	One of the most important "Column-related" decisions you will make is determining which Columns should be required. The following are recommended guidelines for determining which and how many Columns should be required: ■ If the site is primarily used to publish information (small number of content contributors with a large number of "readers"), make all content classification decisions based on whether or not the end user will use the value to find or filter results. In this scenario, don't worry too much about whether or not you have too many required Columns. Remember, if users can find content more easily with better content classification, the content owner or manager will have fewer phone calls requesting information that distract them from their daily work. Because it's their job to provide information, they usually won't mind if they have to spend additional time entering required fields for portal documents. ■ If the site is a collaboration site where the objective is to get users to change their behavior from storing reusable assets on their local or shared drives and putting them in team sites or publishing pages on the portal, assume that most users will have about 30 seconds of patience available when they are saving or uploading content. That means you'll probably be able to have, at most, 5 required Columns. ■ When applicable, include default values so that the user only has to enter a Column value if his content is different from the expected norm. This is an example of a scenario where you may want to consider creating a folder structure for your content. For example, if you have a large repository of project deliverables and each document needs to have an associated Project Name, you can create a folder for each project and assign a default value for Project Name that is unique for each folder. This will make

Best Practice	Recommendation
	it easier for users to comply with a requirement to post their deliverables in the repository because they will not have to add Project Name as an attribute. This may seem contradictory given that as a general rule, we don't like to encourage the use of folders in document libraries. However, as you can see, there are some scenarios where the use of folders for metadata "inheritance," a great addition to SharePoint 2010, will give you a "best of both worlds" capability to find and share content.
Follow the basic principles of good data design.	Make sure that ■ Each metadata property is unique and that each property is really necessary to describe the content. ■ List values represent a single category of knowledge. For example, a Column defining "color" might include values such as red, blue, and green, but not an entry such as plaid. Instead, define a second category for "pattern" to present values such as stripes, polka dot, and plaid. ■ The list of values for an attribute is complete— so that users are not forced to pick an inaccurate field. ■ Choice values in a drop-down list are mutually exclusive. ■ Required Columns appear "above the fold" for data entry if they do not have a default value. ■ Default values are entered judiciously. Many users accept default values without reading them. This unconscious choice can skew filtering and search results. ■ The use of "fill-in" fields in list choices is avoided where possible.
Use descriptive, meaningful labels.	Try to use terms that your users will recognize. Do not make up a label value—use the "old" term if that's what people know.

(continues)

Table 5-1 Metadata Column Best Practices *(continued)*

Best Practice	Recommendation
Use singular nouns for Column names.	For example, use Document Type, not Document Types.
Use a logical order in value lists.	For the most part, list values should be in alphabetical order to help users quickly scan items. If you need to sequence or sort lists using another sort order, you can insert a number in front of a text term. For example: 1-Design, 2-Development, 3-Train, 4-Deploy. Note that you can create a custom display order for Managed Metadata, so this guideline applies only to site and list Columns values that are not derived from Managed Metadata term sets.
Avoid using None, N/A, or Other as metadata values if possible.	If you must use these options, add them to the end of your metadata list, even if the value is out of alphabetical order.
Consider using a Document Description in document libraries (and encourage users to complete it).	Adding a brief description (abstract) to documents helps users figure out if they should open or download a document when they are scanning documents in a list. This helps avoid the extra time required to open a document to actually see if it's useful.

Managed Keywords: The New Column You Get "For Free"

Out-of-the-box document libraries in SharePoint 2010 include the following Columns that were also included in SharePoint 2007: Title, Created By, Modified By, and Checked Out To. In addition, document libraries now include a new Column called Managed Keywords.

In SharePoint 2010, there are three ways an attribute can be assigned to a document:

- When a content contributor or editor selects or adds a value in a Column defined by the content designer. This is a form of authoritative metadata—it is assigned by the content contributor in a structured field.

- When a content consumer assigns a "social tag" to a document. A social tag (described in more detail in Chapter 7) can be any value entered by the user. As the user starts typing a value, SharePoint provides a list of previously used social and managed terms (keywords), and the user can select from this list. Because any user can add social metadata, these tags (or keywords) are not considered authoritative, but they can be used to filter content in search results.
- When a content editor adds a Managed Keyword. Managed Keywords are authoritative tags because they are added by users with content editing privileges, but the source of their values includes both the managed terms for the site as well as the social data values used by other content contributors and "visitors." You can think of Managed Keywords as social tags assigned by a content editor. (Just to make things a little more interesting, if you choose, you can prohibit users from adding their own Managed Keywords to items by requiring them to select from existing values.)

Like any other Column, Managed Keywords help users find content in a library. However, unlike other Columns, the values of Managed Keywords are more flexible and less structured, which provides a very dynamic way to quickly react to evolving terms, opportunities, and emerging business needs.

More than one Managed Keyword can be assigned to the same document by default; they act like a check box attribute. However, there are some conventions that must be used to assign Managed Keywords:

- Separate values with semicolons.
- Do not use commas to separate values. Commas in a list of Managed Keywords will automatically be replaced with semicolons, so for example, if you enter "X, Y, and Z" as your keyword, SharePoint will replace your entry with three separate values (and the third will be called "and Z").
- Use an ampersand (&) or spaces to separate words that should be combined as a single keyword.

Managed Metadata

Managed Metadata is a hierarchical group of enterprise-wide or centrally managed terms that you can first define and then use in Columns in Content Types or lists and libraries. Managed Metadata is a new type of Column that you can use to assign metadata to an item in SharePoint 2010. SharePoint 2010 uses three terms to refer to Managed Metadata:

- **Managed terms**. Think of managed terms as the controlled vocabulary that you will use to assign metadata to content across your solution. Not all metadata values need to be stored and managed as a managed term. Good candidates for managed terms are metadata that have valid values that can or should be organized hierarchically, metadata that is likely to be used in multiple lists and libraries across your solution, or metadata for which there is a restricted list of values from which users can select. As an example, your list of product names is a good candidate for a managed term. Sharing a restricted list of product names across the enterprise ensures that all users will assign the same spelling and name for each product. When you add new products, you can add them in one place and have them available immediately in your entire solution.
- **Managed keywords**. As described in the sidebar, managed keywords are words or phrases that have been added by any user to SharePoint 2010 items—either formally in a managed term store or informally as "social tags." While managed terms can be organized hierarchically, managed keywords are all stored in a flat term set called the Keyword Set.
- **Term store**. The term store is the database that is used to store both managed terms and managed keywords.

With Managed Metadata, you can create a "local" label for the shared values. For example, one part of your organization may refer to your external partners as business partners. Another part of the organization may call them third-party organizations. A third part may call them vendors. Even in an ideal world, each part of the company may have valid reasons for referring to these external parties by different names, even though the actual values—the names of the external companies—are the same. In SharePoint 2007, you would have had to try to get everyone to agree to the same label and values and used either manual processes, custom code, or third-party products to ensure that everything stayed synchronized across multiple sites and Site Collections. In SharePoint 2010, you can use Managed Metadata to create the shared list of values once, use the *values* to help group similar content in search results, but allow each department to refer to the "external people who might be business partners, vendors, or third-party organizations" by whichever Column label makes sense in their context. We talk more about creating a term set in the next section of this chapter.

Managed Metadata is "consumed" in a Managed Metadata service. You must have at least one Managed Metadata service to share Content Types and managed terms across more than one Site Collection. If you have users that need to keep their term sets private so that other users cannot see them, you will need an additional Managed Metadata service to hold the term store with the private term sets. Then you will need to associate the Site Collection with the Managed Metadata service that holds the term stores approved for that Site Collection.

The Term Store Management Tool is used to create and manage terms and term sets. (Term sets are groups of related terms.) With appropriate permissions (generally, Site Owners with full control privileges), you can use this tool to

- Create a new term set or delete one that is no longer needed.
- Add, change, or remove terms.
- Create a hierarchy for terms and identify which terms in the hierarchy can be used to assign tags to content and which terms are just used for grouping terms. (You typically will want to use only the "lowest level" in the term hierarchy for tagging.)
- Define alternate terms (synonyms) so that if users use different terms for the same thing or you are introducing a new term to replace an old one, "taggers" will be able to use their familiar term to find a tag, but the new authoritative term will actually be assigned to the document.
- Import terms from an existing list. Unless you only have a few terms to add to your term set, you will probably want to use the import capability to add your terms. You act on each term independently in the Term Store Management Tool, so while it is convenient to use for updates to existing terms, you will not want to use it to add a large collection of terms.

- Change managed keywords into managed terms by moving them into a term set. This capability allows you to evolve your managed terms over time. In other words, you don't have to make yourself crazy trying to define all your managed terms up front. Yes, you should invest some time to plan your initial managed terms, but you can change your mind later on. However, you will need to assign someone to pay attention to how keywords are being used across the site.

There are some helpful worksheets on the Microsoft Web site that you can use to document and plan potential term sets for your solution. You can download the Term Set Planning Worksheet at http://go.microsoft.com/fwlink/?LinkId=163487&clcid=0x409. Table 5-2 shows how this worksheet could be used to organize a small set of sports-related products. (The list of product names was borrowed from eBay.) As part of the planning exercise for a term set, you will want to look for existing places where potential term set values are stored (such as product lists, regional office lists, or department lists) and organize the values into a meaningful hierarchy. This process should include a data "clean-up" exercise where you will remove duplicates and rationalize terms (select one term to be the primary value and then identify synonyms for alternative values). Standardizing terms may require negotiating. When it is clear Òthat differences are minor (such as different abbreviations or spellings for the same value), our best advice is to use the "get over it" approach—pick a primary term, make the others synonyms, and move on with your life.

Figure 5-5 shows the first step in creating a new term set, accessed from the drop-down list associated with the Site Collection in which you want to create the term set in the Term Store Management Tool. This tool can be accessed from either Central Administration or from within Site Settings.

Figure 5-6 shows how the term set defined in Table 5-2 is instantiated. The term set Name and Description are identified, along with an Owner, a Contact, Stakeholders who should be notified before major changes are made to the term set, and whether or not new terms can be added to the term set and whether the term set can be used for tagging.

If you plan to manually add terms, or if you need to assign synonyms for terms after you have imported a term set, you will use the term properties

Table 5-2 Planning a Term Set

	Level 2	Level 3	Level 4	Level 5	Level 6	Level 7	Description	Available for Tagging	Synonym of
Golf								No	
Golf	Bags							Yes	
Golf	Balls								
Golf	Books								
Golf	Clothing & Shoes								
Golf	Clothing & Shoes	Shirts						No	
Golf	Clothing & Shoes	Shirts	Short-sleeved shirt				Short sleeved shirt with a collar	Yes	
Golf	Clothing & Shoes	Shirts	Long-sleeved shirt					Yes	
Golf	Clothing & Shoes	Shirts	Polo shirt				Short sleeved shirt with a collar	Yes	Collared shirt Short-sleeved shirt
Golf	Clothing & Shoes	Pants						No	
Golf	Clothing & Shoes	Pants	Short Pants				Appropriate for warm weather.	Yes	
Golf	Clothing & Shoes	Pants	Long Pants				Appropriate for colder days on the course.	Yes	
Exercise & Fitness								No	
Exercise & Fitness		Boxing						Yes	
Exercise & Fitness		Yoga						Yes	

editing screen shown in Figure 5-7. For "parent" terms in the hierarchy, you will see a tab called Custom Sort that allows you to specify a custom sort order to child terms. Using a custom sort order ensures that terms appear in consistent order, even if the default label for a term is changed.

Figure 5-8 shows how a description for a managed term appears to the user in Columns with a type of Managed Metadata. The description helps guide the user to select the most appropriate tag for the document.

Figure 5-9 shows how the completed worksheet in Table 5-2 appears in the SharePoint 2010 product managed term set. Once the product term set is defined, it can now be referenced in a Column where the type is Managed Metadata to control the list of values for this term.

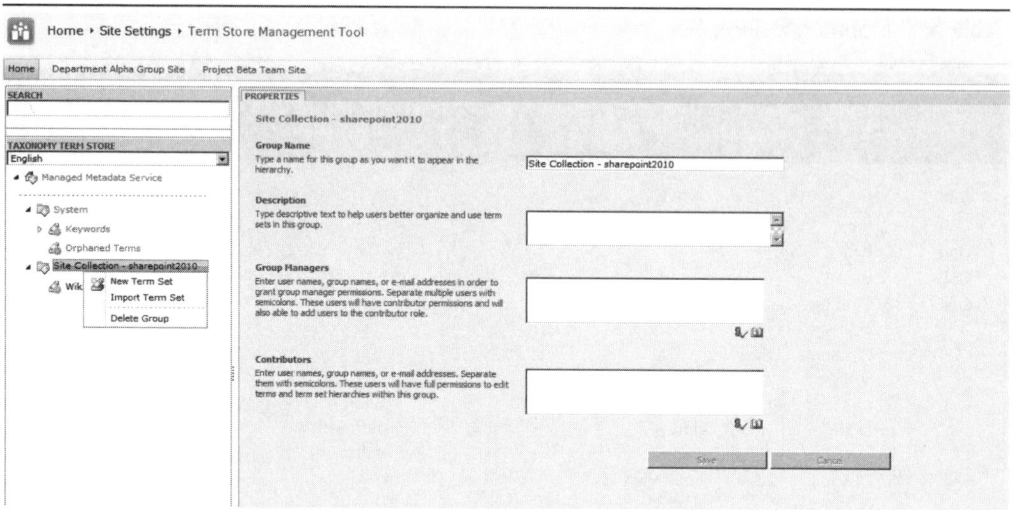

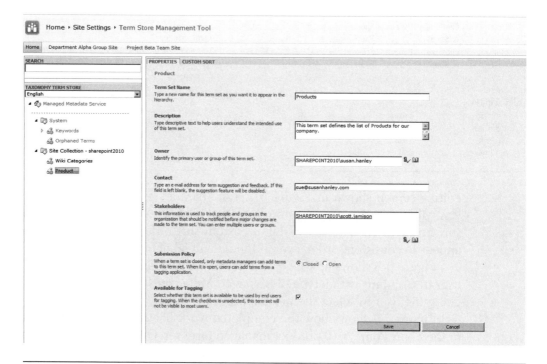

Figure 5-5 Create a term set

Figure 5-6 Define the term set properties

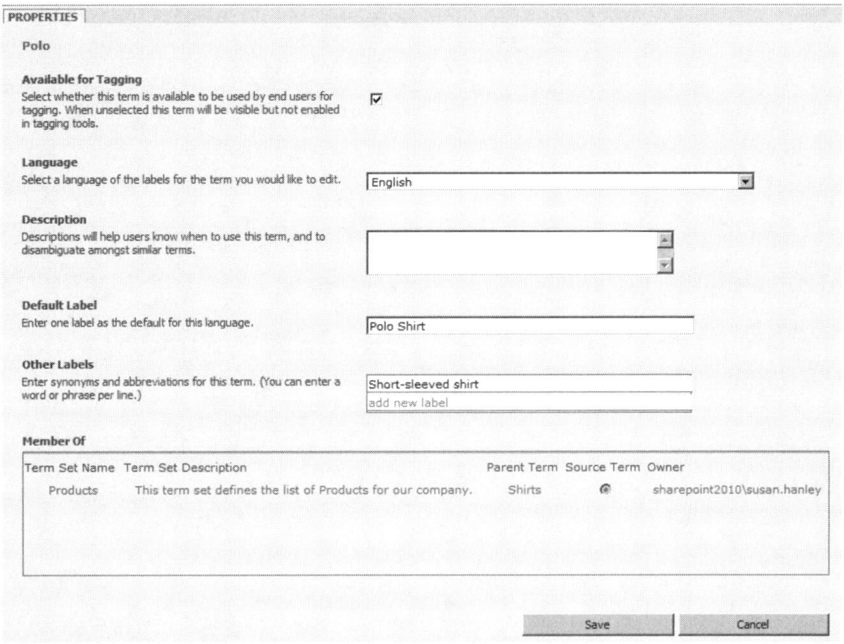

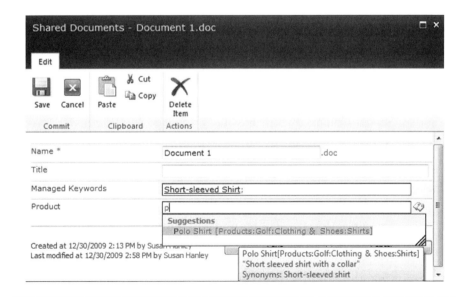

Figure 5-7 Define managed terms

Figure 5-8 Descriptions for managed terms help users assign the most appropriate term

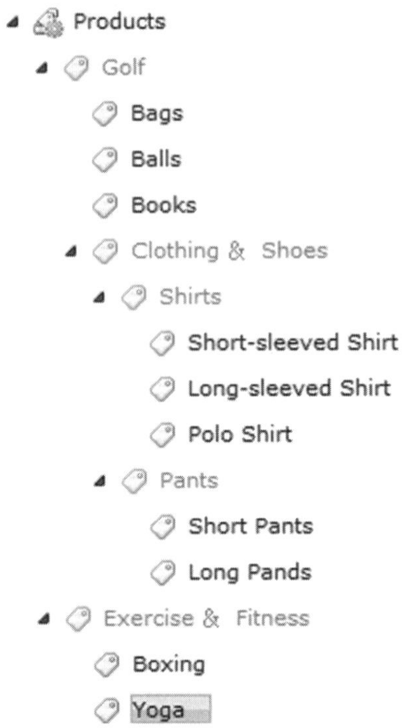

▲ 🏷 Products

   ▲ 🏷 Golf

      🏷 Bags

      🏷 Balls

      🏷 Books

     ▲ 🏷 Clothing & Shoes

        ▲ 🏷 Shirts

           🏷 Short-sleeved Shirt

           🏷 Long-sleeved Shirt

           🏷 Polo Shirt

        ▲ 🏷 Pants

           🏷 Short Pants

           🏷 Long Pands

     ▲ 🏷 Exercise & Fitness

        🏷 Boxing

        🏷 Yoga

Figure 5-9 Product hierarchy

Figure 5-10 shows how the product term set appears to users when it has been associated with a Column called product in a document library. In this example, you can see an instance where the user is attempting to assign a product value of "Collared shirt" to the document. Notice that since Collared shirt has been declared a synonym for "Polo Shirt," this term is available as a tag. The actual tag value that gets assigned to the document is Polo Shirt, not Collared shirt, because Polo Shirt is the primary term.

One of the best features of managed terms is that when you manage term values in a term set and you change the value for a term for any reason, the value will be updated automatically in all the locations where you have used that term. For example, let's say that you accidentally typed "puter" instead of "putter" in the example here. By the time you realize that the term has been misspelled, several hundred documents have been added and assigned the incorrect term. When you change the spelling of puter to putter in the term set, all of the documents with the incorrect

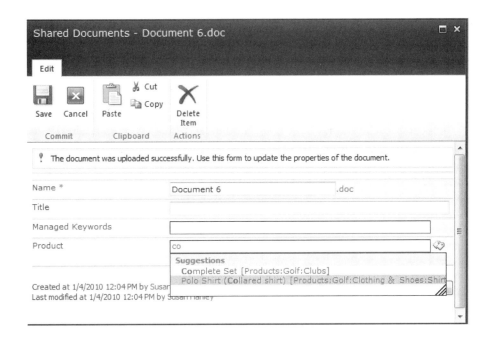

Figure 5-10 Synonyms help users use familiar terms to assign metadata

spelling will be automatically corrected, *even if you don't open them*. This feature will be particularly useful in organizations like pharmaceutical firms where a drug starts out as a compound and may get several interim names before it gets an official brand name prior to public launch. When the drug is approved, a single change to the term store is all that it takes to assign all content tagged "compound ABC" to "blockbuster drug." The term compound ABC can also be added as a *search* synonym for blockbuster drug so that a single search for either term will return all relevant documents, even if the document metadata or content has not been updated with the new managed term. This feature alone should encourage you to carefully plan your use of Managed Metadata.

It may not be necessary to run out and hire a consultant to support this process (though it's not a bad idea for your first deployment). If your organization has a corporate library staffed with someone with a library science degree, you already have a great resource with the relevant knowledge and experience to guide the planning and implementation of your managed terms hierarchy.

Table 5-3 Recommended Actions to Maintain Your Information Architecture

Problems	Solutions
End users may incorrectly assign Column values to content, or when users can't find a "bucket" in which to place their new content, they may put it in a miscellaneous topic, which makes searches and queries far more difficult.	Assign Content Managers (or Content Stewards) to ensure that new content is assigned correctly. Content Managers can be domain experts who allocate a portion of their time to review new contributions to the site or library.
	Content Managers can also be librarians, specialists who help design meaningful taxonomies, tag content as it appears, and maintain the information architecture over time.
	Leverage automated classification software if the volume of content is too large for librarians to study and classify manually.
When the system allows end users to add Column values of their own, they may create a redundant value or concept.	Establish governance policies for managing the information architecture's structure and adding new documents into document libraries, adding new Site Columns, and adding new Column values. Use Managed Metadata to control list values.
	Governance policies should define who does which tasks, procedures for performing tasks, and feedback mechanisms for suggesting changes and improvements.
New terms may get added that are merely synonyms for existing terms, creating unnecessary redundancy.	SharePoint includes a search substitution thesaurus that allows you to define synonyms for terms that are automatically substituted during a search. You can also define synonyms for managed terms as shown in Figure 5-6.
The organization can change direction so that the information architecture becomes less relevant to the business.	Revise the information architecture on a regular basis. At a minimum, conduct an information architecture review once a year (or more frequently if content is being added continuously or major organizational or business changes have occurred). Note that this is less likely to happen if you organize your sites functionally as recommended in the "Site Architecture" section.
Old or irrelevant content may remain on the portal because content owners are not actively engaged in a content recertification process.	Maintain the content itself by archiving old documents and monitoring content usage so that content that is not current or is no longer relevant does not appear in search results. Consider mandating at least an annual content recertification process as part of your content management strategy.

Maintaining Your Information Architecture

When you first deploy a content or knowledge management solution, the information architecture is well-structured, and usually content is appropriately catalogued because designers and application sponsors have taken a lot of time to ensure that the initial implementation is successful. Over time, new content enters the system, along with new knowledge areas, and before you know it, the well-structured information architecture devolves into chaos. When the information architecture becomes less relevant, so do the applications that depend on it. When that happens, users become frustrated, and management wonders why they continue to make investments in the solution.

Even though features such as Managed Metadata give you more opportunities to control your information architecture, it is still important to pay attention to your IA to ensure it evolves with your business and user needs. There are many reasons that an information architecture can degrade over time. The key to overcoming the challenges associated with maintaining your information architecture is to recognize up front that maintaining your information architecture requires a continual investment. Building a successful information architecture is not a "build it once and walk away" process. There are several business process recommendations that can help you manage and maintain your information architecture: Table 5-3 on page 160 provides a list of some of the reasons an information architecture can degrade over time and proposes several mitigating strategies to overcome these problems.

Key Points

Keep the following key points in mind as you plan your information architecture:

- Effectively plan and deploy an information architecture for your solution; this should be an iterative process. Assume that you will not get it right the first time out of the gate and plan to engage users in a series of deployment reviews to evolve the architecture based on user needs and organizational changes over time.
- Conduct usability tests before you deploy your solution to make sure that your information architecture makes sense to end users.

- Leverage Content Types and Columns to manage metadata at the portal level, using inheritance to propagate changes throughout the solution.
- Take advantage of the new metadata management features of SharePoint 2010, especially the ability to share Content Types across Site Collections and the ability to create managed terms.
- Weigh the end-user experience over the content contributor experience in most information architecture decision trade-offs.
- Ensure that maintaining your information architecture is a continuous investment—don't assume that you can design your architecture and walk away. The information architecture and portal content needs continuous nurturing in order to remain relevant and valuable.
- Consider adding a new role to your solution team for an enterprise data architect (or enterprise "taxonomist") to ensure that someone is accountable for ensuring that your information architecture is maintained.

MAKING ENTERPRISE CONTENT MANAGEMENT WORK: DOCUMENTS AND RECORDS

Enterprise content management (ECM) is a widely recognized IT-industry term for software technology that enables organizations to create, capture, manage, secure, store, retain, destroy, publish, distribute, search, personalize, present, view, and print digital content related to organizational processes. Whew—that's a mouthful. So what does this mean? In short, it means storing document content electronically and then making sure it is managed appropriately.

With the 2010 release, SharePoint finally becomes a true document management system. Prior to SharePoint 2010, many companies used SharePoint as a document collaboration environment, only to purchase a more expensive system (such as Documentum or FileNet) to provide actual document management features. In fact, one of the great features that WSS 3.0 and MOSS 2007 introduced to many organizations was the ability to enable many content owners across an organization to create and manage information. While this model eases some of the traditional bottlenecks associated with Web masters managing all content, it poses several new challenges. First, consistency was hard to enforce. Different users could apply different metadata or inconsistent security around content (this includes pages as well as documents and other types of content). In addition, with many owners come varied processes for managing how content gets published and ultimately removed. Finally, with this inconsistency around process and control came a potential conflict with corporate compliance mandates.

SharePoint 2010 changes the way document and other data are managed by easing the burden associated with effective content management of corporate data. Because ECM is now embedded in the main SharePoint feature set, users can take advantage of traditional ECM processes like document management and records management, all within a familiar user interface. This allows users to participate in the management of documents and records without changing the way they work. This chapter contains the following key sections:

- Getting Started with ECM
- What's New for ECM in SharePoint 2010?
- Document Management
- Records Management

Getting Started with ECM

Before we dive into some of the functionality associated with ECM, let's look at some of the key terms we use throughout this chapter:

- **Enterprise Content Management (ECM).** Includes features like Document Management (DM), Forms Management, Web Content Management (WCM), Digital Asset (or Rich Asset) Management, and Records Management (RM)
- **Document Management**. Document management refers to the active usage of "living" documents, along with a set of capabilities, such as check-in, check-out, and version control—capabilities designed to put structure around your living documents. These are documents authored by individuals and teams and exist in a state whereby they may be changed or moved at any time.
- **Records Management**. Records management refers to managing the life cycle of documents and other content (Web pages, physical assets, and so on) that exists in an official, stable state. By life cycle, we mean the organizational rules pertaining to creation, security, review, revision, auditing, archiving, and disposal. Typically, these are items that the organization has effectively authored and should not be changed. A document may move from a normal state and later become a record. Records are often archived, tracked, and audited. The most common scenario for Records Management is legal/regulatory compliance—ensuring that a document is retained/unchanged/purged according to a predictable, known schedule.

■ **Document Set**. A collection of documents that share document management and records management requirements managed together as a single entity.

With these terms defined, let's dig into the main pieces of ECM within SharePoint 2010. For this discussion, we focus the ECM topics to two main components: Document Management and Records Management. (We've moved Web Content Management to its own chapter—see Chapter 12, "Putting Your Site on the Web").

What's New for ECM in SharePoint 2010?

Let's take a high-level view of what's new for ECM in SharePoint 2010. These are new or enhanced features in SharePoint 2010 that will dramatically improve the management and/or support of your content.

Document IDs

At the Site Collection level, you can enable the use of system-assigned identifiers. Once this feature is enabled, each document in the Site Collection will get its own unique identifier. This identifier can then be used to identify documents, either through a direct link, page navigation, or a search. In SharePoint 2007, if a document is moved within SharePoint, all references to it would break. With a document ID, each document now has a permanent path, independent of how many times it is moved. This provides a dependable method for retrieving the document. This is a very powerful feature for those wishing to point users directly to specific documents on their sites. Because this feature is managed at the Site Collection level, there are additional settings that should be undertaken to ensure that document IDs are unique across all Site Collections. This is described in further detail in the following sections.

Document Sets

In many document management scenarios, users might produce several documents to accomplish one task or produce one deliverable. For example, your company might need to create a proposal that consists of a Word document, a PowerPoint presentation, and an Excel-based pricing spreadsheet. As such, it might be beneficial to manage a set of documents that need to be treated as one. This is where the concept of a *document set* becomes valuable. A document set is implemented as a Site Collection feature and needs to be activated prior to use. Activating this feature creates a new Content Type that allows you to group together multiple documents in a single set. The Content Type is effectively an enhanced folder, so it can support things like versioning, retention, workflows, and applying metadata. The big advantage here is that the entire collection of documents is effectively treated as one when part of a business process.

Managed Metadata

Managed metadata services play a large role in effectively tagging content. SharePoint 2010's managed metadata service (or "term store") provides a simple means of centrally managing a keyword taxonomy and providing an easy-to-use interface for updating and leveraging the keyword hierarchy. In addition to a central store of terms, this service provides many useful items: "type-ahead" on keyword selection (which works as an auto-complete function), easy management of the keyword associations, synonym management, and security trimming that allows for the decentralization of metadata ownership.

Content Type Syndication

In SharePoint 2007, creating custom Columns and Content Types was done at the Site Collection level. Custom code was needed if you wanted to use the same Content Type across more than one Site Collection. In SharePoint 2010, there's a new service that syndicates Content Types across many Site Collections. This enables you do define consistent Content Types across your entire enterprise.

Content Organizer

With the content organizer, SharePoint 2010 will automatically process content based on rules. This enables you to set up rules, such as specifying a Drop-off Library where users can centrally upload documents, and have the system automatically create subfolders to partition items so that no folder has too many items, as well as send documents to a specific location based on document attributes. We show you how to configure the content organizer later in this chapter.

In-place Records Management

Records management involves "locking down" a version of a document to provide an immutable snapshot of that document at a point in time. This means that SharePoint 2010 can manage items as auditable sources of corporate content. With SharePoint 2007, this meant having to move that document to another location and/or tightening the security around that item. With SharePoint 2010, documents can be treated as records either in a central location or in-place. As such, you have the choice of sending a document to a Records site (and leaving a Permalink to the new document location in the original library) or marking the document as a record within the context of the original document library. The latter option gives contributors more flexibility in managing document and "locking" them down when each reaches a final state. Doing this provides a proper audit trail and eliminates some current business processes associated with physically moving documents to new locations for archiving.

Now that you have an idea of what was added in SharePoint 2010, let's review how to get the most out of the document management and records management features.

Document Management

Technically, document management has been a core piece of SharePoint since its inception, with features such as Document Libraries and Custom Columns (Metadata). Some might argue that prior versions of SharePoint offered "document collaboration" or perhaps document management "lite." The new document management features that have been added in SharePoint 2010 bring SharePoint's document management capabilities up to par with industry standards. This section discusses each of the key document management features, how and when you'd use them, and then provides a step-by-step walkthrough of configuring a typical configuration for document and records management within SharePoint.

Document Libraries

A document library is simply a SharePoint list that is designed to accommodate documents. In SharePoint, *libraries* are designed to hold large items such as documents, images, videos, and reports, while *lists* typically hold structured data. In most cases, a document library provides the best place to store and manage document content, with features such as versions, check-in/out, and tagging.

Note   Document libraries are also used to hold Web pages. For example, every team site in SharePoint 2010 has a library called Site Pages. This library holds the pages that display the user interface to the user, including Home.aspx, which is the start page for the site.

Item-level Security

One of the features introduced in SharePoint 2007 was the ability to configure permissions at the item level. This prevented administrators from having to create more document libraries. Why? Without item-level security, all documents in a document library were under the same security rule. This meant that outliers were forced into separate document libraries with unique security definitions. Not only did this make little sense to end users (who had to look for similar documents in multiple locations), but it also meant the replication and maintenance of dual metadata lists. This was both cumbersome and confusing.

WSS 3.0 introduced item-level security, which allows items and folders to be managed at the item level. This means that a single document library can hold a collection of similar (by content) documents that have different security definitions. Users looking at the list may see different documents based on their security privileges. In addition, security can be applied not just for viewing but for editing as well. In this case, specific users can edit only certain documents in the list. Again, one document library manages a collection of similar content, but the visibility or accessibility is being managed at the item level.

However, even though you *can* secure content at the item level, our recommendation is to use item-level security as little as possible due to the administrative burden that it puts on site administrators.

Versioning Settings

Version management is a core component of any document management system. It involves tracking the history associated with each group of changes made to a particular document. Like SharePoint 2007, SharePoint 2010

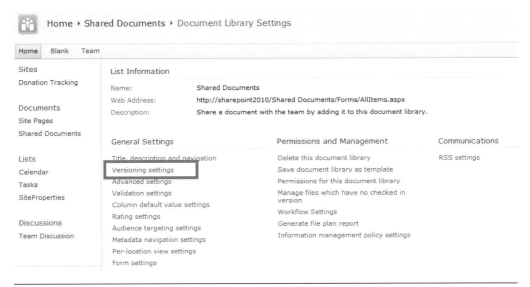

Figure 6-1 The Document Library Versioning Settings provide content approval, version history, draft item security, and check-out requirement options for a document library

offers the ability to keep no prior versions, major versions only, or major and minor versions. A major version number is associated with a version that has been published. A minor version number is associated with a version that is in progress, will be published, but is not yet published. SharePoint tracks changes to both content inside a document and to the document's metadata properties.

Major and minor versioning is an option for documents (and other list items) under the Versioning Settings for a document library. Here, you can determine whether items should have major versions only (or minor versions as well), how many versions of each type to keep, and the visibility of minor documents. See Figure 6-1. Let's discuss each of these in more detail.

Content Approval

There are a number of versioning settings to discuss, the first of which is Content Approval (see Figure 6-2). You can think of this setting as a one-stage approval process. When this setting is enabled, all major-versioned documents need approval from a particular user role before they can be

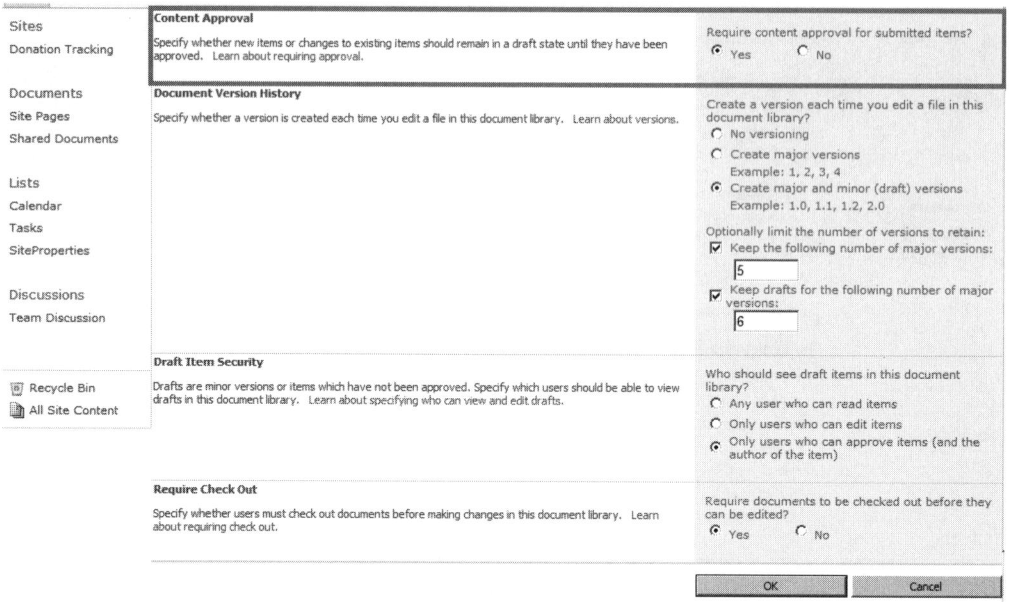

Figure 6-2 Content approval enables you to require major versions of items to be approved before they are visible

seen by most users. New and changed items remain in a pending state until they are approved or rejected by someone who has permission to approve them. If an item or file is approved, it is assigned an Approved status in the list or library, and it is displayed to anyone with permission to view the list or library. If the item or file is rejected, it remains in a pending state and is visible only to the people with permission to view drafts. Minor versions (drafts) don't require approval. These settings apply to what gets returned in search results as well; if you don't have permissions to see "pending" items, they will not be returned in the search results.

Document Version History

Depending on the options selected in this section of your library settings, SharePoint will track revisions to items in this library or list. Libraries can track both major and minor versions. Lists and libraries can also limit the number of versions that people can store (see Figure 6-3).

Tracking both major and minor versions provides a more detailed way to track the version history of an item. Major versions are more likely to represent a milestone, such as when a file is ready to be viewed by a wide

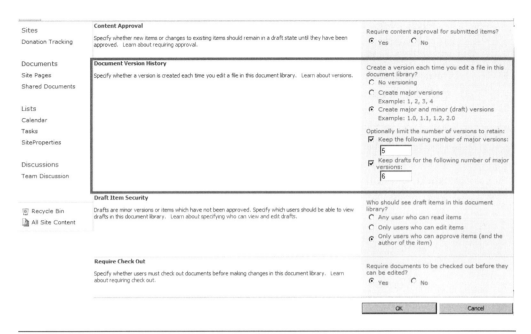

Figure 6-3 Versioning enables you to save the various changes to an item over the course of its editing history

audience. A minor version is typically used as a routine increment, such as a version that a user saves or checks in while he or she is still writing the content. When you want to view the version history of a document, major and minor versions make it easy to identify the stages of the document's development.

When versioning is enabled, versions are stored by default as a minor versions unless you designate them as major versions. When users save a file and close it, the version is tracked as a minor version. Users must publish the item in order for it to become a major version.

If you check out files before working on them, you can designate which type of version you are checking in. You do not have to publish a file if you designate it as a major version when you check it in.

Versions are numbered when they are created. When tracking major and minor versions, the major versions are whole numbers, and the minor versions are decimals. For example, when you first create or upload a document, the document is versioned as 0.1. If you revise it, the document becomes 0.2 (then 0.3 and so on) until you first publish it to create version 1.0. The next revision cycle creates version 1.1, 1.2, 1.x … until you publish its next major version (2.0).

Let's walk through an example to illustrate how the version numbering might work. Let's assume that a user creates a new file in a document library; the document is labeled 0.1. When the user publishes the document, it is then labeled version 1.0. When that document is checked back into the document library, version 1.1 is visible to team members but not seen by the organization. (Note that the specific visibility of draft items depends on the Draft Item Security setting, described in the next section.) The rest of the organization continues to see only version 1.0. Same with a second draft, tagged as version 1.2. Finally, when the document is published, version 2.0 is created, and it supplants version 1.0 from a visibility perspective so that everyone sees version 2.0.

Again, let's recap:

- Version 0.1 (created at check-in; visible to author and/or approval team only)
- Version 1.0 (created when published; visible to all after approval takes place)
- Version 1.1 (created at check-in; visible to author and/or approval team only)
- Version 1.2 (created at check-in; visible to author and/or approval team only)
- Version 2.0 (visible to all)

The power in the major/minor functionality is the ability to manage the document revision process within the portal (versus on a local drive) while at the same time ensuring that a document is not made available until complete and approved.

Note that if you choose to limit the number of versions that SharePoint stores, the oldest versions are permanently deleted when the limit is reached and not sent to the Recycle Bin.

Draft Item Security

The Draft Item Security setting enables you to control which groups of people can read drafts (see Figure 6-4). As discussed in the previous section, drafts are the minor versions of a file and are created in one of two ways: either when a minor version of a file is created or updated in a library that tracks major and minor versions, or when a list item or file is created or updated but is not approved in a list or library in which content approval is required.

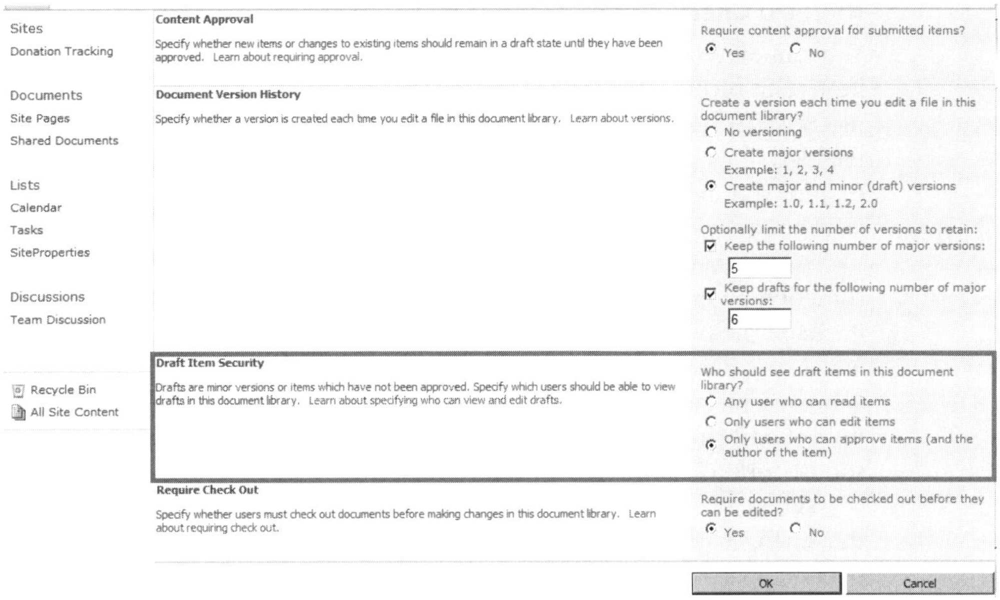

Sites
Donation Tracking

Documents
Site Pages
Shared Documents

Lists
Calendar
Tasks
SiteProperties

Discussions
Team Discussion

Recycle Bin
All Site Content

Content Approval

Specify whether new items or changes to existing items should remain in a draft state until they have been approved. Learn about requiring approval.

Require content approval for submitted items?
- ⦿ Yes ○ No

Document Version History

Specify whether a version is created each time you edit a file in this document library. Learn about versions.

Create a version each time you edit a file in this document library?
- ○ No versioning
- ○ Create major versions
  Example: 1, 2, 3, 4
- ⦿ Create major and minor (draft) versions
  Example: 1.0, 1.1, 1.2, 2.0

Optionally limit the number of versions to retain:
- ☑ Keep the following number of major versions:
  5
- ☑ Keep drafts for the following number of major versions:
  6

Draft Item Security

Drafts are minor versions or items which have not been approved. Specify which users should be able to view drafts in this document library. Learn about specifying who can view and edit drafts.

Who should see draft items in this document library?
- ○ Any user who can read items
- ○ Only users who can edit items
- ⦿ Only users who can approve items (and the author of the item)

Require Check Out

Specify whether users must check out documents before making changes in this document library. Learn about requiring check out.

Require documents to be checked out before they can be edited?
- ⦿ Yes ○ No

[OK] [Cancel]

Figure 6-4 The Draft Item Security setting enables you to control which groups of people can read drafts

You can specify which groups of people can view drafts—either by enabling all users with read access to view them or by restricting it to only users who can edit items. This enables you to specify different settings for the group of people who can view the rest of the items in your list or library, such as the major versions of files or the files or list items that are approved.

When content approval is required, you can specify whether files that are pending approval can be viewed by people with permission to read, people with permission to edit, or only the author and people with permission to approve items. If both major and minor versions are being tracked, the author must publish a major version before the file can be submitted for approval. When content approval is required, people who have permission to read content but do not have permission to see draft items will see the last approved or major version of the file.

If you plan to use minor versions and content approval, then we recommend configuring the Draft Item Security in such a way that only editors and/or approvers see draft items. This ensures that general site users don't see unapproved versions of documents.

Require Check-out

You can also configure the document library to require check-out before items can be edited (see Figure 6-5). Requiring check-out prevents multiple people from making changes at the same time. When this setting is enabled, new files are initially set as checked out. The person who creates or adds the file must check it in before other people can see it. Check-out is also required to update metadata properties on the file.

When check-out is required, a file is checked out automatically when someone opens it for editing. When a file is checked out, no one can edit it except the person who checked it out (with the exception of coauthoring, which provides multiuser editing of the same document). Changes that someone makes to a file while it is checked out are not visible to others until the file is checked back in. This is true regardless of whether the person is working on the file locally or on the server.

When a user checks in a file, he is prompted to enter comments about the changes that he made. If a library tracks versions, the comments become part of the version history. If both major versions and minor

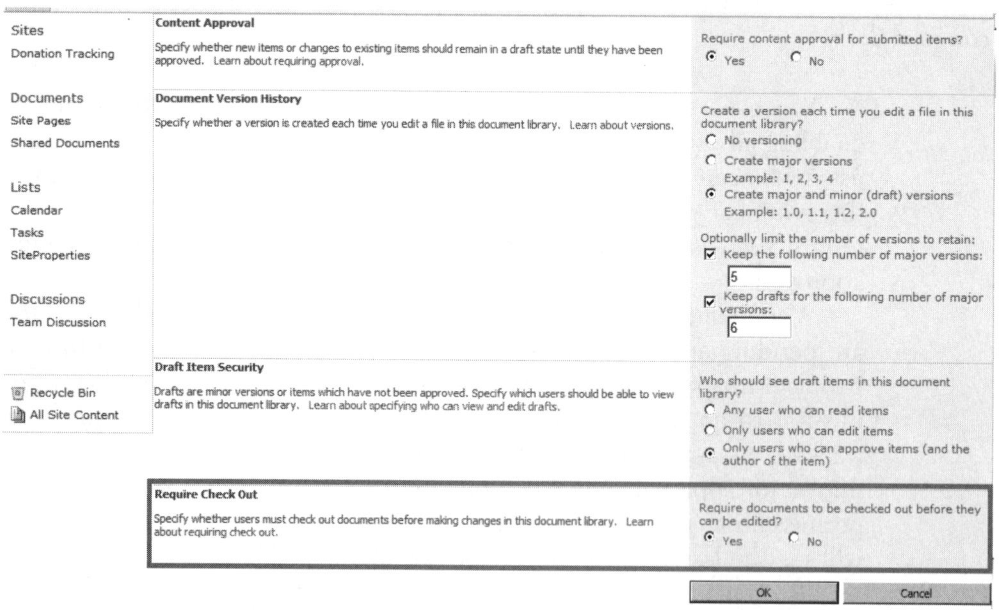

Figure 6-5 The Require Check-out setting enables you to require check-out before items can be edited

versions are tracked, the user is prompted to choose which type of version they are checking in (major or minor).

Document Sets

A new feature in SharePoint 2010 is called Document Sets. Using this feature, documents can be organized into a collection of related documents that can be managed as one. In effect, document sets are folders with which you can:

- Share metadata across documents
- Version the document set itself (instead of the individual documents)
- Initiate workflows for the whole document set
- Set permissions on the document set
- Create a welcome page for the document set

Document sets are implemented as Content Types. To enable document sets, go to Site Actions → Site Settings. Next, under Site Collection Administration, click Manage Site Collection Features and activate the Document Sets feature (see Figure 6-6). After you have the feature

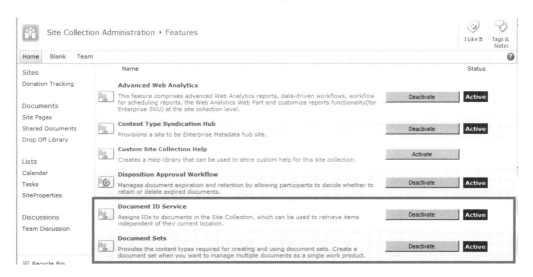

Figure 6-6 The Document Sets feature and the Document ID Service feature are each enabled at the Site Collection

enabled, you can go to the document library's Advanced Settings page and enable management of Content Types. Finally, add the Document Set Content Type to the library (Figure 6-7).

So when do you use document sets? Mainly you want to use document sets when you want to treat a number of documents as a single item with common metadata, permissions, and workflow. For example, you might be creating a proposal for a customer. This proposal itself might be a Word document, while you'll also deliver a PowerPoint presentation, a video presentation, and an Excel spreadsheet for financial analysis. In this scenario, you would probably want all of the items to share the same metadata (customer name, opportunity ID, and so on).

Another example of a document set is when you have a presentation that is associated with supporting materials in spreadsheets. Document sets allow you to keep all the related content together and ensure that users can find documents in the context of their "family."

When a user navigates to a document set, she will see information about the document set and can view and upload documents associated

Sites
Donation Tracking

Documents
Site Pages
Shared Documents
Drop Off Library

Lists
Calendar
Tasks
SiteProperties

Discussions
Team Discussion

Recycle Bin
All Site Content

List Information

Name: Shared Documents
Web Address: http://sharepoint2010/Shared Documents/Forms/AllItems.aspx
Description: Share a document with the team by adding it to this document library.

General Settings

Title, description and navigation
Versioning settings
Advanced settings
Validation settings
Column default value settings
Rating settings
Audience targeting settings
Metadata navigation settings
Per-location view settings
Form settings

Permissions and Management

Delete this document library
Save document library as template
Permissions for this document library
Manage files which have no checked in version
Workflow Settings
Generate file plan report
Information management policy settings
Record declaration settings

Communications

RSS settings

Content Types

This document library is configured to allow multiple content types. Use content types to specify the information you want to display about an item, in addition to its policies, workflows, or other behavior. The following content types are currently available in this library:

Content Type	Visible on New Button	Default Content Type
Document	✓	✓
Asset	✓	
Video	✓	
Document Set	✓	

Figure 6-7 The Document Set Content Type must be added to the document library before you can create one

with the set (see Figure 6-8). In addition, there is a special tab in the ribbon that appears when a user enters a document set (see Figure 6-9). This ribbon selection enables the user to create a version of the set (see Figure 6-10), start a workflow on the set, and manage permissions on the set as a whole.

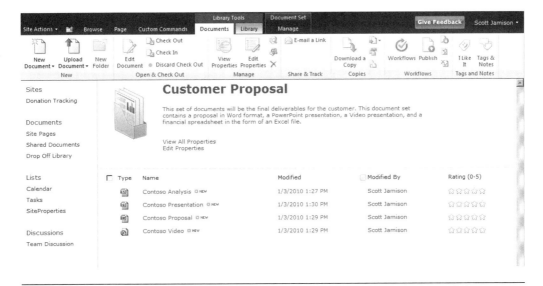

Figure 6-8 Document sets enable you to capture a version of a collection of documents, selecting either the latest of all documents within the set or only the latest published versions of the documents

Figure 6-9 When viewing a document set, a special tab in the ribbon enables you to edit properties on the set, configure permissions, e-mail a link to the document set, capture or review versions, and initiate workflows

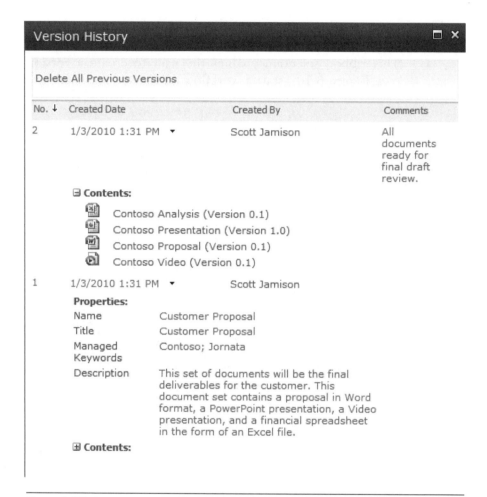

Figure 6-10 Document sets also enable you to capture a version of a collection of documents, selecting either all documents within the set or only published documents

Document IDs

The document ID service enables you do assign unique IDs to documents within a Site Collection. You can then search for and retrieve documents based on ID independent of location. To use this feature, you have to enable it within the Site Collection (refer to Figure 6-6). When you do, you can click the Document ID settings page within Site Collection Administration (see Figure 6-11).

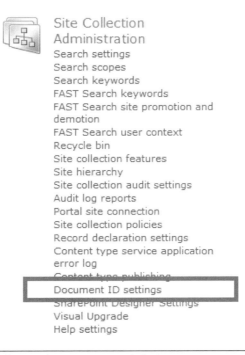

Site Collection
Administration
Search settings
Search scopes
Search keywords
FAST Search keywords
FAST Search site promotion and
demotion
FAST Search user context
Recycle bin
Site collection features
Site hierarchy
Site collection audit settings
Audit log reports
Portal site connection
Site collection policies
Record declaration settings
Content type service application
error log
Content type publishing
Document ID settings
SharePoint Designer Settings
Visual Upgrade
Help settings

Figure 6-11 To configure document IDs, click the Document ID settings link
within Site Collection Administration

There are two options within the Document ID settings page (see Figure 6-12). The first setting is vitally important—it enables you to configure a prefix that will be applied to all documents within the Site Collection. Why is this setting so important? Provided you use unique prefixes across your Site Collections, it will ensure that your document IDs will be unique across Site Collections. The second option enables you to specify a search scope that is used for looking up documents using the ID field.

As a best practice, make sure that each Site Collection has a unique document ID prefix properly configured. Don't just make something up; instead, use consistent prefixes according to your document management policies. Your governance committee should approve all document ID prefixes used in your enterprise; this will ensure that all document IDs assigned by SharePoint are globally unique.

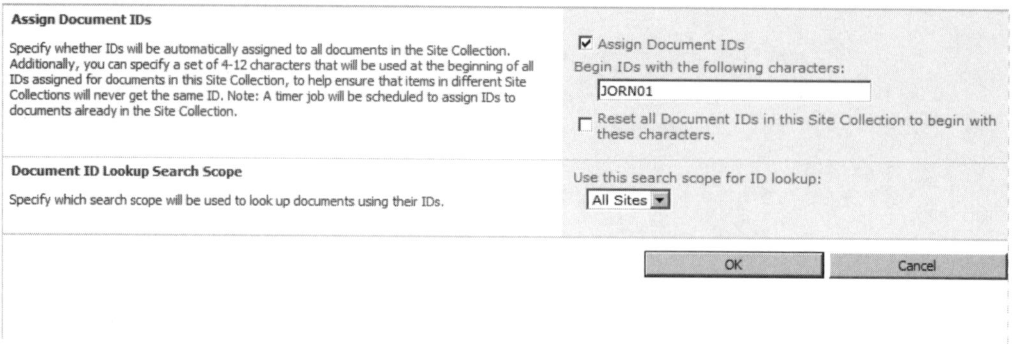

Assign Document IDs

Specify whether IDs will be automatically assigned to all documents in the Site Collection. Additionally, you can specify a set of 4-12 characters that will be used at the beginning of all IDs assigned for documents in this Site Collection, to help ensure that items in different Site Collections will never get the same ID. Note: A timer job will be scheduled to assign IDs to documents already in the Site Collection.

☑ Assign Document IDs

Begin IDs with the following characters:

JORN01

☐ Reset all Document IDs in this Site Collection to begin with these characters.

Document ID Lookup Search Scope

Specify which search scope will be used to look up documents using their IDs.

Use this search scope for ID lookup:

All Sites ▾

OK   Cancel

Figure 6-12 To configure document IDs, click the Document ID settings link within Site Collection Administration

Managed Metadata

With managed metadata, SharePoint 2010 enables you to create centrally managed taxonomies and use them across lists and document libraries. In addition, users are able to navigate by using the metadata items. As an example, you might want to tag proposal documents with a custom property called Offering, which consists of one of the following: product, service, or training. To do so, you can create a new Column in SharePoint called Offering Type and select Managed Metadata as the Column's type. This enables you to point the new Column at a managed term set in the term store. When users enter information into this property, they are able to select from a hierarchical view of preset value choices (see Figure 6-13).

You can also use the managed metadata type to provide hierarchical navigation for users. For example, users can get a navigation tree (see Figure 6-14). If a user selects Service under Offering Type, SharePoint will apply a filter to the current view, only showing items that are tagged with a service offering type. In addition, users can use the Key Filters text box to type in the value of an offering, thereby applying the filter.

To configure metadata navigation, click the Configure Metadata Navigation link within the settings for the document library. Here, you can configure three items (see Figure 6-15):

- **Configure Navigation Hierarchies**. You can set navigation fields based on the following types: Content Type, choice, managed metadata. The properties of all Columns that satisfy one of those three

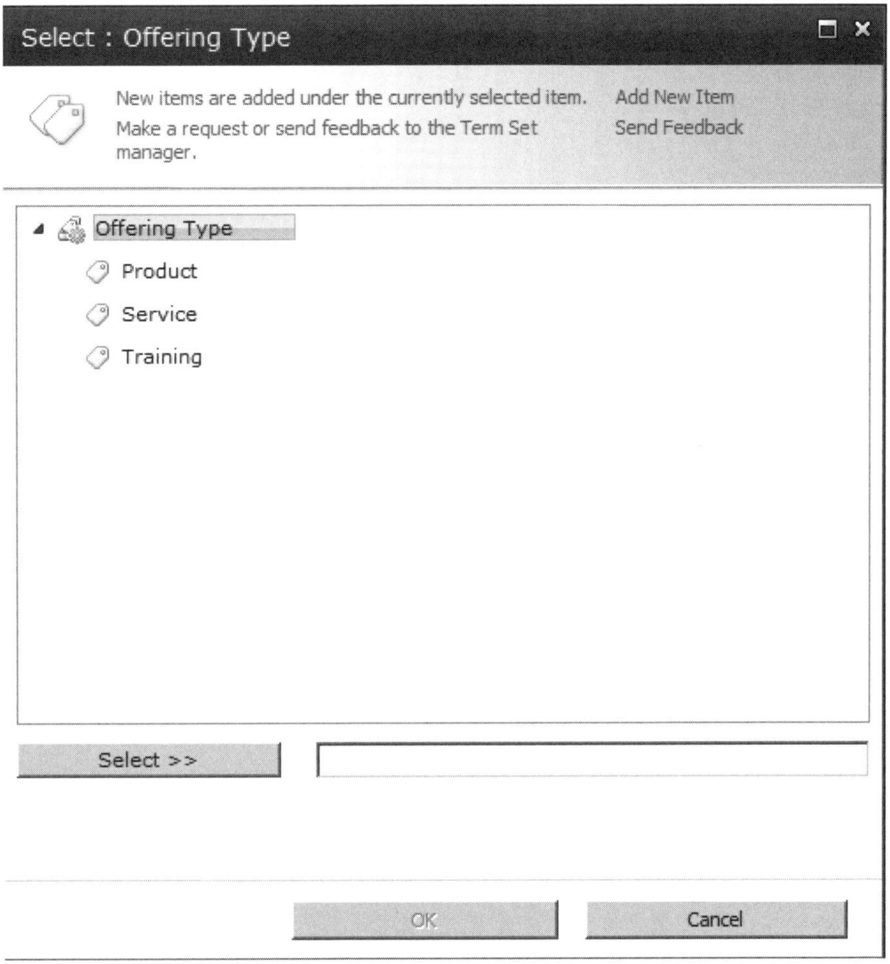

Select : Offering Type

New items are added under the currently selected item.   Add New Item
Make a request or send feedback to the Term Set   Send Feedback
manager.

- ⊿ Offering Type
  - Product
  - Service
  - Training

Select >>

OK   Cancel

Figure 6-13 The managed metadata Column type enables users to select from a set of predefined, centrally managed terms

types are enumerated here. You can choose any/all fields that you want users to navigate by using the tree view.

- **Configure Key Filters**. In addition to the tree view, you may want users to type in filter information for fast filtering. You can indicate which fields you want SharePoint to maintain an index on for filtering.
- **Configure automatic Column indexing for this list**. Typically, you'll want SharePoint to manage Column indices on the list.

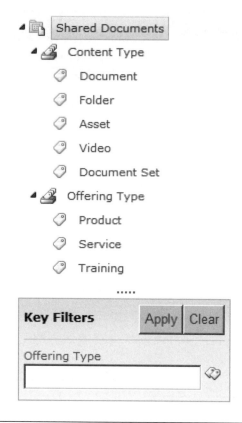

Figure 6-14 Metadata-based navigation in SharePoint 2010 provides a way for users to navigate lists and document libraries by using metadata

Workflow

One of the biggest new features in the last version of SharePoint was the introduction of out-of-the-box workflows. SharePoint 2010 continues to enhance the workflow capabilities within SharePoint. Workflow is a framework for defining rules and associated actions on a list entity (like a document). Workflow rules can be based on metadata (for example, Create Date < 1/1/2005 or Status= 'Approved by Manager') and can trigger actions like document approval, removal, or movement. The biggest advantage of workflow implementation is the consistency and structure it offers. Workflow rules are defined, and then SharePoint manages the actions based on criteria that are met. From a document management perspective, workflow is interesting

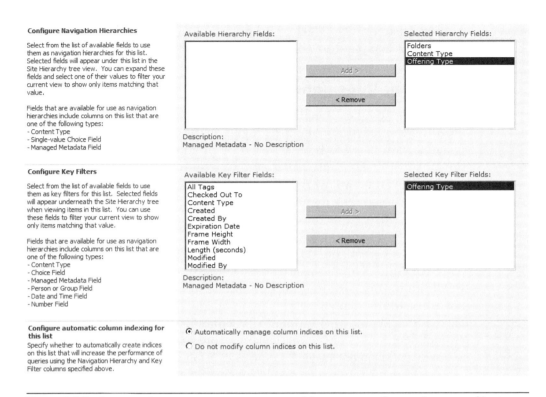

Configure Navigation Hierarchies

Select from the list of available fields to use them as navigation hierarchies for this list. Selected fields will appear under this list in the Site Hierarchy tree view. You can expand these fields and select one of their values to filter your current view to show only items matching that value.

Fields that are available for use as navigation hierarchies include columns on this list that are one of the following types:
- Content Type
- Single-value Choice Field
- Managed Metadata Field

Available Hierarchy Fields:

Add >

< Remove

Description:
Managed Metadata - No Description

Selected Hierarchy Fields:

Folders
Content Type
Offering Type

Configure Key Filters

Select from the list of available fields to use them as key filters for this list. Selected fields will appear underneath the Site Hierarchy tree when viewing items in this list. You can use these fields to filter your current view to show only items matching that value.

Fields that are available for use as navigation hierarchies include columns on this list that are one of the following types:
- Content Type
- Choice Field
- Managed Metadata Field
- Person or Group Field
- Date and Time Field
- Number Field

Available Key Filter Fields:

All Tags
Checked Out To
Content Type
Created
Created By
Expiration Date
Frame Height
Frame Width
Length (seconds)
Modified
Modified By

Add >

< Remove

Description:
Managed Metadata - No Description

Selected Key Filter Fields:

Offering Type

Configure automatic column indexing for this list

Specify whether to automatically create indices on this list that will increase the performance of queries using the Navigation Hierarchy and Key Filter columns specified above.

⊙ Automatically manage column indices on this list.

○ Do not modify column indices on this list.

Figure 6-15 The metadata navigation settings enable you to configure document filtering based on metadata Columns, providing automatic filtering based on filters

in that it enables content administrators to define rules for how humans interact with documents within SharePoint.

SharePoint 2010 contains a few out-of-the-box workflows that represent common workflow scenarios. One of them is an approval process. In this case, one or more approvers must confirm the validity of document content and acknowledge their acceptance through a formal process. The SharePoint-based workflow manages the process of notifying each approver of the requested action, captures the response, and notifies the next approver on the list of the request.

As stated earlier, workflow is a huge advance in the document management capabilities offered with SharePoint 2010. It presents the framework for introducing a set of well-defined actions, with or without intervention, as they apply to SharePoint. In addition, actions can be defined so that appropriate activity can occur and be logged as documents are altered.

See Chapter 11, "Making Business Processes Work: Workflow and Forms," for complete coverage of workflow in SharePoint 2010.

Document Information Panel

One of the toughest challenges in building a document repository is ensuring that each document is tagged with well-defined metadata to make certain it is easily discovered by organizational members. With the breadth of content that is often created in a corporate environment, this can be an overwhelming task. (Ask anyone who has tried to manage a document management system!) Content contributors are much more focused on the details within a document than thinking about how best to classify it. Content discovery, after an item has been submitted, is an afterthought. Why is this bad? Search engines, even the best ones, cannot deliver optimal results if little is known about the content. In addition, it is hard to group similar content if linking attributes are not consistently managed. This leaves many organizations stuck. They have a SharePoint environment that contains the majority of business critical documents but no easy way to find or associate key content.

Why is document tagging so difficult? Mainly it is because the tagging process happens too late in the document submission process. Just after a user uploads documents, he/she is asked for a bunch of metadata. When users are in a hurry, they leave off metadata to save time. Once a document is in the repository, it is very unlikely that it will ever be tagged again by the author. How can SharePoint 2010 make it easier to get authors to assign metadata?

This Document Information Panel (DIP) is an interface within the Office 2010 products (Word or Excel or PowerPoint) that shows the metadata requirements for that document in the Office interface. A content contributor can update metadata as he/she is creating the document. Think about the power in that. SharePoint 2010 has moved the metadata entry process earlier in the document life cycle, closer to the author of the document who, in many cases, has the best knowledge of which attributes apply.

By providing an easier means of assigning document metadata, directly in the environment in which the document is created, the DIP can increase the quality of metadata associated with documents. This additional data has far reaching impact as it offers a better user experience in terms of content "findability" (search, for example). In addition, it provides the data required to implement stronger audit policies around specific types of content.

For an example of the Document Information Panel, see the "Walkthrough: Configuring Enterprise Document and Records Management" section in this chapter.

Document Center

One of the final items to note regarding document management is the Document Center, which is a site template that enables you to centrally manage documents in your enterprise. Where most sites contain document libraries that are geared toward supporting that particular site only, the Document Center is for centrally managing documents.

What does the Document Center template provide? It's essentially a template that has two key lists: a document library and a task list. This Document Center site template also enhances the default settings in the document library to support strong content control. For example, check-out is required before editing, major and minor versions are enabled, support for multiple Content Types is enabled, document sets are enabled, metadata navigation is enabled, and auditing is enabled to track content changes over time. The site template also provides a custom welcome page that facilitates easy upload and search (based on document IDs) for users (see Figure 6-16).

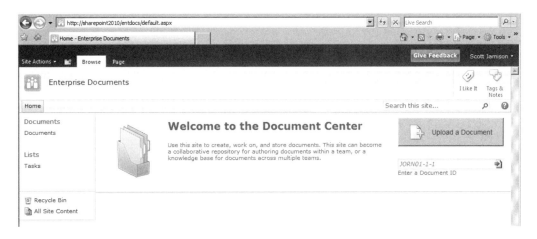

Figure 6-16 The Document Center template enables you to create a site specifically geared toward enterprise document management

Use the Document Center site template for documents that need to be managed in a centralized way. Use a team site template with document libraries to store documents where users are actively collaborating.

Records Management

Records Management in SharePoint 2010 enables you to manage business documents that are necessary for regulatory compliance, business continuity, or historical interest. Records management is not new to SharePoint 2010, but it has been enhanced to allow both in-place records management in addition to the ability to move documents to a specific records center (leaving a permanent link to the new physical location in its place). In a nutshell, records management involves declaring a record, setting polices, and auditing around documents. It's an effective way to ensure that historical content is maintained, not deleted, and does not burden search engines and content navigation.

Record Declaration

To start off, which will you use: in-place records declaration or the records archive? You'll likely use both and will need to decide which and when. There are certain items you need to consider:

- Record retention rules
- Which users can view records
- Ease of locating records (collaborative users versus Records Manager)
- Maintaining each version as a record—do you need this?
- Records Auditing—how often will you audit records?
- Site organization (and number of sites used)—what does your IA look like?
- E-discovery
- Security

If you plan to use a records archive, you will need someone in a records manager role to ensure that records are managed well and that rules are followed. Your records manager will need to work closely with your general counsel, compliance officers, and information architect to ensure protected content is properly identified. For some content, they will likely set up a records archive using the Records Center template (Figure 6-17). Other content could be managed using in-place records management as described in the next section.

You can also declare records in-place. This requires you to enable a Site Collection-level feature called In-place Records Management (see Figure 6-18). Once you enable in-place records management, you can then enable manual declaration of records either at the Site Collection level or at the document library level (under Record declaration settings). You can also automatically declare items as records when they are added to certain lists or libraries. After you enable manual declaration of records, users will see a new action in the ribbon that allows them to declare items as records (see Figure 6-19).

Figure 6-17 The Records Center template enables you to create a site specifically geared toward enterprise records management

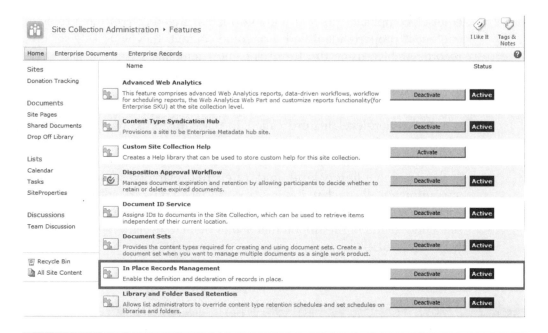

Figure 6-18 You can enable in-place records management through a Site Collection-level feature

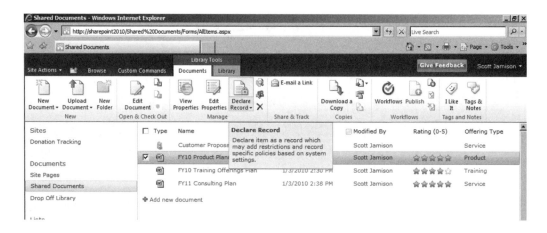

Figure 6-19 Once the ability to manually declare a record is enabled, users can declare records in-place

Auditing

For many organizations, especially those in industries that require a high level of regulatory compliance, storing documents in a repository is not enough. It is just as important to manage the activity around those documents. Activity management is all about auditing or recording the details around what happened to a particular document across its life cycle. Examples of audit information include things such as: Who added particular sections and when? When was this document approved and by whom? What did this document look like on a certain date? What are the rules around document retention?

An even more granular audit requirement is the ability to record viewing statistics associated with a particular document. Let's say you have a new corporate policy that requires executive approval prior to publishing. The information in the document is so sensitive that you may want to know who viewed this document prior to its approved state. As you can see, auditing spills over into accountability. Because of this, it is important to have a robust records management solution in place to properly track and record all details associated with portal content.

SharePoint 2010 delivers on the goal of effective records management by providing a system that allows auditing on documents or any list item. SharePoint 2010 provides auditing capabilities for tracking specific events like when a document was opened or viewed, when a document was edited, when a document was checked out, and even when a document was moved to a new location. All of this is built right into the SharePoint 2010 system interface and is easily configured as part of a list or library definition.

In addition to item-level auditing, SharePoint 2010 also provides auditing at a specific site level. This is an especially interesting feature as it allows site managers to track when security changes were made within the site and when metadata associated with a particular document were altered. Think about the impact of such a feature! Administrators can be assured that policies about site security and/or document definition can be effectively monitored and enforced. This is how the term *compliance* gets introduced in the SharePoint 2010 feature set.

Only administrators can see details on audit data. Content contributors, whose activities are be tracked, do not have access to audit reports. In addition, no one is allowed to edit or alter audit data. This lockdown ensures that audit trails are always complete and accurate.

In addition, audit policies themselves can be audited so administrators can assess how well certain policies are being followed. This rules-based approach is yet another reason why SharePoint can support restricted and sensitive information. Everything is monitored; polices are always tracked.

Information Management Policies

We've briefly talked about applying audit policies to specific document or list items in SharePoint 2010. One of the obvious questions is, how do you ensure that these policies are in place, in all the right places? SharePoint 2010 provides the ability to set Information Management Policies as a means for administrators (or records managers) to define the proper audit policies as well as apply them to all relevant locations so no one has to worry about these policies extending into new sites or documents.

As with most SharePoint 2010 functionality, Information Management Policies management is built right into the interface. This allows administrators or records managers to define policies directly in the Site Settings of a particular document or site. In the Permissions and Policies section, there is a link for Information management policy settings. This is where policy is defined and applied.

Setting and administration of Information Management Policies is intended to be simple and intuitive. No special skills are required to define policies. For end users, the experience is just as simple. When a policy is in place around a particular document, the user is made aware by a notification bar at the top of the document. All other functionality is the same as if there were not an Information Management Policy in place.

While there are several Information Management Policy use cases, let's look at a specific example associated with an expiration policy. Very much like metadata capture, document expiration is critical to the overall effectiveness of portal document delivery. Few documents should live forever (at least in the context of the corporate portal). Over time, most documents become less relevant and therefore should be either reviewed and revised or moved out of the mainstream. Without rules and policies in place, this becomes an overwhelming burden for document administrators. Who can be responsible for investigating all documents for usefulness?

SharePoint 2010 introduces the ability to have multistage expiration policies, which is a set of rules for executing activity on a particular document or group of documents. This is a two-step process.

The first step is to define *when* a document will encounter an expiration trigger. This is most easily done with logic against known metadata (another reason to properly tag content!). While most rules will be date driven (for example, expire after 180 days), any metadata can be used to drive expiration, including a Records Retention Code.

The second step in the policy definition is to define *what happens* to the document when the criteria are met. This can take many forms; you can delete the document from the repository or perhaps launch a SharePoint-based workflow that can move that document to an archive location. By setting expiration rules, administrators and records managers can ensure that the portal always contains relevant and timely data. See Figure 6-20 for the compliance details on an item; note that the item has a multistage retention policy.

Figure 6-20 You can view the compliance details on any document, where you can see the document's scheduled retention policy, record and hold status, and audit information

Walkthrough: Configuring Enterprise Document and Records Management

Let's say you've set up your SharePoint environment and want to ensure that the resulting documents in your sites are properly managed. What is the best way to configure this? This section walks you through an example of setting up and configuring a document library, complete with the necessary items for proper content management. You configure Content Types, use those Content Types in a document library, enable records declaration, and enable appropriate retention policies. You then create a new menu item in the document library that allows users to submit documents to the records repository.

Step 1: Define Metadata by Using SharePoint Site Columns

If you are going to define a document retention policy and configure records management, we assume that you want to tag your documents with meaningful metadata. The metadata you define will be unique to your organization's needs. For this example, we assume three properties: Cost Center, Product, and Fiscal Year. The best way to create metadata Columns is to define Site Columns, which are defined by using the Site Settings page from a top-level site (see Figure 6-21). We use the Site Columns when we create Content Types in the next step.

To create a Site Column, click the Create button (see Figure 6-22). You will be able to enter a name, datatype, and other information. When you've entered your custom Site Columns, you can use them to define a Content Type.

Step 2: Define Content Types that Use the Site Columns

In this step, you use the Site Columns that you created in Step 1 to define custom Content Types. Content Types enable you to define specific classifications of documents by defining a name, a document template, a list of metadata properties that should be captured, and even workflows that should act upon this content. Examples of Content Types include Expense Reports, Purchase Orders, and Proposals; they can be any document that your organization uses and that has unique content management attributes (see Chapter 5 for more information about planning your Content Types). In this example, we create a Purchase Order Content Type. To define a Content Type, click the Site Content Types option within Site Settings (see Figure 6-23). Click Create, which presents you with the option of creating a new Content Type (see Figure 6-24).

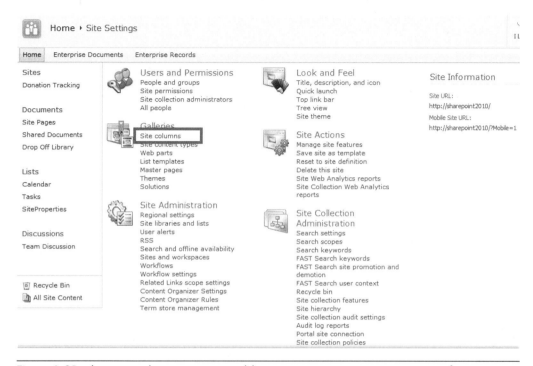

Figure 6-21 The Site Columns option enables you to create custom properties for a Site Collection

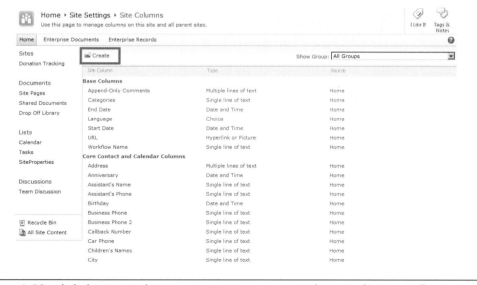

Figure 6-22 Click the Create button to create a new Site Column in the Site Collection's Site Column Gallery

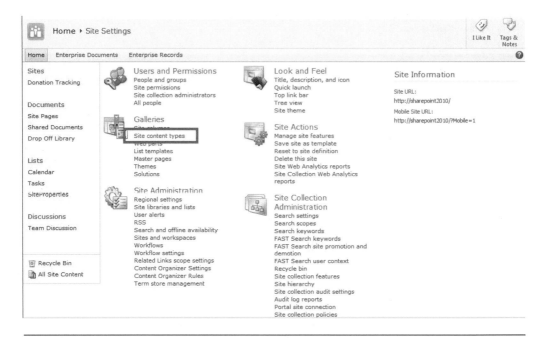

Figure 6-23 The Site Content Types option enables you to create custom Content Types for a Site Collection

Figure 6-24 Creating a new purchase order Content Type

After your Content Type is created, you can configure additional properties (see Figure 6-25) by clicking the name of the Content Type from the Site Content Types configuration page. Here you'll want to add the Site Columns you created in Step 1; simply click the Add from Existing Site Columns link, selecting your Site Columns to add (see Figure 6-26).

Next, click Advanced Settings, which enables you to associate a document template with the Content Type. Once you've associated your template, you'll have a reusable Content Type that will enable your organization to have a consistent template and collection of metadata for purchase orders, no matter where those documents are stored (provided you syndicate the Content Type for other Site Collections to use and add the Content Type to the document library, both of which we do in Step 3).

Step 3: Add the Content Type to a Document Library

Create or locate a document library. Under Advanced Settings for the library, enable Allow management of Content Types (see Figure 6-27). This lets us add our Content Type to this document library. On the Document Library Settings page, click Add from existing site Content Types in the Content Types section (see Figure 6-28).

On the Add Content Types page, select the Purchase Order Content Type and add it to the document library (see Figure 6-29). Users are now able to create new documents with your custom Content Type directly from the new menu (see Figure 6-30). The Document Information Panel will automatically provide users the ability to enter metadata properties from within Word 2010.

At this point, you are able to better manage documents because they are using consistent templates and metadata Columns. Searches will be more effective. Now it's time to set up in-place records declaration.

Step 4: Enable In-Place Records Management

To allow users to declare records in-place, you configure the Record Declaration settings for the library (see Figure 6-31).

As you have seen in this section, the document management and records management features in SharePoint 2010 enable you to create a repository to retain business documents that are necessary for regulatory compliance, business continuity, or historical interest. The ECM

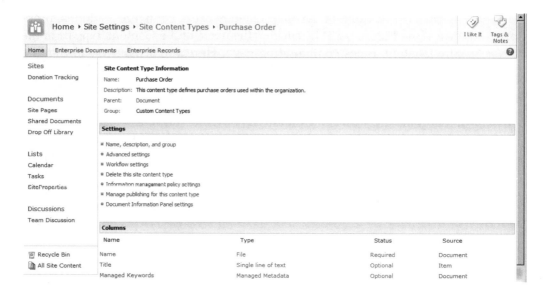

Figure 6-25 The Site Content Type Information page enables you to configure additional properties for your custom Content Type. Use the Information Management Policy settings to enable retention and auditing and the Document Information Panel settings for enabling metadata entry within Office 2010.

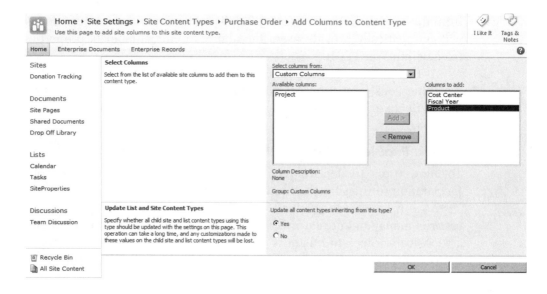

Figure 6-26 The Add Columns page enables you to add Site Columns to a Content Type

Home ▸ Shared Documents ▸ Document Library Settings ▸ Advanced Settings

I Like It   Tags & Notes

| Home | Enterprise Documents | Enterprise Records | |

Sites

Donation Tracking

Content Types

Specify whether to allow the management of content types on this document library. Each content type will appear on the new button and can have a unique set of columns, workflows and other behaviors.

Allow management of content types?

⦿ Yes   ○ No

Documents

Site Pages

Shared Documents

Drop Off Library

Document Template

Type the address of a template to use as the basis for all new files created in this document library. When multiple content types are enabled, this setting is managed on a per content type basis. Learn how to set up a template for a library.

Template URL:

Shared Documents/Forms/template.dot

Lists

Calendar

Tasks

SiteProperties

Opening Documents in the Browser

Specify whether browser-enabled documents should be opened in the client or browser by default when a user clicks on them. If the client application is unavailable, the document will always be opened in the browser.

Default open behavior for browser-enabled documents:

○ Open in the client application
○ Open in the browser
⦿ Use the server default (Open in the browser)

Discussions

Team Discussion

Custom Send To Destination

Type the name and URL for a custom Send To destination that you want to appear on the context menu for this list. It is recommended that you choose a short name for the destination.

Destination name: (For example, Team Library)

URL:

Recycle Bin

All Site Content

Folders

Specify whether the "New Folder" command is available. Changing this setting does not affect existing folders.

Make "New Folder" command available?

⦿ Yes   ○ No

Search

Allow items from this document library to appear in search results?

Figure 6-27 You must enable management of Content Types in the document library in order to use a site Content Type

Content Types

This document library is configured to allow multiple content types. Use content types to specify the information you want to display about an item, in addition to its policies, workflows, or other behavior. The following content types are currently available in this library:

Content Type	Visible on New Button	Default Content Type
Document	✔	✔
Asset	✔	
Video	✔	
Document Set	✔	

Add from existing site content types

Change new button order and default content type

Figure 6-28 Once Content Type management is enabled, a new option to manage Content Types is available

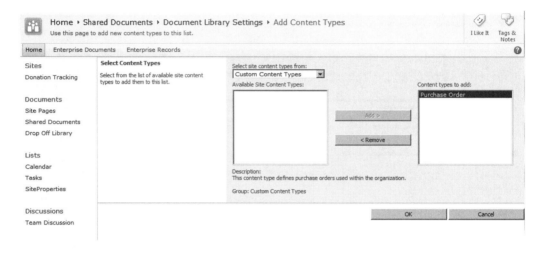

Figure 6-29 Add the site Content Type to the document library

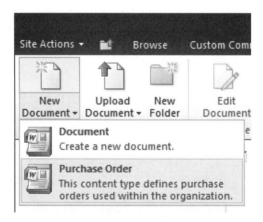

Figure 6-30 Content Types become available on the document library's New menu, making it easy for organizations to encourage template and metadata usage

features of SharePoint 2010 enable you to set polices and auditing around documents. It's an effective way to ensure that historical content is maintained, not deleted, and does not burden search engines and content navigation.

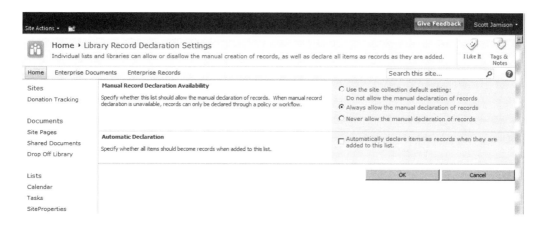

Figure 6-31 To enable the ability for users to manually declare records, you must enable the setting at either the Site Collection or library level

Key Points

This chapter provided some recommendations for using the ECM features of SharePoint 2010. In general, our recommendation is to

- Define site Columns and Content Types to standardize your metadata across the organization, using Content Type syndication to keep your document types consistent.
- Use a team site template with document libraries to store documents where content is being actively updated by a team. Use the Document Center site template for documents that need to be managed in a centralized way.
- As a best practice, make sure that each Site Collection has a unique document ID prefix configured. Your governance committee should approve all document ID prefixes used in your enterprise; this will ensure that all document IDs assigned by SharePoint are globally unique.
- If you have a records manager, use the Records Center site template for storing and managing records. If you don't have a formal, centralized records manager, in-place record declaration will be easier for users to manage.

GETTING SOCIAL: LEVERAGING COMMUNITY FEATURES

SharePoint 2010 communities include a collection of features that allow people to work together in new ways. Calling these features "communities" is probably a good choice of terms even if you don't immediately know what it means. A possible alternative, "social software," has the potential to sound trivial or, even worse, out of place in a business environment. Approaching a business executive with a project to implement social software inside the organization could be a career-limiting move. While you're thinking about improved collaboration and knowledge sharing, executives are thinking about time-wasting activities like Facebook and fantasy football. Are their fears real? Maybe, especially if they read the article in the October 26, 2009, issue of *Computerworld* that reported on a UK study that said employees using Twitter, Facebook, and other social networks in the office are costing UK businesses more than $2.25 billion in lost productivity.[1] Of course, that is not the whole story. Moreover, it's not totally clear that the time spent on these sites (an average of 40 minutes per day in the study) is not work-related. So before we get started talking about how to use the community features in SharePoint 2010, let's spend some time reviewing the value proposition for these features and how they may benefit your organization. As we talk about these features, we use the more widely known terms *social computing* or *social technologies*, but you don't need to use the "s" word when you describe them to your colleagues. You can call these features SharePoint Communities or even Web 2.0.

As you consider how to best take advantage of the community (or Web 2.0) features in SharePoint, keep in mind that using them is optional.

---

1. Sharon Gaudin, "Study: Facebook, Twitter Use at Work Costs Big Bucks." *Computerworld.com* (October 26, 2009), accessed December 20, 2009, http://www.computerworld.com/s/article/9139902/Study_Facebook_Twitter_use_at_work_costs_big_bucks.

For the most part, you can enable some features without enabling them all. You can choose to enable the features over time after you have figured out your governance model and communications messages about how these features are both applicable and beneficial in your environment.

Most organizations recognize that success depends on people working together. Social technologies allow users to interact and share information in ways that help them work together more effectively. As more and more people embrace social technologies in their private lives, they will expect to find this functionality in the tools they use at work. While these technologies may spark raised eyebrows or even outright fear in many business executives, it's very clear that social computing is the new black.

This chapter includes four key sections:

- Getting Started: Developing a Strategy for SharePoint Community Features
- Social Networking: Engaging People
- Social Data: Enhancing Value with User Contributed Content
- Social Sites: Providing a Structure for Collaborative Conversations

Getting Started: Developing a Strategy for SharePoint Community Features

The absolute worst way to get started with the community (social) features of SharePoint is to jump right in because someone in the organization has said, "We should be doing Web 2.0," or because it's hip, cool, or "the 'millennials' expect it." Sure, leveraging community features might help attract new talent to the organization, but the features still need appropriate context and organizational support. Even more importantly, it's not about the tools themselves that helps organizations get business results, *it's what the tools let users do* to solve real business problems. If you are not already leveraging this type of technology in your organization, you need to approach the community features in SharePoint the same way you would approach any other project involving an emerging technology or one that is new to your organization: You need to have a business problem to solve. This probably bears repeating: You need to have a *real* business problem to solve for which social computing technologies can be an effective solution enabler. Otherwise, you will have very limited chance of success. You need to define your desired outcome and then ask, how can SharePoint community features help address this problem? If you haven't done so already, it's probably time to read (or reread) Chapter 1, "Getting Started." In that chapter, we talk about clearly identifying the outcomes you are trying to achieve with your SharePoint deployment. As you think about how and when to deploy SharePoint Community features, consider the following key steps:

- Clearly identify the business problem.
- Identify use cases.
- Be prepared to respond to barriers.
- Define your governance plan.
- Define a "do-able" pilot project.
- Prepare a launch and communications plan.

Clearly Identify the Business Problem

It's important to clearly associate a business outcome objective with any collaboration technology, but especially for the "scary" social technologies. Following are some of the business problems that social technologies can help address:

- **Providing improved access to internal experts**. In many organizations, people complain that it just takes too much time to figure out "who knows about" a particular topic. Expertise is often needed quickly, and even the most connected people in the organization may not know who to contact for every possible topic. User profiles and expertise search help to quickly connect people who need help with people who have the knowledge to help them.
- **Building relationship capital**. It often takes several months if not years for new employees to develop the social networks necessary for them to be effective and productive. Relationship capital—who knows whom—is an underdeveloped asset in many organizations. Often, people have trouble solving problems because the right people in the organization don't connect. Features such as the organization chart browser help employees understand formal relationships in the organization, and social "tags," ratings, and blogs help people understand more informal knowledge relationships so that they can quickly figure out how to get to the tacit expertise distributed across the enterprise.

- **Improving the connection between people and the content and processes they need to get their jobs done**. Authoritative metadata improves search results significantly, but not all organizations have a good plan for assigning metadata to content. User-assigned tags help add additional context to content even when there is authoritative metadata available. Ratings can also help identify useful content, as long as there is a clear governance model for using this feature. Blogs help employees share innovative ideas across organizational boundaries—a frequent issue in large, global organizations where people often complain, "I know someone must have already addressed this issue some place in the organization, I just have no clue how to find them."

- **Identifying new opportunities for mentorship and knowledge sharing**. In large, geographically dispersed companies, it's difficult to match up existing experts with emerging experts. User profiles and blogs help people identify opportunities for mentoring relationships on their own.

- **Allowing users to add content to information stores**. When users add tags to content, they help make the information more useful to themselves, but if they allow the tag to be exposed publicly, they may also make the information more relevant to others and improve the relevance of search results for the entire organization. Social tagging is a very personal activity—users generally do it so that they can personally find or group information in a way that is meaningful to them. However, the added benefit of social tags is that they may also help others find information—either because they help improve search results or because users may "discover" what someone else is thinking about or working on through the activity feeds that show what that person is tagging.

- **Moving conversations out of the limited range of e-mail and hallways and into online spaces where more people can benefit**. A lot of tacit knowledge transfer happens in the private space of e-mail and hallway conversations. Blogs and wikis help make some of these conversations more public, helping to address the "holy grail" challenge of knowledge management: sharing knowledge that is not yet available in formal repositories. In addition, status updates can provide a real-time way of connecting people in the organization without generating extra e-mail traffic.

- **Making it easier to recruit and retain new, Internet-savvy employees**. We said earlier that deploying SharePoint community features shouldn't be done just because younger employees expect to see them. Simply having the functionality available doesn't guarantee that it will be used effectively. That said, the availability (and active use) of social technologies can help your organization attract and retain the next generation of employees who are familiar with and expect to use this type of technology at work.

Note that we're primarily talking about internally facing business problems because this is where we know the majority of our readers are focused.

Identify Use Cases

One of your key goals for social computing inside the organization is to make it "real" for executives and other key stakeholders. This essentially means being able to describe the scenarios or stories where using the SharePoint community features can add value to the organization's objectives. Turning these stories into hard dollar values will be difficult, but remember: the social features are already included in SharePoint, so the only additional investment required is in the training and support required to get people to use them.

Professional services companies use user profiles and social tags to identify internal expertise to quickly assemble the best qualified teams for a client engagement. Large global companies with distributed IT staff members use blogs to share "how I did it" stories and software code across the enterprise so that people don't reinvent the wheel. Organizations all over the world, in the public and private sector both, use wikis to collaboratively create software documentation and "Wikipedia" type definitions that can be shared and updated by a broad community of participants.

You will need to identify use cases that apply in your own organization. Start with your list of business objectives and derive use cases from that list and from the stakeholder interviews you conducted at the start of your SharePoint project.

Be Prepared to Respond to Barriers

Even with well-described, relevant, and meaningful use cases, you may still see some resistance to deploying the community features. Use the ideas in Table 7-1 to help respond to some of the potential barriers you may encounter.

Table 7-1 Suggested Responses to Resistance to Deploying Community Features

Possible Objection	Response
If we allow any user to contribute content (to a discussion board or a wiki or a blog), we risk exposing inaccurate information. This objection is one of the barriers often expressed in organizations where executives are concerned about allowing employees to have blogs. It may also be a concern in an environment where content is collaboratively edited in a wiki. The concern is often not that users will intentionally post inaccurate information, but that they might be misinformed and unintentionally post information that is not correct.	Blogs and wikis tend to be "self-policing," especially if multiple users have edit privileges. If everyone in the organization has edit privileges and can correct incorrect entries, then the risk of incorrect information being exposed is temporary—only until someone catches and corrects the error. Moreover, unlike on the Internet, on an internal intranet site, inappropriate or incorrect content can always be removed by the Site Administrator. The question you need to ask is whether or not this risk is any greater than it would be if a user asks a question in another way and gets an answer from someone who is misinformed. While the exposure risk may be smaller considering only two people are involved in the conversation, the potential damage is probably greater in the direct conversation because there is no opportunity to catch the error unless the person asking the question seeks a "second opinion." Blogs and wikis are actually more transparent than e-mail, where far more damaging conversations can take place. In other words, social technologies make it *easier* to catch problems, not harder. A possible strategy to gradually decrease barriers might be to start by limiting users who can have blogs to subject matter experts and similarly restricting edit privileges on wiki sites until the organization is more comfortable with the technology and explicit positive results can be demonstrated. You may also want to consider a graphic identity marker or a disclaimer on each blog page to indicate that it is a blog to differentiate it from vetted content or an approval workflow on wiki content.
If we allow people to post anything they want in their profiles or on their blogs, they may talk about inappropriate topics or about other people or about information that can't or shouldn't be universally shared.	This barrier may be a legitimate concern in some organizations, especially those where "ethical walls" apply. In general, most organizations already have a policy regarding the appropriate use of corporate IT resources, and this policy typically already covers the type of content expressed in this objection. If it doesn't, then it's time to update the policy, not necessarily ban the activity.

Possible Objection	Response
	As a general rule, most people will do the right thing when it comes to sharing online. One of the reasons that you may see a "flame war" on the public Internet is that people are often anonymous on the Internet and can hide behind pseudonyms. This is not the case inside the organization where a general best practice is to ensure that all users "own" their comments and content. It would defeat the purpose of connecting people to other people inside the organization if anonymous contributions were the norm. Even if contributions are allowed to be anonymous in some circumstances, it is almost always possible that at least the system administrator will be able to see who is posting what content. With a documented policy and user names associated with content, this barrier becomes much less of a real risk.
I don't want to share what I know in a blog because then someone might take my idea and use it without giving me any credit. We've heard this as a barrier in organizations with a culture that rewards and values innovation and individual contributions over collaboration and teamwork. The barrier is often expressed about collaboration solutions in general, not just social technologies.	One of the important concepts of knowledge management is that knowledge is an asset that you don't lose when you give it away—if I share my knowledge to help you out, I still have the knowledge to share again and reuse for myself. People are naturally wired to be helpful but sometimes, organizational norms and reward structures create artificial barriers that limit the success of solutions that promote sharing. It's actually harder to not assign credit to others or at least identify the source of an idea when it comes from a dated blog post or shared document given that the evidence for an idea or concept is easy to find. To mitigate this barrier to successfully deploying social technologies, it may be necessary to look at how people in your organization are rewarded—how they are measured for both regular and incentive compensation. Some of the barriers to collaborative technologies are not risks associated with the technology itself but the fact that the behaviors encouraged by the technology are not perceived as valuable in the organization.

(continues)

Table 7-1 Suggested Responses to Resistance to Deploying Community Features *(continued)*

Possible Objection	Response
If we allow people to create blogs, post notes and comments, and narrate their work in a status update, we might create additional discoverable content that would have to be turned over as part of a lawsuit.	This is probably a valid risk but no more so than any other type of content in the organization, especially e-mail. Remember that unlike e-mail, social content is *always exposed*. In other words, there are many opportunities to correct inappropriate content or remove it simply because it is "social," not private. While there may be additional legitimate risks if community content is exposed in your public facing Web site or extranet environment, internally this content is likely to be far less problematic than e-mail. Most organizations have every employee sign an "appropriate use of internal technology resources" contract when they join the organization. Some have employees re-sign this agreement annually. The bottom line is that most people know how to behave online and will do the right thing. If they don't, the content is both easily identified and removed.
Status updates and notes will be used for trivial purposes and provide a distraction from the main event: work.	There are plenty of opportunities for people to become distracted at work. As mentioned earlier, in general, people understand what is appropriate at work and will do the right thing. If they don't, there are already performance measures in place to ensure that employees get their work done on time. In addition, by adjusting their preferences, users can control the information they share and see. The best mitigation strategy for this objection is a success story—an example of a situation where a connection made via social technologies helped benefit a project team or an individual or the organization as a whole. If you're responsible for the deployment of the community features of SharePoint, your project plan should certainly include a plan to capture and evaluate metrics. Be sure to include success stories as a qualitative metric for your initiative.

Are these possible barriers real? Yes, they are, and we've heard them, so it's important to think about how they might come up in your organization. However, it's also true that none of us has heard of any real negative outcomes in any organization. Intranets are not anonymous, and if you remember back to the guiding principle discussed in Chapter 4, "Planning for Governance," as an employee of the organization, everyone is responsible for intranet content.

Define Your Governance Plan

Hopefully, you thought about your governance plan when you were reading Chapter 4. If you have not yet thought about how you want to approach governance for the community features, it's time to do it now. The most important general governance policy when it comes to community features is to not allow users to post anonymous content. To get value from community features, people need to know who is posting content. "Owning" your content on the intranet helps ensure that everyone plays by the rules and makes it very easy to ensure that governance policies are followed. Your governance plan will need to include specific guidance for at least these community features: My Sites, ratings and tags, and blogs and wikis.

My Sites

Spend some time looking at the out-of-the-box profile content available in My Site (the user's personal portal site). There are four sections to the profile: Basic Information, Contact Information, Details, and Preferences. Many of the profile fields are the same as in MOSS 2007, but there are some significant new fields for which you will want to define governance policies.

Basic Information (see Figure 7-1) includes the About Me description along with Skills and Interests and a new field called Ask Me About where users can enter topics where they are essentially saying, "I can help you with this topic." Your governance plan should have a suggested format for About Me descriptions and provide examples of well-written descriptions. Decide whether or not you want to include Skills and Interests in the profile. Some organizations find that the loosely structured field for Skills is too informal and unstructured to be of much value. In this case, it is helpful to replace the Skills list with a more structured list of suggested Skills so that users select meaningful values. In one organization, a user entered "Jack of All Trades, Master of None" in his skills list. Not only is this entry not helpful, but because a comma was used as a separator differentiating two separate skills, this user actually was identified with two separate skills: Jack of All Trades and Master of None—so even the joke didn't work. At a minimum, you need to provide guidance regarding what types of skills are relevant if you choose to use this field. Another new field in this section is the Time Zone field, which is used to show the local time on the user's profile page. You should probably be less restrictive about interests because this field can have just as much value when used to expose personal interests as it can for professional interests.

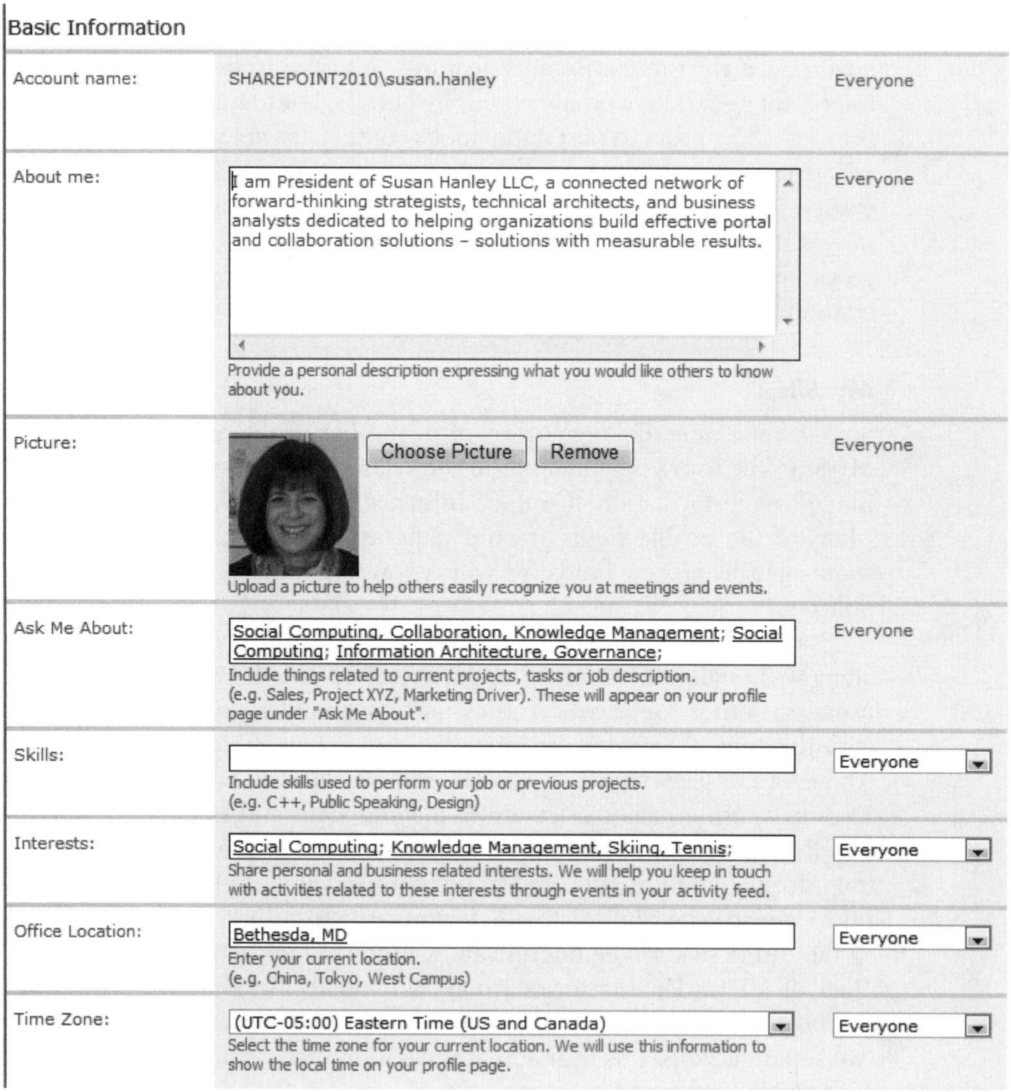

Basic Information		
Account name:	SHAREPOINT2010\susan.hanley	Everyone
About me:	I am President of Susan Hanley LLC, a connected network of forward-thinking strategists, technical architects, and business analysts dedicated to helping organizations build effective portal and collaboration solutions – solutions with measurable results. Provide a personal description expressing what you would like others to know about you.	Everyone
Picture:	Choose Picture Remove Upload a picture to help others easily recognize you at meetings and events.	Everyone
Ask Me About:	Social Computing, Collaboration, Knowledge Management; Social Computing; Information Architecture, Governance; Include things related to current projects, tasks or job description. (e.g. Sales, Project XYZ, Marketing Driver). These will appear on your profile page under "Ask Me About".	Everyone
Skills:	Include skills used to perform your job or previous projects. (e.g. C++, Public Speaking, Design)	Everyone
Interests:	Social Computing; Knowledge Management, Skiing, Tennis; Share personal and business related interests. We will help you keep in touch with activities related to these interests through events in your activity feed.	Everyone
Office Location:	Bethesda, MD Enter your current location. (e.g. China, Tokyo, West Campus)	Everyone
Time Zone:	(UTC-05:00) Eastern Time (US and Canada) Select the time zone for your current location. We will use this information to show the local time on your profile page.	Everyone

Figure 7-1 User profile: Basic Information

The Ask Me About field is particularly important to address in your governance plan. For example, at what degree of knowledge is it appropriate for a user to say that you can ask them about a topic? How well do you have to know something before you should declare this expertise to your colleagues? Do you want users to declare that you can ask them about any topic in which they are interested or only those in which they have some degree of expertise? The answers to these questions will likely vary based on the nature and even size of your organization, but you will want to provide some guidance to users about what is or is not appropriate based on the outcomes you are trying to achieve. Topics that users identify in their Ask Me About profiles are weighted higher in search results, so it is important to clearly identify what type of information should be included in this part of the profile. If expertise location is among your business objectives, you might want to think about the following guidelines for users:

- Add a topic to your Ask Me About profile if you have advanced knowledge of that discipline, even if you haven't yet had a chance to use that knowledge in your current role. This should mean that you have used the discipline extensively and can assist others in applying it to complex problems or that you are a true expert—you are experienced in all aspects of the discipline and are able to develop creative solutions to complex problems and can educate others.
- Also add a topic to your Ask Me About profile if you know the discipline is new or new to the organization, even if all you can do is answer basic questions and direct inquiries to people with more expertise.

Content in the Ask Me About field appears in a user's profile page under the Ask Me About heading. In addition, this field has some special properties when your organization has deployed Outlook 2010 with SharePoint 2010. In Outlook 2010, users can select to enable knowledge mining from outgoing (sent) e-mail messages (Outlook → Options → Advanced). When enabled in both Outlook and SharePoint, users see a set of suggestions under the Ask Me About field in the profile. The suggestions are terms that are "mined" from the outgoing messages in Outlook using a ranking algorithm that identifies frequent topics in e-mail messages. The suggested topics are displayed only to the user on his or her profile and are not shared with others unless the user "consents" to share them by explicitly clicking a suggested term. When clicked, the term is added to the user's Ask Me

About content along with any manually added terms. In this way, SharePoint helps capture and expose employees' tacit knowledge, which helps support real-time expertise location. Your governance plan should explain how e-mail content is used to suggest terms, show users how to "turn off" profiling for e-mail messages, and assure users that their suggested terms are secure—they are exposed to only the user until the user chooses to add them to the profile.

Figure 7-2 shows the fields in the Contact Information and Details area of the My Site. These fields were all available in MOSS 2007. You will certainly want to provide guidance about adding information to the Past Projects field if you are going to use it. This property is very difficult to keep up to date if users are expected to maintain it manually. As a general rule, it is better to eliminate a field rather than allow it to go stale, so if you plan to use this profile attribute, be sure that you have an organizational process that ensures that it will be maintained over time.

Many organizations worry about privacy issues when it comes to exposing birthdays, even if you are only exposing month and day. Be sure to check with your HR department, but in our experience, people really like to know this information about their colleagues—again, month and day only! Most HR departments allow the information to be shared as long as providing it is "opt in." As with all personal fields in the My Site profile, you have the

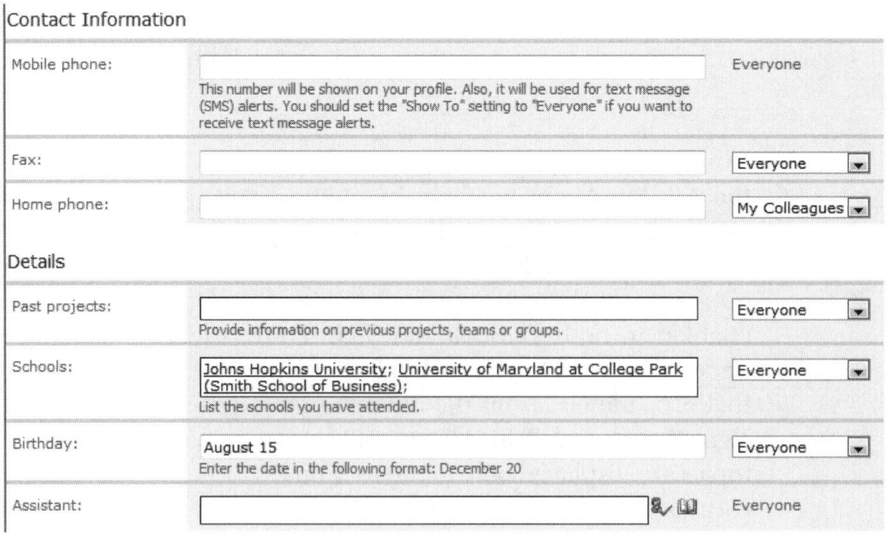

Figure 7-2 User profile: Contact Information and Details

option of removing them from the profile, but if you choose to use them, be sure to define your governance policies for their use and maintenance.

One challenge organizations often express when deploying My Sites is getting people to create their initial profiles. It's very frustrating to search for people in organizations where some users have a well-defined profile and others have virtually no content. Consider hosting a profile building "jam session" to encourage users to create their initial profiles. One organization created a rap video to get employees to update their profiles and showed the video at an all-hands meeting. In the back of the conference room, they created several "kiosks" (tables with laptops) where users could update their profiles during breaks and after the meeting ended.

The last section of the My Site profile allows users to set their preferences about how they want to be notified about the events associated with their profiles such as when people leaves notes on their profiles or when they are added by other users as a colleague. The Preferences fields allow users to control the amount of information they receive to prevent information overload and ensure that they are focused on the community information that they find most helpful. Figure 7-3 shows the available Preferences settings in the user profile.

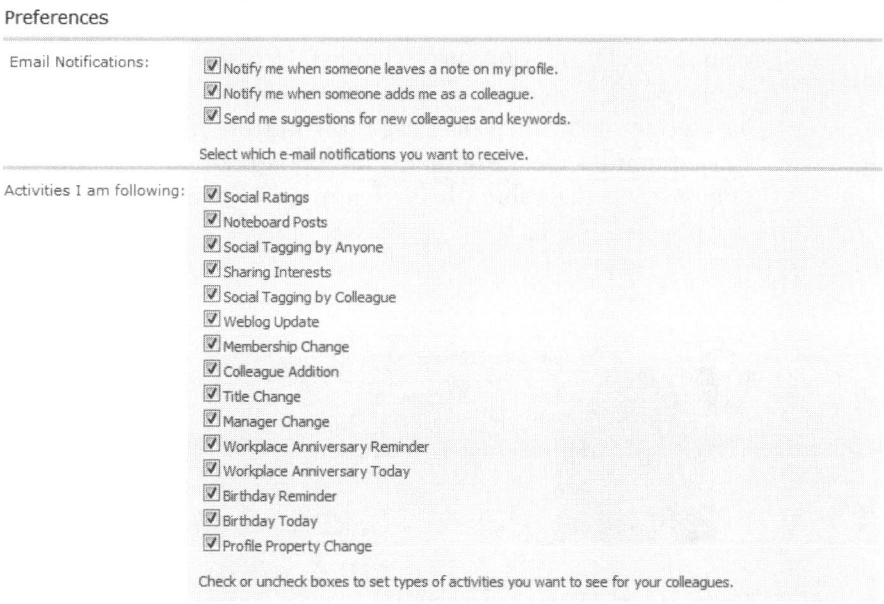

Preferences

Email Notifications:	☑ Notify me when someone leaves a note on my profile.
	☑ Notify me when someone adds me as a colleague.
	☑ Send me suggestions for new colleagues and keywords.
	Select which e-mail notifications you want to receive.
Activities I am following:	☑ Social Ratings
	☑ Noteboard Posts
	☑ Social Tagging by Anyone
	☑ Sharing Interests
	☑ Social Tagging by Colleague
	☑ Weblog Update
	☑ Membership Change
	☑ Colleague Addition
	☑ Title Change
	☑ Manager Change
	☑ Workplace Anniversary Reminder
	☑ Workplace Anniversary Today
	☑ Birthday Reminder
	☑ Birthday Today
	☑ Profile Property Change
	Check or uncheck boxes to set types of activities you want to see for your colleagues.

Figure 7-3 User profile: Preferences

The My Site also includes an area where users can post brief status updates similar to Facebook or Twitter. These "opt in" status updates are combined with the automatically tracked updates to provide an activity monitor that allows community members to keep track of work product and progress. Your governance plan should include guidance to help new micro-bloggers create meaningful posts. One suggestion is to ask users to "narrate their work," posting updates when they complete a major activity or are struggling with a problem. This might encourage colleagues to comment on or add value to someone else's activities. You may also suggest that people post help questions to their status updates when they are struggling with difficult problems. People are basically wired to be helpful. If someone notices a status post from a colleague who clearly needs help, it's very likely that she will respond, just as she would on her private social network or if she'd been asked for help in a more "traditional" way. Not all users will be immediately comfortable with micro-blogging, and that is okay. Over time, users will identify which updates are most useful and will find opportunities to share. Figure 7-4 shows the status updates on the user profile. To update status, the user simply starts typing in the conversation area. The simple user experience and concept that is familiar to users of Facebook and Twitter can help gain adoption and successful outcomes from the use of this feature. In Chapter 1 we talk about developing a metrics program to formally measure the success of your SharePoint solution. When your community features have been deployed for a few months, poll users to find examples of where people have gotten new ideas or received help from a status post. These success story examples (real examples, not "potential" stories) can help not only demonstrate the value of this feature, but can help encourage adoption (try it, you'll like it) from new users.

Figure 7-4 My Site: Status update

Ratings and Tags

Ratings and Tags allow users to create content on any site where these features have been enabled. Your governance plan should help users understand when and why to add this content.

Social tags allow users to add their own personal metadata to content in the solution, which supplements the authoritative content assigned by content owners. Users can say, "I like it," by simply selecting the content they want to tag and clicking the "I Like It" smiley face tag in the upper-right corner of the page, or they can add their own personal terms by clicking the "Tags and Notes" icon. The tag might describe what the content contains or what it does or just the user's personal term for the topic covered by the content. Because these tags are intended to be personal, you don't want your governance plan to be overly directive about what users should do. However, considering that social tags can have an impact on search (they can boost search results and are displayed in the refinement panel in search results), you should provide examples of meaningful tags on your organization's content so that users understand their value and how they work.

Ratings are more controversial and probably deserve more thorough attention in your governance plan. Scott shares a story about how Microsoft created an internal knowledge base for employees to share intellectual property (IP) with their colleagues. They enabled ratings on the site, but at first, people were reluctant to apply the ratings because they felt that the they were about rating their colleagues, not the work, and people were reluctant to rate. Eventually, the deployment team changed the guidance around rating and asked users to rate "Is this content IP?" rather than the implied "What do you think about this content?" (which users interpreted as "What do you think about this author?"). The change in direction gave users permission and guidance to be more subjective about what they were rating, and participation increased. Both ratings and tags are discussed in more detail in the remaining sections of this chapter.

Blogs and Wikis

Many of the barriers to social computing described earlier are expressed in the context of blogs and wikis. The objections rarely play out with any negative consequences, but they are very real to the executives who express them. Your governance plan should explicitly address policies and content for blogs and wikis, including how content will be maintained.

Wikipedia provides an excellent resource for governance policies for enterprise wikis that are known as the "5 pillars of Wikipedia." These rules define how conflicts will be resolved and prescribe a code of conduct for all contributors.[2] Consider assigning a "moderator" for each wiki site. The moderator is an individual who agrees to be accountable for providing oversight to the wiki site, periodically checking to see that content pages are complete, that the site's organization still makes sense, and that content is appropriate.

Define a "Do-able" Pilot Project

A small deployment pilot for an audience predisposed to adopt new technologies is a good way to create a successful outcome for SharePoint community features. Your goal is to find a community that is going to create an initial critical mass of information with a well-connected and vocal leader. As you deploy more broadly, users will see and benefit from this initial content and hopefully be inspired to contribute themselves, especially if your vocal leader uses every opportunity to talk about the benefits. Building support from the ground up allows you to attract rather than mandate participation. Look for a community that may already be using social technologies as a good candidate for your pilot.

Prepare a Launch and Communications Plan

Use the feedback from your pilot to help plan an organization-wide launch plan. Be sure to capture user stories focused on how the community features helped them do their jobs more effectively. Use these stories in your communications activities to help spread the value proposition across the enterprise. Consider how you might want to use incentives to drive initial participation. One organization offered prizes for users who completed their profiles by a certain date.

As discussed in Chapter 10, "Making Search Work: Content, People, Data," the most successful solutions are designed so employees can use them easily without the need for special training. However, you can't assume that everyone in the organization will be familiar with social technologies and how to use them effectively, even if the technology itself is very intuitive. Your launch plan will need to ensure that users understand the value

---

2. http://en.wikipedia.org/wiki/Five_pillars_of_Wikipedia.

proposition for the technologies as well as how to use them to help them be more effective. For example, encourage users to use status updates to narrate their work and share major milestones. Make sure users understand the best practices for tags and ratings that are described later in this chapter.

Consider that the successful adoption of most of the SharePoint community features requires the organization to change—and for individual users to change the way they work. Therefore, it's especially important to be patient. You may be able to launch your pilot in a very short period of time, but the organizational and cultural changes required to sustain a social computing initiative take time, sometimes as long as several years, and you may need to wait a while before their use becomes pervasive. At the same time, remember that you don't need 100% participation to achieve value with social technologies.

Social Networking: Engaging People

My Sites are the hub for interacting with people in SharePoint. The My Site is an individual SharePoint site where users can customize both content and design and specify some of their contact information. In SharePoint 2010, the My Site has been significantly and dramatically enhanced to provide additional social networking functionality. Each user has "full control" over his My Site, which is a secure site that exposes his profile, status, and other attributes but where the user has control over whether or not most personal attributes are publicly available or kept private. To set up a My Site for the first time, users click My Content in their profiles.

User Profile

The profile, as discussed in the preceding section, is where users can declare both their interests and expertise so that other people in the organization can make connections or just learn more about them. The more information a user chooses to share in their profile, the richer the potential social network and professional relationships he can build. Figure 7-5 shows an example of a user profile on a My Site. Some organizations are not comfortable allowing or encouraging users to attach personal information to their profiles. Before you encourage users to add their interests in basket weaving, rock climbing, and extreme sports, be sure to verify that you are not violating any privacy laws or norms. However, unless there are legal reasons for not including personal information in the user profile, our best advice is to go for it—allow users to add what they are comfortable sharing. Don't make a big deal about it and don't try to decide what types of interests are appropriate—trust that your users will know what is good to share with their work colleagues and what might best be kept private. You can also trust that the community will quickly identify if someone has shared something that is not appropriate. Social privacy norms are changing, and what might not be comfortable for a 50-something to share might be very comfortable and accepted for a 20-something. One thing we have repeatedly heard from organizations that have deployed My Sites as an "experiment" to see how users react is that one of the most valued parts of the My Site is the interest profile—people like being able to learn more about their colleagues based on their expressed interests.

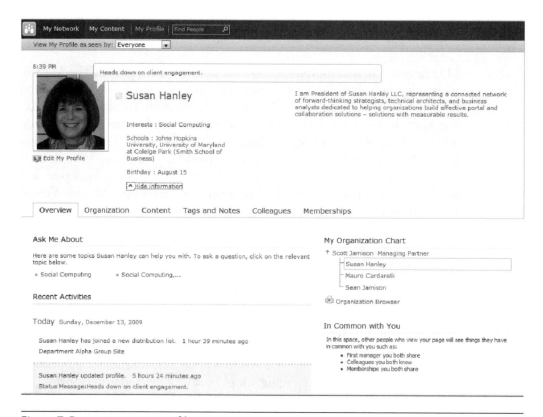

Figure 7-5 My Site: User Profile

Status Updates and Activity Feeds

Status updates allow users to describe "what's happening." Status updates are not intended to be used for verbose activity descriptions, but rather quick updates of milestones or tasks that let others know what someone is working on or thinking about. Consider asking team members working on key projects to post brief status updates once or twice a day so that colleagues know where they are on tasks without having to send an e-mail or make a phone call to check in.

While status updates allow users to deliberately share a status, activity feeds monitor users' actions so that their colleagues can see not just what they explicitly share, but what actions they have taken, such as adding tags, updating their profiles, or rating documents. By adjusting the privacy settings when you take an action monitored by the activity feed feature (for example, by selecting the Private box on a tag or note), users can control what shows up in their activity feeds. By editing the Preferences in their profiles (see Figure 7-3), users can choose which types of activities they wish to monitor for others. This capability ensures that users can manage both the privacy of what they do and the information that they want to see—two important capabilities that may help eliminate user adoption barriers in your organization.

Figure 7-6 shows an example of some activity feeds in Sue's sample profile. Notice how the activity feed includes a direct link to both the content that she's tagged and the terms that she has used. Clicking the content link takes the user to the document or site that has been tagged or rated. Clicking the tag name takes the user to the tag profile, shown in Figure 7-7. This functionality allows users to connect to people and make connections between people and content, which adds context and credibility to information assets, increasing their value to individuals and the organization as a whole. The activity feeds let people stay in touch and also helps them know what is going on with their colleagues. In this way, activity feeds help achieve the objective of improving the way knowledge assets are leveraged in the organization.

Organization Browser

Traditionally, the most popular area of almost every organization's intranet is the company directory. People want to know basic contact information for their colleagues and where they fit in to the organization. SharePoint

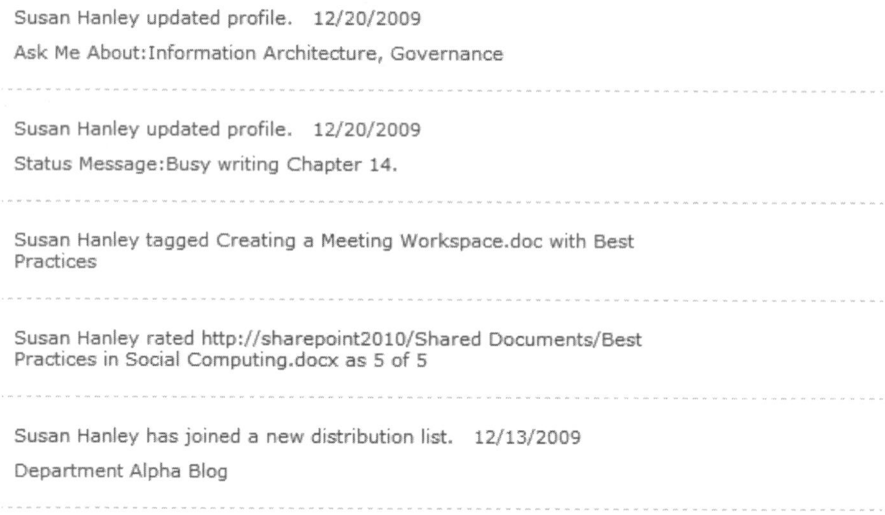
Susan Hanley updated profile. 12/20/2009
Ask Me About:Information Architecture, Governance
Susan Hanley updated profile. 12/20/2009
Status Message:Busy writing Chapter 14.
Susan Hanley tagged Creating a Meeting Workspace.doc with Best Practices
Susan Hanley rated http://sharepoint2010/Shared Documents/Best Practices in Social Computing.docx as 5 of 5
Susan Hanley has joined a new distribution list. 12/13/2009
Department Alpha Blog

Figure 7-6 Activity feed examples

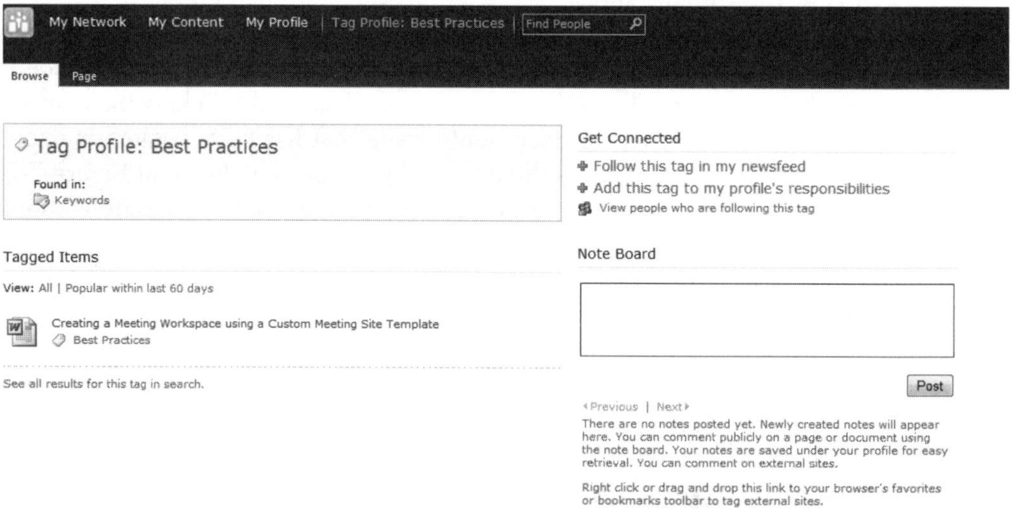
My Network
My Content
My Profile
Tag Profile: Best Practices
Find People
Browse
Page
Tag Profile: Best Practices
Found in:
Keywords
Get Connected
Follow this tag in my newsfeed
Add this tag to my profile's responsibilities
View people who are following this tag
Tagged Items
View: All | Popular within last 60 days
Creating a Meeting Workspace using a Custom Meeting Site Template
Best Practices
See all results for this tag in search.
Note Board
Post
Previous | Next
There are no notes posted yet. Newly created notes will appear here. You can comment publicly on a page or document using the note board. Your notes are saved under your profile for easy retrieval. You can comment on external sites.
Right click or drag and drop this link to your browser's favorites or bookmarks toolbar to tag external sites.

Figure 7-7 Tag profile

Figure 7-8 Organization browser

2010 adds a new "organization" feature that exposes the formal organization of the company in a visually compelling Silverlight display.

Figure 7-8 shows a simple organization browser. The "organization
picker" can be customized by the SharePoint administrator to show how
people are organized in many ways—by division, by product line, by
account, by department, or by location.

Content

The Content section of the profile allows users to add content to their personal sites. The Content area is essentially equivalent to a "private drive"
on a network share. By default, there are two very clearly labeled document libraries in the Content section: Personal Documents and Shared
Documents. The Personal Documents library is automatically created with

unique permissions and is only visible to the user and the SharePoint administrator. The Shared Documents library is "open"—documents posted to this library are displayed on the user's public home page. One perceived risk of moving from "private drives" to personal sites is the problem of inadequately trained users exposing personal or other sensitive content by mistake. These two libraries, with security "predefined," help minimize that risk while providing the benefit of helping to engage people with shared content.

Memberships

The Memberships section of the profile shows the sites where a user has member (contributor) privileges. Figure 7-9 shows an example of the Memberships tab of the My Site. By selecting Edit Memberships (see Figure 7-10), users can select categories in which to group their sites and edit privacy settings to choose to share or not share any group memberships with their colleagues.

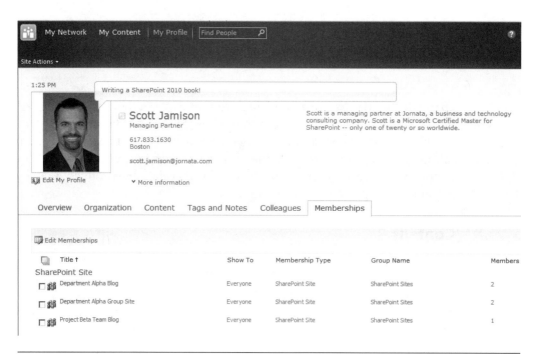

Figure 7-9 Memberships

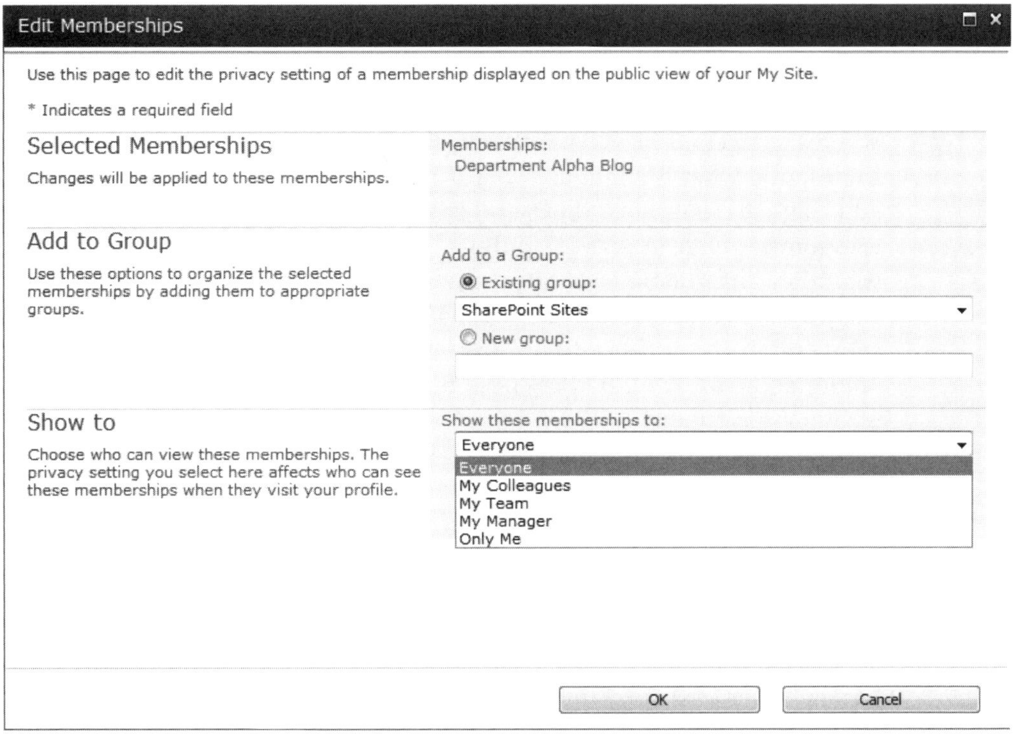

Figure 7-10 Edit Memberships

Social Data: Enhancing Value with User Contributed Content

Ratings, tags, and notes allow users to contribute content to SharePoint even when they don't have update privileges for a site. This "social" data is not meant to be authoritative; it is meant to be "value-added" content to help add context for users. These new features bring a new level of user participation and interaction to your SharePoint solution, allowing users to not only discover content in new ways but also to understand what others think about that content. While ratings and tags (which include bookmarks and notes) are both forms of social data, your organization may have very different comfort levels with these two types of social data. It's important to remember that you don't have to implement these features all at once or all together.

Tags and Notes

Tagging content is the assignment of descriptive words or categories—terms that mean something to the person doing the tagging. When users add a tag to content in SharePoint, they are essentially adding metadata to describe what it contains, what it does, or what it is about. When they add tags to content, they are extending the formal organizational taxonomy, which improves content "findability." Tags help expand your solution's information architecture over time and, most importantly, extend the responsibility for evolving the information architecture to everyone in the organization. This helps associate content with new and emerging terms even before these terms are formally added to the organization's taxonomy.

Social tagging has a lot of hype—both for SharePoint 2010 and on the Internet in general. Despite the hype, few people actually do it, so even if your organization is reluctant to deploy this feature, adding it doesn't necessarily mean anyone is going to use it! Why should you consider encouraging the use of this functionality? Because effective collaboration is not just about getting content in; it's also about getting content out. Adding user-defined tags helps narrow searches or clarify search results so users have a better chance at finding what they need. You don't have to encourage users to think about the rest of the organization when they tag—I can add tags for myself—so *I* can find the content later. If it helps everyone else, that's okay too, but you can encourage users to think about tagging as "it's all about me" functionality. In this way, you don't have to spend too much time worrying about whether or not people are tagging everything correctly; a user-defined "folksonomy" doesn't have to be perfect because it is meant to be personal. In some industries, such as pharmaceutical or legal firms, a carefully planned and monitored taxonomy, vetted by content experts, is absolutely critical. However, don't let that scare you off—you can easily "tip toe" into the world of social tagging; social tags do not add authoritative metadata, but they do enrich your content with informal insights that can help make sure that relevant content is discovered, even in industries that also have formal taxomomies.

As described earlier, the simplest form of tagging is the "I like it" tag. Tagging a page or document with "I like it" might help you find it later or inform your colleagues of content you find useful, but it's not nearly as helpful as assigning a more descriptive tag to a document or page by using the Tags & Notes feature. When you select an item and click Tags & Notes, you can quickly see how other users have publicly tagged the content

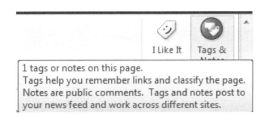

Figure 7-11 Hovering or clicking Tags & Notes quickly identifies whether an item has a tag

(see Figure 7-11). (Note that because users can elect to make any tag private, for their own personal use, you can only see "public" tags.)

When you select an item to tag yourself and start to enter a tag, you will see a list of suggested tags based on how you or others have previously used similar terms. As shown in Figure 7-12, when you tag content, you can see who else has tagged the content, what terms they used, and when they did the tagging.

Tagging a document is pretty straightforward—hover over the document until the selection check box appears, select the box, and then click Tags & Notes. To tag a SharePoint page or site, simply click the Tags & Notes icon. However, it is also possible to tag external content—for example, an external Internet site. To tag an external site, right-click Tags & Notes and select Add to Favorites. When you are on the external site you want to tag, click Tags and Note Board in your browser Favorites to see the prompt to enter your tag. As shown in Figure 7-12, each user has the option to make an individual tag private by selecting the Private: Do not show my tags on this item to others check box. If you initially create a public tag and then later make it private, it will be removed from your profile and activity feed, and other users will no longer see the tag. One key "feature" to keep in mind: If you tag a document created by someone else or someone tags a document that you created and you rename the document, the hyperlink in the activity feed or tag profile referencing the document will break. This doesn't mean that you should never rename a document, but it does mean that there can be implications for users when you do so.

Figure 7-13 shows how to associate a note with content. Notes are associated with content just like tags, but notes do not affect search results and do not become part of the term store associated with your site. Notes add context to content, and while they are technically part of the metadata associated with your content, they are used to *inform* users about the

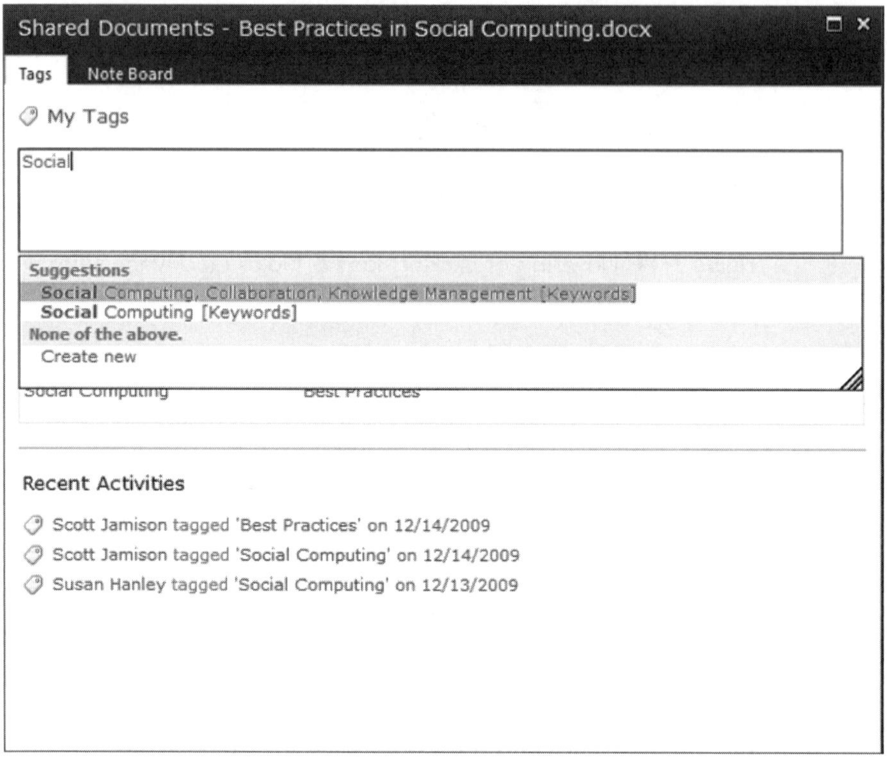

Figure 7-12 Entering a tag

content, not to help them *find* content using browse or search. (Refer to Chapter 5, "Planning Your Information Architecture," for more information about how tags are leveraged as part of your site's information architecture.) Adding a note to content will show up in your activity feed, but if you delete a note from a piece of content, it does not delete the activity feed; in other words, even if you delete the note, the addition of the note shows up in your activity feed but not the activity of deleting the note.

A cool, new built-in Tag Cloud Web Part for SharePoint 2010 (see Figure 7-14) allows you to visually show tags on a site in a compelling way. In the tag cloud, the importance of a tag is shown with font size—more frequently used tags are larger. Each tag term is a hyperlink to the tag profile.

Tag clouds don't necessarily offer a better or more intuitive way to find content. When they are used appropriately, tag clouds can help provide site users with an instant illustration of the main topics on a site or in the

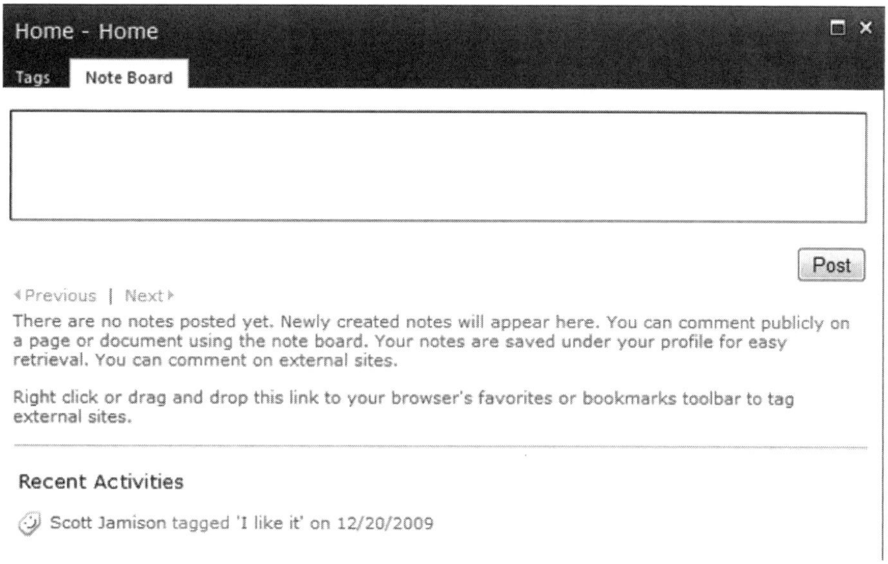

Home - Home

□ ×

Tags | Note Board

[ ]

Post

‹Previous | Next›

There are no notes posted yet. Newly created notes will appear here. You can comment publicly on a page or document using the note board. Your notes are saved under your profile for easy retrieval. You can comment on external sites.

Right click or drag and drop this link to your browser's favorites or bookmarks toolbar to tag external sites.

Recent Activities

Scott Jamison tagged 'I like it' on 12/20/2009

Figure 7-13 Entering a note

Tag Cloud

Social Computing Best Practices I like it Portal Enterprise 2.0

Figure 7-14 Tag cloud

case of your My Site, the main topics that you have cared enough to tag. The main advantage of tag clouds is that they showcase the most important or popular topics dynamically, which is not possible with more traditional static navigational approaches.

Ratings

The ratings feature allows users to rate content and then exposes the ratings as metadata that can be sorted, filtered, and queried. Adding ratings to content theoretically makes it easier for users to find high-quality content. In practice, if you choose to enable this feature, you will need to be sure that users understand what should be rated and what criteria should be used to assign a rating.

Ratings are supported for the following items:

- List items
- Document library items
- Publishing pages

The default values for "ratings" are between 1 and 5. Ratings are stored in the same database as social tags. Ratings share some information with social tags, such as user and item URL. However, ratings data is stored in a separate table in the database.

To use ratings in a specific Site Collection, you first activate the ratings service. Activating the ratings feature adds two Site Collections: Average Rating and Rating Count in a Column group called Ratings Columns. When these Columns are enabled, you can:

- Add the Columns to a Content Type and then add them to all items that have that Content Type.
- Add the Columns manually to enable rating content on a specific list or library.
- Add the Columns automatically to a list or library by using the Enable Rating setting (see Figure 7-15).

Ratings are off by default in lists and libraries. To enable items to be rated, the list or library owner will need to set the Allow items in this list to be rated? list setting. Enabling ratings adds the ratings fields (average rating and number of ratings) to the Content Types currently on the list and to the default view. You will need to add at least the Rating Column to other list views if you want users to be able to see or rate content in a Web Part or any other view. If you add new Content Types later and they don't

Rating settings	Allow items in this list to be rated?
Specify whether or not items in this list can be rated.	○ Yes ⦿ No
Enabling ratings adds the ratings fields (average rating and number of ratings) to the content types currently on this list and to the default view. If you add new content types later and they don't already contain the ratings fields, you will need to add the ratings fields to them either manually or by returning to this page and updating the list. Disabling ratings removes the fields from the list (but not from the underlying content types) and from the default view.	
	OK Cancel

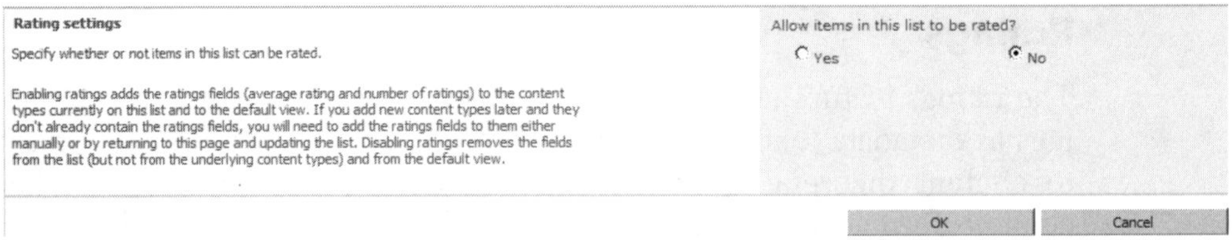

Figure 7-15 Enable Rating setting

already contain the ratings fields, you will need to add the ratings fields to them either manually or by returning to Rating Settings field and updating the list. Disabling ratings removes the fields from the list (but not from the underlying Content Types) and from the default view.

Users add ratings to an item in a document or list by dragging the cursor across the stars (see Figure 7-16) until they settle on the desired rating. The same star display shows the average rating and is also used to submit a rating. The average rating shows up in blue on the star display. As the user pauses over a star, the star changes to yellow to reflect the rating the user submits when the mouse is clicked. If the user moves the mouse off the stars, the control displays the average rating again. Some users may find this behavior to be a little confusing at first, so be prepared to explain what happens when they submit their ratings. Once a rating is submitted, the display reverts back to the average rating, so a user may wonder if his rating "stuck." To see how you personally rated an item, you move the cursor back over the star display and a window pops up to show your personal rating.

When the User Profile Service Application—Social Rating Synchronization Job Timer Job—runs (part of Central Administration), it will synchronize ratings across the implementation. This means that ratings may not be visible to others immediately. As additional ratings are added to content, the average rating shown will change, dynamically reflecting how users have rated the content.

While rating content is simple and works pretty much the same way it does on familiar sites such as Amazon.com, you will need to ensure that users understand your objectives with content ratings. As mentioned earlier, you need to clearly define the context for ratings—do you want users to rate how much they like the content (which might be appropriate when you are asking users to help choose among several alternatives), or do you want users to rate the value of the content for a specific purpose? Be sure that your document library description clearly tells users what ratings mean in the context of your library if you choose to enable this feature.

Rating (0-5)

Figure 7-16 Rating scale

Social Sites: Providing a Structure for Collaborative Conversations

Blogs and wikis have been enhanced significantly in SharePoint 2010. When a user posts an entry to a blog, it appears in the Recent Activity section of the user's My Site, increasing the opportunity for connections and collaboration. Blogs and wikis help achieve collaboration and knowledge transfer objectives in many ways, but most importantly, they help ensure that the right conversations happen at the right times. Both types of sites help create conversations, but blogs are typically for one-to-many conversations, and wikis are typically for many-to-many conversations.

Blogs

Each user in the organization can have her personal blog linked to her My Site. This makes it easy for people to find the blog and easy for the user to post new entries. Attaching the blog to the My Site helps to ensure that the blog is the user's authentic voice. "Management" blogs written by people in the Marketing department are generally perceived as propaganda, and we don't recommend using blogs in this way. A better alternative for Marketing messages is news. That said, SharePoint 2010 makes it very easy for you to set up a "team blog," which can be a great way of posting progress updates (the SharePoint at Microsoft team has a team blog at http://blogs.msdn.com/sharepoint) and insights for departments, project teams, or, if done authentically, your executive team. Team blogs are typically created as subsites of a team or department site. Our general rule for blogs of any type: Keep them authentic.

The blog template in SharePoint 2010 is new and includes blog-specific navigation. For example, you can sort posts by category and date. There is also a new "About this Blog" area where the blog author(s) can provide an introduction and purpose for the blog. Encourage all blog owners to use this feature to describe their blogs. Remember that context is the key to successful collaboration, and the more context blog authors provide, the more useful their posts will be to others.

As with the rest of SharePoint 2010, one of the first new features you will notice in the blog template is the ribbon interface. One of the most significant blog improvements is the ease of entering rich media (both images and video) to a blog post.

The first time a user creates a blog (by default, creating a blog is a part of the My Content area of the My Site), he sees the screen in Figure 7-17. The instructions are self-explanatory, and you really shouldn't need to provide much guidance. Adding a post is also intuitive.

Figure 7-18 shows the user interface for creating a new blog post. By default, content approval is enabled for blog posts, but posts by the blog author are automatically approved. (We're not quite sure about why this is the case because it doesn't seem to mean anything.) As with any list, you can turn off content approval in List Settings. When you create a new blog from your My Site, the appropriate security is enabled for you—only you can add posts, and anyone with read access to your My Site can add comments. Both posts and comments are stored in lists where you can edit permissions and add workflow.

As described here, you can also create a blog site from a team site. When you create a blog site from a team site, you will need to set permissions for the blog manually. To do this, navigate to the Comments list and set unique permissions so that site visitors can add comments, and do the same to the Posts list if only a subset of site contributors can post blog entries. In a team blog, you may want to initiate some type of content approval workflow for posts if you are concerned about representing "authoritative" content in the blog.

Figure 7-17 Creating a new blog

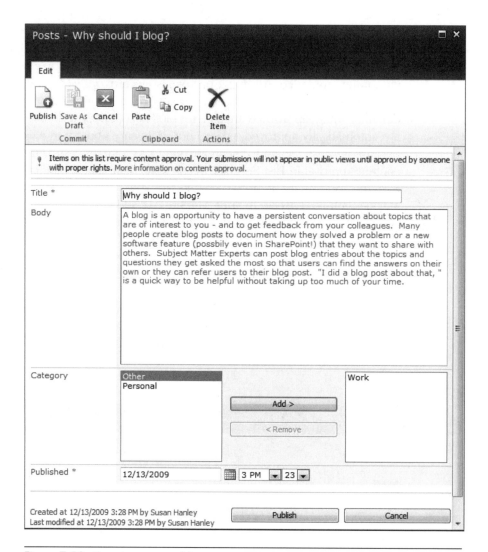

Figure 7-18 Creating a new blog post

Wikis

The success of social computing features depends on participation, not technology. Wikis are technology that help users participate without any formal knowledge of Web programming or even Microsoft Word. While blogs are designed for more structured knowledge exchange, wikis enable a more flexible collaborative experience by allowing every participant to have an equal "voice."

In SharePoint 2010, there are two varieties of wikis:

- **Team sites**. In SharePoint 2010, the Team Site template is essentially a wiki.
- **Enterprise wiki sites**. The enterprise wiki feature in Microsoft SharePoint Server 2010 provides a template that adds page rating, Managed Metadata, and customization capabilities. You can use Microsoft SharePoint Designer 2010 to customize page layouts and implement specific and consistent branding by changing master pages.

Team Sites

The Team Site template in SharePoint 2010 is essentially a wiki. The home page of the team site can be edited using the same functionality used to edit any wiki page. This means that users can see a live preview of changes that they are making as they make them. Figure 7-19 shows the home page of a team site in Edit mode (note the highlighted editing items in the ribbon). To update the welcome message, all you need to do is type; there is no longer a need to open a content editor Web Part and use the rich text editor to change content because the wiki page itself is essentially a rich text editor. In addition to using the wiki Web Edit functionality to edit the team site, users can add Web Parts using the Insert link in the ribbon (see Figure 7-20) to create a rich user interface that combines the features

Figure 7-19 Editing the home page of a team site uses a wiki interface

of a SharePoint 2007 team site with the superior wiki editing experience in SharePoint 2010. This makes it easy to create visually compelling Web pages with little or no knowledge of HTML and combine the structured content of a Web Part with the flexible editing experience of a wiki.

The new Team Site template provides a flexible way to create content (with the wiki editor) that also allows you to take advantage of the structure and security in a more traditional collaboration site. In a more typical wiki environment, all users have both read and write privileges. However, in a wiki-based team site, the site owner (user with Full Control privileges) can designate which users can edit content and which users can only read content. In addition, site owners can view previous versions of a wiki entry to see when and by whom changes were made as shown in Figure 7-21. As with document versions, you can reinstantiate prior versions of wiki pages if necessary. Essentially, the new Team Site template supports shared editing but with more control than an enterprise wiki site.

Other site templates, such as the Group Work Site, do not have a wiki page as a home page. However, if you enable the Wiki Page Home Page feature on your site, you can automatically create a wiki home page similar to the team site.

Enterprise Wikis

An enterprise wiki (see Figure 7-22) combines the basic features of team sites with additional features such as page ratings. To create an enterprise wiki, you need to ensure that Publishing features are enabled for your Site Collection. If you anticipate that the enterprise wiki will have a lot of traffic and content (for example, for an enterprise-wide acronym database), then you should consider configuring it as a single Site Collection and perhaps

Figure 7-20 Insert ribbon on the team site home page

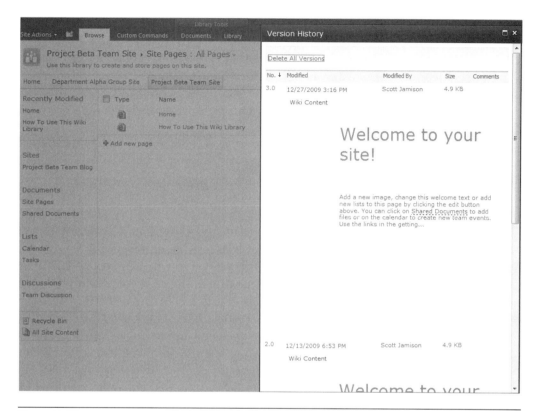

Figure 7-21 View prior versions of a wiki page

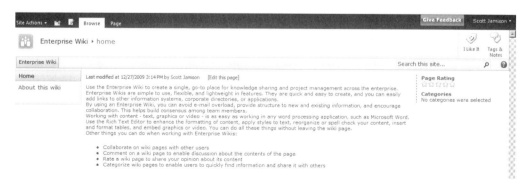

Figure 7-22 Enterprise wiki home page

also a single, dedicated SQL Server database. You can also create an enterprise wiki as a subsite of an existing site if you want to take advantage of the wiki editing features but do not anticipate a large amount of content. Once you have created an enterprise wiki, you cannot convert it or migrate it to the standard wiki format on a team site without using custom code. Therefore, you need to be sure that an enterprise wiki is the right site template for your site.

"We should be using wikis" is not a good enough reason to implement an enterprise wiki site. As discussed throughout this book, you should select both features and functionality based on the business problem you are trying to solve, not because the feature sounds good or is being hyped as Web 2.0. An enterprise wiki is a good solution when you want multiple users to contribute and update to a shared repository. For example, you might want to use an enterprise wiki to enable employees to contribute content to a shared repository of tips or ideas for new products. The most successful wiki sites are relatively unstructured, so if you decide that you need more structure for knowledge sharing, consider using a custom list or a team site to share content.

As with any SharePoint site, you need to carefully consider who is allowed to contribute content to an enterprise wiki. You can certainly use an enterprise wiki to share updates to content that not everyone can update—for example, an HR manual database that can only be edited by users in HR. Even though this type of site should have limited users with edit privileges, the wiki template may still be appropriate because of the ease with which nontechnical users can create Web pages. For shared wiki sites where many users can edit, you may also want to consider assigning a "wiki moderator" to periodically review the content of the enterprise wiki, especially as the site gets up and running because you will not have the benefit of shared corrections and updates until multiple users have an opportunity to review and update content. Remember: If you start to identify a requirement for more control and selective access as you plan your enterprise wiki, you will want to seriously consider whether an enterprise wiki is, in fact, the right solution to solve your business problem.

As discussed earlier in this chapter, you need to plan your governance model carefully for an enterprise wiki site, probably more so than for any other site type, because with shared editing capabilities, you have a greater risk of conflict—where one user edits a page and then another user changes it, potentially resulting in a "flame war." The publishing infrastructure provides several ways to control content, including assigning permissions or using a workflow to add an approval process for wiki entries. However, adding an approval process to your wiki site may discourage users from contributing content, so you will need to carefully plan before you deploy your wiki site.

Considering that editing and contributing to a wiki will likely be an unfamiliar task for many users, be sure to incorporate a training and communications plan for your enterprise wiki site. Deploying an enterprise wiki only creates meaningful value when multiple people are engaged and contributing. Therefore, it's a good idea to get some early adopter users to add "starter content" to any enterprise wiki before you launch to the rest of the organization.

Key Points

As you think about how you will "get social" in your SharePoint deployment, remember:

- Using and benefitting from social computing (Web 2.0) functionality in SharePoint 2010 often requires improvements in organizational information competencies, especially the ability to distinguish authoritative versus speculative or opinion-based content. Be sure to incorporate educating users in this core competency as part of your social computing deployment plan.
- As with any other new technology, to be successful with social computing, *you need to have a business problem to solve*. Be sure that your SharePoint strategy includes business problems that can be solved with social computing features. Reread Chapter 1 as well as the first section of this chapter for business ideas you can leverage.
- Social computing features can be both fun and also provide a compelling way to encourage collaboration and sharing. Don't be afraid to go slowly with "baby steps" as you deploy social computing functionality in your organization. Identify early adopter people and projects and take the time to collect user stories that build both the business case and value proposition for these features.
- Don't allow perceived risks to stop you from trying this functionality. Provide basic ground rules, plan carefully, and remember that it's really hard to find any good examples of horror stories of social computing disasters inside the enterprise. Unlike the public

Internet, if inappropriate or inaccurate content gets posted, you can easily take it down. Moreover, if you are careful about ensuring that your users have the appropriate information literacy skill to distinguish between authoritative and opinion content, your actual risk should be minimized.

- Don't try to look for hard and fast ROI on your social computing investment, but look for progress toward your overall business goals, which might include a reduction in e-mail traffic or an improved business process.

- Above all, be patient. Organizational change takes time. Plan a persistent communications plan (refer to Chapter 9, "Getting Ready to Launch: Planning for Training and Communications") and tolerate a few mistakes—it may not be easy to get adoption of every feature, so you may have to try a few different approaches.

CHAPTER 8

PLANNING YOUR SECURITY MODEL

Planning security for your solution is about balancing and optimizing the various security elements for all of the people who will use the solution, including content contributors, content users, and administrators who manage and maintain security groups. It also involves defining a model that works for the current business requirements but is also defined well enough to grow and be altered as requirements and content change. There is no single best way to design security and manage security groups. Each business scenario is different. Because the risks associated with getting your security model wrong are pretty big—two main issues come to mind: 1) not allowing appropriate access and 2) allowing inappropriate access—we often find ourselves suggesting that planning security should come with the same kind of warning you see on television shows with crazy stunts: "Don't try this at home." In other words, if this is the first time you are implementing security for SharePoint, it, try to get support from someone who has in-depth knowledge of SharePoint security best practices. In this chapter, we share as many of these best practices as we can, but it's really important to remember that almost every planning decision has to be carefully considered from multiple perspectives to arrive at the best solution for the situation. If you delegate design privileges for sites or site collections within your solution, you need to remember that it's not enough to train "site designers" in information architecture best practices; they must also understand how SharePoint security works and best practices for both creating and maintaining a security model or plan. In one of our client organizations, users are not given new sites or site collections until they prepare and document a security plan for their sites that can be reviewed with a senior-level solution architect. This approach is one that might be worth emulating because it ensures that a "site designer," working with an experienced information architect or security specialist, collectively define the security model for the site or solution. In another organization, site administrators are required to attend internal training to ensure they understand both SharePoint site administration and, specifically, security best practices before they can assume full control of a single SharePoint site.

Note   There is no single best way to design security and manage security groups. Each business scenario is different. But users should be trained if you give them rights to administer security.

In this chapter, we discuss security planning from the perspective of the business owner of the solution. Some of the implementation tasks may require support from your technical solution administrator, but ultimately, planning security is a business responsibility, so that is the perspective we use to describe how to think about your security model. This may seem like an overwhelming task for nontechnical resources who perceive security management as something IT has always owned. It's not. Very much like a file system folder, security management in SharePoint is about determining who should and should not have access to various types of content. This chapter contains the following important sections:

- Overview of SharePoint Security Elements
- Defining and Documenting SharePoint Security
- Maintaining Your Security Model

Overview of SharePoint Security Elements

Securing SharePoint sites consists of granting *permissions* to *people* who usually belong to *groups* and then assigning those permissions to *securable objects*. Simple, right? We review each of these key security elements, which are shown in Figure 8-1, in the discussion that follows.

Securable Objects

Securable objects consist of all of the solution elements to which permissions can be applied. For example, you can apply permissions uniquely to a site collection, a subsite or site within a site collection, a list or library, a folder, or an individual item in a list or library. By default, permissions are inherited in your site hierarchy. For example, security permissions for the

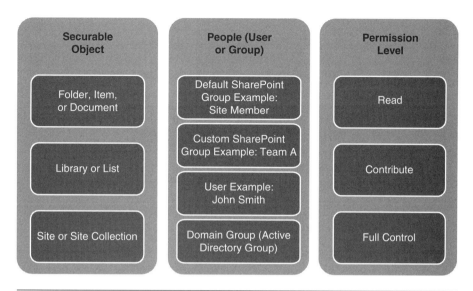

Figure 8-1 SharePoint security elements

top-level site are inherited by all subsites unless you explicitly "break" the inheritance. Permissions for the site are inherited in each object (list or library) on the site, and permissions for documents or list items are inherited from the library as shown in Figure 8-2.

As a general best practice, you always want to apply security at the "highest" level possible in your solution because it's easier to manage and maintain security in fewer places. The menu option used in SharePoint to apply unique permissions is Manage Permissions. It's easiest to understand how security permissions have been applied if permissions are the same for all elements of the site. This is clearly not always possible or practical, but it should be a guiding principle for your security model. Another reason for minimizing security exceptions in SharePoint is that the interface does not easily show you where permissions have been "broken."

Because there is no visual trigger that highlights a specific item (or list or site) that is secured differently than its peers, it can be difficult to quickly identify or change where item-level security has been applied. For example, if you are the site or list "owner" (with Full Control permissions), the only way to tell if a document has unique permissions is to examine permissions in the context of the document. If you need to update security permissions for individually secured items, you will need to update each item independently. If you are the "help desk" person trying to help an end user navigate to a list or library, you will need to remember that your permissions

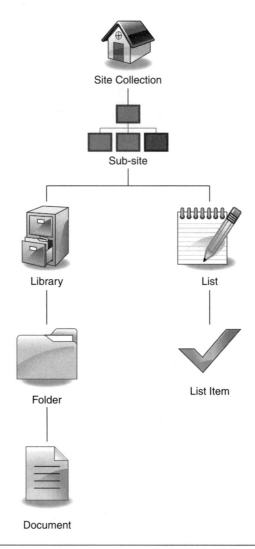

Figure 8-2 Permissions in SharePoint are "inherited" by default

may be different than the end user's permissions inside the same list or library, so you may see more or fewer documents than the person you are trying to assist. If you find that you have a security model that contains many item-level exceptions, you may want to consider documenting the exception in the item metadata or using a third-party solution for SharePoint security analysis and management.

Because security permissions are shared in all documents in a document library, if you have permissions to edit one document in a library, you have permissions to edit all documents in that library unless security has been "broken" (managed) for an individual document in the library. By editing we mean the ability to alter or delete those documents. If you store documents in folders, security in the folder is inherited into each document in the folder. This is one reason that you may want to use folders in a document library—to apply shared editing permissions to separate groups of documents and minimize the use of item-level permissions. This is one example of how security has an impact on your user experience and content topology. Introducing folders to manage collective security may solve authorization issues but may introduce an inconsistency in how content is managed (for example, other libraries may group documents by metadata). Consider this when balancing security management and usability.

Security Trimming

Any object that you secure in SharePoint is secure in both a "browse" and "search" scenario. If a document, list, or site has unique permissions, users who do not have access to the object will not see it in lists or search results. This is called *security trimming*. If an unauthorized user attempts to access this content directly via a URL link, that user will be denied access and prompted for alternate credentials. Security trimming also impacts search results. If two different users execute the same exact search, they may see different results based on their permissions. Security does not affect the relevancy of results; only the number of items that are returned.

Security Exceptions

While not technically part of SharePoint, Information Rights Management (IRM) offers another way to secure items stored in SharePoint. Microsoft IRM allows users to create a persistent set of access controls that live with the content itself rather than the location where the item is stored. IRM services can be used, for example, to protect an individual item from being downloaded or printed. When enabled, IRM security takes precedence in a list or library. For example, if an authorized user opens a rights-managed document from a document library where the IRM protection does not allow documents to be e-mailed, the user would not be able to send that document to another user, even if that person also has access to the SharePoint library. Instead, the person would have to go to the library and download the document directly. For more information about IRM and SharePoint 2010, refer to http://msdn.microsoft.com/en-us/library/ms458245(office.14).aspx.

There are several objects in SharePoint that *cannot* be secured. These include views, Audiences, Web Parts, and list Columns. Be sure to consider the following implications about which objects can be secured and how security is inherited:

- Because you cannot secure an individual view of a document library, you cannot use unique views to "get around" the fact that you cannot secure an individual Column in a list. For example, you may want to have a Column in a list that shows financial numbers that you don't want all users to see. You cannot secure the financial Columns using Manage Permissions or secure a *view* that doesn't display the financial Columns. In this scenario, you should consider using an alternate means of sharing the sensitive data. For example, one approach might be to use Excel to store the information and secure the Column in Excel. You can then use Excel services to display the information in a SharePoint Web Part. (See Chapter 13, "Making Business Intelligence Work," for a description of how to leverage Excel Services.) Another approach would be to show the protected data in a separate list, using an event handler to keep the two lists synchronized.

- You cannot secure a Web Part, but you can use an Audience to *target* a Web Part so that it only shows up to users who "belong" to that Audience. (Note that the content displayed in a Web Part is always secure, but security cannot be applied to the Web Part itself.) Targeting a Web Part using an Audience does not secure the content displayed in the Web Part—you must secure the object displayed in the Web Part by managing permissions on the content. This is an important distinction. Audiences are used to "personalize" presentation and effectively manage screen real estate with relevant content. Use Audience targeting to feature information, not to protect it.

People and Groups

In the context of SharePoint, "people" are individual users who need access to a SharePoint site and can be defined individually or as a member of a group. A group is a named collection of people (users) in SharePoint.

While individual people can be granted permissions inside of SharePoint, it is generally more desirable to first add that person to a group and then grant permissions to the group. That way, new users can be added in one place, the

SharePoint or Active Directory Group, and they will automatically get all the permissions associated with that group. This methodology is also helpful in two other ways: 1) it is easier to replicate security (for example, our new resource should have the same access as Mary) and 2) it reduces the amount of legacy security that accumulates over time (Tom has left the company but his name is still associated with a collection of sites across our environment).

In SharePoint, there are two types of groups that you will work with:

- A **Domain Group** is created outside SharePoint in Active Directory.[1] A Domain Group (also called an Active Directory or AD Group) is defined for the entire enterprise and can be used in any site collection in SharePoint or to manage access for other applications used by your organization. Domain Groups are generally created by a security administrator in your IT group, but some organizations allow business teams to request the creation of a new Domain Group that they can manage themselves. Domain Groups are most often created to represent persistent roles or geographic groups of people inside your organization. If you can, you should take advantage of existing, automatically maintained Domain Groups to assign permissions for your site. For example, if there is already a Domain Group for Managers and you have content or sites that are for Managers only, you should use this existing group in your site. When new managers are added or if someone is no longer a manager, you will not need to worry about (or be responsible for) adding or deleting them from the group. If your organization allows you to create Domain Groups that are not automatically populated, you may have to manage "comings and goings," but you will still only need to do so in one place. It is not always possible or practical to have an Active Directory group for individual sites in SharePoint. This is especially true if you are creating highly granular, low membership groups. You should not clutter AD with SharePoint-specific groups. You should also avoid creating AD groups that cannot be repurposed (that is, used in multiple security applications in and out of SharePoint). In these instances, you are better served leveraging SharePoint security groups.
- A **SharePoint Group** can be defined by a Site Collection Administrator or a user with Manage Permissions privileges and can

---

1. Active Directory is the Microsoft directory service used to manage access to a network and many applications including SharePoint. Active Directory includes profile information about the employee such as name and e-mail address. Individual entries in Active Directory are combined into Active Directory Groups.

be used to secure objects within a single site collection only. Groups created in SharePoint for one site collection can only be used within that individual site collection and must be separately created and maintained if needed in another site collection. All SharePoint Groups are created at the site collection level and are available to any subsite or other securable object in the site collection.

SharePoint Groups can include Active Directory Groups and/or individual users. However, SharePoint Groups cannot include other SharePoint Groups. There are two types of SharePoint Groups: Default Groups and Custom Groups. The primary advantage of SharePoint Groups is in situations when you chose to deviate from the inherited security of a parent site and assign unique permissions to a site. In this case, SharePoint will create the appropriate groups for Owners, Members, and Visitors, and the administrator can manage security by assigning membership for these groups.

Figure 8-3 summarizes the different types of security groups in SharePoint and describes the characteristics of each group.

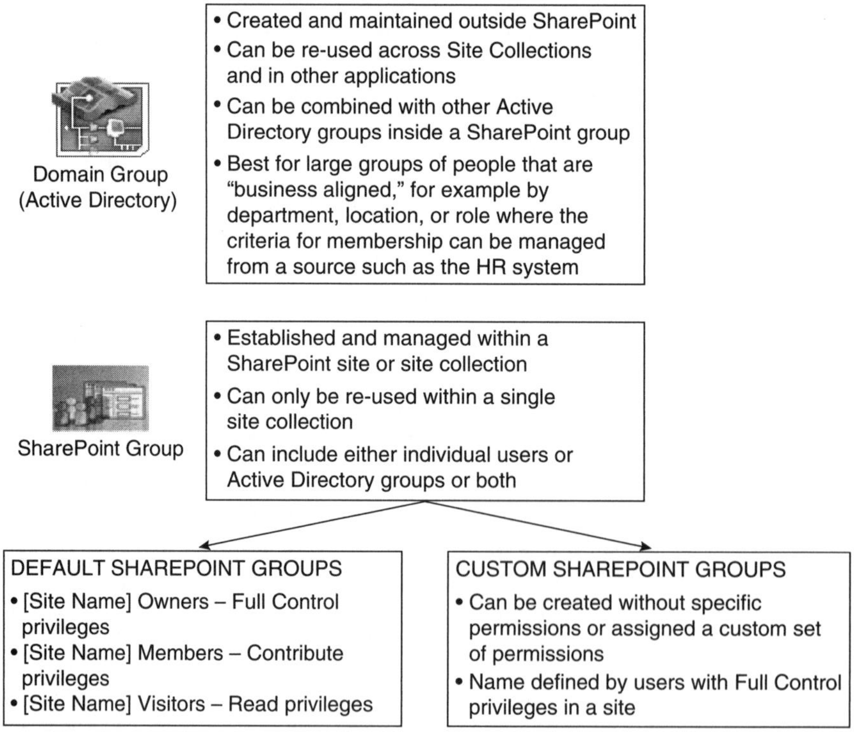

Domain Group
(Active Directory)

- Created and maintained outside SharePoint
- Can be re-used across Site Collections and in other applications
- Can be combined with other Active Directory groups inside a SharePoint group
- Best for large groups of people that are "business aligned," for example by department, location, or role where the criteria for membership can be managed from a source such as the HR system

SharePoint Group

- Established and managed within a SharePoint site or site collection
- Can only be re-used within a single site collection
- Can include either individual users or Active Directory groups or both

DEFAULT SHAREPOINT GROUPS
- [Site Name] Owners – Full Control privileges
- [Site Name] Members – Contribute privileges
- [Site Name] Visitors – Read privileges

CUSTOM SHAREPOINT GROUPS
- Can be created without specific permissions or assigned a custom set of permissions
- Name defined by users with Full Control privileges in a site

Figure 8-3 SharePoint Security Groups

Default SharePoint Groups

SharePoint provides several *default* SharePoint Groups for team sites as shown in Table 8-1. Each of these SharePoint Groups is associated with a default permission level. (Refer to the next section of this chapter for a detailed review of permissions and permission levels.)

Additional default security groups are created if you use templates other than the Team Site template in SharePoint or if you activate publishing features for a site. Table 8-2 shows the additional default SharePoint Groups provided in sites created with the Publishing template or when publishing features are enabled. You may enable publishing features for your site but decide that you do not need any of these security groups. If that is the case, you can leave these groups with no members. In most cases, we discourage the deletion of any default security groups as requirements may change and these groups may be brought to bear further in a site's evolution.

In addition, SharePoint includes several special users and groups for administering SharePoint sites:

- **Site Collection Administrators** have an "all-access pass" to every element of content and all site permissions. In addition, they are recorded as the contact for the site collection and can audit site content, enable site collection features, and monitor site and search usage. You cannot hide content from a Site Collection Administrator,

Table 8-1 SharePoint Groups and Default Permission Levels for Team Sites

Group Name	Default Permission Level
Owners	Assigned *Full Control* permission level for [Site Name]. Generally, there will be a small number of users in this group.
Designers	Assigned *Design* permission level for [Site Name]. You might use this group to give users permissions to design the structure of the site without giving them permission to assign security or create subsites. In practice, we don't find this default group used very often.
Members	Assigned *Contribute* permission level for [Site Name]. More users will be in this group. For team sites, it's likely that all eam members will also be included in the site's Members group.
Visitors	Assigned *Read* permission level for [Site Name]. Generally, the largest number of users will be in this group.
Viewers	Assigned *View* permission level for [Site Name].

Table 8-2 SharePoint Groups and Default Permission Levels for Publishing Sites

Group Name	Default Permission Level
Restricted Readers	Assigned *Restricted Read* permission level for [Site Name]. This group is rarely used and is most often leveraged when users should have a very limited visibility into presentation page content only.
Style Resource Readers	Assigned permissions that allow the member to have read access to the Master Page Gallery and Restricted Read to the Style Library. This group is used for design team members who may want to see associated styling elements.
Quick Deploy Users	Assigned permissions that allow the user to contribute to the Quick Deploy Items library plus Limited Access to the rest of the site.
Approvers	Assigned *Approve* permission level for [Site Name]. This group is used for content publishing purposes. Members have the authority to see, validate, publish, or reject/propose content changes prior to public consumption.
Hierarchy Managers	Assigned *Manage Hierarchy* permission level for [Site Name].

so if you have content that needs to be visible only to members of the executive committee, you will need to designate a member of the executive committee as the Site Collection Administrator. You need to designate individual people, not a group, as Site Collection Administrators, with the ideal number being more than one, but no more than a handful of users. It is recommended that Site Collection Administrators (or any administrator) be named users and not service accounts. Using service accounts eliminates auditing capabilities as you can't track changes to specific resources.

- **Farm Administrators** control which users can manage settings for the server farm. By default, Farm Administrators do not have access to site content, though they can take ownership of a site if they want to view content. This group is used only in Central Administration; you won't see this group in any individual site collection.

- **Administrators** have the same privileges as Farm Administrators, but they can also install new products and applications, deploy Web Parts to the entire farm, create new Web applications, and start services (such as a search crawl). This group does not have access to site content by default and is not visible in an individual site collection.

Custom SharePoint Groups

The out-of-the-box security groups in SharePoint are essentially a combination of "role" and "permissions." Also, the SharePoint model is inclusive and not exclusive. That is, you cannot define activities that users or groups are not allowed to perform. For example, the Members group has the Contribute permission level by default, so people often associate the Members group with Contribute permissions, even though this doesn't have to be the case. There may be situations where you have different groups of people who need different access permissions to various objects in your solution, and it may not be possible or practical to create an Active Directory group for them. While you can add multiple Active Directory Groups to a SharePoint Group, you cannot "nest" SharePoint Groups. If the same group of people need different permissions in different sites (for example, Contribute in one and Read in another) and you can't use an Active Directory Group, you will want to create a custom SharePoint Group. You may also want to create a custom group because the terms Visitors, Members, and Owners just don't make sense in your organization. As a best practice, when you create a custom SharePoint Group, choose a name for the group to reflect the people in the group and their collective "role" in the organization, not their security permissions. This is hard to explain without an example, so please continue reading to the section of this chapter where the step-by-step planning process is described to see an example of a situation where you might want to create custom SharePoint Groups. As a general practice, you always want to give a person or group the least amount of permissions to effectively achieve the required business functionality … and no more. This certainly creates additional administrative overhead, but it is a core tenet of ensuring the stability and security of a SharePoint environment.

Permissions

Individual permissions (such as view items, open items, edit items, and delete items) are grouped together into permission "levels," such as Contribute, which allow users to perform specific actions. You can also create custom permission levels, but when you do this you may make managing a site more difficult, and you will also make it more difficult to audit your site's security. That doesn't mean that you shouldn't create custom permission levels, but it does mean that you should carefully document all the permissions levels that you create for your site. In addition, you should validate any custom security groups as being essential. One we have seen often is a custom security group that offers content contribution but does not have deletion rights. (Note that the Recycle Bin may minimize the need for this type of customization.) Individual permissions are assigned to one or more permission levels, which are in turn assigned to individual users (if you absolutely have to) and/or SharePoint Groups (the preferred approach).

The out-of-the-box or default permission levels for team sites include

- **Full Control** provides administrator access to the site. This permission level contains all permissions. This permission level cannot be customized or deleted. As a general rule, you will only allow a user to have Full Control privileges when they have demonstrated an understanding of how SharePoint works, SharePoint best practices, and, most importantly, your organization's governance model. This user can give anyone else permissions, including Full Control.
- **Design** allows the user to create lists and document libraries, edit pages, and apply themes, borders, and style sheets in the site.
- **Contribute** allows the user to add, edit, and delete items in existing lists and document libraries.
- **Read** allows read-only access to the site. Users and groups with this permission level can view items and pages, open items, and download documents.
- **Limited Access** is a special permission level that is automatically assigned to users who have access to some areas of the site but not all areas. For example, a user with Contribute access to a document library on a subsite will appear in the permissions list of the home page as having limited access permissions. This does not allow him to view anything on the home page unless he belongs to a group that has home page access. Limited Access is automatically assigned by SharePoint when a user or group is provided unique access to a specific securable object. This permission level cannot be customized or deleted.

The out-of-the-box or default permission levels for publishing sites include

- **Manage Hierarchy** allows users to create sites and edit pages, list items, and documents. This permission level does not include permissions to approve items, apply themes and borders or style sheets, or create groups. However, this permission level is otherwise very similar to Full Control.

- **Approve** allows users to edit and approve pages, list items, and documents. You will most likely use this permission only in publishing sites.
- **View** allows users to view pages, list items, and documents. Document types with server-side file handlers can be viewed in the browser but not downloaded.
- **Restricted Read** is designed to give users access to a specific list, document library, item, or document without giving them access to the entire site. Previous document versions and user rights information are not available to people and groups with this permission level.

It is possible to create "custom" permission levels based on business needs. Custom permission levels, like securable objects that require unique security, will add complexity to the maintenance of your security model. Some individual permissions have dependencies, but in general, SharePoint will not allow you to delete an individual permission from a permission level if other individual permissions depend on it. With 32 individual permissions, you can see that creating custom permission levels can get very complicated. If you do create custom permission levels, be sure to carefully document and describe what you have done and why you have created the custom levels. Examples of possible "custom" permission levels that we have seen in practice include

- **Editor (or Restricted Contributor)**. For users who can upload and edit documents but cannot delete documents. This custom permission level can help ensure that users cannot accidentally delete a document but still have the capability to upload and edit them. To create a custom Editor permission level, start by creating a copy of the Contribute permission level and then remove (uncheck) the Delete Items and Delete Versions permissions. Users without delete permissions will not be able to edit the document Name (file name) after uploading the document. If the Name needs to be changed, a user with Contribute, Design, or Full Control permissions will have to make any necessary changes to the Document Name. Users with custom Editor permissions (add, change, but not delete) can edit other metadata properties.
- **Manage Permissions**. For users who need to manage permissions for the site or library but not necessarily have Full Control access. By default, a user must have Full Control permissions to manage security for a site. However, you may want to delegate the responsibility for managing security to a user who should not have Full Control

access to the site. In this case, create a custom permission level that starts with the Contribute set but *adds* the Manage Permissions user permission. This custom permission level will allow users to upload, edit, and delete documents and manage user access without having full control. You'll want to be careful about creating this type of access because in addition to allowing a group with this custom permission set to add and remove users from Groups, they can also create new groups and change permissions on existing objects. As with Full Control, only highly trusted and trained users should have the ability to manage permissions on your site.

Use the following best practices for creating and managing permission levels:

- If a custom permission level is needed for a SharePoint site collection, *always start with an existing permission level* and then either add to or delete from that set of permissions to create the custom permission level.
- Try to create short, meaningful names for each custom permission level and be sure to add a description that summarizes what type of access is associated with the permission level. In some cases, it is helpful to prepend your organization's name to customizations to have them stand out as unique and personalized.
- As a general rule, *do not change the "default" permission levels*. Remember the saying "You touch it, you own it." SharePoint does not offer any indicator that shows alterations to native security levels. If a similar permission level is needed and you are tempted to modify one of the default permission levels, follow this process instead:
  - Start with a copy of that permission level and make a custom permission level.
  - After copying the default permission level, make additions or deletions to individual permissions.

Defining and Documenting SharePoint Security

This section describes a process you can use to work through the steps required to properly secure your site (or site collection). We recommend that you complete and document your security model *before* actually creating groups or assigning permission levels in a site collection. The following are the steps described in this process:

Step 1. List and describe where unique security is required.
Step 2. List and describe who needs access.
Step 3. List and describe the permission levels.
Step 4. Define and create the SharePoint Security Groups you need.
Step 5. Apply security permissions.

Step 1: List and Describe Where Unique Security Is Required

A well thought out security model is crucial for the successful assignment of security in any SharePoint site collection. To simplify the ongoing management of security of each site collection, it is important to determine which parts of a site collection have common security requirements and which parts have unique requirements. This should happen in a review of security with your business sponsor. As discussed in Chapter 4, "Planning for Governance," you need to carefully consider the implications of "over-securing" content. If every site is locked down for Read access, it will be hard to achieve your knowledge management objectives. Also remember that SharePoint security is inclusive—you need to fully understand the requirements associated with protecting highly secured content and know what should never happen (for example, security breaches).

As you think about creating the permission structure for each site collection, you need to carefully balance the ease of maintaining and administering the security model with the need to control specific permissions for individual securable objects. As a general rule, try to manage security *at the site level*. If there are particular items that contain sensitive information that must be even more secure than the site as a whole, you can apply security to individual securable objects. But remember, applying detailed security permissions at the object level can be a very time-consuming task. SharePoint 2010 includes the capability to identify how permissions have been assigned in your site collection (see the next major section of this chapter), but "unpacking" permissions is a group by group, site by site, object by object process, so the more complex your model, the more complex it will be to examine and maintain security. You will not be able to tell just by looking at a document library or site whether unique security has been applied (without the use of third-party administration tools)—you will have to examine the settings for the object or group to see how it has been secured. This is why it is easier to maintain security at the site level: You have only one place to look when you need to understand how security has been applied.

Consider each part of a site when determining the security assignments for the top level site, the subsite, and document libraries and lists. Document the overall site security model and note the parts that require unique security levels. One way to initially document the security that will need to be applied is to start with the site architecture diagram and add a visual indicator to define where unique security is needed. As discussed in Chapter 5, "Planning Your Information Architecture," there are several tools you can use to create a site architecture diagram, including PowerPoint or Word if the diagram is not very complex. Figure 8-4 shows a simple site architecture diagram that includes an indicator (the words UNIQUE or INHERIT) to show where unique security permissions will be applied.

Notice that the Discussion Board on the home page is in **bold**. This is a visual cue that the Discussion Board will have different security than the rest of the home page—all employees have Read access to most of the content on the home page, but they can contribute to the Discussion Board. The same would be required for surveys. You could also create a "node" in your diagram for each object in the site and use dotted lines or different colors to indicate where unique security is required. Planning security is an iterative process, and you may find that you need a more text-based approach to evolve your model. The remaining examples show a

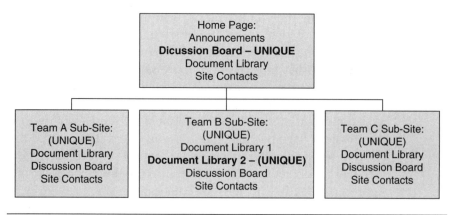

Figure 8-4 Site architecture diagram with security indicator

series of tables you can use to design and document your security model. Table 8-3 shows an example of the first level of your security model for an intranet—where you describe each securable object and document whether it needs unique or inherited permissions. Starting with a table like the one shown in Table 8-3, facilitate a conversation with the business sponsor about the types of permissions that are needed for the site. In general, a similar approach can be used to prepare the security model for an extranet (that is, externally accessible site for content presentation or collaboration with partners or customers), but more care would be required to define shared and exclusive partner/client areas.

Note that this example assumes a home page where a small number of individuals can contribute content but a large number can read content.

Table 8-3 Sample Security Table

Securable Object	Description	Unique or Inherited Permissions
Home	Top level site in the hierarchy	Unique
	Everyone in the company can see the home page, but only the people in the *marketing department* can edit most content on the page	
Home/Discussion Board	Discussion board on the home page that anyone can contribute to	Unique
Home/Subsite for Team A	Subsite for just the Finance Team	Unique
Home/Subsite for Team B	Subsite for the Marketing Team where only a few people will edit	Unique
Home/Subsite B/ Document Library 2	Private library where Marketing Department will work on documents before everyone else in the company can see them	Unique
Home/Subsite for Team C	Subsite for Human Resources where all users can Read but only members of HR can edit	Unique

The home page is a site where the primary purpose is communications. On the home page, there is a discussion board that every user can contribute to even though they only have Read permissions for the rest of the content on the home page. We use this example in the description of the security planning process in the remaining steps in this section. As we go through the steps, we expand the columns in the table. At the end of the steps, we will have documented our security model for this site collection.

When planning security keep in mind the following:

- Security of each object is inherited from its parent unless inheritance is explicitly broken. For example, by default, every object (for example, list or library) on a site has the same security as the site itself. If a user has Contribute access to the site, they have Contribute access to every object on the site. Similarly, if a user has Contribute access to a document library, she has Contribute access to every document in the library unless unique permissions have been applied to a document.
- Permissions from the parent can be reapplied if previously broken. However, any special permission levels that were previously created at the object level will be removed when permissions from the parent are reapplied.

Given these characteristics, think about the following regarding security as the site is designed:

- Try to design the site to allow assignment of permissions at the site level.
- If security at the object level is required, consider security for an entire object (an entire list or library, for example) before securing individual items. This may mean creating a second document library (or a folder within a library) if you need unique permissions for a particular group of documents.
- Always consider navigation. If you assign unique security to a nested subsite, you must ensure that the user has a navigation path to it. That is, if a user has access to a subsite but does not have any access to the parent site he/she will have no way to get to this site. This is why it is good practice to examine your security model from the top down (that is, home page to lowest level subsite) then in the reverse (lowest level site back to home page).

Step 2: List and Describe Who Needs Access

The next step is to carefully consider who needs access to a site collection or part of a site collection. The easiest way to document this is to add columns to the table created in Step 1 to identify who needs what type of access to each securable object in the site collection. This is shown in Table 8-4.

This step may require several revisions as the plan is reviewed with key stakeholders for the site and as the site design evolves. It should account for expected functional growth and anticipated security changes.

Step 3: List and Describe the Permission Levels

Next, evaluate the out-of-the-box permission levels to ensure that that they meet your needs. As described earlier, permission levels are the collection of individual permissions that describe what users can and cannot do with the securable objects on a site. You can use a table structure like that shown in Table 8-5 to describe the permission levels needed for your site. In our scenario, we do not need any custom permission levels, but you can use the example in Table 8-5 as a reference.

Step 4: Define and Create the SharePoint Security Groups You Need

Create a custom SharePoint Group when there is a group of users in a site collection that need different permission levels in different areas of the site where it will be confusing to call the group Members in one part of the site and Visitors in another or where it is not possible or practical to create a Domain Group for these users. When you create a custom SharePoint Group, it is best to choose a group name with a business-oriented name—such as Marketing Team—rather than a permission-oriented name like Member or Visitor. Create your custom SharePoint Groups at the top level of the site with *no* permissions. Then, add specific permission levels to the custom group at the specific securable objects where unique access is needed within the site collection.

For simple sites and most team sites, you can begin by using the default SharePoint Groups (which are [Site Name] Owners, [Site Name] Members, and [Site Name] Visitors) and assign permissions at the site level. In our example, by examining the security requirements, we decide that we want to create a custom SharePoint Group called Marketing

Table 8-4 Sample Security Table with Access Defined

Securable Object (level in the site hierarchy)	Description	Unique or Inherited Permissions?	People or Roles that Need Access	What Do These Users Need to Do?
Home	Top level site in the hierarchy Everyone in the company can see the home page, but only the people in the *marketing department* can edit most content on the page	Unique	Entire Company Members of the Marketing Team Fred and Sally	Read Contribute content Design or manage the entire site collection
Home/Discussion Board	Discussion board on the home page that anyone can contribute to	Unique	Entire Company	Contribute content
Home/Subsite for Team A	Subsite for just the Finance Team	Unique	Members of the Finance team John (Site Owner for this site)	Contribute content Design or manage this site
Home/Subsite for Team B	Subsite for the Marketing Team where only a few people will edit	Unique	Members of the Marketing Team Bob, Jane, Seth Sarah (Site Owner for this site)	Read Contribute content Design or manage this site
Home/Subsite B/ Document Library 2	Private library where Marketing Department will work on documents before everyone else in the company can see them	Unique	Members of the Marketing Team	Contribute content
Home/ Subsite C	Subsite for Human Resources where all users can read but only members of HR can edit	Unique	Entire Company Members of the HR Team	Read Contribute content

Table 8-5 Permission Levels for this Site

What Are the Permission Levels for This Site?	Describe Each Permission Level
Full Control	Administrator rights—all permissions.
Design	Create lists and document libraries, edit pages and apply themes, borders, and style sheets in the site.
Contribute	Add, edit, and delete items in existing lists and document libraries.
Read	Read-only access to the site—view items and pages, open items, and documents.
Manage Permissions	CUSTOM: Create and change permission levels on the site and assign permission to users and groups.
Editor	CUSTOM: View, add, and edit items or documents in lists, document libraries, and discussion comments; cannot delete items.

because we want to create a clearly named group of *people* that we can maintain as a group but assign different *permission levels* to this group depending on the securable object within the site. Whether or not you use custom or default security groups, you will generally follow a model similar to the inverted triangle shown in Figure 8-5. In general, you should assign users only the permissions they need to do their jobs.

Most of your users will belong to a group with Read permissions. Fewer users will belong to groups with Contribute permissions. Do not add every user as a member of the [Site Name] Owners SharePoint Group. Only a few users should have Full Control privileges. Because Full Control users can change other's permissions, it is easy to lose control of the site if too many people have Full Control permissions. Do not confuse business ownership of a site with the default security group called [Site Name] Owners. In most cases, the business executive who is the "owner" or sponsor of the site is not going to have Full Control privileges for the site. Use the naming best practices described earlier to name the custom security groups you create for your site.

SharePoint allows you to quickly give everyone in your company access to a site collection by assigning Read privileges to "all authenticated users."

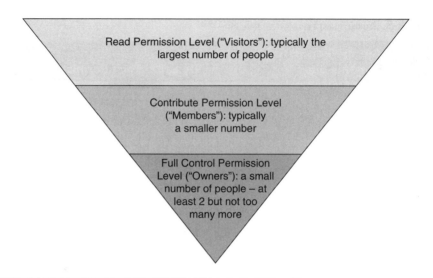

Read Permission Level ("Visitors"): typically the largest number of people

Contribute Permission Level ("Members"): typically a smaller number

Full Control Permission Level ("Owners"): a small number of people – at least 2 but not too many more

Figure 8-5 Assign users only the permissions they need to do their jobs

Before doing this, think about the impact. This gives *everyone* with credentials Read access. This may include contractors, consultants, and other temporary help. If this is not appropriate, you will need to adjust your security application. This would hold true for other areas of your intranet like a Human Resources site or an employee directory.

Step 5: Apply Security Permissions

Security is assigned *from the perspective of the securable object*. Therefore, in the last step of the process, permissions and objects that need security are combined with any existing Domain Groups and Default or Custom SharePoint Groups.

In this step, extend the security table to include the securable objects requiring unique security (from Step 1), the security group name (owners, members, visitors from this Step 4), the permission level (from Step 3), and the people who need access (from Step 2) in a table similar to Table 8-6. This complete security table example is shown in Table 8-6. Note that as a best practice, you should save your security plan and any other administrative documents for your site in a secure document library only visible to users with Full Control or Design privileges.

In this example, two custom SharePoint Groups are created for Marketing and HR because these groups of people have different levels of

Table 8-6 Sample Complete Security Model

Securable Object	Description	Unique or Inherited Permissions	Security Group	Permission Level	Who Is in This Group?
Home	Top level site in the hierarchy	Unique	*Home* Visitors	Read	AD Group for the entire company or AD group that contains employees only.
	Everyone in the company can see the home page, but only the people in the *marketing department* can edit most content on the page		*Home* Members	Contribute	No one—so this default group can be deleted.
			Marketing Team	Contribute	People who work in Marketing. Users are added and maintained by the Site Owner in SharePoint.
			Home Owners	Full Control	Fred (IT Resource). Sally (SharePoint Super User).
Home/ Discussion Board	Discussion board on the home page that anyone can contribute to	Unique	Discussion Board Visitors	Read	Not explicitly used—Read access inherited from parent.
			Discussion Board Members	Contribute	AD Group for the entire company.
			Discussion Board Owners	Full Control	Not explicitly used— inherited from parent.
Home/ Subsite for Team A	Subsite for just the Finance Team	Unique	Team A Site Visitors	Read	No Visitors for this site—need to remove permissions for the "parent" Visitors group when this site is created.
			Team A Site Members	Contribute	Individual members of the Finance team added to this "default" SharePoint Group for this subsite. There is no need to create a custom SharePoint Group for the Finance Team because they *only* have unique privileges on this one site.
			Team A Site Owners	Full Control	John (Team Leader or Project Manager).
			Home Site Owners	Full Control	Inherited from the parent level, includes Fred and Sally. It's usually a good idea to share this group across all subsites and ask the subsite owner not to remove permissions for this group on an individual subsite.

(continues)

Table 8-6 Sample Complete Security Model *(continued)*

Securable Object	Description	Unique or Inherited Permissions	Security Group	Permission Level	Who Is in This Group?
Home/ Subsite for Team B	Subsite for the Marketing Team where only a few people will edit most of the content	Unique	Marketing Team	Read	People who work in Marketing. Set up and managed at the top of the site collection. Note that the "parent" SharePoint Groups will be removed from access for this subsite because it is an exclusive, private site for the Marketing Team.
			Team B Site Members	Contribute	Bob, Jane, Seth (Implementers, Content Creators).
			Team Site B Owners	Full Control	Sarah (Site Owner for this site).
			Home Site Owners	Full Control	Inherited from the parent level, includes Fred and Sally.
Home/ Subsite B/ Document Library 2	Private library where Marketing Department will work on documents before everyone else in the company can see them	Unique	Marketing Team	Contribute	People who work in Marketing.
			Team Site B Owners	Full Control	Sarah (Site Owner for this site)—inherited from subsite.
			Home Site Owners	Full Control	Inherited from the parent level, includes Fred and Sally.
Home/ Subsite C	Subsite for Human Resources where all users can Read but only members of HR can edit	Unique	Entire Company	Read	AD Group for the entire company.
			HR Team	Contribute	Members of the HR Team.
			Home Site Owners	Full Control	Inherited from the parent level, includes Fred and Sally.

access in different areas of the site collection. For all other securable objects, the default groups created by SharePoint are used. In addition, we explicitly removed permissions for any security group that was initially inherited from the parent (top level) site but should not have permissions for the uniquely secured object.

Maintaining Your Security Model

It may be overly ambitious to expect you to keep your security model up to date, but if there is any documentation worth maintaining as you evolve your site design, this is the one to try to maintain. In fact, it may not be a single document but a collection of completed document templates (if you choose to decentralize security management). If you always follow the best practice of assigning users to groups rather than assigning permissions to individuals, maintaining the document won't be too difficult because you will only need to make an update if you add a new group or a add unique permissions to a securable object. Is it realistic to assume that you can keep the security model document current in a dynamic environment? Probably not. So you will definitely want to take advantage of the ways SharePoint 2010 allows you to "unpack" your security model directly in your site. Here's what you can do pretty easily:

- Check the permissions that have been assigned to a group across the entire site collection.
- On an individual object, display the permission levels and how those permissions were applied (for example, "given directly" or "given through the [Site Name] Members group").

Here's what you can't do with the native interface: check the permissions that have been assigned to an individual across the entire site collection (which should give you the best incentive possible to try to always put users in a group and avoid giving users individual permissions) or audit who has made security changes to various securable objects.

Checking Permissions Assigned to a Group

To examine how permissions have been assigned to a group across a site collection, you must have Full Control privileges. At the root of the site collection, select Site Settings, Users and Permissions, and then "People and groups." Highlight the group in the quick launch and select Settings/View Group Permissions. You will see a list similar to the image in Figure 8-6, which enumerates the permissions for the Home Visitors group in a sample site collection. The list shows the URL of each securable object and the permission level that has been assigned to each group. Notice that this group has Read access to the Team Beta blog site, but that

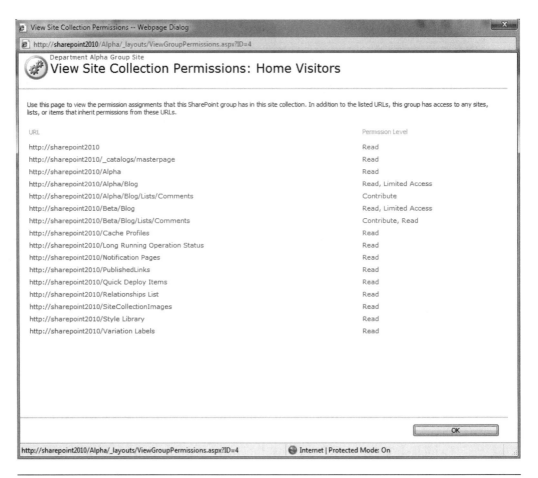

Figure 8-6 View Site Collection permissions for a Group

they have Contribute permissions to the Comments list. This explicit permission level assignment allows people who only have Read access to the entire site (the default permission for the default SharePoint Visitors Group) to post a comment (Contribute) to the Team Beta blog but not generate a new post.

Displaying Permission Levels on an Object

To examine permission levels for an individual object, you have to navigate to the object and look "under the covers" to find out how permissions have been assigned. If you have a very complex security model, you will have to turn over a lot of covers to audit the security across the entire collection.

From the individual object where you want to display permissions, navigate to the settings for that object.

- For a site, this will be found under Site Settings, Users and Permissions. Click Site permissions to access the Check Permissions button. Note that People and Groups will show individuals and site groups that are available to the entire site collection, not just the current site.
- For a Document Library, select List Settings and then the Permissions for this list option under Permissions and Management.

When you click the Check Permissions button, you will see the permissions that have been granted for a group or a user of that object. While you cannot check an individual user's permission across the entire collection, you *can* check a person's individual permissions inside a given object. However, you will not be able to identify that user Chris has Contribute permissions for most documents in a document library but only Read for a specific more secure document without examining each document to see where unique permissions have been applied. Save yourself some audit pain—if you are going to secure individual documents or items in a list or library, write down what you did in your security model and keep it current. Better still, put more secure documents in a separate document library with more restricted access. Another best practice tip is to create a test user account and use it for security validation. If you are someone with security application privileges, you automatically have access to the associated content. To verify security changes you make, add the test user as a member of the appropriate security group. Log in as that test user and validate that the content is accessible. Remove the user from the group and test again to ensure content is no longer accessible.

Figure 8-7 shows the results of the Check Permissions action from the perspective of the Comments list on the Team Beta Blog site shown in Figure 8-6. You can only enter one user or group name at a time when you check permissions. When permissions were "managed" for this list, the Site Owner left the Read permission level checked and then also checked the Contribute permission level, which is why you see that this group has both Contribute and Read permissions. Note that the "highest" set of privileges will always apply. Because the Contribute permission level is the same as the Read permission level with additional permissions to add, edit,

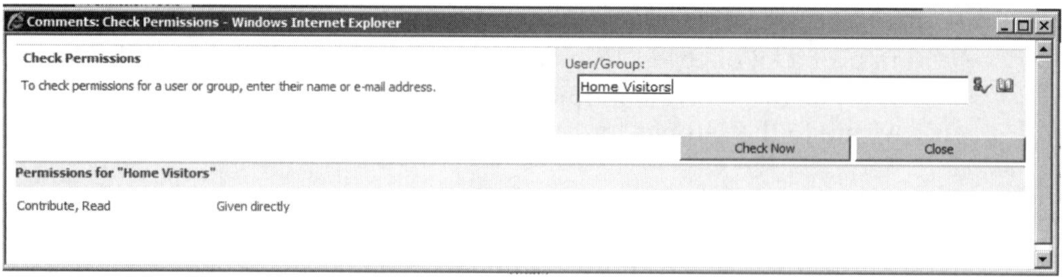

Figure 8-7 Check permissions for a securable object: one Group at a time

and delete items and versions, it would have been OK to uncheck the Read permission level in this example, as shown in Figure 8-8.

The concept of "highest" set of privileges will always apply is an important one. This means if a user is a member of two groups, Group A and Group B, where Group A has Read access to a site and Group B has Contribute access, then the user is a contributor. This is sometimes confusing from an administration perspective but can be managed somewhat by limiting the number of security groups applied to a securable object.

Troubleshooting

This section contains some examples of reported issues and questions with security application in SharePoint and the associated potential resolutions/answers. This list is not exhaustive but is intended to demontrate some additional learning elements associated with Share Point secuity management.

- **"SharePoint is denying me access to a site."** First, it is very important to note that SharePoint handles *authorization* but not *authentication*. You can't get to a SharePoint site without first being authenticated (that is, associated with valid credentials). Once SharePoint knows who you are, it applies security to determine whether you are authorized to see all, some, or none of the content. If a user does not have access rights, a dialog box is presented so alternate credentials may be entered. After three failed attempts, the dialog box is removed, and the user is redirected to an error (or access denied) page. The security model would need to be altered to grant this user the appropriate access.

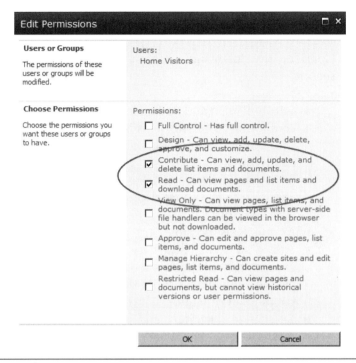

Figure 8-8 Edit permissions

- **"Certain users can no longer access their team site, and security has not been changed."** There is a scenario worth mentioning here. If a site contributor places an image on the site and the image is located (and secured) in a different location, then that security is applied at the time of page rendering. So in this example, a user may be prompted with the security dialog box because that user does not have access to that image. This is why security must be well-mapped in early stages where, in this case, an openly available image library has the necessary read access.
- **"How do I know if I have site administration rights?"** The quickest and simplest indicator is the Site Actions button. If you see it on a site, you have access to the underlying administration pages. If you don't, then you don't!
- **"How do I know if I have contribution rights to a library?"** Similar to the previous point, if you see the library's tool bar with the associated contribution actions in the ribbon, then you do.

Key Points

Consider the following recommended actions when you think about security:

- Carefully plan and document your security model before you begin configuring your site. This involves defining the security associated with the full-site topology as well as the necessary roles and security exceptions.
- Try to apply security at the "highest" level, preferably the site. Pay attention to the concept of permission inheritance as you plan and apply security.
- As much as possible, try to avoid giving access permissions to individual users. Always try to ensure that users will be assigned to groups and that permissions are assigned to groups, not individual people. This makes support and maintenance simpler and reduces the amount of clutter that is left behind when staff depart.
- Be sure to document and justify all custom permission levels you create for your site.
- Use the "principle of least privilege" to assign permissions to users. As a general rule, only give users permissions that they need to perform their roles. Your business sponsor may be the effective "owner" of your site, but that doesn't mean that you should give your business sponsor Owner (Full Control) privileges for the site. Think about a variation of the phrase that is often associated with the Hippocratic Oath for assigning security permissions: "First, don't assign permissions that allow a user to do harm to the site" as you place users into security groups.
- If you are not using a default security group created automatically by SharePoint, it's a good practice to delete the group from your site collection so that users are not confused about whether or not the group is actually used or has any members. You can always re-create the group if you decide you need it later.
- If you need to create custom permission levels, start by making a copy of an existing permission level and then add or remove individual permissions. Don't go overboard with creating custom permission levels or you will make yourself crazy trying to understand and maintain your security model.

- Be sure to create a process or plan to monitor security as your solution evolves.
- Don't give service accounts or generic user accounts security privileges. An effective security audit includes the ability to associate any task with a specific individual.
- Factor security into any navigation strategy. In travelling from site A to site B, a user must have at least Read permission to all nodes in that path or the navigation fails.
- If you can, try to keep the security model document up to date. If that becomes too much of a challenge, use the processes described in the "Maintaining Your Security Model" section to review permissions and access on a regular basis. At a minimum, try to document where and why you have applied individual item-level permissions in a list or library—you don't necessarily have to document how you have secured each item, just the "method to your madness!"

CHAPTER 9

Getting Ready to Launch: Planning for Training and Communications

One of the most important lessons we learned from deploying SharePoint 2007 was the importance of training and persistent communications. Despite what we all hoped would be a very intuitive interface for end users, not all Site Designers followed or even understood design and usability best practices. As a result, some users were confused and disappointed with the product. Moreover, many organizations adopted a "build it and they will come" approach to both training users and communicating the benefits and value of their new SharePoint solutions. It is even more important to avoid this mistake for SharePoint 2010.

- The new "ribbon" interface in SharePoint 2010 will create a consistent and familiar user experience for some users. But if your organization has users who have not yet migrated to Office 2007, this may be their first look at a brand new interface. The ribbon may initially provide a very unfamiliar user experience for users who are used to Office 2003, and your training and communications plans should account for this possibility. Note that you may also want to take advantage of the "visual upgrade" migration option for SharePoint 2010. This migration strategy, discussed in Chapter 17, "Planning Your Move from SharePoint 2007 to 2010," allows you to migrate the back-end infrastructure of an existing SharePoint 2007 solution without enabling the front-end user experience, which gives you additional time to execute training and communications strategy.
- With new end-user features such as social tagging and content rating, SharePoint 2010 end users have an even larger role to play in

the success of SharePoint solutions. Effective training is even more important than ever before.

You need to remember several critical lessons about training and communications for SharePoint 2010, which are the key sections contained in this chapter:

- Training
  - One size does *not* fit all. Training needs to be targeted to the end user's role in the organization and role or responsibility with regard to the solution.
  - You need to adapt to the learning style of the learner. Educational experts know that not everyone learns in precisely the same way. This is especially true for busy adults. You will get the best outcomes from your training initiatives if you can offer training in multiple ways: classroom, online, "just-in-time" via computer-based training (CBT) or short online videos, quick reference "cards," and so on.
- Communications
  - Communications planning does not end at solution launch.
  - Communication needs to be persistent so you do not miss out on the ongoing opportunity to enhance the value of your solution and to provide consistent reinforcement of best practices for taking full advantage of the solution and its content.

In this chapter, we share lessons we learned from both successful and unsuccessful SharePoint deployments for two different but very related activities: training and communications. The following are the key sections contained in this chapter:

- Training
- Communications

If you think that training and communications are not your job, think again. If you are involved in the planning, design, or development of a new SharePoint solution, you should always have the end user in mind. Therefore, everyone is responsible for training and communications.

Training

SharePoint 2010 can be a very intuitive product for some users, but this will definitely not be the case for all users in your organization. While the flexibility of SharePoint can be a valuable selling point, in the hands of an inexperienced designer, your site can be much less intuitive for your users. Be careful not to underestimate the amount of training users will need—especially users with site design permissions, even if their sites are only used by a small group of people. However, keep the following in mind: If your solution requires extensive training for the typical user, you've probably made some fundamental design mistakes. As a general rule, your goal is to design solutions that don't require training for "every day" use.

Your training strategy should encompass all aspects of your new solution—not only the SharePoint 2010 technology but also business processes impacted by SharePoint 2010. Users who are very familiar with MOSS 2007 will be especially interested in learning about things that have changed in SharePoint 2010, so a critical component of your training plan will need to include specific "upgraded features" training for those users.

This section discusses the following key elements of your training plan:

- **Audience**. Who should be trained and what training content is appropriate for each audience
- **Timing**. When training should be offered
- **Approach**. Examples of successful training approaches that can be considered for your training plan

Audience

Develop a training program for SharePoint 2010 that carefully addresses the specific needs of each constituent community based on their role in the organization and their role in the context of the solution. If you implement personal sites (My Site), all users will have Contribute (or Edit) permissions for at least that area of the portal. This means that every user in the organization should know *something* about best practices for organizing information. However, not all users will have the same level of interest, so your training plan will need to be adjusted accordingly. While you may *think* that everyone wants to learn everything that they can about SharePoint, in practice this doesn't always turn out to be the case. Think about how you can structure your training plan so that you offer multiple levels of training for users with varying degrees of both interest and time. One successful approach that several organizations have adopted is to create a "SharePoint Basics" offering that introduces all users to the solution, shows them effective search techniques, and explains the basics of your content organization and site navigation schemes. This introductory topic shouldn't require much more than about an hour to deliver. The Basics offering can then be supplemented with additional training content based on user interest and role.

Timing

Training for SharePoint 2010 is ideally scheduled immediately prior to the launch of your new solution and on an ongoing basis as users need new and expanded skills. Some users, particularly users who are responsible for loading the initial content, will need to be trained (either formally or informally) prior to the start of content conversion. The majority of users, particularly those with Read access, should be trained just before or at the time of your solution launch.

One of the biggest training challenges, of course, is figuring out just what users need and just when they need it. There is no single best answer to this challenge because each solution is different. It's really hard to figure out what is "just enough" when it comes to training for SharePoint. It depends on the user's role, how frequently they will use the skill, and a host of other factors, including their learning style. If your user community includes a significant number of engineers or scientists, it is likely that no matter how much or how little you teach them about SharePoint, they will try and figure out what else it can do! As you plan training, the important thing to remember is that you want to engage the natural curiosity of your user community *before* they propagate a "wrong" or ineffective approach by exploring on their own. We've seen too many cases where eager end users "discover" a feature and share it with their colleagues even if there is actually a much simpler or more effective feature for that problem. You will need to negotiate a careful balance between overwhelming the user with too much content while making sure that each user has enough knowledge to get her job done. If you have nontechnical users who will be given Full Control or Design privileges on a SharePoint site, it is important to empower them with site design best practices training, not just how to use SharePoint features. These new "Site Designers" should be familiar with the guiding principles documented in your governance plan (see Chapter 4, "Planning for Governance") and information architecture fundamentals (see Chapter 5, "Planning Your Information Architecture").

While you will definitely need to develop a training plan that is specific to your organization's needs, you will not always need to develop training material. There are many commercial SharePoint training offer-ings as well as documentation and online training that is available at Microsoft.com. Many training companies seem to find it most effective to teach SharePoint classes as multiday events. Unfortunately, not all training participants will be able to participate or find this type of training effective. For the most part, we have seen only limited success with this type of train-ing if large communities need to be trained. Furthermore, many user groups find it difficult to schedule that much time away from their job duties.

Identifying a more effective delivery approach is challenging. Should you consider multiday training options for *all* of your SharePoint users, even if the class is called SharePoint Basics? Absolutely not. Should you consider it for *some* users? Definitely yes. For the majority of your users, you will need to consider frequent "minitraining" events that allow users to consume training "just in time," as they need it.

Here are some suggested approaches for just-in-time SharePoint training:

- **SharePoint Basics**. Online or in-person brief introductory training to be offered in conjunction with the launch of your new solution and then at additional intervals for new employees or people who want a refresher.
- **Online, topic-based, computer-based training**. Look for some of the SharePoint training companies to update their MOSS 2007 video training offerings for SharePoint 2010—and additional "on demand" training from Microsoft Office online. Short, topic-focused training videos or online training can be delivered to users just as they need the knowledge in the course of doing their work. The ideal training modules require no more than 10 minutes to "consume" and can be accessed by users as they are trying to accom-plish specific tasks. While you can certainly develop these modules on your own, it's worth checking out the existing offerings, even if they reflect a "generic" SharePoint solution. In some cases, you can work with the solution provider to customize the materials for your specific implementation.
- **End user documentation, delivered online or in print form**. Some users will not be comfortable without written documentation. Many successful organizations create "generic" documentation for key tasks such as uploading and assigning metadata to documents or changing security permissions that they make available to teams to

use "as is" or customize for their sites. Others create formal documentation only for tasks or processes that are customized in their deployment. Still others "create" documentation for their environment by linking to existing Microsoft documentation on the various SharePoint features. As you think about the approach that will be most successful in your organization, keep in mind that to be useful, your documentation needs to be consumable. This means that you should think about small documents rather than 20-page "books" that no one will ever read. In addition, remember that to be valuable, documentation should be delivered in context. This means that while you may want to create a document library or site for user documentation, you should *link* to each relevant chunk of documentation from the site where the user will need it—create links in the context of where users will do their work. For example, on a page where a user will submit a form, provide a link to the document describing how to submit the form.

- **Recurring training events such as regular meetings or "lunch and learn" sessions**. One very successful organization implemented a regular "Get Sharp on SharePoint" weekly training event. Each week, they planned and delivered a 30-minute online meeting focused on a unique SharePoint topic such as search, creating your personal SharePoint site, assigning metadata, and so on. The first 15 minutes of the meeting was typically devoted to a presentation, and the second 15 minutes provided an opportunity for participants to ask questions and share experiences (either on the topic of the day or not). Each meeting was recorded so that users could replay the video at any time. The combination of real-time, online topic-based training plus recorded playback was extremely effective in both introducing and reinforcing key topics. Because the topics were publicized as part of the communications plan, users could plan their participation based on their interest and workload.

- **"Office hours" consulting sessions**. Several companies offer recurring "drop-in" help centers where users can bring their SharePoint design or usage concerns to their internal SharePoint experts. This effectively provides one-on-one private training to supplement other just-in-time training offerings.

While not always considered part of training, another key resource for just-in-time training is your Power User community and SharePoint Center of

Excellence team (see Chapter 4). A powerful way to deliver training just at the moment that a user needs it is to offer a "live" person for quick questions. Creating an Ask the Experts discussion forum, establishing a best practices wiki with a searchable repository of tips and tricks, publishing a list of SharePoint subject matter experts in your own organization, and adding links to SharePoint training in your default site templates can also help support your training program.

Approach

Training should be tailored to how each constituent community will use SharePoint 2010 to do their jobs. To maximize the effectiveness of your training plan, you may want to consider training a few employees from each department or business unit or office in a "train the trainer" scenario and ask them to train their peers. You may also want to identify some initial candidates to become "power users" of SharePoint 2010 and consider providing additional, in-depth training for these individuals. Ideally, the "power users" should be distributed across the organization so that they can provide first-level support and ongoing training to members of their local department, business unit, or office.

Each organization will have unique business roles that may require specialized SharePoint 2010 training. Don't kid yourself—certain types of users will absolutely require custom approaches to training. For example, in a law firm, you should not plan to deliver the same training to both partners and paralegals. In a hospital, clinicians and administrators will probably have different training needs and learning styles.

In general, there are three types of user roles for a SharePoint 2010 solution: Visitors (readers), Members (contributors), and Owners (designers). These roles are generally described using SharePoint 2010 terminology for the permissions that users have on a given page or site.

- **Visitors** have Read permission only for the specific page or site—at least for the "authoritative" content. One of the unique training challenges for SharePoint 2010 is that you may have certain types of content (for example, social tags or ratings) that any user can add to a page or site, even if they only have Read permission for the primary content. These users will need training in when and how they should add social content as well as, and even more importantly than, training in the organizational governance policies for this type of information.

- **Members** generally have both Read and Contribute permission. These users will need the same training as Visitors but must also understand how to add content and how to assign metadata to contributed content and the governance policies for content contribution.
- **Owners** typically have Design permission, which means that they have the ability to modify the structure, lists, libraries, and content metadata for the site in addition to being able to add content. These users need a comprehensive set of "how to" training for SharePoint 2010 as well as a complete understanding of all of your governance principles and policies. In addition, any user with Design privileges needs to understand some basic information architecture and Web site usability best practices.

As you roll out SharePoint solutions inside your organization, you are making an implied assumption that your users have basic "information literacy" skills. This may not always be the case in all organizations. Because SharePoint 2010 includes so many social computing ("Web 2.0") features, your training plan may need to address the needs of users who have not yet mastered each of these basic skills. Refer to the sidebar for a list of some of the basic information literacy skills you will want to ensure are part of the core competencies of your solution users.

Information Literacy Competencies for Successful Collaboration and Portal Solutions

Some of the basic information literacy skills that are important for your solution users to have include

- **Locating.** The ability to understand and use IT-based tools required to conduct research on the Internet, including basic search competencies (narrowing or expanding search scopes, understanding metadata concepts)
- **Evaluating.** The ability to distinguish between authoritative and nonauthoritative information sources (for example, social tags versus other types of metadata) and current versus old information as well as the ability to critically evaluate the strengths and weaknesses, benefits, and costs of information technologies
- **Communicating.** The ability to format and publish ideas electronically, both in document format as well as on blogs and wiki pages

along with the ability to classify and organize information in ways that benefit both personal and shared retrieval (understanding the fundamental concepts of "findability")

- **Learning**. The ability to adapt to and make use of continuously evolving innovations in information technology, including the ability to determine how to apply emerging technologies inside the business

Table 9-1 summarizes the basic training requirements for each general SharePoint 2010 role.

Table 9-1 Summary of Suggested General Training Requirements for Out-of-the-Box SharePoint Roles

Training Concept	Visitors	Members	Owners (Site Designers)
Overall navigational and content structure of your solution.	✓	✓	✓
Basic concepts of your governance plan (for example, guiding principles for use and responsibilities for content accuracy).	✓	✓	✓
Basic security concepts (permission levels).	✓	✓	✓
How to set personal settings (regional settings, for example).	✓	✓	✓
Navigational concepts (tabs, breadcrumbs, links, "back button").	✓	✓	✓
Overview of common Web Parts in your solution (as applicable): Calendar, Document Library, Tasks,	✓	✓	✓

(continues)

Table 9-1 Summary of Suggested General Training Requirements for Out-of-the-Box SharePoint Roles *(continued)*

Training Concept	Visitors	Members	Owners (Site Designers)
and so on. Be sure to review not just what each Web part does, but how you are using the Web Part and the business benefit it provides.			
Personalizing views and setting up alerts.	✓	✓	✓
General best practices for search as well as key search features (such as best bets) and leveraging metadata filters in document libraries. Ensure that users understand best practices for finding content when ■ I know it exists, and I know where it is. ■ I know it exists, but I don't know where it is. ■ I don't know if it exists.	✓	✓	✓
Introduction to social computing best practices.	✓	✓	✓
Uploading documents and applying metadata (include best practices for file naming).		✓	✓
Updating and deleting documents (implications of deleting documents, best practices for "editing in place," when to create a document set, and so on).		✓	✓
Best practices for creating Web content—your organization's "Style Guide" (which may already exist for your intranet or Web site)		✓	✓

Training Concept	Visitors	Members	Owners (Site Designers)
Details of your governance plan—especially focusing on design principles, policies, standard design frameworks.			✓
Information architecture best practices (how much metadata is "enough," when folders are appropriate, page layout best practices, best practices for creating new "nodes" in your navigational hierarchy, and so on).			✓
Comprehensive SharePoint 2010 "how to" training (features and functions).			✓ Note: Not all Site Designers may have privileges to completely structure a new SharePoint site. It is likely that it will not be necessary to provide detailed feature training for every Site Designer.

Table 9-2 lists additional "advanced" training topics that should be offered for special solution roles and other users based on interest and business need.

Another key role that you should be sure to consider in your training plan is your Help Desk. You will need to factor the skills and abilities of your Help Desk personnel along with the Service Level Agreement expectation when you consider how much training to provide Help Desk personnel. If they will be expected to answer "How do I ..." questions, then they should have the same training as your Site Designers. If they will primarily answer "access" questions and transfer more specific SharePoint questions to a solution-specific expert team, then this may not be necessary. However, just like any new solution, you need to be sure that your Help Desk is prepared to provide support as soon as you launch. Be sure to consider Help Desk personnel training upfront—not as an afterthought.

Table 9-2 Summary of Suggested Special/Advanced Training Topics for Special SharePoint Roles

Training Concept	Power Users	Content Stewards
Information architecture best practices, particularly focused on document and content metadata.		✓
Comprehensive SharePoint 2010 "how to" training (features and functions)—you may want to consider formal, in-person training for Site Designers and perhaps offer Web-based training for Power Users.	✓ (based on interest and job relevance)	

Communications

Don't assume that your new SharePoint 2010 solution is going to launch itself—a communications plan is absolutely essential for successful solutions. One mistake many organizations make is that they leave communications planning to the end of their project plans and forget to engage the internal marketing and communications teams early enough in the project so that they can have an impact. The other big mistake that organizations make is assuming that communications planning is over once the solution is launched. A good communications strategy must be persistent; until your solution is embedded into the fabric of your organization, you should use every opportunity to promote awareness of both the features and benefits of the solution. Everyone in your organization is listening to the same radio station: WIIFM (what's in it for me). Your persistent communications plan needs to ensure that you are constantly promoting the value of your solution to ensure that the business benefits that are so critical to your organizational success can be realized.

The communications strategy should promote both awareness and the value of the new SharePoint 2010 solution. Your communications plan will likely include some awareness activities that begin during design, but the majority of activities will begin just before you are ready to launch the solution and continue persistently. Communications activities must also be an active part of sustaining user acceptance throughout the entire life of the solution, and thus your plan needs to include not just communications when the solution launches, but also ongoing activities that keep the portal and collaboration tools "top of mind" throughout their lifetime. As you begin to think about your communications planning, be sure to

- Leverage existing expertise and experts to help develop your communications plan. Work with your internal communications or marketing teams to develop both communications messages and materials. Consider what activities and messages have worked in the past and think creatively about new ways of engaging users and solution contributors.

- Leverage existing newsletters and "town hall" or business unit meetings to deliver key messages about the solution, collaboration tools, and other productivity initiatives. You can also demonstrate the solution "live."

- Draft a memorandum for the CEO or similar high-level executive to send when you are ready to launch. Active sponsorship by key business executives can go a long way toward getting users over initial reluctance to try the new solution.

- Tailor messages in communications plans for each target audience. For example, messages may be different for field personnel versus home office personnel because the value of the solution and collaboration tools and the business reasons for using them may be different based on the various roles and locations in the organization. The same user will leverage the solution for different reasons at different times, and the communications plan should address these different scenarios. An attorney in a law firm will play the role of "employee" when she uses the company portal to update the beneficiary of her 401K plan. However, the attorney will approach the same portal as a business stakeholder when she uses the portal to find last month's billing for her current clients. Make sure that both the communications medium and the message are targeted to your audience and the roles they play in the organization. In the attorney example, this might mean designing a communications message for all employees that reminds users that the company portal can be used for basic HR self service. In addition, this could also mean designing a completely separate message targeted to just attorneys that describes how Attorney Smith used the portal while on the phone with a client who was requesting additional work to quickly identify that this client was 60 days past due and that this timely information resulted in an immediate collection of the past due amount. Work with key individuals within each business group to ensure messages and medium work for their locations and roles.

- Consider a fun activity, such as an intranet scavenger hunt, to get users excited about the new solution. For example, one organization created a portal treasure hunt that provided participants with a list of 10 questions whose answers could be found by either searching or browsing for content within the solution environment. One question asked users to find the author of a specific document published to the portal. This answer was found by searching or browsing for the document and then examining metadata properties to identify the author. Another asked users to find out what would be offered for lunch in the cafeteria on a date two weeks into the future. This answer was found by navigating to or searching for the cafeteria menu, which was published monthly, and looking in the document for the lunch item on the date. A third question asked users to identify who to call for questions related to medical benefits. This answer could be found in several ways including searching for the term "medical benefits," which turned up a Frequently Asked Question with the answer to this question or by navigating to the HR page and looking at the Key Contacts list for the medical benefits expert, whose name and contact information were prominently featured. Users who turned in correct answers for all 10 questions were entered into a drawing for a dinner for two at a local restaurant. The activity not only promoted the new intranet, but it also walked new users through some valuable information seeking activities for which the solution could provide quick and accurate results.

- Encourage influential executives to talk about the solution and, better yet, use the solution for information distribution instead of sending e-mail. One successful organization found an executive who decided to refuse to respond to e-mail messages that included attachments that should have been added as links to documents in the portal. When he got an e-mail with an attachment, he politely replied to the sender that he would read their e-mail when the attachment was referenced as a link to a document in the portal. This helped rapidly enforce the "one copy of a document" and "no more e-mail attachments" guiding principles.

- Eliminate any paper-based or e-mail distribution for regular reports or targeted communications if they can be found on the portal. For example, you may want to consider eliminating paper-based newsletters if you can use the portal to create targeted news items or simply post the existing newsletter to the portal and allow users to print it only if they want a paper copy. (This will not only help drive users to your solution, but it will also help support your organization's "green" initiatives!)

- Promote enthusiasm and eagerness by including high-value content and functionality in the first release. One important activity is to ensure that you have correctly identified a "killer application" and critical content for the first release of SharePoint 2010. This will be a key component of your plan if you are migrating from MOSS 2007 because users will want to understand the benefit (to them) of the upgrade. Be sure that you are implementing at least one type of content or application that users really want and have not been able to get before—this is the "wow" factor that helps encourage user adoption. For example, your portal might include a dashboard integrating information from different applications that provides a comprehensive view of a customer or an account. Your portal might also include a collection of links to all of the resources a new employee needs to quickly get up to speed in your organization. Identify valuable content or applications that users can only get on the portal to encourage users to try it. Design specific communications to promote the use of this content.
- Manage user expectations about what SharePoint 2010 is and isn't, emphasizing that it is a platform that is designed to evolve over time. Communications vehicles should emphasize and reiterate this point and should focus on the objectives of this first release and ask users to provide feedback regarding metadata (Did we get it right?), satisfaction (Are users happy with the end-user experience, and can they find what they are looking for?), and training (Do we need more?). Make sure you have a contact on each page so users know who is responsible for content.
- Remember that communications is an ongoing activity—you need to think about messaging beyond the initial launch, after the solution is operational as well. It will be difficult for your users to learn and appreciate all of the features of SharePoint 2010 in a single newsletter or training class. An ongoing communications effort provides additional opportunities to promote the features and functionality of SharePoint 2010 as well as your specific implementation.

A good communications plan identifies the method, the message, and the audience for each element. A good plan also includes activities for multiple phases of solution development, including messages that you may communicate during design, pilot, launch, and post-release. Use the structure in Table 9-3 as a starting point for developing your own communications plan. You can consider some of these suggested activities as well as others that are

Table 9-3 Communications Activities for New SharePoint Solutions

Communications Element/ Item/Medium	Description	Audience	Key Messages	Expected Outcomes	Timing	Responsibility
Article in Newsletter	Brief article (with no major commitments regarding timing) that talks about the plans for the new solution	Organization	Acknowledgment of stakeholders who participated in the initial interviews Key benefits of solution Status of project Initial deployment plan—where we are with pilots, etc. Expectations for new processes For more information call …	Awareness raised about the project Expectations managed regarding enterprise rollout and impact on individual users	During design	
Presentation at leadership team meeting(s)	Brief presentation and demo of new solution	Organization Leadership	Solution will deliver real business value to departments Search works! Navigation adds value Examples of business value demonstrated in early pilot experiences	Build awareness and commitment Build enthusiasm for using the solution Gain commitment for supporting solution launch	Likely to be towards the end of the pilot	
"Scavenger Hunt" (or similar activity)	Fun and engaging activity to get users to try the portal—could have a prize or prizes at the end	All of Organization	Solution is here Solution is useful Solution can help you be more effective in your job	Increased awareness, enthusiasm 50% participation (example only)	At launch	

Communications Element/ Item/Medium	Description	Audience	Key Messages	Expected Outcomes	Timing	Responsibility
Offer desktop wallpaper featuring an image representing new solution	Wallpaper graphic to offer to users to put on their desktops	Organization	Awareness of portal	Increased awareness Increased usage	Send a link to users (can repeat as necessary)	
"Give Away" For example: Laminated "cheat sheet" Magnet Post-it pads Chocolate bar imprinted or wrapped with the solution logo (a personal favorite, even if it only has a temporary existence)	Tangible item to remind users to try the solution	Organization	Solution is here Solution is useful Solution can help you be more effective in your job	Increased awareness	At launch	
Posters in break rooms	Poster or flyer posted in break rooms promoting the portal and usage scenarios	Organization	Solution is here Solution is useful Solution can help you be more effective in your job	Increased awareness	At launch	
Survey—use SharePoint survey Web part	Online survey to gather feedback regarding solution usage and value	Organization	Management wants to hear from users	Useful feedback Increased buy-in from users	30–60 days after launch	

(continues)

Table 9-3 Communications Activities for New SharePoint Solutions *(continued)*

Communications Element/ Item/Medium	Description	Audience	Key Messages	Expected Outcomes	Timing	Responsibility
E-mail to all Content Stewards/Site Owners	Memo to Content Stewards to provide reinforcement about the importance of keeping content current and relevant and following best practices	Content Stewards	Check your sites on a regular basis—look at content itself and metadata assignments	Improved content management Better search results	Monthly	
Demonstration at "all-hands" meetings	Brief demo and presentation about the solution at face-to-face meetings that occur during the first few months after launch	Organization	Solution is live! Opportunity to deliver value to your organization Demonstration of key features—improved search, etc.	Awareness and commitment to using the solution	As opportunity is identified	
Intranet promotion within the solution	Promote the portal within the portal using content on the home page	Organization	Feature key new content	Increased awareness Just-in-time learning	As opportunity is identified	
E-mail to Site Stewards and Site Designers with a learn, apply, join message	Message to encourage Stewards and Designers to get trained and join the Power Users community	Site Stewards and Site Designers	Learn (get trained!) Apply (best practices and standards) Join (the Power Users community)	More knowledge distributed across the organization Improved "findability" and search results	At initial launch and then periodically thereafter as part of ongoing communica-tions	

specific for your organization. Note that each activity suggested in the table has been successfully deployed in at least one organization. You will need to consider whether or not these activities might work in your organization but try not to limit yourself to what has been done in the past. Think about the culture of your own organization as you consider various options.

Key Points

As you prepare your training and communications plans, consider the following takeaways from this chapter:

- Think about the story of the Three Bears as you create your training plan. Too little training and you run the risk of ineffective SharePoint sites. Too much training and people will feel like they are drinking from a fire hose. Your goal: Use the suggestions in this chapter to try to get your training "just right."
- Train just enough and just in time. Consider offering training "topics" to supplement basic SharePoint training so that users can focus on areas of interest at the time that they need to learn more about a topic. SharePoint 2010 has even more features and functionality than SharePoint 2007. This will definitely be overwhelming to many users. To ensure that people retain and can process what they learn, think about how both training and communications can be offered in "consumable chunks."
- Provide training in more than just how to use the various SharePoint features. Make sure that training covers best practices that define which features to use in a variety of business scenarios.
- Supplement training in "why" and "how" with a set of reusable examples of common configurations such as sites to manage a team, sites to manage a project, or sites to provide or publish information.
- Explain the concept of metadata and show examples of document libraries "before" (with folders) and "after" (with metadata) so that users can understand how using metadata instead of folders improves content "findability." Do not use generic examples—make sure all examples include real data from your organization.
- In general, don't try to train all users in all features at one time. Consider introducing more advanced SharePoint 2010 functionality over time (for example, the ability to target content via audiences, the ability to set up document and meeting workspaces, and the ability to set up and personalize a My Site) so as not to overwhelm users with too much information. Consider targeted groups, however, for more advanced functionality.

- Think about communications as a "lifetime," not "one-time," process.
- Use the suggested format (and ideas) in this chapter to help jump start your communications and training plans.
- Focus on value to the user in your communications and training messages, emphasizing "what's in it for me" and the business benefit of participation in the solution.

PART II

OPTIMIZING

CHAPTER 10

MAKING SEARCH WORK: CONTENT, PEOPLE, DATA

For the 2010 product generation, Microsoft has several search offerings. These include SharePoint Foundation 2010, Search Server 2010 Express, Search Server 2010, SharePoint Server 2010, and FAST Search Server 2010 for SharePoint. Although we compare the various products at the end of this chapter, keep in mind while reading that our focus is SharePoint Server 2010.

This chapter contains the following key sections:

- Search as a Business Capability
- Using Search
- How SharePoint Search Works
- Analyzing and Designing Search
- Configuring Search
- Monitoring and Enhancing Search
- SharePoint 2010 Search: What's New? Limitations? Flavors?

Search as a Business Capability

Search is an important capability for business productivity. Throughout the course of a day, business users spend a significant amount of time retrieving documents and looking for information that can make their jobs easier. In some cases, browsing Web sites or navigating file shares for information can be effective; however, with search users can quickly access information from multiple sources and discover or recover information with less effort.

From a portal perspective, search is something that is often taken for granted. With the abundance of powerful search tools on the Web such as Google or Bing, people expect to find things very easily. Because of this, business users often expect their company search to "just work." The satisfaction standards are very high, and the tolerance for poor results is low. Fortunately, SharePoint provides many search features that make it possible to deliver a rich and complete search experience. But be forewarned: no tool is magic—you need to plan and execute in order to make it work effectively.

As with the other aspects of the SharePoint platform, search can be used for a wide range of business purposes. In the case of an intranet solution, search may be one of many features used to drive efficiency and consistency. In the case of an enterprise search portal solution, search just might be the primary purpose for a SharePoint deployment.

While planning, it is important to clearly define what the role of search is in your SharePoint project. This definition should be explained in a scope statement of the project plan for the portal or search project. The project plan should include an executive overview, value proposition, and some boundaries around the scope of the project and the approach to be taken in designing search. The project plan should describe the search solution in terms of the value it adds to the business. The effectiveness of the search solution depends on the quality of the resulting search solution as well as proper integration and adoption by the business. For these reasons, it is vital that that executive sponsors support concepts in the project plan. With backing from the executives and enough creative space to progressively elaborate during the search implementation process, the project team will be able to fully leverage the native functionality of SharePoint 2010.

Using Search

Search may be implemented as feature of a Web portal, or in the case of an enterprise search portal, it can be deployed as a stand-alone tool. In any event, SharePoint provides a familiar keyword search as is available on the Web. As a user, you can type in a word or phrase, press a button, and view results. Beyond using a search box, you may also experience search, contextually, without even knowing it. Search results Web Parts can be configured on portal pages with predefined queries. As you navigate to a page that has a search results Web Part preconfigured, you can view security trimmed links (search results) to relevant documents, people, and other information.

SharePoint 2010 search results contain several elements of information. Each result includes a URL link, a teaser (brief description of result), author name, date, and the size of document. If the desired search result is not immediately visible in the result set, there are refiners available to further drill and filter the results set. By default, refiners appear within a navigation panel on the left side of the search results page and provide a structured view of results, grouped by Result Type, Site, Author, and Modified Date. An example search results page is shown in Figure 10-1.

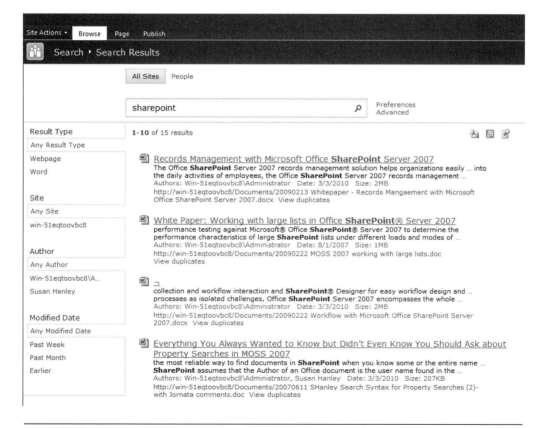

Figure 10-1 SharePoint automatically collapses duplicate results. When two nearly identical documents appear on a results page, only one will display. This result will contain a View duplicates link. By clicking the link, you may view all duplicates for this result.

Keywords

Keywords are the terms that a user enters in the search box to issue a search request. A keyword can actually be a simple term, which is a single word. For example, issuing a search on **contract** may yield a specific set of results. This is the most common way to search.

Keywords can also be issued as a phrase. A phrase includes two or more words separated by spaces and enclosed in quotation marks. If you don't include the words in quotation marks, SharePoint will search for either the first term *or* the second term. For example, a search for **statement of work** (without quotation marks) would return all results with the word **statement** or **work** in them. On the other hand, a search for **"statement of work"** would only return results containing that exact phrase in full.

Property Filters

Property filters allow a user to reduce the result set based on criteria defined in metadata properties. Common properties that are leveraged for this type of query include content source, author, and file type.

To retrieve a result set filtered by location, users can use the site keyword, which lets you filter results to those from a specific URL address. For example, to request results from only https://inside.mycompany.com, you could issue a search query including the term, **site:https//inside.mycompany.com**. Here are some other examples:

Author
author:Scott
author:"Scott Jamison"
author:"DOMAIN\sjamison"
Scope
scope:Discussions
scope:"Healthcare Documents"
File extension
filetype:xlsx
filetype:docx
filetype:pdf

Prefix Matching

Prefix matching allows you to search using only a partial beginning of a word or phrase. For example, a search for **"door*"** would return documents containing **doorway**. Because this method of using an asterisk in a keyword search only works for prefixes, a search for **"*way"** would not yield **doorway** results. Prefixes do work with property queries. For example, **author:mic** would return documents authored by people with the first names beginning with Mic, including Michael, Michelle, Michaela, and Mickey.

Inclusions and Exclusions

SharePoint keyword syntax allows you to specifically include or exclude search results having a particular word or phrase. Included terms allow you specify that you require certain terms to be in the result set; this is denoted by a plus sign (**+**). For example, if you are searching for information about Nevada laws but only want items that include the phrase "speed limit," you could issue a search for **Nevada + "speed limit"**. Similarly, you can exclude search results that contain a particular word or phrase using the minus sign (**−**). (Be sure to put phrases in quotation marks so that SharePoint knows that the words need to be found together.)

Boolean Expressions

SharePoint 2010 supports the use of Boolean expressions such as AND and OR. If you are searching your personal site for a spaghetti sauce recipe you uploaded, you might search for **tomato AND garlic AND oregano**.

Numeric Values

When you are searching for numeric values, you may be interested in providing an operator to limit the result set. SharePoint does support various formats for crawled properties, such as text, integer, date and time, binary data, and Yes/No. Supported search operators on numeric properties include $<$, $>$, and $=$. If you are searching customer order documents in a library that has a numeric Order Amount Column, you might try **Order Amount > 1000**. This will return results that have a number greater than 1000 in the Order Amount Column. Keep in mind that Managed Properties must be created and mapped to Crawled Properties prior to a full crawl before you can search for values in a custom document library Column or custom site Column.

URL Searches

When a user submits a search, the search box Web Part routes the user to a corresponding search results page. Included in the URL redirection is the query information. You can actually reproduce any keyword search that is produced from a search box Web Part simply by encoding the query in a URL. This technique is used primarily for development purposes, but it also has some practical uses for end users. For example, if you wanted to e-mail a hyperlink to a colleague so that he could view a search result, you could send him the complete URL containing the encoded search query. Note that the results may be different for that user because of security trimming.

To build a URL that contains a search query in it, first identify the URL of the search results page. It typically follows the following format: http://<server>/SearchCenter/Pages/results.aspx. If that does not match your environment, work with your search administrator to determine the correct URL.

Next, you can append the various search parameters.

Entering **k** lets you specify the keyword, which can be a single word, phrase, or prefix. For example, to search for **amaretto**, you would issue a request of **http://Portal/SearchCenter/Pages/results.aspx?k=amaretto**.

Entering **s** lets you specify the search scope. You can specify multiple scopes if necessary. Here is an example: **http://Portal/SearchCenter/Pages/results.aspx?k=stethoscope&s=HealthcareSites%2cMedical Journals**.

Alerts

Users can subscribe to search result sets. By default, search results pages contain action links called Alert Me and RSS. These action links allow the user to subscribe to the result set in using her preferred method. Figure 10-2 shows a subscription for a specific search term.

Using Advanced Search

In a default Search Center site, you may click an advanced search link to bring you to a search page containing a more sophisticated search box. An

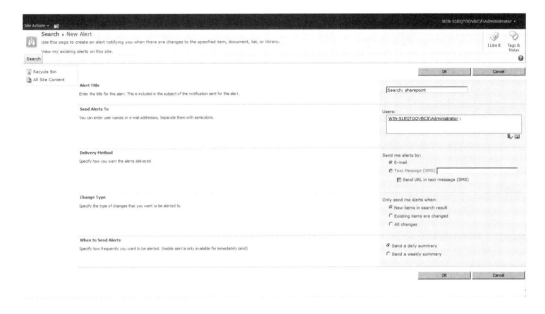

Figure 10-2 Alerts subscriptions can be configured for individuals or groups

advanced search box not only provides support for keywords, but also provides other options to specify a search query more granularly. Figure 10-3 shows an advanced search box.

Searching from Within Office

It is also possible to issue searches from within Microsoft Office applications. This assists with searching a company intranet, for example, for documents and other content without leaving the work you currently have open. To perform a search right from within Word, right-click a word and choose Look Up …. Office will then open the research pane, providing the option to look in a number of sources.

To search from Microsoft Word, you may need to add your SharePoint search as one of the search providers. To do this, you can begin by selecting the Research Options link at the bottom of the research pane. Next, click Add Services button and enter the URL of your intranet search Web service. The default name is http://<server>/_vti_bin/search.asmx. Microsoft Word should find your search service and present you with a confirmation. Click Install to add the service to the research pane.

Figure 10-3 The advanced search box can be configured to include custom property filters

How SharePoint Search Works

In addition to understanding how to use search functionality from an end-user perspective, it's also helpful to understanding the moving parts behind the scenes. This section covers two key components: the front-end components that drive the user experience and the back-end components that power the indexing and search query results.

The User Experience

In a SharePoint Site Collection, search pages, search Web Parts, and navigation elements are combined to create the search user experience. From an end-user perspective, the search box might be considered the primary component of search. The search box Web Part is one of seventeen or more search Web Parts which ships with the product. There are search box

Web Parts such as Advanced Search Box, People Search Box, and the Search Box, as well as search results Web Parts such as Federated Results, People Search Core Results, Search Core Results, and Top Federated Results. Each Web Part is configurable using a Web Part tool pane. In addition to search Web Parts, SharePoint also includes search page layouts for Advanced Search, People Search Results, Search Box, and Search Results.

Each search box is configured to point to a corresponding search results page, where the search results will display when an end user performs a query. The results page contains multiple Web Parts for displaying the results, as well as other elements, such as action links, to provide a rich user experience.

As the Site Collection components make up the user experience from a look-and-feel perspective, the search services actually determine which items are most relevant to a user's search query. Relevance is a measure of how well items in the index meet the user's criteria. With each search request, SharePoint retrieves matches, calculates a rank value for results from the index, and then returns the results to the search results Web Part in an XML format. The search results Web Part formats the raw XML into something more user-friendly by way of its XSL style sheet. The search results style sheet is configurable through the Web Part tool pane and customizable in SharePoint Designer. By default, search results are sorted in an order of rank value in descending order. In other words, the most relevant items display at the top of the search results page. Relevancy and rank are calculated by SharePoint using complex algorithms, which weigh and process a variety of ranking parameters such as frequency of search term, file type, click distance, URL depth, and language consistency.

Site Templates

SharePoint 2010 provides three site templates that can be used for search. These templates provide the navigation, page layouts, and Web Parts required to create a visual search experience. Figure 10-4 shows the search center site template options.

- **Enterprise Search Center**. A site for delivering the search experience. The Welcome page includes a box with two tabs: one for general searches and another for searches for information about people. You can add and customize tabs to focus on other search scopes or results types.

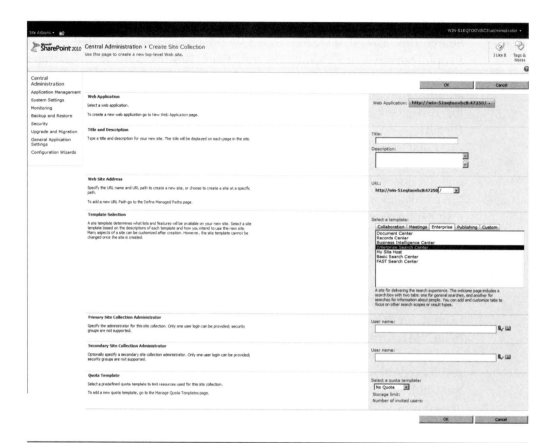

Figure 10-4 The three Search Center site templates are available in the Enterprise group of site templates

- **Basic Search Center**. A site for delivering the search experience. The site includes pages for search results and advanced searches.
- **FAST Search Center**. A site for delivering the FAST search experience. The Welcome page includes a search box with two tabs: one for general searches and another for searches for information about people. You can add and customize tabs to focus on other search scopes or result types.

Index and Query Components

When a user performs a search query, SharePoint is able to locate and retrieve the content from an index. Acting much like an index you might find in the back of a text book, SharePoint maintains an index of text from the crawled content. By default, the index is located in the Windows file system of the servers, which are running either the SharePoint search index service or the SharePoint search query service. The default path to the directory is C:\Program Files\Microsoft Office Servers\14.0\Data\Applications\GUID. Within a subdirectory, files store the unique keywords from crawled items as well as other pointer information. Gather logs, noise word files, and thesaurus files can also be located within subfolders of this directory location.

Where the index files are stored in the file system, a SQL Server database, called the Metadata Property Store, stores property information (used in scopes and filters) as well as security definitions for the crawled content.

Content sources contain address information (URL, UNC, and so on) and instruct SharePoint where to crawl. The index and property stores are populated by the index engine when content sources are being crawled. Crawling can be initiated manually or according to a schedule. Content sources are configurable within the Search Service Application, which is accessible from the Central Administration Web application. SharePoint 2010 supports the following types of content sources:

- SharePoint sites (this includes People)
- Web sites
- Fileshares
- Exchange public folders
- Line-of-business data
- Custom repository

Analyzing and Designing Search

An effective first step for designing a search solution is to identify stakeholders, business unit representatives, and sponsors who are responsible for providing guidance, resources, and funding for the project. Organize some detailed questions for them and then conduct interviews to facilitate the elicitation of business requirements.

Ask the business representatives the following:

- What types of content will be searched?
- What is the content used for?
- Where is the content stored?
- How much effort has been spent in cataloging content?

- What types of content can search help uncover?
- What are some example search queries that you might run?

Business Analysis

It is important to maintain a holistic mindset to requirements gathering because certain revealed information can ignite and expand subsequent conversations. You will discover how search impacts individuals and teams, as well as the enterprise as a whole. This approach results in a more solid foundation for the initial definition of search, which improves the search deliverables and limits future rework. The consequence to poor planning with search is that valuable information may be missed or not presented in an intuitive and useful way.

To promote good planning, interview business representatives and conduct focus group activities. The goal of eliciting feedback is to gather as much useful information about business needs as possible. This process should include free and open discussions and not be constrained by assumptions about the scope of the search implementation, the limitations of the software, or any other reason why a particular idea may or may not be implemented. The requirements analysis is not a scope definition exercise, and you are not obligating the business to any particular feature or capability. Instead, your goal is to completely understand what search capabilities the business needs and wants. During the pursuit of this information, it is acceptable and encouraged to explore the users' day-to-day processes and ask questions about how they do their jobs and what ways they think search could improve their jobs or somebody else's.

While gathering requirements, it is important to keep in mind that useful information can be contained in various forms, both structured and unstructured. The "right" answer to a question might exist in a document, a discussion thread, or a wiki. Business users expect a search engine to interrogate all possible sources in the pursuit of the answer. By understanding what the sources of information are and how to retrieve the right answers from the various content formats, you can effectively define the functional requirements of SharePoint search.

Creating a Business Requirements Document

The interviews and discussions can produce a plethora of information about search. You will need to figure out a way to consistently extrapolate and organize the requirements, feedback, ideas, and explanations that are provided. So before beginning the interviewing process, invest time in developing document templates and surveys for collecting and organizing the search requirements from the various facets of the organization. A benefit to documenting consistently across groups is that you can more easily merge the requirements from the disparate groups into a single document at a later time, grouping related information. An easy way to get started with building a search requirements document template is to add a section that identifies the types of content that business users might need to search for. This is a fundamental inquiry that will apply to everybody you meet with about search. As an example, Table 10-1 lists various types of content and provides a column where you can indicate whether or not a need exists.

The business capabilities that the SharePoint search features provide can only realize maximum potential if the proper analysis and planning efforts have been invested into the other facets of SharePoint. To leverage metadata properties most effectively, the business should have a common nomenclature and utilize consistent Column naming throughout its SharePoint portals and sites. These properties, in turn, can be configured as managed properties and then can be used within search scopes, which can greatly enhance the end-user experience.

Creating a Design Document

When you have completed the business analysis and planning process, you will need to translate the business needs to native SharePoint search functionality. Create a design document that contains sections that closely map to the SharePoint configurations. The design document is valuable because it not only represents what you need to do to build your solution, but it also doubles as an administrator document, which the support staff can reference and use to better understand how search has been configured.

While the process of designing the functional requirements of a SharePoint search solution initiate from the business-user perspective, the approach taken in configuring search runs a completely opposite course. When configuring, you should start with back end and gradually make your way to the user experience at the end of the process. First in the configuration sequence is the infrastructure, where you configure the necessary storage and processing resources. Next, you move into SharePoint Central Administration where you configure the farm-wide settings and server topology. Next, you go into the Search Service Application and configure search settings. Finally, you move into the Site Collection where you

Table 10-1 Example of Information to Gather to Define Search Requirements

Searching for ...	... in This Location	Need Exists? (Y/N)	Description of Content
Documents	SharePoint sites		
■ PDF	Fileshares		
■ Word	Exchange public folders		
■ Excel	Lotus Notes databases		
■ PowerPoint	Local hard drives (C:\)		
Web Content	SharePoint sites		
■ Text	Internal Web sites		
■ Links	Internet Web sites		
SharePoint List Items	SharePoint sites		
■ Custom Items			
■ Issues			
■ Tasks			
Discussions	SharePoint sites		
	Exchange Public Folders		
	Notes Databases		
People	SharePoint Profile Database		
	Active Directory		
	Exchange Address Book		
	LDAP directory		
	HR System		
Structured Business Data			
■ Database Records	ERP Database		
■ Transactions	CRM Database		
	Project Management Database		
	HR Management Database		
	Learning Management Database		
	Time and Billing Database		
	Issue Tracking Database		
	Accounting Database		
	Custom Database		

configure subsites, pages, Web Parts, and the navigation. The design document should flow in the direction of the configuration, from the back end forward to the end-user experience.

To effectively design and document a search solution, you must be very familiar with configuration steps and have in-depth understanding of the business requirements. The design document merges these knowledge areas into one cohesive artifact, which is why it is a critical component to the overall approach. Table 10-2 through Table 10-6 provide a starting point for creating a SharePoint search design document. These tables resemble the actual configuration screens within SharePoint, which make the process of configuring search a whole lot easier. And by having the configuration documented upfront, you can race through the configuration while making only minor adjustments to the document as you go, rather than trying to write a document from scratch and configure at the same time—or worse, try to backfill the documentation later.

Planning

To understand what is required to configure search, you may benefit from first breaking this topic into manageable parts. Search configurations occur at the following areas:

- Server/infrastructure
- Central Administration, Farm-wide Settings

Table 10-2 How Unique Content Sources May Be Configured

	Content Sources	
Title	**Type**	**Start Address**
Local Office SharePoint Server Sites	SharePoint sites	https://centraladmin.domain.com/
People	SharePoint sites	https://mysite.domain.com/ sps3s://mysite.domain.com/
Corporate Portal	SharePoint sites	https://inside.domain.com/
Extranet Portal	SharePoint sites	https://outside.domain.com/
Search Portal	SharePoint sites	https://search.domain.com/
Public Web Site	Web sites	http://www.domain.com/

Table 10-3 Crawl Schedule for Each Content Source

Content Source	Crawl Schedules Full Crawl	Incremental Crawl
Local Office SharePoint Server Sites	Not Scheduled	Not Scheduled
People	At 2:00 AM on 15th of every month	Every 12 hour(s) from 6:00 AM for 12 hour(s) every day
Corporate Portal	At 2:00 AM on 15th of every month	Every 5 minute(s) from 6:00 AM for 12 hour(s) every day
Extranet Portal	At 2:00 AM on 15th of every month	Every 5 minute(s) from 6:00 AM for 12 hour(s) every day
Search Portal	Not Scheduled	Not Scheduled
Public Web Site	At 4:00 AM on 15th of every month	Every 12 hour(s) from 6:00 AM for 12 hour(s) every day

Table 10-4 Document Your Service Account Credentials

URL	Crawl Rules Include or Exclude	Service Account
://centraladmin.domain.com/	Exclude	
://search.domain.com/	Exclude	Refer to Service Account Documentation
:///*brokensites.aspx	Exclude	
:///*rejectedsites.aspx	Exclude	
*://*allitems.aspx*	Exclude	
*://*allforms.aspx*	Exclude	

Table 10-5 Metadata Property Mapping Illustrates How Managed Properties Are Configured to Map to One or More Crawled Properties

Managed Property	Type	Use in Scopes	Include Values from	Crawled Property	Include in Index
	Integer	Yes	Single	SharePoint:isdocument (Integer)	Yes
				SharePoint:isdocument (Integer)	Yes
CustomIsDocument				Basic:22(Integer)	Yes
Created	Date and Time	No	Single	Basic:15(Date and Time)	Yes
				Office:12(Date and Time)	Yes
	Text	Yes	Single	Ows_Created_x0020_By (Text)	Yes
	Text			Office:4(Text)	Yes
Created By	Text			Mail:6(Text)	Yes
	Text	Yes	Single	FileExtension(Text)	Yes
				Ows_FileType(Text)	Yes
Fileextension				Ows_File_x0020_Type (Text)	Yes
Filename	Text	Yes	Single	Basic:10(Text)	Yes

Table 10-6 You May Require Numerous Scopes, Each Having Several Rules Each—It Is Important to Capture These Settings in a Document

Scopes		
Scope Name	Excel	
Target Results Page	Default	

Rules		
Scope Rule Type	Value	Behavior
Property Query	FileExtension = xls	Include
Property Query	FileExtension = xlsx	Include
Property Query	FileExtension = xlt	Include
Property Query	FileExtension = xlsm	Include

- Central Administration, Search Service Application
- Site Collection

Following the business analysis activities, you should have a good idea what content sources need to be included in the search solution. Use the content source information to plan for capacity. Investigate each content source, calculating the total size of the content in each source. Keep track of the current size as well as an estimated size using future milestone dates. When calculating the size of content stored within SharePoint Web applications, keep in mind that SQL Server content databases consume more space than just the size of the content itself, as database files (.mdf) and log files (.ldf) require additional overhead. With this information you can begin the technical analysis and design of the search infrastructure, including defining the following requirements:

- Accessibility requirements
- Capacity and storage requirements
- System performance requirements (remember to monitor the systems being crawled)
- Hardware requirements (servers, storage, processor, memory, network)
- Service Level Agreements (SLA) and availability requirements
- Disaster recovery

SharePoint search is a resource-intensive service, and so hardware needs to be sized accordingly. Storage requirements can vary greatly, depending on the size of the SharePoint farm, amount of content being crawled, nature of the content, as well as the use of properties. It is advisable to refer to online resources, such as Microsoft TechNet (http://technet.microsoft.com) or MSDN Blogs (http://blogs.msdn.com) for credible guidance on estimation approaches for infrastructure components. Table 10-7 provides some detail on capacity planning requirements.

Beyond the crawled content, you must plan to allocate storage for the search service application components. These include

- The inverted index files (located on index servers)
- Propagated index files (located on query servers)
- Search Service Application Crawl Store database (located on the database servers)

Table 10-7 Storage Estimates for Capacity Planning

Content Storage Estimates			
Title	Current Size	Estimated Size Now +1 Year	Estimated Size Now 3 Years
Local Office SharePoint Server Sites	100 MB	100 MB	100 MB
People	500 MB	500 MB	500 MB
Corporate Portal	2 GB	4 GB	6 GB
Extranet Portal	4 GB	5 GB	6 GB
Search Portal	100 MB	100 MB	100 MB
Public Web Site	500 MB	500 MB	500 MB
Space Required for Additional Content Source TBD	5 GB	10 GB	20 GB
Total Corpus	**~12 GB**	**~21 GB**	**~34 GB**

- Search Service Application database
- Search Service Application Property Store database
- SharePoint WSS Search database
- SQL Server Temp database

There are several components that make up SharePoint search topology. Among these include an Administration Component, a Crawl Component, Index, Databases, and a Query Component. With respect to servers in a server farm, SharePoint search components may be configured to run together on one system or spread apart on separate systems. This topology is defined within the SharePoint Central Administration, Modify Topology panel and must be configured prior to using search.

The optimal topology configuration depends on many variables. Hardware resources such as storage, CPU, disk I/O, memory, and network play an important role in planning the topology. Other factors might include available hardware, budget for future hardware, number of users, geographical characteristics, performance requirements, amount of content being crawled, nature of the systems being crawled, operational responsibility assignments, high availability requirements, and disaster recovery requirements.

The topology can adapt and scale as needs change. For example, to scale out from a single server topology, a general rule of thumb is that the SQL Server role would be the first component to separate onto its own server. Next, the indexing engine as it is processor-intensive, leaving only the Web Front End role and Query Server role remaining on the original server. Next, another SharePoint Web front end can be added and optionally dedicated for crawling purposes so that the users are not competing with the crawler for system resources. The environment can continue to scale by adding hardware nodes and reconfiguring the topology. As with capacity and performance planning, the infrastructure planning does require a detailed analysis of the environment because every situation is different.

Configuring Search

Having the design document will greatly streamline the configuration process because the important questions will have already been answered. This section provides an overview of the configuration approach as well as explanations about certain configuration tasks.

Configuration Overview

After the SharePoint Server 2010 installation has been completed, see the following list that delineates the approach to configuring search. This sequence is significant because certain configurations depend on previous configurations. For example, crawled properties depend on a full crawl, managed properties depend on crawled properties, scopes depend on managed properties, and Site Collection settings depend on scopes.

- Configure the server topology and farm-wide settings in the Central Administration, Farm-wide Search Administration page.
- Install third-party iFilters and custom document icons (for example, PDF).
- From the Central Administration, Search Service Application, configure the following:
  - File types
  - Content sources
  - Crawl schedules

- Crawl rules
- Crawler impact rules
- Authoritative pages
- Perform a full crawl of content
- Metadata properties (after full crawl completes)
- Search scopes
- From Central Administration, create a search center Site Collection.
- Within the Site Collection, configure the following:
  - Subsites
  - Search pages and search result pages
  - Search box and search results Web Parts
  - Keywords/best bets
- In the file system, configure the thesaurus files (optional).

Adding and Configuring Content Sources

Content sources are managed from the Central Administration, Search Service Application, Manage Content Sources page. As described in the previous section, you need to make content available to search queries by crawling the desired content to build the content index so that the information is searchable. Content source can be added and configured to instruct SharePoint to crawl the following types of locations: SharePoint sites, Web sites that are not SharePoint sites, file shares, Exchange public folders, line of business data, and custom repository. You can specify one or more start addresses (URLs) for each content source. A start address is the top of the content's hierarchy. For example, a root folder in a file share, folder structure is considered a start address.

It is possible have only one content source with many SharePoint start addresses in it; however, this configuration is less flexible than if you were to add a separate content source for each major starting address or SharePoint Web application. Configuring separate content sources provides greater control because it allows you to distinguish content within search scopes, allows you to set unique crawl schedules for different start addresses, and allows you to start and stop crawls on one start address without interrupting others.

Aside from start addresses and content sources, the content source configuration screen also allows you to specify if you would like to crawl only the starting address versus all content below the starting address.

To add a new content source, click the New Content Source link on the Manage Content Sources Screen to get the Add Content Source page. Here, you supply a name for your new content source. From here, you name the content source, provide a start address, and establish the crawl schedules. This process is shown in Figure 10-5.

To configure a content source for SharePoint sites, select SharePoint Sites as the content source type. Enter the URLs in the form, http://intranet. Next, configure the crawl settings and set up a schedule. Keep in mind that a high-intensity crawl may impair that underlying system and the network as well. Unleashing a crawl of network shares could also consume enough

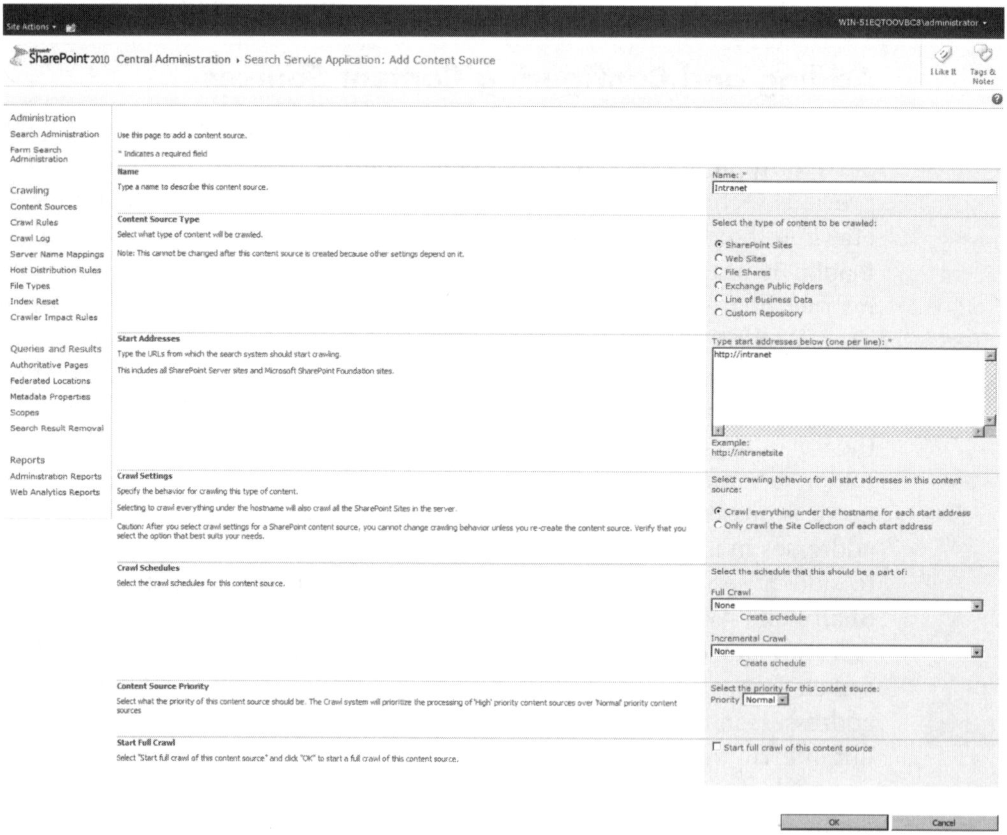

Figure 10-5 Add a content source from Central Administration → Search Service Application → Add Content Source

bandwidth to be noticeable to workers on the network. Furthermore, if you are backing up the search components of the SharePoint farm or the crawled systems, try to run these backup operations during periods when the crawl is not running. These tips help to reduce contention on the SharePoint servers as well as the servers storing the crawled content. It is also a good practice to document the system operation schedules, such as backups and crawls, and keep this information for reference. On an ongoing basis, crawl behaviors should be measured and monitored. You should keep track of the amount of content in the content sources as well as the amount of time it takes for a crawl to complete on the content source. If a content source grows, backups will take longer, and a job schedule overlap can occur, creating a contention. Reviewing and adjusting the crawl schedules should be considered as a regular responsibility for the support team. Figure 10-6 shows the crawler impact rules.

Federated Locations

Federated locations allow users to expand their searches to include content that is either in a remote SharePoint environment or retrievable by public Web sites that support OpenSearch 1.0 or 1.1. For example, if Bing is configured as a federated location, users searching from their SharePoint

Figure 10-6 Crawler Impact Rules can be used to throttle the intensity of the crawler on each content source and are configured within Central Administration and accessible from the Search Service Application page

search portals will retrieve results both from the local SharePoint index as well as from Bing. Federated locations are configurable from within the Central Administration → Search Service Application Manage Federated Locations page.

Authoritative Pages and Demoted Sites

Authoritative page settings prioritize locations in the content index so that results from those sites are more (or less) likely to appear ranked highly in the result set. Authoritative page settings are configured in the Search Service Application. Pages can have one of four ranking levels (most authoritative, second level, third level, and sites to demote). By default, all top-level pages for Web applications are added as most authoritative. You can move the top-level pages to other authoritative page levels or remove them from authoritative page settings completely.

When planning authoritative page settings, group sites into the three levels by importance. In addition, group the sites that are not likely to be relevant as sites to *demote*. Demoted sites will typically appear toward the end of the search results after all other relevance weighting factors have been considered. Don't try to assign an authoritative page to every single site. Start with obvious ones and then adjust the authoritative page settings based on feedback from users and information in the query logs and crawl logs. Authoritative pages and demoted sites are configurable from within the Central Administration → Search Service Applications → Specify Authoritative Pages screen.

Metadata Properties

When SharePoint crawls content, it includes stored property values in a database; these are crawled properties. Managed properties are the set of properties that are provided to the user as part of the search user experience (the ones that users can filter on, and so on). These map one-to-many to crawled properties. Some managed properties are created by default while in others, administrators must create and map. For example, if you crawl the file extension for documents, you must explicitly specify that the file extension crawled property be included in the index. This is done in the service application, under the metadata properties, crawled properties panel. Next, you must create a managed property called File Extension and map it to the appropriate crawled property. Creating a managed property allows users to leverage the property in keyword searches and allows scopes to leverage the managed property as a filter.

Search Scopes

A search scope provides a way to filter search queries by enabling users to focus their queries on a subset of the total index. Ideally, a search result will appear in the top 20 results when a user issues a query. By providing scopes, users can easily apply filters to their initial queries, making this benchmark much easier to reach.

Scopes can be configured to filter search results by content address, managed property (for example, issue status = unresolved), or content source. For example, a scope might allow a medical doctor to search on all items in the Medical Records Scope, where the Medical Records scope limits the results to items that are documents, located in a Records Center, having the file extension of PDF.

Note Scopes may be created within the Search Service Application as a shared scope or within a Site Collection as a local scope.

To help determine your search scopes, review your information architecture to identify Content Types and properties that people want to search. Create shared scopes for content in the information architecture that is relevant for more than one Site Collection being hosted in the farm.

To create a search scope, go to Search Service Application within Central Administration. Click View Scopes. Click New Scope. Enter a title, description, and keep the default results page. Once the scope is created, click Add rules.

Search scopes can contain one or more rules that are applied to all content in the currently selected search scope to determine what is included in search results.

You can set rules by

- Web address (location)
- Properties (managed properties)
- Content source (why it is beneficial to be using separate content sources for start addresses)
- All content (everything in the index)

For example, to set up a scope that only returns information from a specific site, add a Web Address rule where the Folder equals the site URL. This will provide a filtered search list that is scoped to a specific set of content.

Search User Interface

Once the search service application is configured, the next step is to create the user interface for search. When designing the search experience, a decision that needs to be made is whether to create a stand-alone search portal or integrate search features into an existing portal, such as an intranet or content management portal. The Search Center site templates may be used in either case. Once the search site structure is determined, there are numerous components within the Site Collection that combine to make up the overall user experience by providing controls to the user for submitting queries as well as the pieces needed to view and interact with results. The components of the search results page in Edit mode include

- Search pages and search Web Parts (basic, advanced, people)
- Search results pages and search results Web Parts
- Scope display groups
- Search keywords

Keywords and Best Bets

Keywords are words or phrases that SharePoint administrators have identified as important. They provide a way to display information and links on the initial results page manually. Created at the Site Collection level, keywords help to prioritize content during search queries to display high-relevance content more prominently in search results. Each keyword should have a definition of the keyword that appears in search results, one or more synonymous search terms, and one or more best bets, which are the URLs that administrators specify as being most relevant for a particular keyword phrase.

Searches that match keywords (or synonyms of keywords) show the specific preselected content (definition(s) and best bet(s)) at the top of search results. Best bets are used highlight or promote search results that the search administrator has determined are more relevant for users of a collection. You should choose obvious keywords to start, leveraging best bets to publicize very popular sites and continue to monitor the effectiveness of the chosen best bets over time.

Monitoring and Enhancing Search

You should continuously monitor how SharePoint search is being used—it will provide the insight required to tweak search results going forward. Go to Central Administration → Search Service Application → Web Analytics Reports → where you can find reports that provide valuable information about how search and other usage patterns.

The Administrative Report Library contains

- Crawl Rate per Content Source
- Crawl Rate per Type
- Query Latency
- Query Latency Trend
- SharePoint Backend Query Latency
- Crawl Processing per Activity
- Crawl Processing per Component
- Crawl Queue

The Web Analytics Reports include

- Number of Queries
- Top Queries
- No Results Queries

In addition to the reports found in the Search Service Application, there are also reports viewable within the SharePoint Site Collection. These include Web Analytics reports and Site Collection Web Analytics reports. Both can provide more information about how content within SharePoint Site Collections is being leveraged by the business. The Site Collection Web Analytics Reports provide additional, search-specific reports such as Number of Queries, Top Queries, Failed Queries, Best Bet Usage, Best Bet Suggestions, Best Bet Suggestions Action History, and Search Keywords.

SharePoint 2010 Search: What's New? Limitations? Flavors?

There are many exciting new features in SharePoint 2010 that go a long way in improving the overall search experience for business users. Individually, each offers incremental value; together they help drive business value from your investment in configuring and optimizing search across your corporate content. These new features include the following:

- **Expanded sorting options**. Sort results by relevance, date oldest, and date newest.
- **Search refiners**. A structured view of result categories allowing you to interactively explore and navigate the top results.
- **Social definitions/social tag ranking**. Click through rates of SharePoint content is monitored and tracked. These statistics are used to influence the relevancy ranking of search results. Ranking improves with use of content.
- **People search improvements**. More user profile information is exposed by default (name, contact information, title, responsibilities, and what the person is working on).
- **New and enhanced Web Analytics and Search Administration reports**.

SharePoint Server 2010 Search Limitations

There are some key limitations that you should be aware of when using SharePoint 2010 for enterprise search:

- There is no configuration for the "Did you mean" feature. While this feature is useful, it is not configurable.
- There is no support for regular expression queries, that is, pattern searches such as xxx-xx-xxxx for social security number.
- There is no graphical user interface for managing the thesaurus. This is done in the file system using the thesaurus files.
- SharePoint does not crawl the text within an image by default. A third-party iFilter is required for optical character recognition.

What Flavor of SharePoint 2010 Search Is Right for You?

At the very beginning of the chapter, we mentioned that there are several options available in the SharePoint 2010 suite related to search (Table 10-8). They range from the very simple to the very robust (for example, FAST). Which is right for your organization? Table 10-8 highlights the key functionality offered in each search option. Remember, the bigger the tool, the more investment you will need to make (in money and time) to implement it properly.

Table 10–8 Comparison of the Features of the Microsoft SharePoint 2010 Search Product Editions

Feature	SharePoint Foundation	SharePoint Server Standard CAL	SharePoint Server Enterprise CAL	FAST Search Server for SharePoint
Site templates containing page and Web Parts designed for search layouts		X	X	X
Search SharePoint sites (same Site Collection)	X	X	X	X
Search SharePoint sites (different Site Collections)		X	X	X
Custom search scopes (local)		X	X	X
Custom search scopes (Shared)		X	X	X
Search Web sites, files shares, Exchange Public Folders, line of business data, custom repositories		X	X	X
Search line-of-business data			X	X
Search custom repositories			X	X
Search people and expertise		X	X	X
Search Rich Web content				X
Security trimming of search results	X	X	X	X
Sort results by date newest, date oldest				X
Sort results by metadata properties				X
Refiners for top results		X	X	X
finers for all results				X
Previewers for results				X
Search alerts (e-mail and RSS)		X	X	X
Advanced user and group contextualization		X	X	X
Basic keywords and best bets		X	X	X

(continues)

Table 10–8 Comparison of the Features of the Microsoft SharePoint 2010 Search Product Editions *(continued)*

Feature	SharePoint Foundation	SharePoint Server Standard CAL	SharePoint Server Enterprise CAL	FAST Search Server for SharePoint
Visual best bets				X
Federated search (remote SharePoint farms and public Web sites)		X	X	X
Federate from Windows 7		X	X	X
Result suggestions		X	X	X
Basic ranking influence		X	X	X
Advanced ranking schema management				X
Social tagging of content influences ranking			X	X
Activity influenced ranking (popular contentranks higher)		X	X	X
Keyword-based document boosts				X
Manually define metadata properties		X	X	X
Advanced property extraction from unstructured content				X

Key Points

There are many key factors that help make the search experience all it can be. No matter what technology you use for search, you will always need to make sure that your content structure, taxonomy, and search engine settings are optimized in order to meet your search goals.

- Invest time in collecting user requirements before you begin designing your search solution. Make sure you are including the right people in your analysis.
- Plan the infrastructure and search server topology in a way that supports high performance and scalability.
- Document the user requirements and the design specifications. For the design specifications, use tables that map closely to the actual configuration screens within SharePoint Central Administration, the Search Service Application, and the Site Collection.
- Promote information architecture best practices for crawled content.

- Teach users how search works and how to use it.
- Use the Administration Reports and the Web Analytics Reports located in the Central Administration Web application to monitor search and site usage patterns so that you can make adjustments to ensure users will find what they are looking for quickly, with a minimal number of clicks.

CHAPTER 11

MAKING BUSINESS PROCESSES WORK: WORKFLOW AND FORMS

Organizations, large or small, typically have a common need: capturing documents and/or data and then acting upon those documents or data through some kind of process. In this chapter, we cover two key elements that SharePoint offers in the way of technology that enables business processes of this type, specifically workflow and electronic forms. This chapter's key sections include

- Getting Started with Workflow
- Workflow Terminology
- Using the Provided Workflows
- Creating Custom Workflows with SharePoint Designer 2010
- Designing Workflows with Visio 2010
- Using InfoPath 2010 to Create Electronic Forms

SharePoint makes use of workflow to enhance the capabilities of document libraries and lists. Workflow features are useful when you want to orchestrate document authoring, review, approval, and publishing processes. SharePoint supports both parallel and serial approval. You can also use workflow in business scenarios—for example, expense approval and purchase order routing. The workflow engine manages the execution of activities. It enables business users to extend SharePoint by providing rules, conditions, and activities.

Getting Started with Workflow

One of the challenges of network drive-based (or even e-mail-based) collaboration is the proper routing of content to the right people at the right time. Typically, coworkers are either blind to activity happening on shared drives or inundated with e-mail discussions about content that they are not actively monitoring. Automated workflows ease this burden by offering a structured means of transporting content, typically documents or forms, to the appropriate reviewers for comments, approval, or publishing. In some ways, think of workflow as a manageable business rules engine that allows administrators to predefine the routing of information across its life cycle. As an example, consider a standard employee reimbursement form. Typically, a manager or supervisor must review or approve the submitted claim before it is processed. This causes two problems: 1) the coordination among employee, reviewer, and finance representatives is sometimes clunky, and 2) there is no auditing maintained around the form activity (for example, who approved the submission? when? why haven't I received my check?). Workflow solves both problems by allowing for the routing and auditing of content.

From a SharePoint perspective, workflow allows for the management of content movement (through a review or approval cycle), auditing of all activity associated with the content, and task list integration that allows users to see what items are pending their review or approval. This is all done in an interface that most employees interact with regularly. Notifications from workflow processes can be e-mailed so users do not have to monitor task lists. In addition, exceptions can be defined, so if unexpected delays in processing occur, someone is notified.

One of the biggest challenges in implementing a successful workflow strategy is not so much becoming an expert in the custom workflow creation process, but rather understanding how to define a clear and accurate business process. Before associating a workflow with a SharePoint list or document, ask

- How do you define the life cycle of the associate business process (who should approve it first? how many people should we ask for feedback from? if this document should go to someone's manager, does the system have that data?)
- What is the current process? What are the benefits of automating this process?
- How do you deal with exceptions (for instance, what if someone is away or sick)?

- How important is it that we log all activity associated with this list item or document? Do we need to look back historically on previous content for insight into the approval process?

Whether it is a simple serial, single-person approval process or a complex workflow associated with many conditional layers and approvers, designing the business rules first will ensure that the right technology decisions are made later. As you see in the coming sections, SharePoint offers some native workflow processes as well as integration with SharePoint Designer custom workflows (and even Visio, .NET-based, or third-party created complex solutions). In every case, it is important to effectively manage the processes and expectations surrounding this business-critical content movement.

Workflow Terminology

SharePoint Server 2010 and SharePoint Foundation 2010 include the capability to use workflows within a list or document library as well as at the site level (that is, not associated with a list item). While both versions offer the same fundamental platform (Windows Workflow Foundation), the difference comes down to what default workflows are offered (see Table 11-1). Beyond the default workflows, custom workflows can be developed using SharePoint Designer 2010 or Visual Studio 2010. Because this book focuses on creating solutions without custom code, we focus on the SharePoint Designer solutions only, which we cover later in the chapter. For now, let's focus on the fundamentals of workflow in SharePoint, including the differences between workflow templates, workflow associations, and workflow instances.

Note After the 2003 Office System was released, Microsoft realized that it would be smart to consolidate workflow engines, so it developed Windows Workflow Foundation (WF), which ships as a free platform component of .NET 3.0. Starting with SharePoint and Office 2007, WF is automatically installed with either and is used as the foundation for SharePoint workflow.

Templates, Associations, and Instances

There are three ways to describe a workflow. A workflow *template* is the initial description of what should happen (steps, conditions, activities, and so on). When you take a template and bind it to a list or library, that linkage is called an *association*. When you add an item to a workflow-enabled list, the workflow that starts up and processes that item is called a workflow *instance*.

Let's say you have a workflow template called Approval. You could associate the workflow template to three separate lists (list A, list B, and list C). Within each list, there are ten items, each in one of the various stages of workflow processing. In this scenario, there is a total of:

- One workflow template
- Three associations (one template x three lists)
- Thirty workflow instances (three associations x ten items each)

Using the Provided Workflows

To get you started, SharePoint provides several out-of-the-box workflows that can be applied immediately to your lists and libraries. While SharePoint Foundation Server 2010 users only get one such workflow (the Three-State workflow), SharePoint Server 2010 users have several to choose from. The advantage of using these workflows is that users can simply apply them directly without waiting for custom workflows to be built and deployed. The provided workflows are designed to be generic enough that they can be applied to many review and approval processes. Table 11-1 lists some of the more popular workflows provided.

Table 11-1 Default Workflow Templates That Allow You to Get Started with Your Workflow Immediately

Name	Description	Use For ...	Available in SharePoint Foundation 2010?
Approval	Routes a document (or list item) to one or more users for approval via a Web-based form.	Generic approval processes in document libraries and publishing sites.	N

Name	Description	Use For ...	Available in SharePoint Foundation 2010?
Collect Feedback	Routes a document (or list item) to one or more users for feedback. Reviewers can provide feedback, which is then compiled and sent to the person who initiated the workflow once the workflow has completed.	Aggregating feedback on a document.	N
Collect Signatures	Routes an Office document to one or more users to collect approval via digital signatures. Note: This workflow must be manually started from within Office 2007 or 2010.	Digital-signature-based approval processes for Office documents.	N
Disposition Approval	Manages document expiration and retention by allowing participants to decide whether to retain or delete expired documents.	Records Management (retaining or deleting expired documents and/or list items).	N
Three-State	Manages business processes and complex workflows. Lets you choose what happens (re: choice fields in a list and its initial, middle, and final states).	Tracking items in a list—things like issues, tasks, and so on. Useful for adding to a task list as stage 2 of an approval workflow to track the actual task.	Y
Publishing Approval	Routes a page for approval. Approvers can approve or reject the page, reassign the approval task, or request changes to the page.	Use for approving Web pages as opposed to documents.	N

Associating a Workflow with a List

By default, workflows are not associated with any of the list templates provided, but using them is a very simple process. To see what workflows are available for your list, let's look at a Document Library.

To associate a workflow, open your document library and select the Library tab under Library Tools in the ribbon. In the settings section on the right, you will notice an icon menu for workflows (see Figure 11-1).

From here, you can select to Add a Workflow to your library. This will open the Add a Workflow page shown in Figure 11-2.

On the Add a Workflow page, you will find several options:

- Select Workflow Template
- Workflow Name
- Task List
- History List
- Start Options

The template list displays all the workflows available to you for your library. For this example we use the Approval workflow for our Annual Newsletter Review. The task list is used to store tasks that are assigned during the workflow (in this case reviewer tasks). The history list is used by the workflow to store messages such as status, errors, and general feedback. See Table 11-2 for start-up options on workflows.

Once you have all options configured and click Next, the Properties page for the workflow opens (see Figure 11-3). This lets you define the default list of approvers among other values such as approval order, notification message, task due dates, and so on. When you elect to let users initiate the workflow manually, these settings can be overridden by the user who initiates the workflow. If you elect to start the workflow automatically, the default settings will always be used when the workflow begins.

Figure 11-1 The workflow menu under Library Settings on the list ribbon allows you to add a workflow to your list

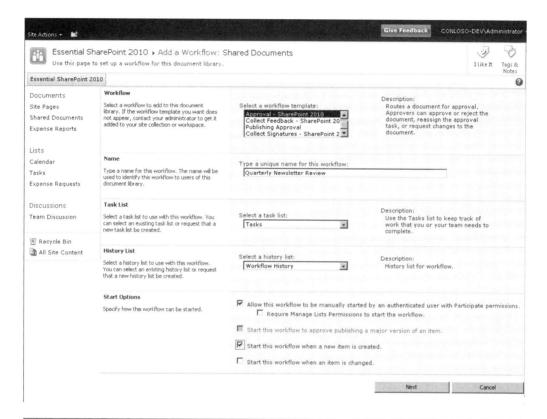

Figure 11-2 The first page of the out-of-the-box workflow wizard lets you configure its name, associated template, and start-up parameters

Had we chosen a different workflow, the options presented to us in the properties page may be completely different. Indeed, certain workflows may not require default properties at all.

Testing Your Workflow

With the workflow association complete, we are ready to test. To test the new workflow, upload a document into your document library or create a new one from the New icon. If you selected a manual start, your workflow

Table 11-2 Workflow Start-up Options Allow You to Control When the Workflow Is Initiated

Name	Description	Use For ...	Notes
Allow this workflow to be manually started.	Lets a user manually initiate this workflow for an item.	Letting users selectively run workflows on items.	The default settings on workflows can be overridden by the user initiating the workflow.
Start this workflow to approve publishing a major version of an item.	This workflow starts when a user marks (publishes) a document as a major version.	Making sure published items get approvals. Uses the content approval feature, which keeps items in draft state until approved.	Out-of-the-box workflows only. Only available for libraries with major versioning enabled.
Start this workflow when a new item is created.	Automatically initiates the workflow when a new item is added or created.	Ensuring workflows always run for newly added items (approvals and so on).	
Start this workflow when an item is changed.	Automatically initiates the workflow when an existing item is modified.	Ensuring that a workflow runs for modified items (approvals and so on).	

will not begin automatically. Instead, a user will have to initiate the workflow. There are two ways to initiate a manual workflow: from the items workflow page, or from within an Office 2007 or 2010 client application such as Word or Excel.

Starting the Workflow from the Item Workflow Page

For workflows that can be started manually, you do so from the item's workflow page (see Figure 11-4). This is accessed from the items context menu using the Workflows option or by clicking the Workflows icon in the ribbon.

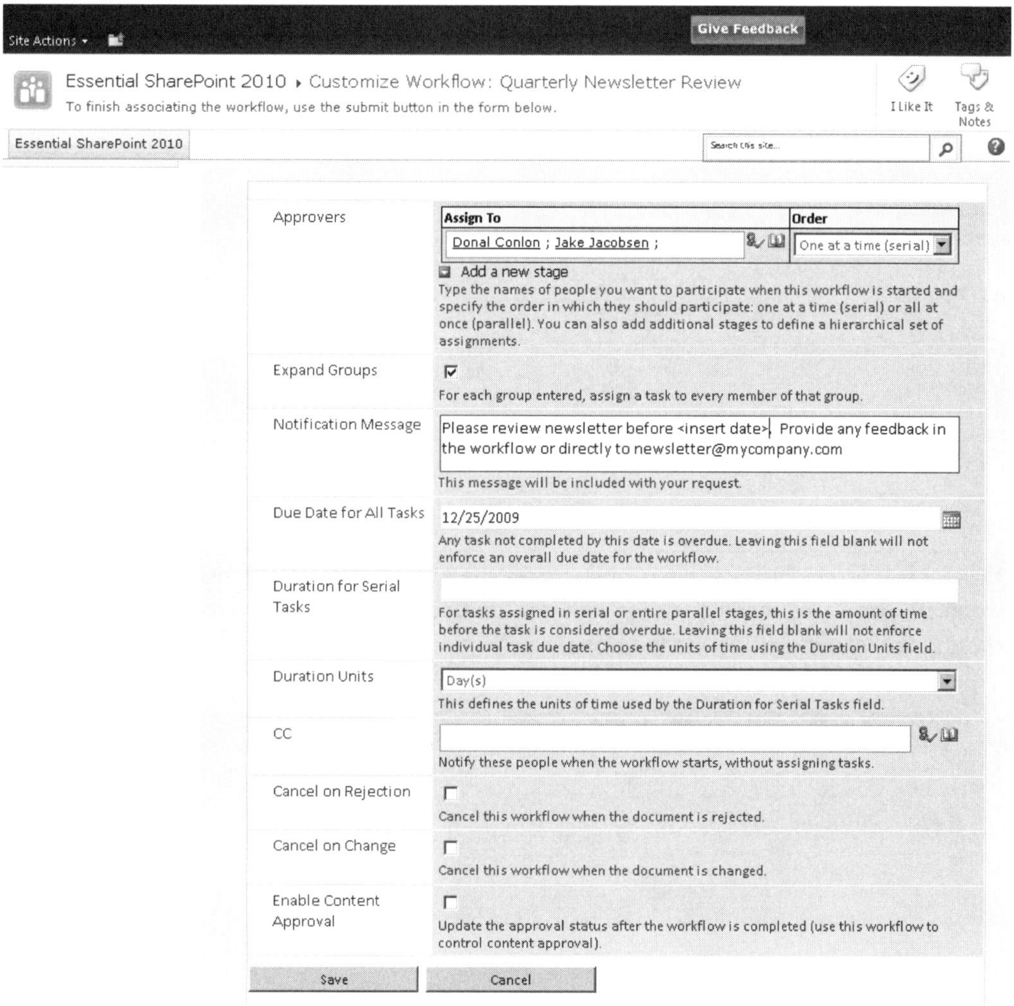

Figure 11-3 Use the second page of the workflow wizard to set default settings for the workflow

The workflows page will display all the available workflows that can be started, as well as any running and completed workflows (see Figure 11-5).

Select the desired workflow, in this case the Quarterly Newsletter Review. Because we are gathering information described earlier (refer to Figure 11-3), we have the opportunity to modify the default values such as

Figure 11-4 Select the Workflows option from the context menu to access the items workflow page. The workflow page can also be accessed by selecting the list item and clicking the Workflows icon in the ribbon.

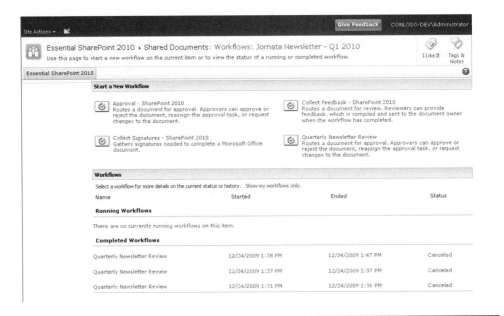

Figure 11-5 The Item Workflow page allows you to select a workflow to start, and also shows running and completed workflows

approvers, notification message, and so on. If the workflow did not require starting values, it would start immediately.

Starting the Workflow from Office 2010 Client

With SharePoint's tight integration with Office 2010, it is not necessary to find the document in the browser to start its workflow. If you have the document already opened, go to the document BackStage (the File tab) and select Share, as you see in Figure 11-6.

From the Share page, you see the available workflows listed at the bottom. Selecting the Quarterly Newsletter Review workflow displays its description and a Start Workflow button. Figure 11-7 shows the dialog requesting the start properties for the workflow, similar to how it would appear if started from the browser.

With the workflow now started, the next task is to check its status to make sure it is running and to see what stage it is at.

Checking the Workflow Status

Once again, we open up the item workflow page. This time we see our workflow listed under Running workflows. Clicking the workflow title

Figure 11-6 The Office 2010 BackStage allows you to start a workflow without having to leave the client application

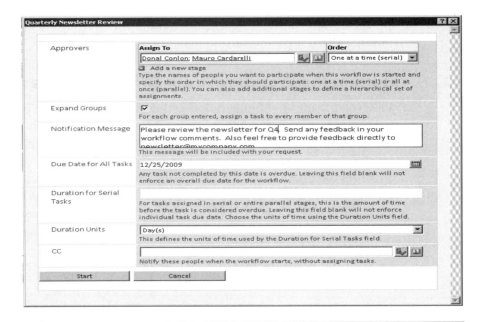

Figure 11-7 Office 2010 client prompts for workflow properties similar to starting the workflow from the browser

will open the information for this workflow instance. Figure 11-8 shows the information page where we can see general status information at the top as well as tasks that have been assigned and a running workflow history.

Note   With Visio Services running, the Workflow Information page can display a graphical representation of the workflow if the workflow originated from Visio. Using this service is discussed in more detail later in the chapter.

It's not very practical for the user to have to check the workflow information page to see what tasks have been assigned to them, and they don't. Typically, when tasks are assigned through workflow, the assignee is notified via e-mail. Figure 11-9 shows the e-mail our assignee received in Outlook. The e-mail contains a link directly to the document for review and also includes a button in the ribbon to open the task where they can (in this case) approve or reject the document.

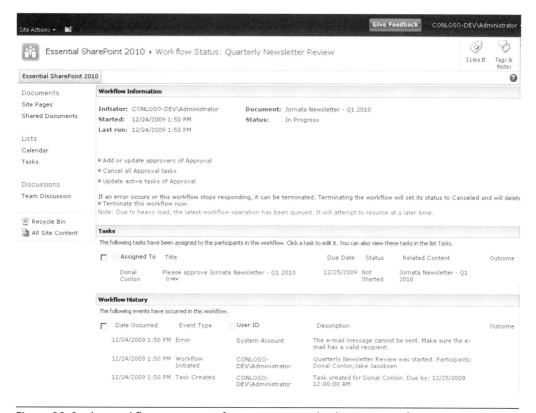

Figure 11-8 The workflow instance information page displays status information as well as task assignments and a running workflow history

As well as sending the e-mail, Office 2010 provides a handy notification bar at the top of the document that also allows the user to open the task directly (Figure 11-10). If he accidentally closes the information bar, there is also a link to the task from the Info page under the File tab.

The task form allows the assignee to fill in feedback and to action the task by approving, rejecting, and so on (Figure 11-11). For our approval workflow, the user can also request a change or even reassign the task.

The workflow templates that SharePoint Server 2010 provides have plenty of functionality that will suit the majority of simple approval workflows. However, the user is not limited to these workflows alone. The next section discusses using SharePoint Designer to take workflows to the next level.

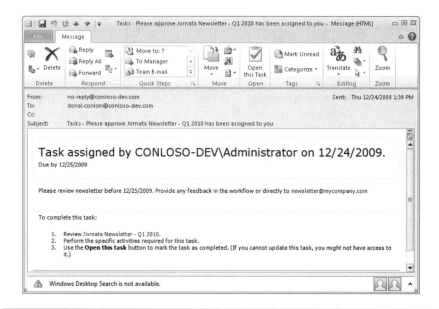

Figure 11-9 The assignee is notified when a task has been assigned to him or her. From the e-mail, he or she can access the item or document directly as well as the assigned task.

Creating Custom Workflows with SharePoint Designer 2010

When you find the workflows that SharePoint provides for you do not quite fit the process, Microsoft SharePoint Designer 2010 gives you the ability to modify them or even design your own from scratch. This gives a business analyst or Power User the ability to create his or her own workflows without requiring the involvement of IT or even a developer. Using a predefined list of activities, the user can whip up a workflow to route her documents for approval, move documents, modify properties, and so on.

Note SharePoint Designer started its life as Microsoft FrontPage. While it was feared by many IT groups because of what damage untrained users could do to SharePoint, it has since evolved into an essential tool for managing SharePoint content by both IT personnel and business users. SharePoint 2010 adds additional controls and settings for IT administrators to have more granular control over who can use SharePoint Designer, what actions they can perform, and on what sites.

Figure 11-10 Office 2010 notifies the user that a workflow task has been assigned to him or her for this document

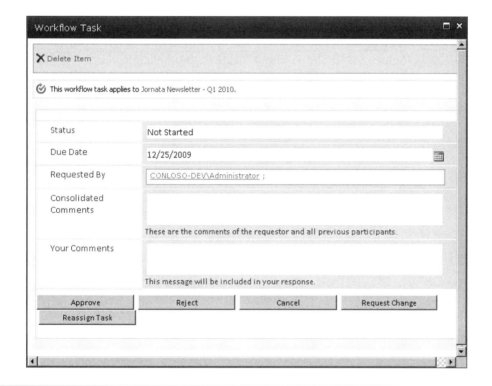

Figure 11-11 The workflow task form allows the reviewer to provide comments and to approve or deny the document

SharePoint Designer connects directly to a SharePoint site and allows the user to manage content in a very rich user interface. The workflow tools within Designer allow the user to develop a workflow specifically for a list, or a generic workflow that can be used by many lists.

Introducing SharePoint Designer (for Workflow Development)

Before we jump in to creating our first workflow in SharePoint Designer, let's take a look at the application to see what we are dealing with. Figure 11-12 shows SharePoint Designer 2010 opened at its home page for our site.

You can see from the home page that you can get a quick overview of the site, including general information, permissions, subsites, and other settings.

In the navigation pane on the left, you see a list of all available objects such as lists and libraries, workflows, site pages, and so on. As you can see, you can browse the majority of objects within SharePoint related to design. With our focus being on workflow, let's open that tab to see what we have.

Figure 11-13 shows the Workflow tab selected. You will notice the options on the ribbon are all related to our workflow tasks. The main pane lists all our available workflows; because we have not created any custom workflows yet, this list only displays the reusable workflow templates

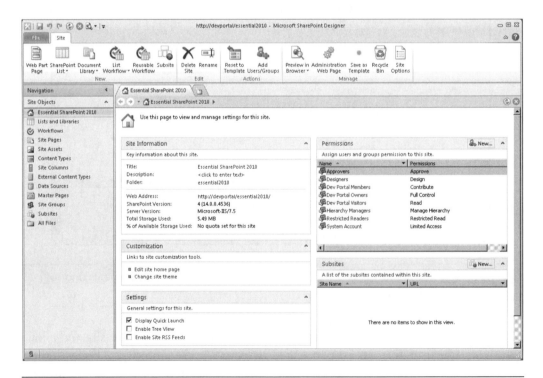

Figure 11-12 The SharePoint Designer 2010 home page for our connected site displays general site information as well as subsites and permissions to the site

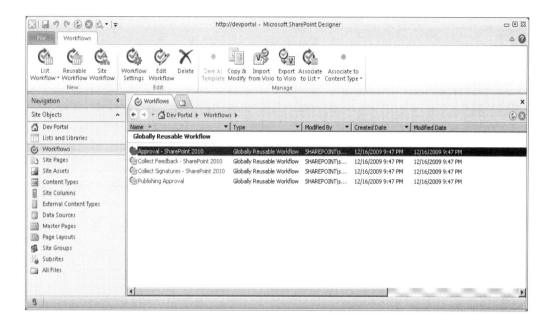

Figure 11-13 The Workflow tab displays our available workflow templates and provides all our workflow options in the ribbon

provided with SharePoint Server 2010. The ribbon keeps us focused on the task at hand by making only our workflow options available.

Clicking any of the workflows listed will open an information page for that workflow template. This gives us a quick overview of information about the workflow, start options, and even the forms associated with the workflow (see Figure 11-14). This is very useful for troubleshooting.

Note You may be wondering why the workflow Quarterly Newsletter Review that we created earlier is not listed. Even though we created a new workflow, we used an existing template (the Approval—SharePoint 2010 template) to create that workflow. If you navigate to the documents library through Designer, you will see it listed in the workflows section for that list.

Workflow Types

When creating a workflow from Designer, there are three options: List Workflows, Reusable Workflows, and Site Workflows. The differences are explained in Table 11-3.

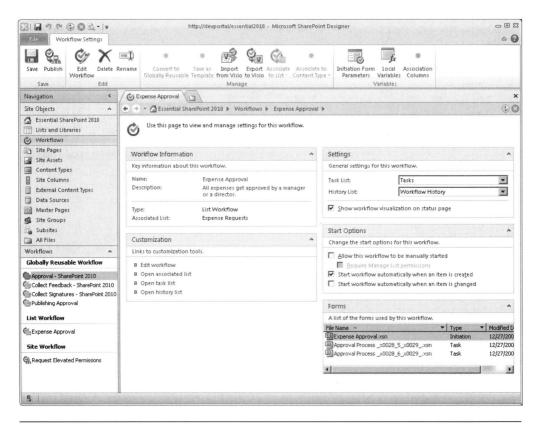

Figure 11-14 The Workflow Information page displays an overview of the workflow, including the forms that it uses

Table 11-3 Three Types of Workflows to Choose From

Workflow Type	Description
List Workflow	Associated directly with a list. Cannot be reused on a different list. Content-sensitive so can work directly with list values.
Reusable Workflow	Not associated with any list. Can be associated with any list once created. Is not content-sensitive.
Site Workflow	Associated with the site and not a list. Can be used for workflows that are not associated with list data. Manually run from the site Actions menu.

Note Site workflows are new to SharePoint 2010. In SharePoint 2007, to achieve the same type of workflow you had to *fake it* by using a list with a single dummy item.

Workflow Association Options

When you create a new reusable workflow, it cannot be used until it has been associated with a list or Content Type. When you open the workflow in Designer, you will have both association options in the ribbon in the Manage section. When you click Associate to List, you will see all the available lists to associate with. Similarly, when you click Associate to Content Type, you will see available Content Types. The benefit of associating a workflow to a Content Type is that it will work for all items using that Content Type in any list where the Content Type is in use.

Workflow Actions

SharePoint Designer ships with a set of actions specifically for SharePoint interaction. This list can be extended by installing third-party actions or even developing your own. Table 11-4 lists all the actions provided with Designer.

Creating a Simple Workflow

We covered the basics of Workflows in SharePoint Designer 2010; let's create a simple workflow to see how it actually works. For our example, we are going to create a *site workflow* that allows a site member to request elevated privileges—so a visitor can request to be upgraded to a member, and a member can request to be upgraded to an owner. All the site workflow will do is e-mail the administrator with the request, so it does not need to be associated with a list item.

For our workflow, we need to

- Define the initiation variable for the requested role.
- Create a step to e-mail the administrator.
- Create a task for the administrator.
- Write to the workflow history.

Table 11-4 Actions to Choose from When Developing a Workflow in Designer

Action	Description	Available in Visio?
Core		
Add a Comment	At the time of this writing, this action does not do anything in the release candidate version of SharePoint 2010.	Y
Add Time To Date	Adds a time period to a date variable.	Y
Do Calculation	Does a basic calculation such as addition and outputs to a variable.	Y
Log to History List	Writes an entry to the workflow history.	Y
Pause for Duration	Pauses the workflow for a defined period.	Y
Pause until Date	Pauses the workflow until a defined date.	Y
Send an E-mail	Defines e-mail recipients, subject, and body.	Y
Set Time Portion of Date/Time Field	Sets time value and outputs to a variable.	Y
Set Workflow Status	Sets status of current workflow.	Y
Set Workflow Variable	Uses a workflow variable to store values.	Y
Stop Workflow	Terminates the workflow.	Y
Document Set Actions		
Capture a Version of the Document Set	Can specify document set with major or minor versions.	N
Send Document Set to Repository	Copies or moves a set to a defined content organizer.	Y
Set Content Approval Status for the Document Set	Sets the status with comments.	Y
Start Document Set Approval Process	Kicks off an approval process for the set for list of users.	Y

Action	Description	Available in Visio?
List Actions		
Check In Item	Checks in the item and provides comments.	Y
Check Out Item	Checks out the item.	Y
Copy List Item	Copies an item from one list to another.	Y
Create List Item	Creates an item and outputs it to a variable.	Y
Declare Record	Declares current item as a record.	
Delete Item	Deletes defined item in list	Y
Discard Check Out Item	If item is checked out it will be discarded.	Y
Set Content Approval Status	Sets status to Approved, Rejected, or Pending.	Y
Set Field in Current Item	Updates field value.	Y
Undeclare Record	If an item is a record, it will be reverted.	
Update List Item	Commits any changes made to item.	Y
Wait for Field Change in Current Item	Pauses workflow until a field value condition is met.	Y
Relational Actions		
Lookup Manager of a User	Gets manager from Active Directory.	Y
Task Actions		
Assign a Form to a Group	Defines a form with simple fields and assigned to list of users.	Y
Assign a to-do Item	Creates a task for a user and adds to workflow task list.	Y
Collect Data from a User	Builds a custom form and outputs values to variable.	Y
Start Approval Process	Kicks off an Approval workflow.	Y
Start Custom Task Process	Kicks off a Task workflow.	Y
Start Feedback Process	Kicks off a Feedback workflow.	Y

(continues)

Table 11-4 Actions to Choose from When Developing a Workflow in Designer *(continued)*

Action	Description	Available in Visio?
Utility Actions		
Start Feedback Process	Kicks off a Feedback workflow.	Y
Extract Substring from End of String	Manipulates a string value.	N
Extract Substring from Index of String	Manipulates a string value.	N
Extract Substring from Start of String	Manipulates a string value.	N
Extract Substring of String from Index with Length	Manipulates a string value.	N
Find Interval Between Dates	Manipulates a string value.	N

Let's get started. From the workflow tab in SharePoint Designer, click the Site Workflow icon in the ribbon to create a new workflow. Figure 11-15 shows the dialog where we enter the workflow name and description.

The main pane starts with a Step 1 for the workflow (see Figure 11-16). The Insert group on the ribbon has options to allow you to add workflow elements such as conditions or actions. Our workflow will have three simple steps, which are described here:

1. Send e-mail. Edit the e-mail to include the user name and site name and send to the administrator.
2. Create task. Create a task for the administrator.
3. Write to history. Track the request in the workflow history.

Before defining the workflow steps, we create an initiation form parameter that will be used for the role requested (member or owner) (see Figure 11-17). From the Variables group on the ribbon, click the Initiation Form Parameters icon and add a new Field called **Requested Permission**. This will be a Choice field where we define our choices: Member and Owner.

Clicking Next allows you to provide the two values for our options: Member and Owner.

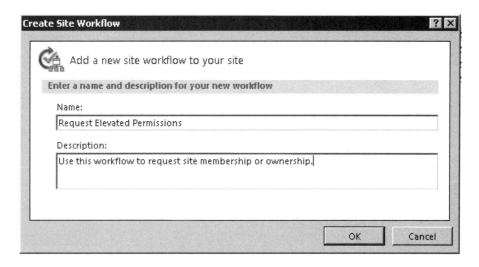

Figure 11-15 The Site Workflow dialog allows you to enter a workflow title and description

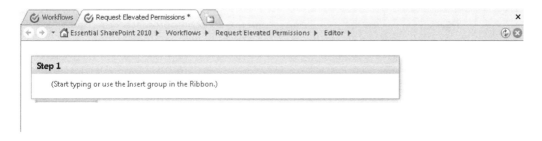

Figure 11-16 The new workflow starts with Step 1. A condition or action needs to be added to this step.

Step 1: Send E-mail

From the Action menu on the ribbon, select Send an E-mail. Click the link in the action to bring up the e-mail dialog as shown in Figure 11-18. We want to include the name of the user requesting the change, the permission level they are requesting, and the site they are requesting access to.

To include values from the workflow such as permissions level, site URL, and so on, click the Add or Change Lookup button at the bottom of

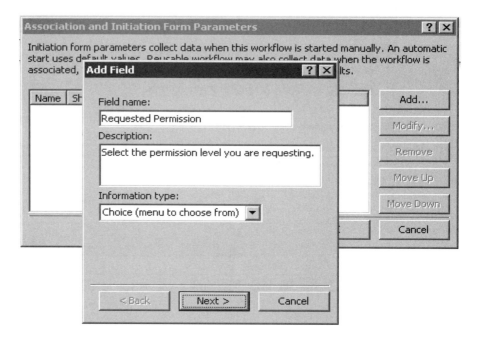

Figure 11-17 Use the initiation parameters to prompt the user for values that you can use in your workflow

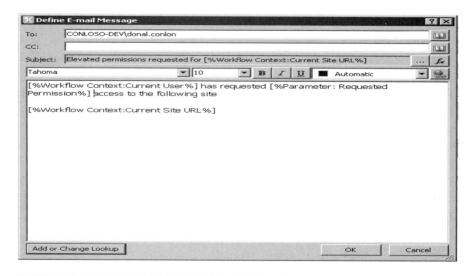

Figure 11-18 The E-Mail Message dialog allows you to specify the recipients and include values from the workflow within the subject or body of the e-mail

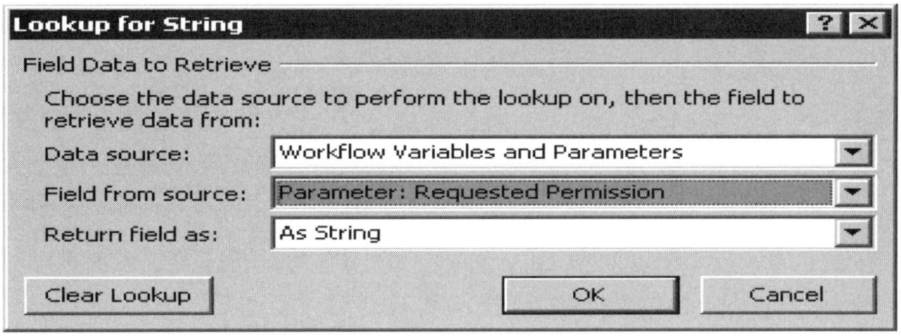

Figure 11-19 Use the Lookup dialog to add values to the e-mail such as workflow variables, list values, or other related properties

the dialog. This allows you to choose values from the workflow variables, the associated task or history list, even values from other lists in the current site. Figure 11-19 shows selecting the Requested Permission variable so we can add it to the body of the e-mail.

Step 2: Create Task

Add another step to the workflow from the Insert section on the ribbon. This step is going to create the action to create a task for the administrator. Select Assign a To-Do Item from the actions menu. Clicking the link in the task action launches a wizard that asks for a task title and description (see Figure 11-20).

Step 3: Write History

The final step is going to capture the request in the workflow history log. Again from the ribbon, add another task and insert the action Log to History List. This way we can see what requests happened when. Figure 11-21 shows the text we are going to write to the history log. Again, we can include values from the workflow using the Add or Change Lookup button.

Figure 11-22 shows the end result of all the workflow steps.

Note The steps are initially listed as Step 1, Step 2, and so on. You can rename the steps by clicking the step title and adding your own value.

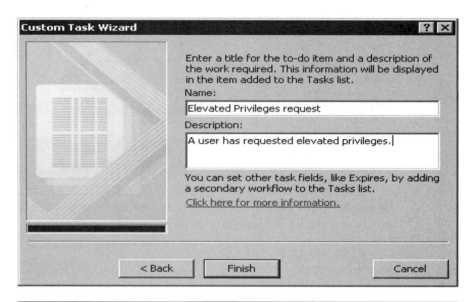

Figure 11-20 The Task wizard allows you to define a title and a description for the task

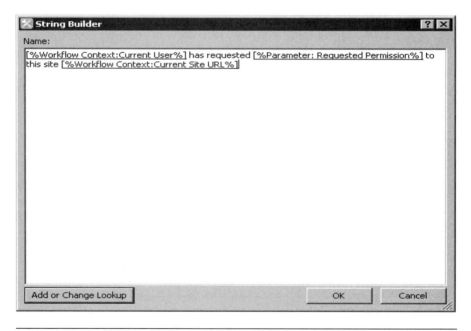

Figure 11-21 The Log to History List action allows you to keep track of workflow activities. You can include workflow properties within the text.

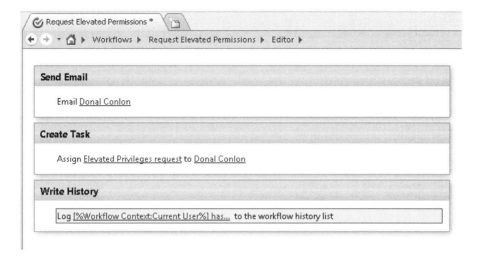

Figure 11-22 The final list of steps for our simple workflow

With the workflow steps complete, we are ready to publish the workflow. Clicking the Publish icon on the ribbon will first check for errors and then publish the workflow to our site.

Testing Our Workflow

From the Site Actions menu in your site, select the Site Workflows icon. This brings up a page that shows all the site workflows (see Figure 11-23), where we can start a new workflow or check the status of running or complete workflows.

Clicking the Request Elevated Permissions icon will kick off the new workflow. Figure 11-24 shows the user being prompted for the access level she is requesting. You can see how our simple workflow variable gets converted into a user-friendly choice field. Once the user selects a value, all she has to do is click the Start button to get the workflow started.

If you remember from our steps, clicking Start will send an e-mail to the administrator, create a task for the administrator, and log the activity to the workflow history log. So let's take a look at all of these. If we return to our Site Workflows page, we now see our workflow in the Running workflows section. Clicking this workflow brings us to the

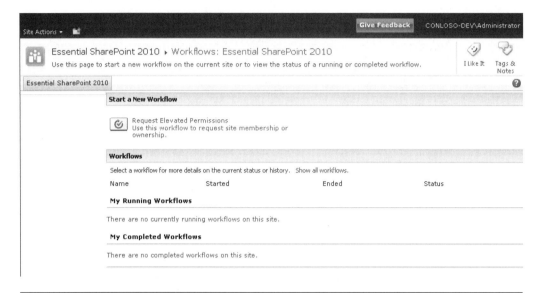

Figure 11-23 The Site Workflows page allows you to start a new site workflow or to track running or complete workflows

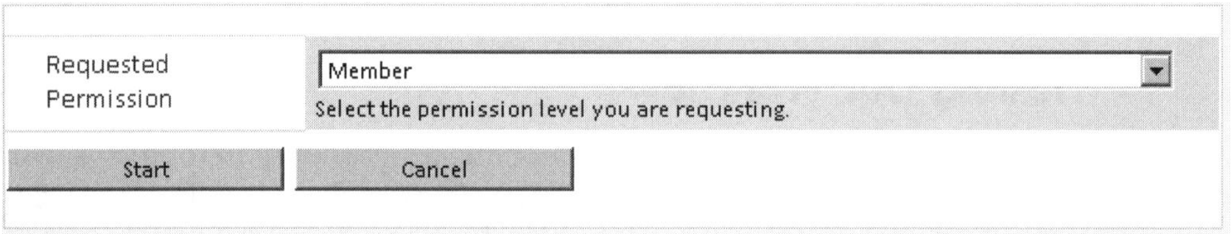

Figure 11-24 The workflow variable you created in SharePoint designer gets converted into a drop-down list allowing the user to select the permission level he or she is requesting

information page for this workflow instance. Figure 11-25 shows our workflow information page where we can see status, the assigned task, and the workflow history entry.

If you switch to Outlook, you see the e-mail that our workflow sent (see Figure 11-26). The e-mail body contains the requested user's name, the requested permission, and a link to the site.

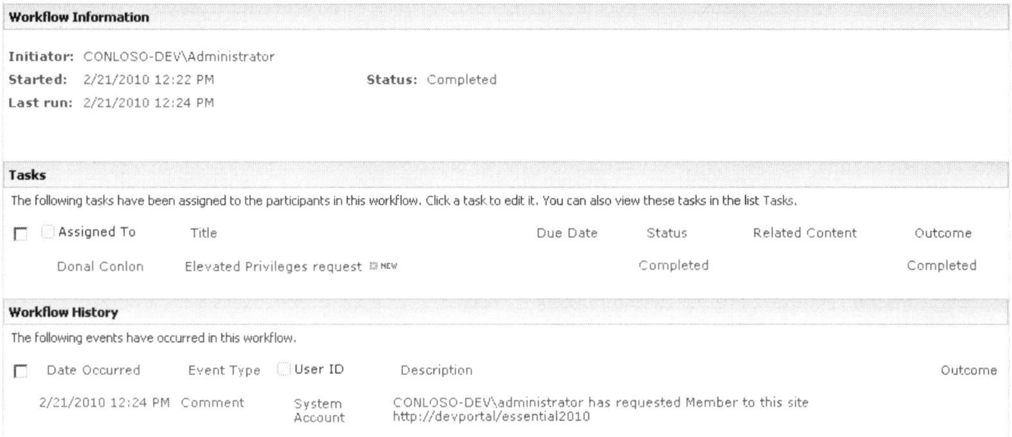

Workflow Information
Initiator: CONLOSO-DEV\Administrator
Started: 2/21/2010 12:22 PM
Status: Completed
Last run: 2/21/2010 12:24 PM
Tasks
The following tasks have been assigned to the participants in this workflow. Click a task to edit it. You can also view these tasks in the list Tasks.
Assigned To
Title
Due Date
Status
Related Content
Outcome
Donal Conlon
Elevated Privileges request
NEW
Completed
Completed
Workflow History
The following events have occurred in this workflow.
Date Occurred
Event Type
User ID
Description
Outcome
2/21/2010 12:24 PM
Comment
System Account
CONLOSO-DEV\administrator has requested Member to this site http://devportal/essential2010

Figure 11-25 The information page for the workflow shows the current status, any assigned tasks, and the workflow history

Elevated permissions requested for http://devportal/essential2010 - Message (HTML)
File
Message
Ignore
Junk
Delete
Reply
Reply All
Forward
Move to: ?
To Manager
Team E-mail
Move
Mark Unread
Categorize
Follow Up
Translate
Zoom
Delete
Respond
Quick Steps
Move
Tags
Editing
Zoom
From: no-reply@conloso-dev.com
Sent: Sat 12/26/2009 12:29 PM
To: donal.conlon@conloso-dev.com
Cc:
Subject: Elevated permissions requested for http://devportal/essential2010
CONLOSO-DEV\administrator has requested Member access to the following site
http://devportal/essential2010
Windows Desktop Search is not available.

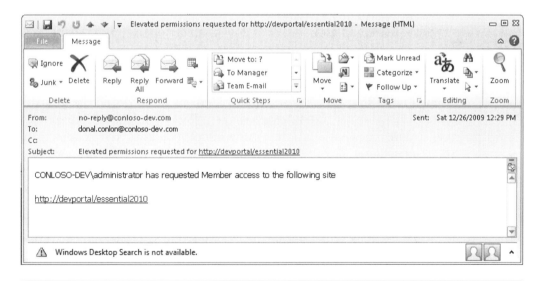

Figure 11-26 The e-mail sent by the workflow contains information about the user, requested access, and the site in question

While this workflow is pretty simple with only three steps, you can see the value in using SharePoint Designer for workflow development without having to get the IT department or developers involved. SharePoint Designer gives the end user many options for developing workflows by providing conditions and several actions. It does not, however, help in visualizing the workflow process itself, as the steps in Designer are linear. The next section shows how Microsoft Visio 2010 can be used to design the workflow, and how Visio Services is used to provide the user a visual representation of the workflow process.

Designing Workflows with Visio 2010

A common practice in organizations is for a business analyst to work with business users in Visio when designing workflows. The end result, a Visio diagram, is handed to a developer where it is then turned into a SharePoint Designer workflow or Visual Studio workflow.

Visio 2010 provides a new template specifically for designing workflows that can be imported directly into a SharePoint Designer workflow. Figure 11-27 shows the Visio 2010 home page where you can select the Microsoft SharePoint Workflow.

Selecting the SharePoint Workflow template opens up the shape stencils specifically for SharePoint workflows. Each of these shapes relate to the actions and conditions that are available in SharePoint Designer. Similar to any Visio diagram, these shapes can be dragged on to the canvas to build out a full workflow solution. Figure 11-28 shows all the available action shapes for a workflow. Each shape reflects a default action, so dragging it onto the canvas has the same effect as adding the action to the SharePoint Designer canvas. It is not possible to define the properties on the shapes, however. For example, adding the Log to history list action does not allow you to define the message you are logging to history. These properties still have to be set after the workflow has been imported into SharePoint Designer.

Even though the properties cannot be set by the workflow designer from within Visio, you can still add details to each step, specifying what any values should be. This additional description can be added directly on the design canvas and will be ignored by SharePoint Designer on import.

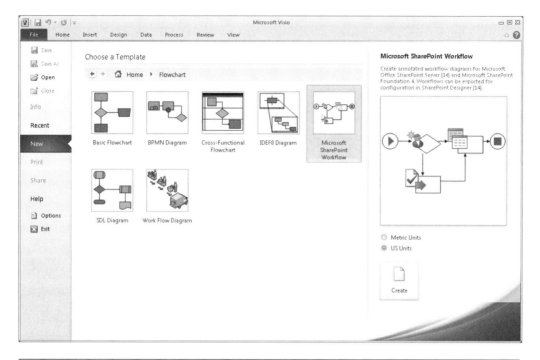

Figure 11-27 Microsoft Visio 2010 provides a new workflow template for creating SharePoint workflows that can be imported into SharePoint Designer 2010

Designing a Visio Workflow

Let's look at an example of how a workflow can start its life in Visio and get transformed into a fully deployed SharePoint workflow solution. The example we are going to use is a simple Expense approval process. A SharePoint list is used by employees to request expense approval. If the amount is greater than $1,000, then the expense needs to be approved by a director; otherwise, it can be approved by the requestor's manager.

Figure 11-29 shows our workflow designed in Visio. As you can see, it is not too complicated, but you can also see how easy it is to determine the approval flow.

You can see that we also added a general description and some detail at each step to assist the workflow developer when filling in the properties in SharePoint Designer. Now all that has to be done is to save this Visio file

Figure 11-28 The Visio shape stencils for SharePoint workflows contain shapes for each of the default actions and conditions in SharePoint Designer

and get it to the workflow developer. Once the developer receives and understands the flow, he can select to Export the diagram from the Process tab in Visio. This will check the workflow for errors and, upon success, will export to a .vwi (Visio Workflow Interchange) file, which can be imported into SharePoint Designer.

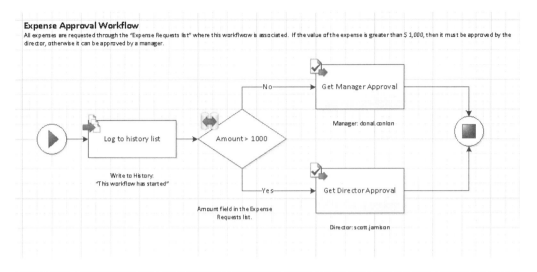

Figure 11-29 The SharePoint workflow shapes allow you to build a diagram using conditions and actions such as log to history, get approval, and so on

Importing the Workflow into SharePoint Designer

From the workflows area in SharePoint Designer, select the Import from Visio icon in the Manage section on the ribbon. Upon import you will have the opportunity to name your workflow and assign it to a list in your site or declare it a site workflow. Figure 11-30 shows what the workflow looks like after import. As you can see, it got all the steps right; all that is left to do is to fill in the blanks (properties). Now would be a good time to print out the original Visio diagram!

You will also notice that an imported workflow has a tag over each step that represents the step in the Visio diagram. This makes it much easier when applying the properties.

We continue as if we started in SharePoint Designer by filling in each property value for each step and publishing the workflow to the site. Before we publish, we want to make one change that is specific to imported workflows. From the workflow information page, you will notice the checkbox Show workflow visualization on status page is now enabled (see Figure 11-31). Checking this will not only render the Visio diagram in the browser, but will also show you the current workflow stage.

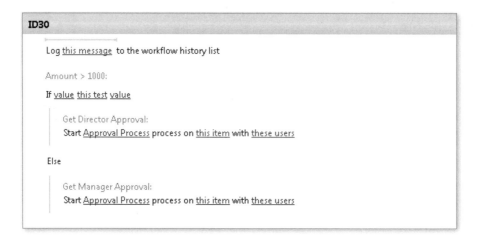

Figure 11-30 The imported workflow has all the steps but does not provide any of the property values

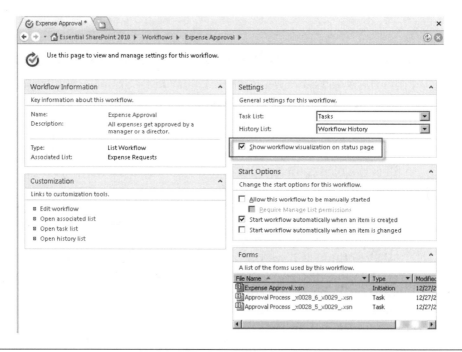

Figure 11-31 An imported workflow allows you display the Visio diagram on the workflow status page (SharePoint Server 2010 Enterprise only)

Note Visio Graphics Services is only available in SharePoint Server 2010 Enterprise edition. If the site you are publishing to does not have this license then you cannot take advantage of the graphic representation of the workflow process.

With our workflow published, we are ready to test by creating a new entry in our Expense Requests list. We have set our workflow to fire on all new items, so all we have to do is save the item and check the workflow status page.

The default view of a list that has active workflows will include a Column containing a link to the workflow. When we create our new item, we will see a link to the workflow in a Column called Expense Approval, as you can see in Figure 11-32. Clicking this link will bring us directly to the workflow status page for this workflow instance.

Figure 11-33 shows our status page. If you remember from our previous workflow, the status page still contains status information, any assigned tasks, and workflow history; with the help of Visio Services, we also have a graphical representation of the workflow at the top of the page.

Together, Visio 2010 and Visio Graphical Services do wonders in not only bridging the gap between business process designer and workflow developer, but also by bringing the workflows to life by rendering them right on the status page and indicating exactly what is going on with the process.

In this workflow, we used a simple list to gather information from the user that we could use in our workflow. However, it is often the case that complex business processes require much more interaction with the data than a simple list will allow. InfoPath 2010 addresses this need, which we discuss in the next section.

Figure 11-32 A list with active workflows will add a Column to the default view for that workflow with a link to the workflow instance for the item

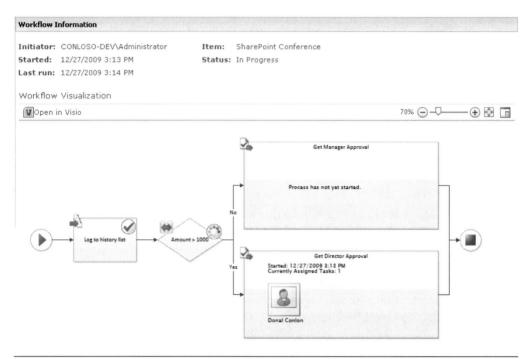

Figure 11-33 Visio Services renders the Visio diagram directly in the browser. Visual indicators tell the current step and what happened at previous steps.

Using InfoPath 2010 to Create Electronic Forms

When you create a new item in SharePoint, you are provided with a form that enables you to enter data into the associated list. Sometimes, however, the default SharePoint forms are not sufficient for capturing data in a complete way because you may need to look up information from other sources, make one choice field be dependent on another, and so on. In addition, users may be used to filling out paper-based forms, so you might want to make a form that behaves like the paper form. For example, you may want to enable job applicants to fill out a fairly complex application form.

So do you really need electronic forms? In most cases, organizations are using SharePoint lists, Word documents, or Excel worksheets. But a real form package gives you rich design, validation, prepopulation of information, multiple roles, digital signatures, and rich security.

Take a look at this list of common issues and see if any of these sound familiar:

- In your existing forms-submission process, do you have challenges around incomplete, inaccurate, or lost information? Do you face challenges around locating that information? Does it take too long for information to make it to its final destination(s)? Forms can drive business processes so that these issues are minimized or eliminated, validating the data by checking it as the user is supplying it.
- Are your users overwhelmed with the number of business processes or sources of information that exist within your company? Electronic information capture helps streamline the complex processes sitting behind forms.
- Are people filling out paper forms that need to be rekeyed? Electronic forms capture data at the source.

If you are experiencing any of these issues, you're probably a good candidate for capturing information via an electronic form. InfoPath 2010 is Microsoft's offering for electronic forms creation and use. In this section, we describe the process of using an InfoPath-based electronic form with SharePoint. We focus not on the technical details of InfoPath, but rather the key integration points with SharePoint.

Note The example in this section requires all users (and the form designer) to have InfoPath 2010 to fill out a form. If you elect to use browser-based forms created with InfoPath (described in the next section), you'll need SharePoint Server 2010 Enterprise.

Introduction to InfoPath

InfoPath 2010 is a client application that lets you visually design forms using layout tables and controls for gathering data such as text boxes, choice fields, buttons, and so on. In addition to quickly formatting a form, InfoPath allows you to connect the form to various data sources such as a database or a SharePoint list. The interface provides a lot of wizard functionality for tasks such as submitting the form, but InfoPath also provides for full customization using Visual Studio Tools for Applications.

Figure 11-34 shows the home page for InfoPath 2010. From the home page you can select from a variety of templates to get started or choose to

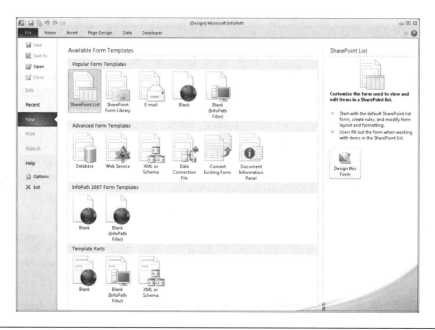

Figure 11-34 The InfoPath home page allows you to select from existing templates, or you can design your own from scratch

design your own. While InfoPath is used to design the templates, it's also used to fill in the forms built from these templates.

An InfoPath form can be used in two ways:

- Gather and send data to a service.
- Gather and save the data to a file (local or on the network).

If the data in the form is saved to a file, it is saved as XML with the form schema. While InfoPath can exist and operate on its own, we are going to focus on how it integrates with SharePoint through the Forms library template and InfoPath Forms Services. Before we discuss integration however, let's start by creating a simple InfoPath form.

Creating an InfoPath Form

From the InfoPath home page, select the blank template. Figure 11-35 shows the new form with a placeholder for the form title. To build the form, we are going to use some controls from the Controls group on the ribbon, and then we are going to use tables from the Insert tab to format

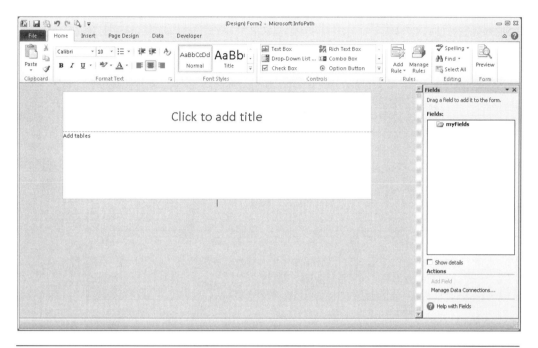

Figure 11-35 The blank template allows you to define your own InfoPath form using controls and tables for layout

the layout. It's unclear why Controls is not on the Insert tab, but that's a question for the InfoPath team.

So using tables and controls, we are going to put together a layout that looks similar to Figure 11-36. The majority of controls are text and date fields; however, the expense fields are wrapped into one very useful control called the Repeating Table. The repeating table control allows a user to add additional rows to the table on the fly—very useful for an expense report.

When you add a control to the form, InfoPath gives it a default name like field1, all of these fields can be renamed to be more descriptive like reportDate. As you add fields, you will see them listed in the Fields panel on the right.

Once all of our controls are added and positioned using the layout tables, all that is left to do is add a Submit button. For our expense report we are going to submit it to a SharePoint Forms library. What this means is when the user clicks the Submit button, the data will get saved as a new item in the library. To do this, we need to create a new SharePoint library

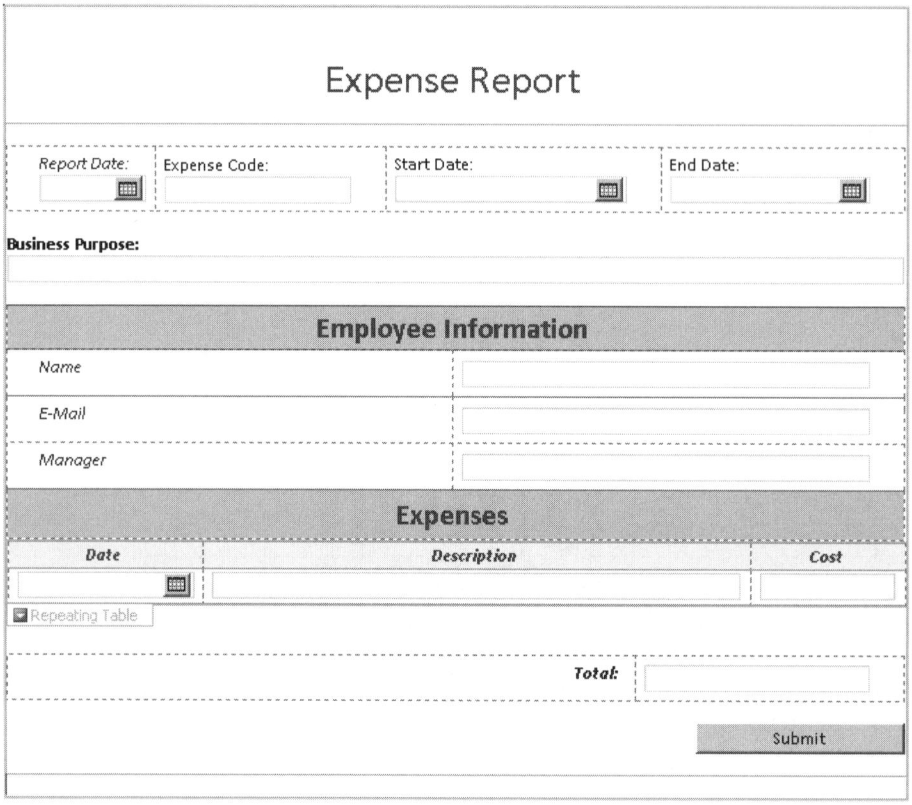

Figure 11-36 Our Expense Report includes date fields, text fields, and a repeating table where additional rows can be added for each expense

using the forms template and then in InfoPath configure the submit action to send the data to our new library.

Assuming we have our Forms library in place (you should know how to do that by now), right click the button and select Button Properties. From the Button Properties dialog, ensure the action is set to Submit and click the Submit Options ... button. Figure 11-37 shows the submit options we have. Here, we select to submit to a SharePoint Document Library. Before we click OK though, we need to configure a data connection to our SharePoint library as in Figure 11-38.

Click Add to create a new data connection for the library. The Data Connection Wizard (see Figure 11-38) steps you through the simple process of connecting to the SharePoint form library we have already created.

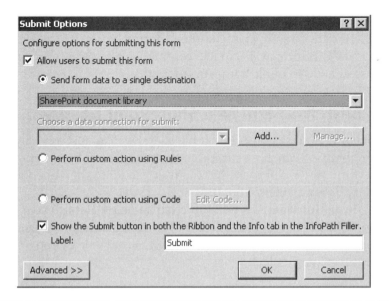

Figure 11-37 The Submit Options dialog allows us to send the data to a SharePoint document library that we define through a data connection

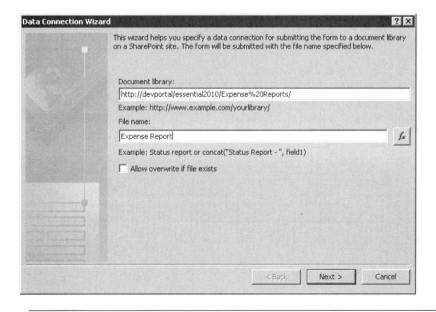

Figure 11-38 The Data Connection Wizard steps through the process of creating a destination for the form data

To recap, we now have a fully designed form that will allow the user to submit data directly to a SharePoint forms library. However, we still need to make this form available in a central place so our users can get to it. For this we need to publish it from InfoPath.

Publish the Form to a SharePoint Library

While we could publish it to a file share, we can just as easily publish it to the library to which we are submitting the data. The benefit of publishing the form to the library is that the user can go to the same location to submit and view expense reports.

From InfoPath, open the File tab and click Publish your form to open the Publish page (Figure 11-39). The publish page has many publishing options, one being to Publish form to a SharePoint Library. This is the one we are going to select.

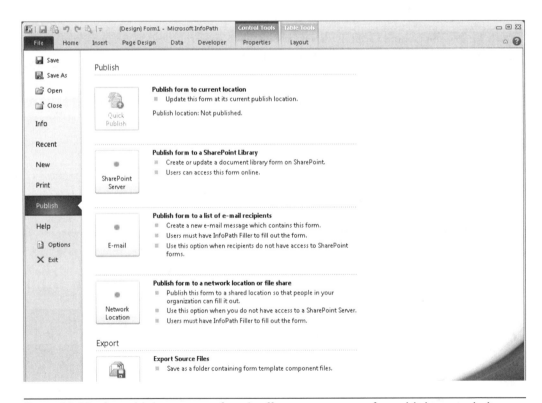

Figure 11-39 The Publish page in InfoPath offers many options for publishing, including publishing to a SharePoint library

The Publishing wizard steps you though the process, asking you for the address of the SharePoint site you're publishing to. Figure 11-40 shows where you can specify whether the form should be Web-enabled and whether you are publishing directly to a library, Content Type, or form template. While we are publishing directly to a library, it is very useful to publish the form to a Content Type that can be used across many libraries. We are going to clear the checkbox and not have the form be Web-enabled. We revisit this later when we discuss Forms Services.

The final steps in the wizard allow you to select from an existing library or to create a new one. Because we have our library already created, we can select it from the list. Once our form has been published, it is now ready to be tested.

Testing the Published InfoPath Form

If we browse to our library and click the New button in the ribbon, our Expense Report form opens in the InfoPath client as in Figure 11-41. You can use the date picker to select dates and add several expenses using the repeating table in the expenses section.

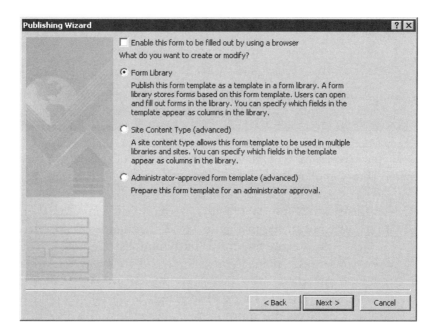

Figure 11-40 The Publishing wizard allows you to specify whether this form should be Web-enabled and whether you are publishing directly to a library, Content Type, or form template

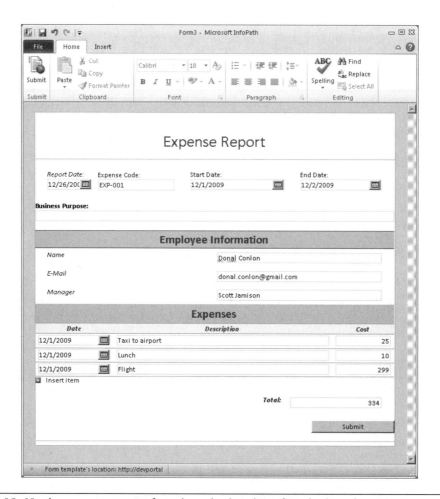

Figure 11-41 The expense report form launched in the InfoPath client from the Expense Reports Forms library in SharePoint

This submits the data results in a new entry in our Expense Reports library, as you can see in Figure 11-42. The fields we specified in Figure 11-36 are now extracted into SharePoint list Columns. This metadata allows you to easily manage these items the same way you would any other item with metadata.

The next step in our expense report application would be to add a workflow and have the appropriate manager be notified so they can review the report. This would follow exactly the same process as we did with our expense request workflow earlier.

Figure 11-42 The Forms library contains a new expense report submitted from InfoPath. Selected form fields get converted into list Columns.

InfoPath Forms Services

SharePoint Server 2010 and SharePoint Foundation Server 2010 both allow you to create forms libraries and to publish directly to them from InfoPath, but each user needs to have InfoPath installed on his or her computer to work with the forms.

SharePoint Server 2010 Enterprise provides InfoPath Forms Services, which can take a published form template and render it as a Web page. This eliminates the need for the user to have the InfoPath client installed.

Looking back to Figure 11-40, when publishing our form to Share Point we chose not to enable form rendering. Let's revisit this, and this time enable form rendering by checking the box Enable this form to be filled out using a browser. Continuing the publication as before, now let's open our form from the Expense Reports library (see Figure 11-43).

The experience in the browser is exactly the same, allowing you to pick dates using a date-picker and even add additional rows for each expense line item.

Note While InfoPath Forms Services can convert many form elements from the client to the browser, it may have difficulty with certain controls depending on how complicated your form is. For this reason, InfoPath provides a Design Checker where you can check compatibility.

The rendered form even includes a Ribbon with standard actions. You will notice a Save icon. This allows users to save the data directly to the library; however, they would be prompted to provide a file name, which is

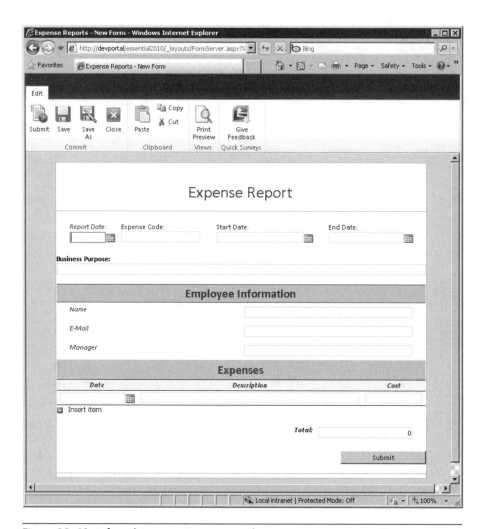

Figure 11-43 InfoPath Forms Services in SharePoint Server 2010 Enterprise allows you to render InfoPath forms directly in the browser

why we choose to use a submit action instead. InfoPath allows you to disable the ribbon for Web forms, which is what we would do in this case in a production environment.

InfoPath 2010 gives the business user tremendous power for creating forms quickly and relatively easily. Even developers can take advantage of the advanced features such as data connections to really bring the forms to life. With the addition of Forms Services, the need for another deployed client can be eliminated, which is always welcome by IT departments.

Should we also mention the new InfoPath forms Web Control Parts in 2010 that can be used for composite applications and mashups?

Key Points

This chapter reviewed the workflow integration in Office SharePoint Server 2010, including the out-of-the-box workflows and those created using Office SharePoint Designer. In addition to designing workflows using Visio 2010 and rendering using Visio Graphical Services, we also covered how to use InfoPath forms with SharePoint. Let's review the key points.

- SharePoint 2010 provides several out-of-the-box workflows including
  - Approval
  - Collect Feedback
  - Collect Signatures
  - Disposition Approval
  - Three-State
  - Publishing Approval
- SharePoint Designer 2010 allows you to modify out-of-the-box global workflows as well as design unique ones.
- Visio 2010 allows you to design SharePoint workflows that can be imported directly into SharePoint Designer 2010.
- With SharePoint Server 2010 Enterprise, Visio Graphical Services allows you to render your Visio workflow in the browser.
- With InfoPath 2010, you can publish form templates to document libraries as well as submit the form data to a SharePoint list.
- With SharePoint Server 2010 Enterprise, you can publish an InfoPath form and have it rendered as a Web form.
- Advanced workflows can be created by using Visual Studio 2010 (which is beyond the scope of this book).

CHAPTER 12

PUTTING YOUR SITE ON THE WEB

Enterprise content management (ECM) is a widely recognized IT industry term for software technology that enables organizations to create/capture, manage/secure, store/retain/destroy, publish/distribute, search, personalize, and present/view/print any digital content related to organizational processes. Whew—that's a mouthful. So what does this mean? In short, it means storing Web or document content electronically and then making sure it is managed appropriately.

ECM played a big part in the overall success of MOSS 2007 intranets and collaboration sites. The native SharePoint features associated with ECM made it easy for all users to manage and publish content to be leveraged by peers across the company. However, did you know that MOSS 2007 was also a widely popular choice for Internet-facing Web sites? Many organizations chose to take advantage of their existing investments in SharePoint to revamp their Internet presence, using the same technology that served its employee base. SharePoint had been a very successful platform for document management—and an HTML Web document is really just another type of document. This increased focus on SharePoint as a Web content management (WCM) solution began with MOSS 2007 and continues in SharePoint 2010.

SharePoint 2010 takes WCM to the next level. It offers a richer functionality suite that makes it even easier to manage, repurpose, deploy, and analyze content distributed to an anonymous access community. Let's look into what got better with WCM in SharePoint 2010 and what new features have been added that will make SharePoint 2010 a more attractive alternative for Internet-facing content. This chapter contains the following key sections:

- Why SharePoint for Internet-facing Web Sites?
- Web Content Management: The Basics
- Content Deployment: Key Terms and Architecture
- What Has Improved in SharePoint 2010 Web Content Management?
- Richer User Experience

- Additional Features
- Customizing the User Experience (UX)
- Putting It All Together: An WCM Strategy

Why SharePoint for Internet-facing Web Sites?

Before we dive into some of the functionality associated with WCM, let's look at some of the key reasons why organizations use SharePoint for their Internet sites:

- **Ease of use**. Part of the appeal of SharePoint has always been its low threshold for entry. Users can be trained very quickly to use specific functionality and require very little training for uploading and managing content.
- **You already own it (business users)**. For those organizations that have already invested in SharePoint as part of an internal collaboration or communication initiative, they can leverage that very same software for allowing designated employees to manage Internet content with no additional training.
- **You already own it (IT)**. Again, for those organizations already familiar with SharePoint, it is much easier to quantify IT support for an Internet-facing site. IT knows how to manage and maintain a SharePoint environment because they already do that for internal usage.
- **Leverage list data**. Web sites do not have to be a collection of static HTML content. SharePoint allows you to easily leverage list data for content presentation. This makes it easier to deploy and maintain dynamic content presentation without having to manage the underlying HTML.
- **Search**. SharePoint has a native search engine that will support the discovery experience associated with looking for keyword matches on your Web site. There is no need to purchase third-party search products to integrate into your WCM solution.
- **Content repurposing**. The life cycle of a document can span the boundary of the corporate firewall. What was once created through employee collaboration can ultimately serve high value to partners, clients, or customers. By leveraging SharePoint for intranet, extranet, and even Internet use, content can be shared naturally, via workflow, from system to another.

And those are just a few reasons! Because of these and many others, SharePoint has gained tremendous momentum in the Internet-facing WCM space. SharePoint 2010 takes advantage of that momentum and raises the bar associated with what companies can do with their Web sites. It is now easier to leverage native capabilities in SharePoint to create a highly dynamic, rich, aesthetically pleasing corporate Web site.

Web Content Management: The Basics

SharePoint 2010 offers the capability to manage Web content (pages, images, and HTML) in an easy way. This allows business users to author and publish Web content quickly and easily without having to involve IT or a webmaster for each and every new page or update to a page. This enables your Internet site to take on any look and feel (unlike the default SharePoint UI that most people think of) and scale to the requirements of the world's most popular Web sites. For example, take a look at Figure 12-1.

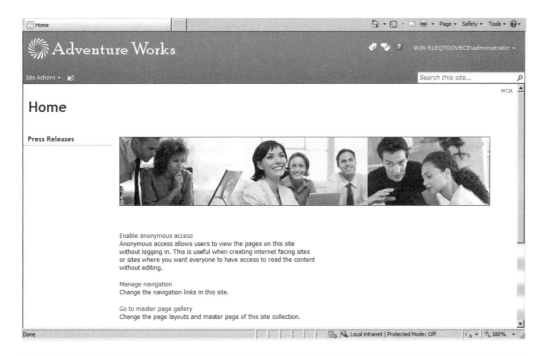

Figure 12-1 SharePoint 2010 can be used for highly branded, content-based pages that are accessed anonymously over the Internet

This is a default SharePoint Web page. For a business user to make a change to the page, it's as simple as clicking the Edit icon (paper with a pencil over it) in the toolbar or by clicking the Page toolbar item and selecting Edit from the ribbon. The result is that the page can be modified in Edit mode (see Figure 12-2), eliminating the need for the user to ask IT to make a Web page modification on his or her behalf. Finally, the page can be run through an approval process (see Figure 12-3), ensuring that changes are reviewed before going live to the Internet.

There are entire books dedicated to creating, managing, and hosting Web content-managed sites, so we won't try to re-create those here in a few pages. Instead, we provide the basics of how SharePoint provides Web content management features.

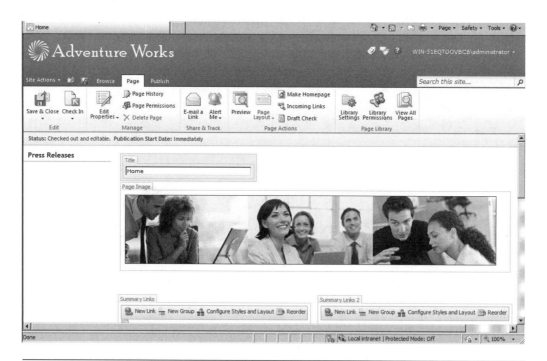

Figure 12-2 Making edits to a Web page is easy with SharePoint 2010. Simply edit content inline on the page.

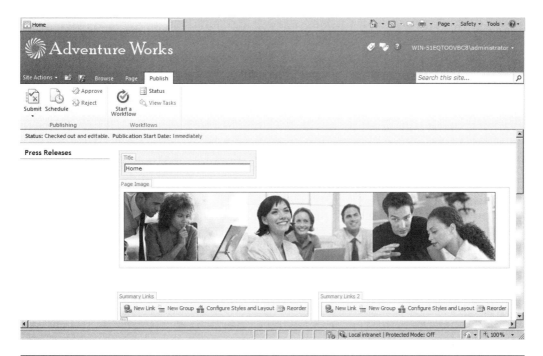

Figure 12-3 Initiating a workflow on a page or pushing out changes for publishing is done with the ribbon functions at the top of the page

Web Publishing 101: Publishing Sites

There are different kinds of site templates within SharePoint (Collaboration, Meeting, Enterprise, Publishing, Custom). The publishing site templates provide additional features that enable business users to create and manage Web content on a page (or create brand new Web pages). For some people, this may sound a lot like a wiki site. Isn't a wiki site also an easy way to create new Web pages and update existing Web pages? Yes. The main difference is that wikis are a geared toward sharing ideas within a community. Wikis provide Web pages that can be quickly edited to record information and then linked together through keywords, but they are far less powerful than the full-fledged WCM pages. For example, take a look at www.xbox.com. This is not a wiki—it is a highly stylized Web site with a number of controls to keep it branded properly. In publishing sites, contributors can work on draft versions of pages and publish them to make them visible to readers. Publishing sites also include document and image libraries for storing Web publishing assets such as site pages and images.

Take a look at a SharePoint 2010 publishing site. Publishing site templates are available in the Content & Data tab (see Figure 12-4). When you've created a publishing site, SharePoint provides a number of new menu options.

Interestingly, the Web publishing features are actually provided by a SharePoint Feature. This means that you can add publishing features to any SharePoint site. First, you must turn on the Publishing feature in the Site Collection. Try the following: Create a regular SharePoint team site. Notice how you get the standard Site Actions options as depicted in Figure 12-5. Next, go to Site Settings. Under Site Administration, select Site Features. The Publishing feature is what helps the SharePoint site to

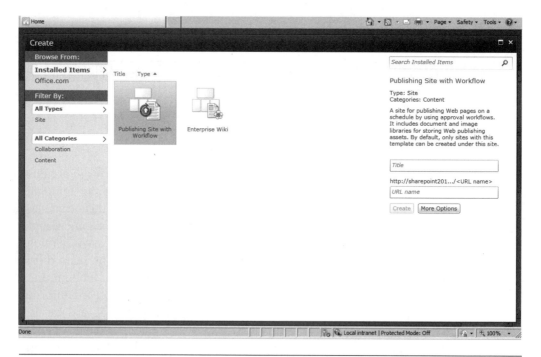

Figure 12-4 The Publishing site template provides page layouts that contain field controls so that business users can add content without affecting the design of the page

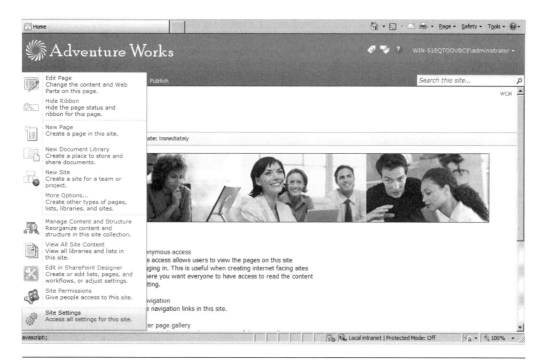

Figure 12-5 Site Settings is available by clicking the Site Actions content menu

support Web publishing features. Enable this feature by clicking Activate (see Figure 12-6). Go back to your site; it will look the same. But if you look more closely, you'll notice some key changes. For example, the Site Actions menu has a number of additional options related to publishing, like Create Page (see Figure 12-7).

Although the Publishing Feature can be used with any SharePoint site, you'll probably plan to use it more to create Internet-facing sites. The Internet Presence template that ships with SharePoint is a good example—it uses a set of master pages, layouts, and styles. However, *your* layout and styles will likely need to be very different from the example template. Hence, when creating your Internet site, you'll probably want to start with a blank slate and build from there. This is an important consideration when planning an Internet-facing site.

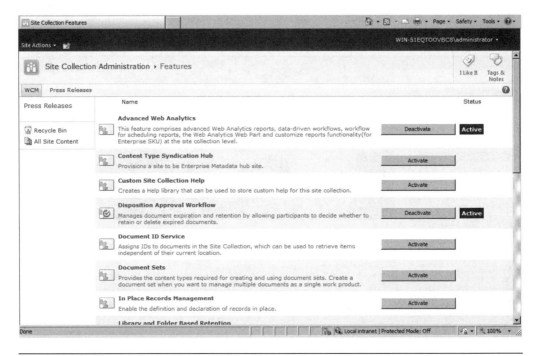

Figure 12-6 The Publishing site feature can be activated in Site Settings

Content Deployment: Key Terms and Architecture

Unlike intranets where changes are made real-time on production content, Internet sites typically require a protective layer around the content. By that, we mean that content is created or edited in one location and then "pushed" to the production system via a deployment process. This protects the integrity and quality of the data and gives testers an environment where they can validate changes.

With SharePoint 2010, there are four key terms to understand with content deployment:

- **Source Site Collection**. Location from which content is being deployed.
- **Destination Site Collection**. Location to which content is being deployed; typically a destination Site Collection has increased security and is more tightly controlled and managed.

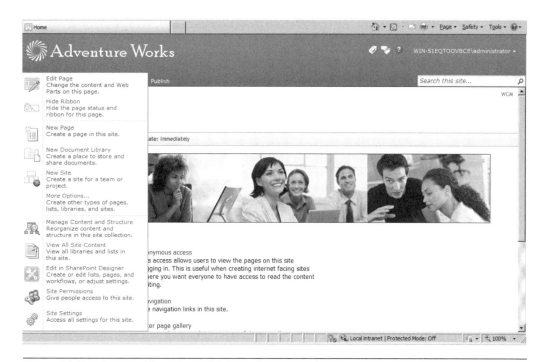

Figure 12-7 After enabling the Publishing feature within a site, users with appropriate permissions will see options to create and manage Web pages

- **Content Deployment Path**. A source Site Collection from which content deployment can originate and a destination Site Collection to which content is deployed.
- **Content Deployment Job**. Copies specified content on a specified schedule by using a specific path. There are three types of jobs: full, incremental, and quick.

With that, the big decision in content deployment is server architecture. This is the process of defining how content will move from your authoring environment to production. There are three configurations to consider.

- **Single publishing farm**. In this configuration, both the authoring and production Site Collections are in the same farm but in different Site Collections (actually different Web applications). This is not typically used for Internet sites.

- **Authoring and production farms**. This involves an authoring farm inside your firewall and an external farm where your production content exists. This is the preferred, simplest choice for Internet sites.
- **Authoring, staging, and production farm**. This involves three farms and is used when more advanced approval processes are in place. In this scenario, content can be validated and approved in an environment that closely matches production but still held separate until final approval occurs.

SharePoint 2010 supports all three scenarios. There is a fourth, live updates on the production site, but this is not typically used in Internet-facing sites. The important thing to note is that there is much more coordination and configuration required when building in a publishing mechanism for site content updates. You will need to decide when automation should be used and when human approval is required.

What Has Improved in SharePoint 2010 Web Content Management?

For those familiar with WCM in MOSS 2007, you'll be excited to learn that a number of things have improved with SharePoint 2010. Let's take a look at some of these:

- **Fewer clicks**. One of the challenges with MOSS 2007 was the use of application pages for managing edits and alterations on Web pages. Users would often get confused by having to execute multiple clicks to make page changes. More importantly, those changes were sometimes made on a different page than the one needing edits. SharePoint 2010 makes it easier to manage Web content by requiring fewer clicks to execute changes and having those changes occur inline on the designated page.
- **Standards and accessibility**. SharePoint 2010 is now XHTML-compliant and WCAG 2.0 AA-level compliant. What does that mean? SharePoint 2010 now offers a better and richer interface for all users, including those with disabilities or impairments.
- **Better workflow**. With the introduction of workflow capabilities offered in Visio 2010, SharePoint Designer 2010, and Visual Studio

2010, users now have more native options for creating and deploying both simple and sophisticated workflows. This makes it easier to manage approval of new content as well as make associated changes to list data.

- **Multilingual support**. SharePoint 2010 users can now switch languages real-time in the interface; this includes navigation items and menus. While this does not offer true translation capabilities (that is, your data from SharePoint lists will not be translated by SharePoint) it does offer a richer means of creating a single Web site to serve a variety of global users with the goal primarily focused on assisting content contributors who are managing content in various languages.

- **Web analytics**. Reporting and analytics are greatly improved. In true Internet fashion, you can analyze visitor data to look for trends, as well as better analytics on user search queries.

- **Search**. The introduction of FAST search in SharePoint offers a significant improvement in how search can be leveraged to better discover Web site content. It is also important to note that the native SharePoint 2010 search has improved with better relevancy calculations and metadata refinement options.

- **Digital asset management**. SharePoint 2010 now has the ability to include and even edit streaming videos and thumbnails. This offers a richer interface for content presentation and another element for what can be shown on your Web site.

Richer User Experience

One of the themes you will hear a lot about with SharePoint 2010 is the notion of a richer user experience. Let's take a minute to explain what that means. Fundamentally, when we talk about ease of use with SharePoint it is centered on allowing users to gain the most functionality with the least amount of intrusion (defined as required training or tools). SharePoint 2010 handles this by offering improvements in two key areas. The first, as discussed earlier, is the ability to make many, if not all, page edits right on the page (fewer clicks). This allows users to easily see the impact of the changes without having to go to a different page or tool to do it. More importantly, for those users of SharePoint who don't necessarily use Internet Explorer, this experience also holds for Safari or FireFox. That's a big deal! Figure 12-8 shows a standard SharePoint Web page in Edit mode. Users with the appropriate permissions can get to this mode in one click and begin to make changes immediately.

Another important improvement in the user experience is the ability to better manage rich content. The Content Editor Web Part (CEWP) is still a very powerful native Web Part based solely on its simplicity. Just type in the box and format the content accordingly. No Web development or HTML skills required! However, in some ways, the CEWP is not needed with WCM. With SharePoint 2010, you can now add content practically anywhere. You are now entering data in field controls, versus the CEWP textbox, and have more freedom to decide where and how HTML is presented.

Also SharePoint 2010 offers the ribbon as a formatting tool so users familiar with Word 2007 (or 2010) will see an instant parallel in creating and managing content in a rich text box. Figure 12-9 shows an example of a Content Editor Web Part.

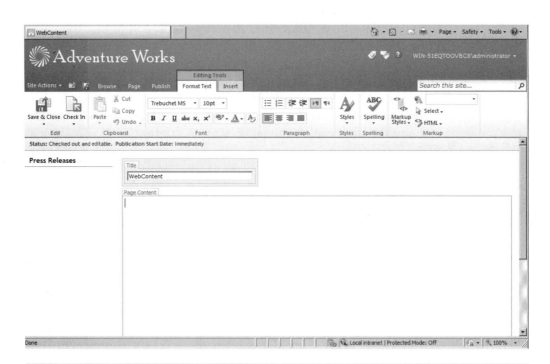

Figure 12-8 Users can make changes to SharePoint Web pages quickly and easily, right in the interface and using a variety of Web browsers

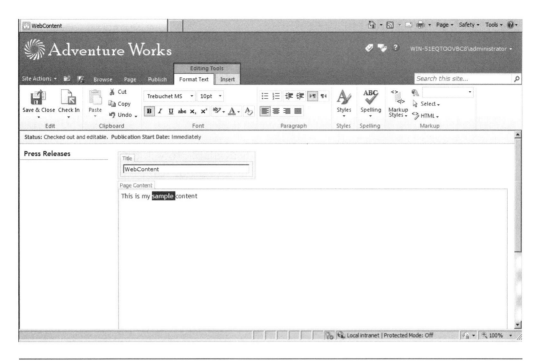

Figure 12-9 Users can make text changes on a page by using field controls

What does this have to do with WCM? Simple. It allows more freedom for managing the content on the Web site; it allows more users to be empowered to make changes and to easily deploy those changes right to the Web. This offers the potential to change the way companies manage their Internet-facing content. Whereas the role of a webmaster for an intranet site was altered with the enablement of the employee community, there is a potential with SharePoint 2010 to change the way Internet-facing content is managed and, more importantly, by whom.

Additional Features

So, you've seen some of the key improvements made with existing SharePoint content management functionality. But there's actually a lot more. SharePoint 2010 has added some additional functionality that now offer more compelling reasons to consider SharePoint for Internet-facing content. Let's look at a few.

Content Organizer

This is a new tool with SharePoint 2010. It allows you to define rules-based logic to help determine where new content should be placed on your Web site. First, let's look at how to enable it. Under Site Settings, pick the Content Organizer Rules. If you don't see it under Site Settings, it may not be activated. Go to Site Features and activate it. See Figure 12-10 to see where this is located.

Rules can be based on any fields available to you on the specific page. These rules can help define where new content will be placed. Think of it like a wizard that understands your site topology. Figure 12-11 shows an example of a rules creation page.

This is a nice way of controlling how new content is placed on your Web site. By setting up a few key rules, you can dictate the automatic placement of new content on your Web site. This allows a consistency in how content is presented and maintained by enforcing an overall topology for content.

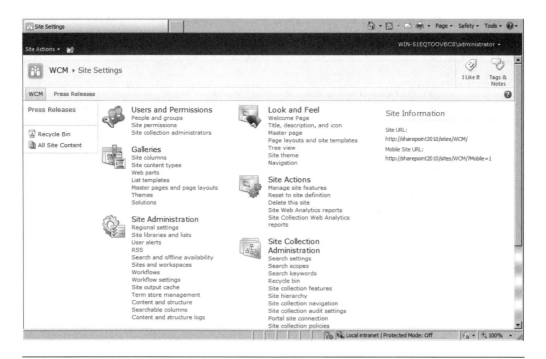

Figure 12-10 You can define content organizer rules by selecting the appropriate link under Site Settings

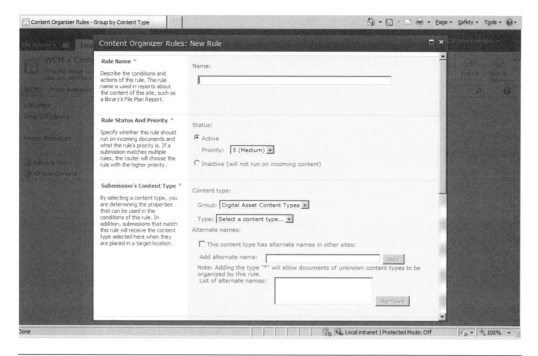

Figure 12-11 Users can create rules to determine where new content will be placed on the Web site

Managed Metadata

We've already talked about one of the key themes in SharePoint 2010—a richer user experience. Well, another important theme is metadata. What does metadata have to do with WCM? Lots. Metadata can be used to provide another means of getting to specific Web content, specifically through search. Don't expect your users to always work their way through your page navigation. They'll want "shortcuts" to key content by simply entering a keyword in the search box. That's where metadata fits in. SharePoint 2010 offers a new Column called Managed Metadata. This lets your users tag pages with the keywords from a defined set and therefore offer an alternate means to getting at Web content. Figure 12-12 shows an example of how you would tag a page with known keywords.

We talk about metadata in more detail in other chapters of this book (see Chapter 5, "Planning Your Information Architecture," and Chapter 6, "Making Content Management Work"), but suffice it to say, it offers a powerful means to help keep your data organized.

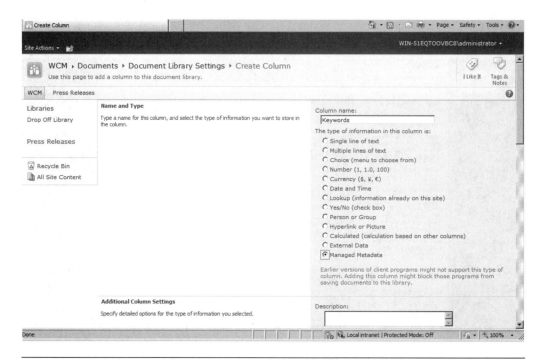

Figure 12-12 Users can create metadata tags for specific pages, thus increasing their "findability" in search

User Ratings

Have you been on sites such as MSDN where you can rate the page that you're on (typically 1–5 stars)? This has become a core part of most Internet sites that interact with customers. You've seen this on sites like Netflix.com and Amazon.com. SharePoint 2010 now offers the same type of functionality. There's a new field Column that you can enable for your Pages library that will automatically offer the display (and tracking) of a page rating. This is the traditional 1–5 stars (where 1 is the lowest rating and 5 is the highest). This has been a core piece of other ECM products for some time and is now a part of SharePoint as well. While this is not something that should be used on every page, it does offer a good feedback mechanism for core content sites that are customer-focused.

Note that user ratings do not work out of the box with anonymous access, so if you plan to use them on your Internet site, you will need to configure usage accordingly.

Web Reporting and Analytics

For those of you who are interested in who is coming to your Web site, where are they navigating, what are they looking for (and if they are finding it!), and what is the more popular content, SharePoint 2010 offers some very compelling tools for analysis. The usage analysis tools in MOSS 2007 have been replaced with a new Web Analytics service that tracks and reports user activity. There is a collection of Web Parts that comes with SharePoint 2010 that will show you this data. There is also an ability to define alerts associated with key usage data so you can be notified when, for example, a search is executed and no results are returned. Note that SharePoint 2010 does not offer trending analysis and is more focused on click activity for specific users.

Social Networking

Yes, social networking functionality should be considered as you look at Web Content Management. Why? Today, with highly popular Web sites like FaceBook and LinkedIn, users have come to expect a sense of community when repeatedly visiting a Web site. Offering core functionality like bookmarking, setting ratings, tagging, and even a personal page will entice users to visit your Web site often. SharePoint 2010 has core social networking tools that will enable you to turn this functionality for a subset or a complete collection of users. You may even leverage things like workflow to allow content submission from external users and an approval process for accepting and sharing it. For additional information about SharePoint 2010 social networking features see Chapter 7, "Getting Social: Leveraging Community Features."

Customizing the User Experience (UX)

In this chapter we've taken you through some functional elements associated with content on your Internet site. However, there is still a big part of WCM that has to do with defining and managing the user experience (UX). In fact, some would argue that the user experience is the true measure of the overall success of a Web site.

What is UX? A user's experience on a Web site can be segmented into four categories: 1) Branding, 2) Usability, 3) Functionality, and 4) Content.

One segment is no more important than the others; they all need to be optimized for users to embrace and appreciate the overall experience of interacting with a Web site. To this point, we've touched upon how SharePoint 2010 offers certain functional elements to make it easier for visitors to navigate and discover information, where the focus has been on making it easy to update and present important content on the Web site. Let's extend our discussion into a key UX segment: branding.

Branding is an essential part of any Web site. It defines the aesthetic appeal and visual presentation of your Web pages. At the highest level, branding provides visitors with an engaging experience (which increases the likelihood that they will buy your product or at least return for another visit). To create a strong impact, remember that branding is about consistency; consistency among the Web pages (in terms of color palette, content organization, layout, and navigation), and consistency with the brand identity (as it relates to an organization's other public materials like print collateral). In addition, graphics, collateral and multimedia are all part of branding and are used to add value to the overall experience.

How does SharePoint 2010 handle branding? There are two key elements: master pages and page layouts.

Working with Master Pages

Master pages define the look and feel and standard behavior that affect all of the Web pages in a Web site. For those familiar with SharePoint 2007 (or .NET 2.0 for that matter), master pages work pretty much the same in SharePoint 2010. The concept is that a master page defines a template for how content will be presented and that template is applied to all associated pages so you don't have to keep building pages from scratch. In addition, the use of a template makes the propagation of changes to all pages quick and seamless.

SharePoint 2010 provides some base master pages as the starting point for branding customization. Master pages are edited and applied with the use of SharePoint Designer (a separate, freely available Office product for Web design). Let's look at a few:

- **v4.master** is the default master page for SharePoint 2010 look and feel. It includes the ribbon and all other UI changes new to SharePoint 2010. If you want to apply a custom branding to the native SharePoint 2010 look, start by making a copy of this master page and edit accordingly with SharePoint Designer.

- **default.master** should be familiar to those who have used SharePoint 2007. It does not have the ribbon and mimics the look and feel of SharePoint 2007. If you upgrade from SharePoint 2007 to SharePoint 2010 you will notice that this master page will be used in your upgraded application.
- **minimal.master** is the master page used for search results. It is a very simple master page and allows you freedom to customize the user experience associated with search.
- **simple.master** is used for login and error pages. You can override this master page if you wish to present a custom login or error screen.

To change the master page associated with your site, go to Site Actions → Site Settings → Master pages. This is shown in Figure 12-13. You can change the master page by altering the selection shown on the Site Master Page Settings, as seen in Figure 12-14.

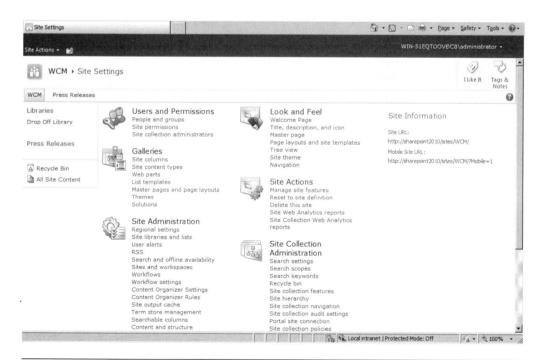

Figure 12-13 Users with appropriate permissions can get to the Master Page screen through Site Settings

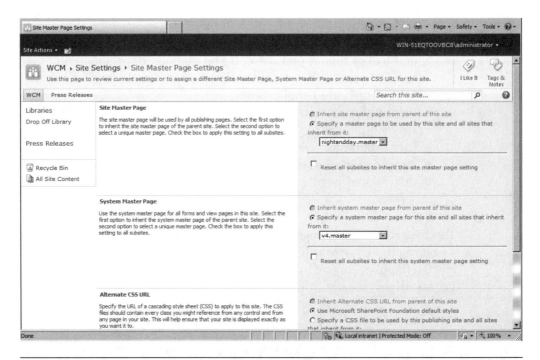

Figure 12-14 You can alter the selected master page for your site by changing the option on the Master Page screen

One important change with SharePoint 2010 is the fact that custom master pages apply to all pages in the /_layouts directory. This includes the system page. For those who struggled with creating a custom system.master page with SharePoint 2007 or were forced to build a custom theme, this is welcome news!

Working with Page Layouts

Master pages are an essential component of a good Web site as they control the consistency associated with look and feel. However, content presentation across an entire Web site might need to be different given that a home page is presented differently than a news page or a product detail page. That's where page layouts come in. Page layouts are page templates that define how a page should look, the fields that are available, and exactly which collections should be present on the page (such as lists and libraries).

In the construction of a Web site, you would develop a collection of page layouts for the various ways you want to present content. In SharePoint Web sites, you will want to turn on the publishing features for your Web site. This will enable the use of publishing page layouts. The use of these page layouts allows content submitters to work directly in their browsers for content management and submit changes for approval when done. The customization of page layouts, like master pages, is done exclusively in SharePoint Designer.

Do you need custom page pages and custom page layouts? The answer is probably yes. Think of the master page as the wrapper around all your Web site pages. This wrapper enforces a consistent look and feel as it relates to content or graphics that are shared across all these pages (for example, header, footer, navigation, and so on). The page layout controls how content is presented that is unique to the page or at least the type of page. As mentioned, you might have one page layout for your home page, another that is used on your various product pages (that may show different content but should show it in a similar way to other product pages), another that is used when only simple HTML is needed, and another when you are pulling data from SharePoint lists.

Creating a Custom Page Layout

Creating a custom page layout in SharePoint 2010 is very similar to how it was done in SharePoint 2007. It involves the use of Content Types and custom Columns. The first step is to create a custom site Content Type. You do this under Site Settings → Site Content Types (as seen in Figure 12-15). Click New to display a data entry page (see Figure 12-16) that requests additional information for the Content Type Name, parent content type from (select Publishing Content Types), Parent Content Type (select Page), and Put this site content type into (select Page Layout Content Types).

After you create a new Content Type, you can create a new page layout from it. Before you do this, make sure your Content Type has any additional custom Columns that you might need for your for content presentation. Now, in SharePoint Designer 2010, open the Web site for which you want to create the page layout. From the menu, select New → SharePoint Content. From the dialog box, click SharePoint Publishing. Click Page Layout and find your new Content Type from the list of Page Layout Content Types. That's it! Give your new page layout a name and

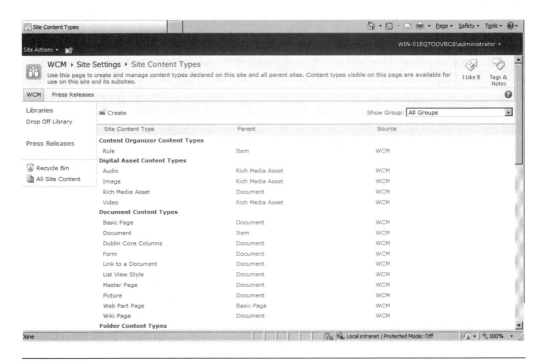

Figure 12-15 To start creating a new Content Type, select Create from the list of existing Content Types

title, and customize the organization of content. Once saved and published, you can use this page layout as the base template for pages that you will create for your Web site.

Remember, page layouts can only be created and edited in SharePoint Designer but can be used for Web page creation by content authors, who are have been given proper access, simply using the browser.

Media Field Control

Another important element in an engaging user experience on a Web site is the use of rich media. SharePoint 2010 offers a number of new ways to include rich media on your Web site. One of these is the media field control. The media field control is built on Silverlight 3.0 and allows you to embed video on your SharePoint site. Like all things with SharePoint, it is also customizable with SharePoint Designer.

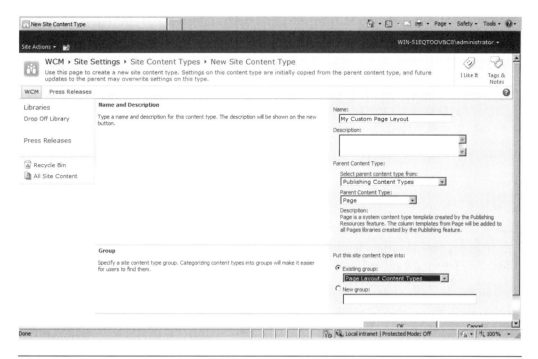

Figure 12-16 You can define a new Content Type by supplying base information like name and parent content type

When would you use the media field control? Let's say you have a news section on your Web site and you would like to include rich media in your page layout. To do this, it is very straightforward. Simply extend the Content Type associated with the specific page layout in use by including a new Column of type Media Field. This will include the option to include a rich media control from the ribbon. The control would point to the source of your video content. That's it! You now have embedded video on your Web page. Of course, this example uses the Media Field control in the context of a page layout. You can also use the media Web Parts that are native in SharePoint if you simply want to add embedded video to a specific page.

Putting It All Together: A WCM Strategy

Okay, let's say you have read the previous pages, are existing SharePoint users (internal only), and are excited about the potential of using

SharePoint 2010 to refresh your Internet presence. Where do you begin? Let's start with some key questions about the current site:

- How much of your current Web content is static HTML?
- Do you post documents on your Web site?
- Who manages and approves content on your Web site?
- What is the process for submitting new content to your Web site?
- Do you track user activity on your Web site?
- What is the competitive advantage of having a new Web site?
- Who "owns" the Web site?
- How much external content is repurposed from internal content?

Do you know the answers to all these questions? If no, then the first step is to assemble a team of representative internal resources that who, collectively, can answer them. Once you have these answers, you are ready for design sessions. The goal of these sessions is to lay out an overall information architecture for your Web content, defining what goes where, who will manage it, how content is deployed, and how you will monitor user activity. Think about some of the new features highlighted earlier in this chapter. All may not be right for you but, as an organization that has already invested in SharePoint, you will recognize obvious gains by leveraging an existing technology and empowering another group of users and consumers. Here are additional questions to ponder once you have more details on your SharePoint Web site:

- How will your users use search to find content?
- Should we "push" content from our intranet to sections of the Web site?
- How important is the site branding?
- Will the site be in multiple languages?
- Will we still use a webmaster, or will ownership be distributed?
- What is the long-term vision for the Web site?

Think about how your employees have changed the way the business processes work inside your organization as SharePoint has been widely used. Extend that now to include changes in how your customers or prospects learn about who you are and what you do based on the content that you present. Dynamic organizations have dynamic Web sites. It's time to stop apologizing for your old static Web site and realize that it is an asset that can be leveraged for competitive business gains.

Key Points

This chapter provided some suggestions for using the WCM features of SharePoint 2010. In general, our recommendation is to

- Enable more users to participate in the management of Web-based content.
- Look at usage analytics and set up key alerts for monitoring activities.
- Use the social networking tools in SharePoint to build a community of users.

CHAPTER 13

MAKING BUSINESS INTELLIGENCE WORK

Ask any CEO, CIO, or CFO what the number one need is for making solid business decisions, and the answer will most likely always come down to one word. Information—the right information in just the right amount at just the right time. Understanding what has happened and what is happening most certainly can help in the process of determining what to do next. This, of course, assumes two key elements about your data: quality and timeliness. Organizations today need to have real-time, visual cues that tell them how they are performing, both operationally and strategically. Reports generated after the fact mean that it's too late to change course if there is a problem. If you can't react fast, your competition probably can, and that's a problem.

This transformation of data to actionable information is at the heart of business intelligence (BI). And while quality and timeliness are essential to building a business intelligence solution, it is also very important to decide how best to present the information gathered. Do you use a report or a chart or scorecard? Telling the story is a big part of getting success with BI. SharePoint 2010 helps in this way by providing users with several options to show information and help facilitate decision making. It is important to state upfront what SharePoint 2010 is *not*: It is not a data warehouse for storing large amounts of corporate data. It is not a data-cleansing tool that will automatically correct bad or incomplete data. Think of SharePoint as a potential *presentation tier* for business intelligence data. It is there to help present key data to all users that will help make getting to the right decisions faster and easier.

This chapter covers key business intelligence capabilities that are provided by SharePoint 2010, including report delivery, dashboards, scorecards, key performance indicators, and server-side Excel calculations and charting. The key sections contained in the chapter include

- Getting Started with Business Intelligence
- Which Presentation Tool Is Right for You?
- Excel Services
- PerformancePoint Services
- Visio Services
- Putting It All Together

Getting Started with Business Intelligence

Business intelligence is very personalized. Independent of the challenges of getting corporate data collected, completed, and cleansed, the "right" delivery method is highly subjective. One user may be satisfied with a static report that simply delivers information; another user wants the ability to drill into specific sections of a report to interact with more detail; another still may want to spend three seconds looking at a picture to determine whether action is required.

With all of that, how do you get started? The first step is to recognize that delivery around BI has evolved. It used to be that you needed to know the users and know what they wanted to see. That's changed. Now, business intelligence is much more about putting tools in the hands of the users and letting them have control over what they see (thus the slogan "BI for the masses"). In the next few sections, we highlight various options for BI delivery in SharePoint, including report storage and delivery, charts, dashboards, scorecards, and key performance indicators (KPIs). In a later section, we discuss your options and how to select the delivery choice that is most appropriate.

Reports

It is pretty safe say that every person in an organization, independent of role or responsibilities, interacts with some type of report. In the "old days" reports were delivered in paper form through interoffice mail or by printing a hardcopy. With technology advances, this has changed so that most report delivery occurs through e-mail attachments or interacting directly with an online system.

At the highest level, there are two types of reports, static and dynamic. A static report is a presentation of information in locked-down view, meaning the reader can only see the information in the format that is shown and is only exposed to the level of detail provided on that report. Think of it as a .pdf file (a 401K statement, for example). The report itself may have been generated from any enterprise system. A dynamic report is more flexible. It allows the user to manipulate the presentation of data and/or access detail that may not have been presented in the default view. Think of a sales performance report. Perhaps the presentation is revenue per region, but the user is allowed to drill into an individual office or maybe request additional supplemental detail by checking a checkbox. Again, this report may have been generated from any number of external systems.

From a SharePoint perspective, the type of report or the data source is irrelevant. Again, think of SharePoint as the delivery tool. How does it help? While we stated earlier that SharePoint is not a data repository, it *is* a document repository. And reports are documents! This means that you can deliver corporate reports by storing them in SharePoint. You may get the reports into SharePoint manually or provide access to a reporting source like Reporting Services or through custom development. The value of placing reports in SharePoint versus e-mailing them directly to users or placing them on a network drive is plentiful. A SharePoint document (report) library

- Can be secured, either at the library or item (report) level. This allows you to easily apply permissions so the reports are only seen by the appropriate resources.
- Is crawled by SharePoint's search engine so reports can be returned in search results.
- Has version control so that as reports are updated, the new version overlays the old and there is no confusion about which is the most current version.
- Can meet compliance requirements through defined document management workflows to control approval, publication, and disposition.
- Is familiar to users in an existing SharePoint environment, so it is easier to train users on how to access new reports.
- Has alerts so users can be notified of new or updated reports.

In addition, SharePoint has very tight integration with SQL Server Reporting Services so that reports generated in SSRS can be shown in the context of a SharePoint portal and can provide users with a single access point for reports and supplemental structured and unstructured data.

Charts

Reports are text-based. That means they contain characters and numbers and are formatted in a certain way for presentation. Another way to show data is in a graph. A pie chart or bar chart can "tell a story" with fewer words and numbers than a traditional report. The value of a chart is that it leverages a visual indicator to quickly highlight specific data elements (i.e., sales are way down this year because the current year bar is much smaller than last year's). Business users have long been familiar with charts through their use of Microsoft Excel. Excel provides an easy way to transform data into a picture.

From a SharePoint perspective, there are three main ways to present these charts as part of a business intelligence solution. The first and simplest is to store the spreadsheet that contains the chart(s) in a document library (similar to the Reports section). This requires very little effort but forces the user to click the "right" file and launch Excel on the desktop. A second choice is to use a third-party charting tool that offers SharePoint integration where the charts are actually Web Parts that have been configured to point to a specific data source and present results in a specific way. The benefit here is that the user interface is much richer, and access to the visual indicators is faster. The challenge is that this requires an additional purchase and at least some level of training in the third-party solution. The final choice is to use Excel Services, discussed later in this chapter. Excel Services requires that the organization has the Enterprise version of SharePoint Server 2010. It allows users in Excel to publish a chart or collection of charts directly from Excel and have them rendered directly into SharePoint. This offers the rich and instant presentation without the overhead of an additional software solution.

Dashboards

Dashboards can be used to show, in real time, how an organization (or, more often, a part of an organization) is performing against *tactical* goals. Most often the metrics that are displayed in a dashboard reflect data that is constantly changing (how many support calls do we have in queue? how many units have we manufactured today?). Dashboards are most often watched by members in the organization who are responsible for specific day-to-day goals.

The information used in a dashboard is usually "raw" data, but in an effective dashboard it is displayed in such a way that there is an instant recognition of performance against a target. So, for instance, if there are fewer than 5 support calls in queue, we can show the number 5 in green; if there are 6 to 20, we can show the number in yellow; and if there are more than 20, we can show the number in red. This commonly understood color scheme provides instant feedback to supervisors or staff members on how they are doing at any moment in time. At a glance, someone can look at a dashboard to spot the trouble areas and do further investigation or take action. The use of gauges or progress bars or charts can also provide visual cues about the information that changes regularly.

The most critical action to perform before setting up a dashboard is to identify which metrics are going to help drive the organization's perform-ance. Too often, information like the current weather or the company's stock ticker is dropped onto a dashboard because they are easy to create. However, unless you are in the snowplow business, a weather dashboard is not likely to provide a metric that drives performance.

Dashboards are not one size fits all. Different people in the organiza-tion need to see different information to understand performance. Sometimes this just means a different level of granularity (how many sup-port calls for software product X versus software product Y versus for all software products), but it can also mean different metrics for different parts of the organization. Because of this, you need to carefully plan so that you are sure that you are providing the right information to the right peo-ple at the right time in your dashboards.

Scorecards

Scorecards are another example of BI tools that can be used to show how an organization is performing against *strategic* goals. The metrics are gen-erally from a snapshot in time rather than real time. The metrics that are contained in a scorecard also can be viewed from an overall organizational level (how are we doing against our revenue goals for the year?) or cascaded down to the individual level (how much have I sold this year?). Scorecards are usually watched most closely at the top level of an organization.

As with dashboards, the most important step in creating a scorecard is to do careful analysis. An organization's strategy is almost always difficult to articulate outside the board room. Scorecards are a way to make strategy real to everyone in the organization. If our strategy is to be the best and most well-known service provider in a specific industry, then we need to identify what metrics the organization should monitor to understand how you are doing against that strategy. Scorecards have been around for a long time, and many organizations think that they have a handle on theirs if they are watching financial metrics. However, it is just as important to watch metrics that show how the organization is performing from a customer perspective, from a business process perspective, and from a learning and growth perspective. The reasons for this are many. Revenue might be going through the roof, but if the staff is leaving in droves, there's a problem. If profits are way up but no one can understand when they should report a critical defect, then we have a problem.

The visual representation of scorecards is similar to dashboards but is usually simpler. The red/yellow/green approach is the most common, given that users are interested in how they are performing against a fixed set of metrics at a specific time period. The visuals won't change in real time but will change on a periodic basis, whatever period makes sense for the overall organization. Usually these periods are monthly because that coincides with financial reporting periods, and monthly reporting is well-ingrained in the corporate psyche.

Let's assume that you have done all of the upfront analysis for your dashboards and scorecards (no small feat, but too large a set of topics to cover here). Once you have SharePoint up and running, enabling collaboration and teamwork across the enterprise, it's time to consider using the platform as a basis for business intelligence. SharePoint provides a rich set of new tools to facilitate building up your dashboards and scorecards.

Key Performance Indicators (KPIs)

A Key Performance Indicator is one element of a scorecard. Organizations use KPIs to monitor business activity and performance. Simply stated, KPIs are metrics (data values) that are compared against a benchmark and scored. KPI indicators (also known as Status Indicators) are intended to spur action. If the sale KPI is red, it indicates that an issue has arisen and that action is required. Status Indicator Lists are one way to implement a simple dashboard or scorecard. A scorecard is more formal and has more rollup and drilldown capabilities that allow for views into supporting metrics. Status Indicator lists in SharePoint are meant to be simpler. They are linear and represent the presentation of a group of items that share a common data point (that is, they all relate to the organization).

Traditionally, corporate executives have used KPIs to get a "pulse" on business performance. Examples include sales pipeline, revenue, and products sold (all for a specific point in time). Ever increasingly, however, all levels of an organization are being exposed to KPI lists as a way to present performance data. Think of project teams being exposed to project performance (utilization or budget versus actual) in a master list. The power of a KPI list is that it presents, in a very simple interface, information about collected data as measured against predefined goals. One of the key challenges about any sort of dashboard or scorecard is that it seeks to aggregate a wide variety of data—data that may come from multiple systems. Worse yet, the necessary data may not exist in any systems—or be very complex to calculate or locate. Presenting the red/yellow/green on a scale is often the easy part. Defining and locating the actual data is the hard part.

In SharePoint Server 2010, Key Performance Indicators are called *Status Indicators*. Status Indicator lists allow you to create a graphical representation of the status of the business activity or performance attribute you are measuring. Like scorecards, a traditional KPI list typically has three main color codings (although it is possible to use a number of graphical icons, including smiley and sad faces):

- **Green**. Positive results against a measurement
- **Yellow**. Borderline results
- **Red**. Poor results

Which Presentation Tool Is Right for You?

Reports, charts, dashboards, and scorecards. Which is best for your users? Remember, business intelligence is highly subjective, so you may need to use some or all in an overall deployment. Table 13-1 may help in your decision-making process.

Table 13-1 Selecting the Right BI Delivery Tool

Requirement	Delivery Tool
Presentation of existing static reports generated from another system	Report: Document library
Presentation of dynamic reports that allow drill down	Report: SQL Server Reporting Services (SSRS) reports shown with Web Parts on SharePoint site
Charts generated and managed by business users that need to be shared with organizational members (SharePoint 2010 Enterprise not being used)	Chart: Spreadsheets in document library
Charts generated and managed by business users that need to be shared with organizational members (SharePoint 2010 Enterprise being used)	Chart: Excel Services
Charts need to be ultra rich with customizable capabilities and can be managed by IT development resources	Chart: Third-party charting tool with SharePoint integration
Executive presentation on health of the business with key metrics measured against previous reporting periods	Scorecard (using PerformancePoint capabilities)
Executive presentation on activities of sales organization, including details on recent closed deals, top prospects, top-performing sales team members	Dashboard (using PerformancePoint capabilities)
Business process diagram that shows stages and analytics associated with performance in each stage	Chart (using Visio Services)

Excel Services

In the last section, we mentioned Excel Services (introduced with Microsoft Office SharePoint server 2007 and improved with SharePoint 2010) as an option for displaying reports. Excel Services is a core component in the

SharePoint 2010, Enterprise Edition business intelligence toolkit. It provides business users the very powerful way to share charts and graphs they own and manage.

We have seen two main trends in business intelligence adoption within major organizations: 1) the vast majority of companies have or are implementing a strategy for business intelligence, and 2) the most popular tool for delivering business intelligence data continues to be Microsoft Excel. Excel offers users (business analysts or knowledge workers who work closely with specific business data) a familiar environment for manipulating corporate data. For years, many software companies have tried to re-create this experience in a Web-based environment with the goal of better leveraging of workbook-based results in a broader medium. Most solutions failed because they could not effectively mimic the simplicity of what Excel offers users. Excel Services, a business intelligence component of SharePoint, looks to change that by validating what business users have known all along—that Excel is a great tool for ad-hoc manipulation of business data. Excel Services, however, takes the concept to a new level by allowing data owners not only to acquire and manipulate business data but, ultimately, to publish it to a Web-based environment that is highly secure and protected.

One of the biggest strengths of Excel Services is that it not only allows users to publish Excel-based content (entire workbooks, individual worksheets, or even a single chart), but it also offers an ability to only publish what the data owner wants seen. As an example, a business analyst may use specific formulas and business logic to take raw data and deliver a set of charts to make predictions or show trends. The analyst would like to share these results with a broader audience but cannot e-mail the workbook without the risk of compromising the formulas and proprietary logic. Excel Services offers a solution by allowing the business analyst to create the chart using native Excel capabilities and then publish only the content from the spreadsheet that he wants to share to a SharePoint portal.

Excel Services in SharePoint 2010 continues to be a major component in the business intelligence integration into SharePoint technologies. It truly offers business users the best of both worlds; users can continue to build and analyze using a tool that is very familiar, and they are empowered to publish results without having to work through an IT department to build custom Web pages or dashboards.

Getting Started with Excel Services

One of the first things to look at is the three core components of Excel Services:

- **Excel Calculation Engine**. This is the main engine responsible for managing the data and calculations associated with workbooks.
- **Excel Web Access**. This is the Web Part within SharePoint that allows the rendering of Excel-based content in a browser-based environment. These can be associated with dashboards and can be connected to other Web parts.
- **Excel Web Services**. These are application programming interfaces (API) that developers can use to program against Excel Services to build custom solutions against Excel workbooks.

How Does Excel Services Work?

Let's take a look at how we can take Excel-based content and publish it to SharePoint. One of the first things we need to do is tell Excel Services where to look for the Excel workbooks we want to render as HTML on our portal. When you define a trusted source file location, you can specify a path to a specific SharePoint-based site or file system file (UNC path) or an HTTP location that is Internet-based.

Note that when you work with SharePoint-based sites you can enable Excel Services workbook acquisition in all underlying child sites as well. The advantage of doing so is that it allows administrators to apply more granular security on subsites when maintaining navigation among Excel charts. There are a several options associated with setting a trusted connection, including limits on a workbook's size and number of calculations.

A trusted file location acts as a master address book that indicates the portal sections or file system locations that are enabled for Excel Services consumption. One of the important things to note here is that this capability is an administrative task. It is assumed that the definition of trusted locations will be managed by a SharePoint administrator and *not* the business users. Later, we talk about the coordination required between business users and SharePoint administrators. It is important to mention, however, that Excel Services is not intended to give business users full control or management of SharePoint security or administration.

Let's assume a sample Excel file contains a worksheet dedicated to salesperson bonus calculations. In this scenario, a manager is using Excel to manage employee compensation based on performance. He is using a formula based on some personal definitions to calculate bonus amounts and show the data in a simple pie chart. The goal is to share the data with the team but not share the formulas associated with the results. How does Excel Services enable this outcome?

- **Business process**. Without Excel Services, the manager would be forced to take manual steps to separate the pie chart from the calculations. This would have included things like hiding a calculation worksheet, copying the chart to another workbook, or generating a PDF file with the chart. All of these require manual steps every time data changes. Obviously, it is in an inefficient process. Excel Services allows for publishing and protection within the same environment.
- **Presentation**. If you look closely at the sample, you'll notice that the table associated with salesperson data has graphical indicators for performance. This is done using Excel's conditional formatting. You should notice that this looks very similar to a KPI list. Conditional formatting in Excel is another way of publishing performance data.
- **Security**. The goal of the publishing exercise is not simply to show the pie chart, but also to protect the formulas and business logic. Excel Services allows a user to publish an entire workbook, a single sheet, or any chart. This is a very powerful tool. Consumers of the content cannot edit the data; the transmission is unidirectional. They can, however, do many things with the end results. This includes sorting and filtering, recalculation, and pivot table capabilities.
- **Ease of maintenance**. Manual manipulation of Excel files is manageable but not very scalable. Yes, it is possible to manipulate the workbook or segment charts through a manual process. This process, however, requires the same effort every time data needs to be republished. One of the biggest advantages of the Excel Services model is that it allows for a continuous "dialog" between producer and consumers through the connection it provides to the data.

We've now created our data presentation, secured the business logic, and published the results to the intended audience—all with no code or direct IT involvement other than initial administration settings. That is the true power and value of Excel Services. It empowers business users to leverage the tools they have (and know) to effectively and securely publish results, all in an effective and efficient manner.

Excel Services can be a great accelerator of business intelligence activity for a business that has invested in a SharePoint environment. As mentioned earlier in this chapter, however, it is not a substitute for coordinated activities between business and technical resources. In a standard corporate setting, business users will continue to "own" and manage the data in an Excel environment. They should be supported by an IT staff that helps them easily connect to backend corporate data as well as provide them with the necessary SharePoint support to securely place Excel files. While the advertisement around Excel Services states a "no code" deployment, it does not include a "no IT" process. It is important to leverage the value of this new and exciting tool within a framework of coordinated business and technology activities.

What's New in Excel Services with SharePoint 2010?

For those familiar with Excel Services from Microsoft Office SharePoint Services 2007, you'll be pleasantly surprised to know that while Excel Services operates basically as before in SharePoint 2010, there are a number of improvements and additions that make it an appealing business intelligence tool.

- **Trusted locations**. Trusted locations are now provided by default with SharePoint 2010. That means there is less dependency on IT administrators to create and maintain trusted locations with SharePoint administration. Thus, business users are more enabled and less dependent on IT staff for publishing spreadsheets.
- **Multiuser collaboration**. Multiuser collaboration allows several business people to edit a workbook at the same time. The Excel Services engine monitors changes made by individual users and applies them in the order that they are made. Thus, the last edits executed will override the previous modifications, and all of it can be kept in the same workbook, thus avoiding the need for serial edits.
- **Slicer feature**. The Slicer feature is a new type of data filter in Microsoft Excel 2010. It is interactive, flexible in design and layout, and always conveys the current filtering state. The Slicer feature allows Excel 2010 users to create rich reports using OLAP data. These reports, in turn, can then be published through Excel Services into SharePoint. The obvious advantage here is the rich presentation of data that has been accumulating through advanced

data analysis. Note that business users must use Excel 2010 to take advantage of this feature.

- **Unattended service account**. Excel Services offers a low-privilege unattended service account for business users to use as a single identity for getting data. This allows all business users to use a single account for data acquisition with Microsoft Office 2010. The big value here is that IT does not need to manage special accounts for data acquisition; nor do they need to incur security risks by sharing username/password with business users interested in "connecting" to data for analysis.

- **Windows PowerShell**. Much like many of the other features and functions in SharePoint 2010, Excel Services activities can be executed automatically using PowerShell scripts. This gives IT tighter control in defining and maintaining a SharePoint 2010 environment, potentially across many farms and environments.

PerformancePoint Services

Those who have followed Microsoft business intelligence technologies will probably recall Business Scorecard Manager, which became a component of PerformancePoint Server. PerformancePoint Server 2007 was its own product and was deployed to a dedicated, stand-alone server. Microsoft has now integrated PerformancePoint Services into SharePoint 2010 Enterprise and extends its capabilities with new and improved features.

PerformancePoint Services in SharePoint 2010 is a performance management service that an organization can leverage to monitor and analyze its business. In an earlier section, we talked about building dashboards and scorecards for graphical presentations of key decision-making data. In SharePoint Enterprise, the definition, construction, and management of dashboards and scorecards is done with PerformancePoint Services. The high-value proposition here is that because PerformancePoint Services provides a rich and easy-to-use way to construct dashboards, scorecards, and KPIs, and SharePoint offers a natural presentation tier for this data, the bar has been raised on the business intelligence capabilities that can be originated within SharePoint. Remember, we talked earlier about using SharePoint to store reports or present information gathered in other places, like Excel. With PerformancePoint Services, we're actually talking about a front-to-back business intelligence solution that offers a full gamut of tools for gathering, analyzing, and presenting corporate metrics.

How Does PerformancePoint Services Work?

Users familiar with PerformancePoint Server 2007 will notice a fundamental change in how PerformancePoint Services works. It no longer is a separate Web application in IIS with its own SQL Server database; it is fully integrated with SharePoint 2010. This means that PerformancePoint Services stores its data in SharePoint document libraries and lists. Because of this, it can naturally take advantage of the features that exist natively with SharePoint, the most compelling being security integration. Very much like Excel Services, PerformancePoint Services is a service within SharePoint that is integrated with the Microsoft SharePoint Foundation; when you have the Enterprise version of SharePoint 2010 running in your environment, you have full access to the capabilities of PerformancePoint without having to install or configure anything new.

Why Use PerformancePoint Services?

PerformancePoint Services is specifically targeted as a Performance Management solution. Performance Management allows business users to monitor and analyze their businesses by presenting key data and metrics that can facilitate change (from business process to product development to staffing).

With PerformancePoint Services

- An organization can use a single platform for "pushing" key business metrics to all employees. The "outreach" component of the PerformancePoint Services tool (and thus SharePoint) is very important in that a company can get data in the hands of decision makers of all levels more quickly and efficiently.
- Individual business users can take advantage of metrics presented via PerformancePoint Services as one component of their collective business activities, meaning that it can be integrated with native collaborative tools in SharePoint to offer context and execution outside the data that is shown.
- IT can provide the business with a single tool for showcasing data that has been aggregated though a master repository such as a data warehouse. By using a tool like SharePoint, which is already highly leveraged for collaboration and communication, IT has fewer systems to support and less effort associated with monitoring and training users in diverse business applications.

PerformancePoint Services provides all of the functionality needed for performance management, including scorecards, dashboards, management reporting, and analytics. Reporting is also integrated with PerformancePoint Services to provide planning, budgeting, and forecasting output. As mentioned before, all of this is done within the context of an existing SharePoint environment offering business users a single interface for collaboration and analysis. The main advantage of PerformancePoint is that users can see more robust scorecards and dashboards and then be able to click a metric to drill down to subdashboards or even the raw data.

What's New with PerformancePoint Services in SharePoint 2010?

There are a number of improvements that Microsoft made to the PerformancePoint functionality as part of the integration with SharePoint 2010. Here are some key elements:

- **Integration with SharePoint**. Dashboards and dashboard items are stored and secured within SharePoint lists and libraries. This offers several important benefits:
  - SharePoint security is now used to manage data access. This makes it a more integrated platform that can leverage an existing SharePoint security model.
  - Because all of the data now exists in SharePoint, it is automatically part of the SharePoint capacity and disaster recovery planning. This offers business users the comfort of knowing that key data will be supported with the same strength of SharePoint management.
  - PerformancePoint Services information is presented in Web Parts, just like all other Web Parts, so they can be managed and even linked in the same way as other Web parts.
- **Better scorecards**. Scorecards have been improved to allow for better drill down into detail information. Business users can even create custom metrics that use multiple data sources. In addition, scorecards now have a richer and easier way to sort and filter data presented.
- **SQL Server 2008**. PerformancePoint Services supports SQL Server Analysis Services 2008. For those organizations that have taken advantage of the enhanced features in SQL Server 2008, PerformancePoint Services can be used to connect to that data.

- **Better reporting**. PerformancePoint Services offers new chart types and more formatting options so reporting can better present the "right" chart or graph to present data.
- **Time intelligence**. One of the more common user requests associated with business intelligence reporting is the ability to more easily manipulate the presentation of data based on time intervals. PerformancePoint Services offers more flexible time intelligence that allows business users to have better control of scorecard presentation.
- **Linked Web Parts**. PerformancePoint Web Parts can be linked, much like other SharePoint Web Parts, so that user interaction on one can automatically alter the presentation of data in another.
- **Dashboard development**. PerformancePoint Services includes a Dashboard Designer that allows business users to easily create and deploy dashboards.
- **Accessibility compliance**. Business intelligence data is intended to be useful to all users, independent of accessibility challenges. PerformancePoint Services offers a more flexible interface to comply with accessibility challenges.
- **Decomposition Tree**. The Decomposition Tree, which can be in a scorecard or dashboard, is a new visualization report type available in PerformancePoint Services. It allows business users to navigate down from higher-level data values into lower-level details to better understand the presentation of those values.
- **KPI Details report**. The KPI Details report is a new report type that displays information about metrics within a scorecard. The KPI Details report is a Web Part in SharePoint 2010 and can be connected to PerformancePoint Services scorecards to offer a more granular presentation of the data behind a metric.

Visio Services

What does Visio have to do with business intelligence? Well, if you recall an earlier definition that stated business intelligence is mostly about "telling a story" with few words, then showing information in Visio diagrams is just as impactful. Business users have used Microsoft Visio for some time to represent corporate data. One of the challenges, however, has been that not all content consumers had Visio on their desktops, so distribution of Visio charts was sometimes a challenge. Visio Services has been introduced with SharePoint 2010. It operates very much the same way as Excel Services or PerformancePoint Services in that it acts as a service in the context of a SharePoint environment.

Why Use Visio Services?

There are three main benefits to using Visio Services:

- A business user can share a presentation of data created in Microsoft Visio in the browser without requiring the content consumer to have Visio installed on his or her desktop.
- Once a diagram from Visio has been deployed, information can be refreshed so that changes made in Visio can automatically be refreshed in the browser presentation.
- Much like Excel Services and PerformancePoint Services, Visio diagrams can be shown in the context of an already familiar SharePoint environment.

Visio Services supports diagrams connected to one or more of the following data sources:

- SQL Server
- SharePoint lists
- Excel workbooks that are stored in SharePoint
- Any ODBC data source that you can normally connect to

Visio Services is an exciting new tool that offers business users an easy way to share diagrams. Because it operates as a service within SharePoint, Visio Services has a very low overhead for IT in terms of management and support. It is important to remember that Visio Services does require both the Enterprise version of SharePoint 2010 for presentation and Microsoft Visio 2010 on the desktop of users who will create diagrams that will be published to SharePoint.

Putting It All Together

At this point, you should have an appreciation for how dashboards and scorecards (and even Visio diagrams) can be enabled in SharePoint, Excel Services and PerformancePoint Services, and Visio Services. But what are the benefits of this technology?

The business benefits of using Excel Services are many. When an analyst can take a key set of charts based on his Excel spreadsheets into the portal for wider consumption, he is able to inform the organization in ways that are not always possible when a spreadsheet gets mailed around. Having a single place where a spreadsheet is stored that can be viewed by the people who are allowed to see it ensures that everyone is getting the same message. Is the spreadsheet that you e-mailed to me on Tuesday the right one, or is it the one that Bob said he got from you on Wednesday? What changed? Do I need to compare the two? If it's only in one place, then there is only one answer. In addition, Excel Services allows an analyst to control and protect the published information. The user is not simply uploading a spreadsheet into a document library; a subset of the data is shared in a controlled and secure manner.

PerformancePoint Services can provide an additional visual layer or veneer on top of large amounts of information. Are we trending up or down? Are we more productive or less? Again, with a single glance, you can tell. You see a problem, you can click on the indicator and see what's driving the trend, and most importantly, you can then do something about it in an informed way. It's all about what the numbers *mean*, not what the numbers *are*. There's a reason that visual representations are more helpful than long lists of numbers. With a single glance, you can tell whether things are good, not so good, or bad.

Visio Services offers the ability to present business intelligence data in a diagram format. Think of the presentation of a business process (or workflow) now integrated with back-end data that shows performance at each phase in the process. That is a very compelling presentation that is not easily done with a chart or scorecard or dashboard. That's where Visio adds another layer of value.

As you start to think about how all this hangs together and how you might deploy business intelligence solutions in your organization using SharePoint, keep a few things in mind:

- **Understand your strategy**. Many times dashboards and scorecards can enforce exactly the opposite behavior than what is intended. Think about a scorecard that tracks the number of new accounts. What is going to happen to your existing accounts? Will they get neglected inadvertently? Using one lever can often have an impact somewhere else. Make sure it is all strategic.
- **Keep it simple**. Giving people hundreds of metrics to watch regularly will hide the messages. Decide on which metrics (or more

likely a combination of metrics) indicate good performance and use those. Build up a high-level dashboard or scorecard for general consumption and listen to what people find helpful or not and go from there. Don't try to build the be-all and end-all solution from day one.

- **Expect things to change**. When the novelty wears off, dashboards can get dull. They need to evolve to both keep people's focus but also to reflect any changes in the organization's underlying strategy or business processes. Having agility in your dashboard and score-card development capabilities will translate into agility against your competition and in the marketplace.
- **Make sure the data is accurate**. A dashboard or scorecard is useless (and dangerous) if wrong. Ensure that data delivery is complete and accurate. Remember, this presentation is driving business decisions.
- **Target an audience**. A dashboard tells a story. That story is specific to certain data elements and is presented to convey a certain message. Keep the messaging focused and target a specific set of users. If dashboard viewers want more metrics, maybe a new dashboard is required.
- **Business intelligence is not about "one size fits all."** Know your user and target the right presentation of corporate data with the one that tells the story in the easiest and most useful way. Take advantage of the robustness and integration that SharePoint offers to map the solutions one-to-few (versus one-for-all).

Key Points

Bringing business intelligence to your knowledge workers is a key feature of SharePoint. Features such as report delivery, Excel Services, and PerformancePoint provide fantastic ways to harness and distribute analytics information. When using SharePoint for business intelligence, remember these key points:

- Dashboards can be used to show, in real time, how an organization (or more often a part of an organization) is performing against *tactical* goals.
- Scorecards are used to show how an organization is performing against *strategic* goals.

- Status Indicator lists (also known as KPIs) are a simple way to map business metrics to existing data values to provide a graphical presentation of performance.
- Excel Services empower business users to publish Excel-based content in an environment that offers visibility without compromising security.
- PerformancePoint Services allows you to provide more advanced business intelligence presentations, allowing you to create and manage metrics for scorecards, dashboards, and KPIs.
- Visio Services allows users to publish Visio diagrams to a browser and to connect those diagrams to corporate data, thus providing a different type of business intelligence solution.

CHAPTER 14

COMPOSITE APPLICATIONS WITH BUSINESS CONNECTIVITY SERVICES

Companies far and wide have always struggled with connecting their users with the business data stored in various locations, such as databases and fileshares, across the organization. As these companies became more successful at getting the data into an electronic format, IT departments were under pressure to meet the demands of the data consumer.

The separation between the data storage and the interface to that data typically required significant efforts in custom software development to provide applications to meet these needs. Once custom development efforts are required, then both time and effort as well as cost and project risks increase significantly.

SharePoint Composites are introduced in SharePoint 2010 to address this issue. Using the suite of client applications (Designer, InfoPath, Excel, Access, Visio) and the composite nature of SharePoint Web part pages, IT departments can significantly reduce the need to be involved in data-driven solutions while still maintaining control over the systems and the data itself.

This chapter contains the following key sections:

- What Is a Composite Application?
- Introducing Business Connectivity Services
- BCS Components
- Types of BCS Solutions
- Getting Started with BCS
- Building a Composite Application

What Is a Composite Application?

SharePoint 2010 provides the user with a suite of applications and functionality to allow them to take more control over how they represent their data. With the help of Visio Services, Excel and Access Services, and using SharePoint Designer, it is possible for these users to build no-code collaborative solutions through browser-based customizations.

Note With SharePoint composites, you can:

- Rapidly create no-code collaborative solutions.
- Unlock the value of enterprise data.
- Maintain control over end-user solutions.

While Visio, Excel, and Access allow the user to work on local data and then publish it to SharePoint, leveraging enterprise data was always a challenge. Microsoft recognized this and filled this gap with Business Connectivity Services.

Introducing Business Connectivity Services

In SharePoint 2007, the Business Data Catalog (BDC) was introduced to much fanfare. It provided a way to bring enterprise data from SQL, ORACLE, and other sources directly into SharePoint. This was the first step in bridging the gap between SharePoint data and external enterprise data. While it was an important step to take, it proved to be difficult to work with and limited in functionality. With SharePoint Server 2010, Microsoft went from a small step to a giant leap replacing the BDC with Business Connectivity Services (BCS).

With BCS, users can read and write data as easily as they interact with a standard SharePoint list. The Business Data Web Parts help expose the external data for building composite applications. Because the data is fully accessible through SharePoint, the same data can now be accessed through Outlook, SharePoint Workspace, as well as the full Office Suite. Other features include the following:

- Expose enterprise data from external sources such as databases, Web services in SharePoint 2010, and Office 2010.
- Map Office Type objects and capabilities such as appointments, tasks, and contacts to external data.
- Enable a two-way synchronization between the external data and SharePoint, allowing the data to be updated as well as consumed in SharePoint.
- Provide offline accessibility to the external data using clients such as Outlook or SharePoint Workspace.

While all this gives the user great functionality flexibility, IT departments need not fret; SharePoint still allows IT to control who gets to create what and where.

BCS Components

The Business Connectivity Services provide many tools for connecting to and managing how we interact with external data. While SharePoint Server 2010 license holders get more goodies, SharePoint Foundation 2010 is certainly not left out in the cold. Figure 14-1 shows the distribution of components between the Office products. Before we explore the various components however, we need to understand the fundamental building block of BCS—the External Content Type.

External Content Types

External data is represented through a new object called an *External Content Type*. With an External Content Type you get to define the following for the data connection:

- External Data Source
- Office Item Type
- Operations
- Fields
- Permissions

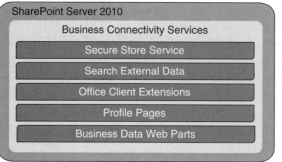

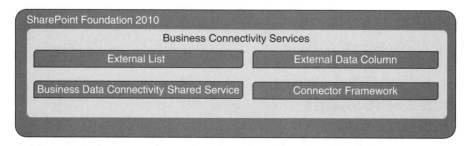

Figure 14-1 Business Connectivity Services provide a number of components, depending on the version of SharePoint 2010

After you have defined your External Content Type, you can use this to work directly within SharePoint lists. In doing so, all the data from the external source will now be available in what appears to be a standard SharePoint list when using a SharePoint *External List*. Using an *External Data Column*, several of the external data columns can be added to other lists.

As you can see, there are many pieces to the BCS puzzle. Table 14-1 explains each of the components in more detail.

Types of BCS Solutions

With the list of components described in Table 14-1, it is easy to see that the user has options when it comes to building solutions. Whatever solution they choose to build will fall under one of the following categories:

- SharePoint Web-based solution
- Simple solution in Outlook 2010
- Simple solution in SharePoint Workspace 2010

Table 14-1 The Many Components of the Business Connectivity Services in SharePoint

Function	Description	SharePoint Foundation 2010	SharePoint Server 2010	Office 2010
External List	Special list type that interacts directly with an external data source	Y	Y	
External Data Column	Special data type allows you to add external data to any list	Y	Y	
Secure Store Service	Handles credential mapping allowing single sign-on functionality		Y	
External Data Search	Exposes the external data to SharePoint search for indexing		Y	
Rich Client Extensions	Allows Office clients to connect directly to the external data through SharePoint		Y	
External Data Web Parts	Several Web Parts that allow you to build composite applications from your external data		Y	
Profile Pages	Expose the external data in a single page for a single item		Y	
Rich Client Components	Works with the rich client extensions to access external data			Y

- Declarative solution in Outlook 2010
- Code-based solution using the BCS API

The SharePoint Web-based solution is the type that will be created the most, and this is the one we investigate for the rest of this chapter.

Getting Started with BCS

What better way to discover what Business Connectivity Services is about than to dive straight in and create a sample application? For this example, we are going to connect to the Customers table in the Northwind database and use it to create a SharePoint external list. When we have our customer list in SharePoint, we will create an external column for our document library and then use all we know to build a composite application.

For our solution we need to

- Connect to the Northwind database.
- Define an External Content Type.
- Create an external list in our SharePoint site.
- Create an External Column for our document library.

All of these tasks will be done from SharePoint Designer, so without further ado, let's open SharePoint Designer and point it at our sample SharePoint site.

Creating an External Content Type

From the Site Objects list in SharePoint Designer, you can see an External Content Types option. Selecting this allows us to create a new External Content Type using the icon in the ribbon.

Figure 14-2 shows all the elements that make up our new External Content Type including general information such as name and office type (Generic List, Appointment, Task, and Post), operations, permissions, associated external lists, and fields.

After naming the Content Type we now need to connect it to our external data source by clicking the link next to the External System label. This opens the Operation Designer page as in Figure 14-2.

Note   The external data source in this example is a SQL database, but SharePoint Designer 2010 provides for connections to a Web service as well as a .NET assembly.

The Operation Designer page in Figure 14-3 shows the page with our database connected. Creating the connection was as easy as clicking the Add Connection button and providing the database server, name, and credentials. You can see the list of tables in our database in the Data Source Explorer. Now that we have located our Customers table, we have to define the operations that will allow us to interact with the data. Right-clicking the Customers table allows us to select from all the operations available (Figure 14-4).

The first option allows us to define all the operations at once. Selecting this option prompts a wizard that enables us to define parameters and

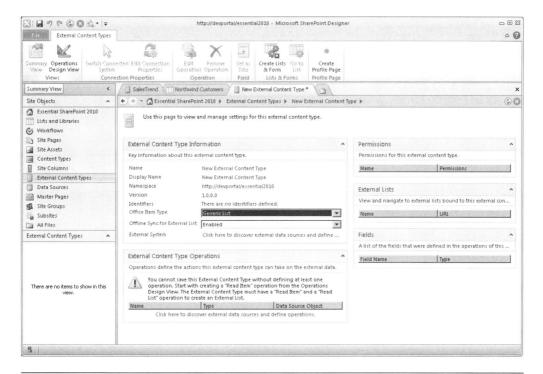

Figure 14-2 The new External Content Type page displays general information as well as permissions, operations, fields, and associated external lists

filters. We are doing a simple one-to-one mapping of a table, so we don't need to apply filters. Figure 14-5 shows the Parameters page where we can select the fields we want to pull from our data source as well as field properties, such as display name, if the field is read-only, and so on.

You may also notice the Office Property option under properties. This allows you to map your inbound columns to Office type properties such as first name, e-mail address, home phone number, and so on. The reason you may want to do this is if you are creating a Content Type using one of the Office types such as contact, task, or other. Having these Content Types makes integration with the Office clients incredibly easy.

After the wizard is complete, you will have a full set of operations defined for your data. Figure 14-6 shows us returning to our External Content Type summary page where can see the fields we selected and the operations we defined.

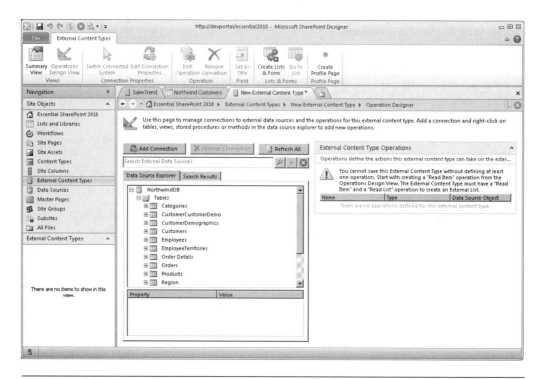

Figure 14-3 The Operation Designer allows you to define and search external connections

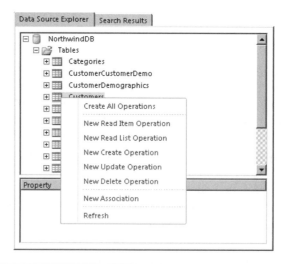

Figure 14-4 The Operation Designer allows you to select from several operations to define for your data source

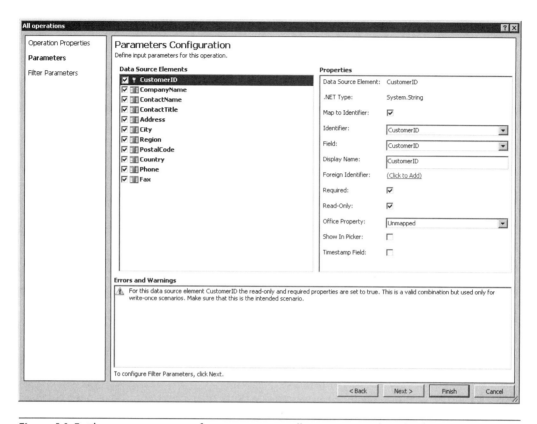

Figure 14-5 The Parameters Configuration page allows you to select the fields to connect with and to define various properties for those fields

We have our External Content Type connected to our external data source, fields selected, and operations defined. We are ready to save the Content Type and put it to use.

Creating an External List in SharePoint

From the External Content Type summary page in SharePoint Designer, you will notice an icon in the Lists & Forms group called Create Lists & Form. Clicking this icon displays a dialog where we specify our external list properties (see Figure 14-7).

Note You have the option to create an InfoPath form instead of the standard SharePoint list form when you define your new external list. This is extremely useful if you plan to extend the form with custom branding or functionality.

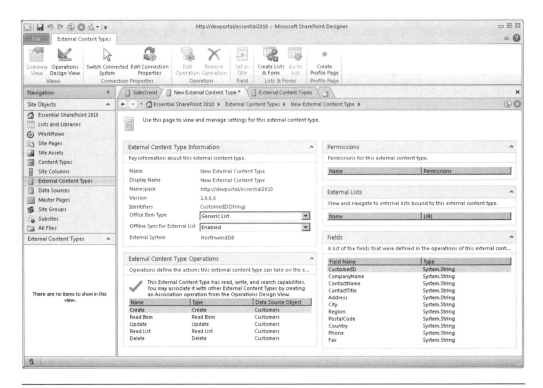

Figure 14-6 The External Content Type summary page after operations have been defined

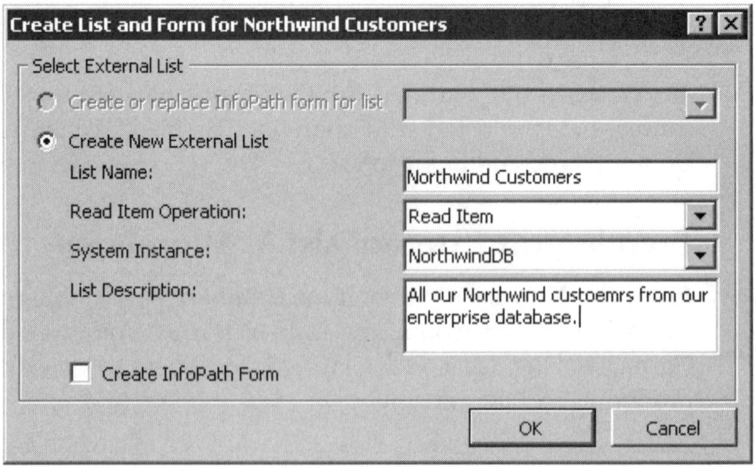

Figure 14-7 The Create External List dialog allows us to specify new list properties

After our list is created, its association to the External Content Type will be listed in the External Lists section of the summary page in SharePoint Designer. Returning to our SharePoint site, we now see a new list containing our Northwind customers as if it were all manually created through the SharePoint UI. Figure 14-8 displays our external list in all its glory.

Now, in case you were reading too fast, let me recap. We opened SharePoint Designer and created a new External Content Type that points to the Customers table of our Northwind database in SQL. We then defined our operations, selected the fields we wanted, and saved the External Content Type with a new name. We then used the External Content Type to create an external list in our SharePoint site, which allows us to read and write all the customer data that is in the SQL table. This is powerful: a complete application without having to write any code!

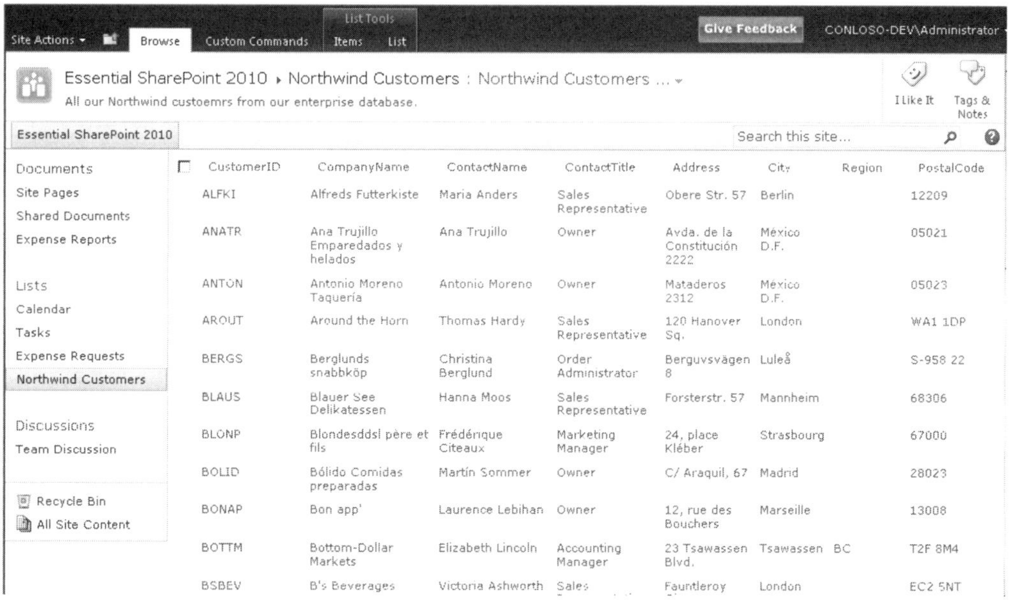

Figure 14-8 The new external list displays the Northwind Customers database table just like any other SharePoint list

---

Note Because the ability to create BCS-based solutions is both simple and powerful, governance is needed. Be sure you have a rigorous test plan, especially for shared environments. Simple changes to the farm, such as a service pack install, need to be validated by your business units who are running SharePoint-based solutions.

There's even more power with BCS. In the next sections, we add even more functionality to our external list by adding custom actions, integrating the customer list with our document library, and finally creating our composite application.

Adding Custom Actions to an External Data List

One restriction with an external list is that you cannot associate workflows with it. However, you can create custom actions accessible from within the ribbon or the list item (context) menu. This allows you to direct the user to a URL and send the list item as a value in the URL query. With this sort of functionality, we can create custom services that can access the list data using the ID and process the external data, all from within the SharePoint list interface.

Let's see an example. Taking our existing customer data, we wish to add a custom action that calls a service that displays a report from SQL Server Reporting Services for the current customer. This service is an asp.net page that takes a single query value—the list item ID.

If we open the newly created external list in SharePoint Designer, we see an icon called Custom Action in the ribbon. This allows us to create a new action for the list item menu. Selecting this option displays the dialog in Figure 14-9 where we can specify the properties of the action.

For our new action, we tell it to Navigate to URL where we specify the URL of our aspx page. Notice we pass the list item ID in the URL using the format {ItemId}. SharePoint converts that to the actual list item ID.

Note Creating the service page for this demonstration is beyond the scope of this book.

Figure 14-10 shows our new action in the list item menu. We could also have specified an icon if we had one handy. Selecting this new action

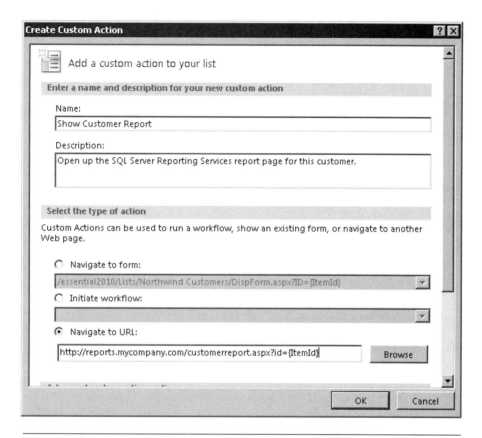

Figure 14-9 Creating a custom action allows you to send the item ID directly to a different service URL

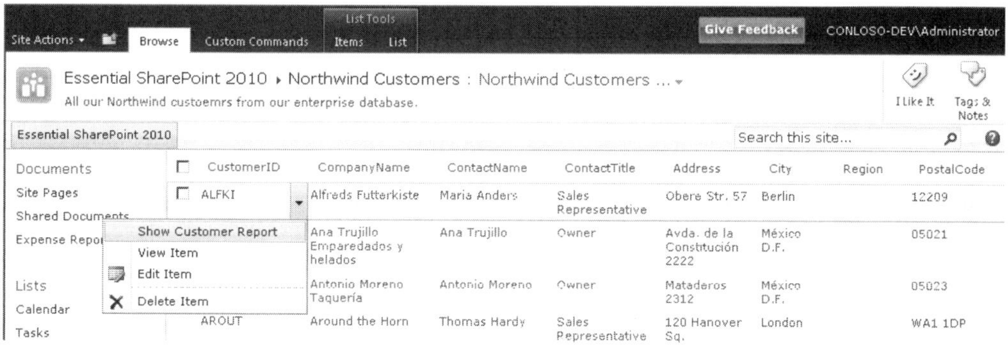

Figure 14-10 It's easy to add custom actions to the list item menu and ribbon using SharePoint Designer

will redirect the user to the aspx page we specified while sending the item ID in the URL. The aspx page can do any number of things now that it has a reference to the item in the list, including starting a custom workflow.

To achieve all that we have achieved without the BCS would have required using a custom code-based solution. What took us a matter of minutes would previously have taken weeks. There is no doubt that BCS is going to be very popular with your business users.

Using an External Data Column

We already have our Customer data in its own list in SharePoint, but what if we wanted to use just one of those columns in a different list? Using a new column type called an External Data Column, we can achieve just that.

In our site we have a document library that we have been using for tracking customer forms such as invoices, presentations, and so on. Rather than using a choice column for the customer reference, we can pull this value directly from our enterprise customer list using the external Content Type we created earlier.

Figure 14-11 shows us adding a new column to our customer documents library. We select the External Data as the Column type, and then we configure that to use the Northwind Customers External Content Type which allows us to select a value from the CustomerID column. That's all there is to it. Now when we pick a customer ID we know it is the correct value.

Building a Composite Application

So far we have built an External Content Type and used that to create an external list in our SharePoint site and also to create an External Data Column in our documents library. With all that done, we have enough to build a simple composite application.

The BCS provides several Web Parts that we can now use to build a composite application. Out of the box, we get the Web Parts listed in Table 14-2.

So let's build a composite application for our customers from Northwind. Our application will contain a filter where we pick our customer, and then the filter will be applied to a data item Web Part and a document library Web Part.

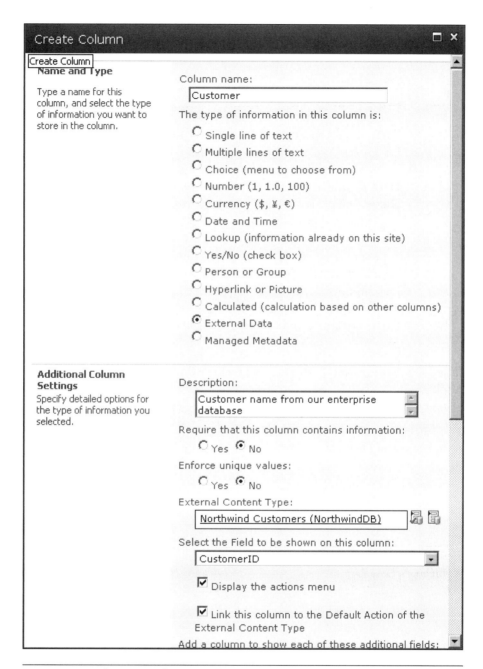

Figure 14-11 The External Data Column type allows you to select values directly from an external source such as a customer database

---

Note The Business Data Web Parts are part of the Enterprise license; to access them you must activate the Enterprise Site Collection Features through Site Settings.

After creating a new page in our site, we edit the page to add our Web Parts as seen in Figure 14-12. All of the BCS Web Parts are in the Business Data folder in the Web Part navigator.

We are going to add the following Web Parts to our page: the Business Data Connectivity Filter, the Business Data Item, and then the Shared Documents list (for this we select from Existing List in the ribbon).

When we have our three Web Parts added to the page, we are going to connect the business data Web Parts to our Customers External Content Type and then configure them all to talk to each other. The Business Data Web Parts are easily connected to the External Content Type using the Web Part properties. Once we have those configured, we use Web Part connections to wire them together. Figure 14-13 shows how to connect the Web Parts. For our connections, the Business Data Connectivity is the *provider*

Table 14-2 Several Web Parts Provided by the BCS to Use to Build a Composite Application

Web Part	Description
Business Data Actions	Displays a list of actions from an External Content Type
Business Data Item	Displays a single item from an External Content Type
Business Data Item Builder	Uses the query string to create a business data item and provides the value to other Web Parts
Business Data List	Displays a list of items from the External Content Type
Business Data Related List	Displays a list of items related to one or more parent items from an External Content Type
Business Data Connectivity Filter	Uses values from the External Content Type to use to filter the contents of Web Parts

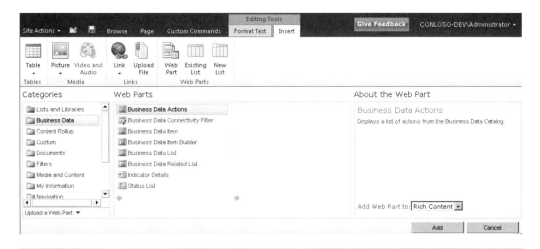

Figure 14-12 The BCS Web Parts can be found in the Business Data category after you enable Enterprise features

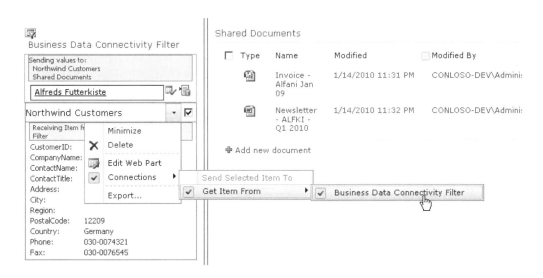

Figure 14-13 Connecting Web Parts allows them to talk to each other, so filter Web Parts can change the content of other Web Parts on the same page

Figure 14-14 Composite application for Northwind customers allows us to select a customer and have their details and documents appear in the other Web Parts

(providing the customer ID to the other Web Parts), with the shared documents library and Business Data Item Web Parts being the *consumers*.

With our connections configured, selecting a customer from the filter Web Part using the little icon to the right displays the customer details in the Business Data Item Web Part and will then filter the Shared Documents Web Part for just those customer documents. Figure 14-14 shows us what our application looks like after a customer has been selected.

The BCS Web Parts give you many options for creating composite applications for integrating SharePoint data with your enterprise data. A typical extension of our composite page would be to use the other Web Parts in the Business Data category to display indicators relating to the customer.

Key Points

Business Connectivity Services is a very compelling feature of SharePoint Server 2010 that allows business users to truly integrate their enterprise data with SharePoint content. With the Business Data Web Parts provided with the Enterprise edition of SharePoint 2010, building composite apps is as easy as dropping them on a Web page and connecting them together. The following list is a review of the key points:

- External Content Types allow you to easily connect to external data from sources such as SQL, ORACLE, or Web Services.
- External lists in SharePoint can display content directly from an external source using an External Content Type.
- External content can be updated directly from an external list as if you are updating a standard SharePoint list item.
- The Column type External Data can be used to integrate a single column from your external source into any SharePoint list.
- Actions can be configured to pass the external item to another application for processing.
- The BCS provides several Web Parts for creating composite applications.
- Web Part Connections allow you to pass data from one Web Part to another.

CHAPTER 15

OFFICE 2010 CLIENT APPLICATIONS

Why are we talking about the Office 2010 client applications in a SharePoint 2010 book? The answer is simple: To maximize the value of your investment in the SharePoint platform, you will want to evaluate and take advantage of the integration and capabilities that are "lit up" through the Office client.

The Office 2007 system added many features that worked "best" with a combination of the 2007 versions of the Office client and SharePoint. These included offline information and easy access to advanced SharePoint document management features such as workflow, metadata, and version control.

There is business value here: If you make it easy for end users to work with SharePoint from within the context of the Office applications that they already spend most of their time in (that is, Outlook, Word, Excel, PowerPoint), then you will give them the incentive to use SharePoint over other tools such as fileshares and e-mail. It's a virtuous cycle: As more properly tagged content is added to SharePoint, the more relevant search results will be, which then drives people to use your SharePoint environment and begin to access the social, business intelligence, forms, and other tools.

With the 2010 release, Microsoft has built upon and extended the role of the Office client in the SharePoint experience. This chapter includes the following key sections:

- What's New in Office 2010?
- Office Client Applications That Connect with SharePoint 2010
- SharePoint Workspace: Taking a SharePoint Site Offline
- Documents and Data Caching
- Backstage
- Other Clients: Office Web Applications and Office Mobile Applications

What's New in Office 2010?

With Office 2010, Microsoft made an important change to how they package the client applications. Most corporations have the Professional Plus version of Office. In Office 2010, this suite has been enhanced to now include SharePoint Workspace (formerly Groove), OneNote, and the Office Web Application companions. The addition of these three applications to the Professional Plus suite is an indication of how important these programs are. This licensing change should enable many companies to have access to these capabilities.

One of the biggest changes that will affect SharePoint is the upgrade and repositioning of Groove. In the 2010 release, Groove has been renamed to SharePoint Workspace. This is more than just slapping a new name on the product. The SharePoint Workspace product has received significant updates and has been newly positioned as the primary rich client for SharePoint. The simplest way to think about this is to consider the relationship between SharePoint Workspace and SharePoint Server to be similar to how Outlook functions as the rich desktop client for Exchange Server.

OneNote has also been improved in 2010. It is a tremendous application for capturing information from various formats (text, audio, images, and so on) and integrating them on one canvas. OneNote has rich integration with SharePoint so multiple people can concurrently collaborate on a page within a shared OneNote notebook and have their changes automatically synchronized and tracked so people can see who changed what section and when. In some ways OneNote is like a wiki editor on steroids and can be used for various tasks such as meeting notes, brainstorming, policies, procedures, and training materials.

Business Connectivity Services (BCS) has also emerged in SharePoint 2010 as the successor to the Business Data Catalog (BDC) that was introduced in SharePoint 2007. BCS enables you to establish a read/write connection with a back-end database such as a CRM (Siebel or Dynamics, for example) or ERP system (such as PeopleSoft or SAP) using tools such as SharePoint Designer or Visual Studio 2010. After being created and published to SharePoint, the BCS connection can be reused by SharePoint lists and the Office 2010 clients (for example, SharePoint Workspace, Outlook, or Word) to view and edit data that is stored in the back-end system. More detailed information on the BCS is provided in Chapter 14, "Composite Applications with Business Connectivity Services."

Also new in 2010 are the Web and mobile application companions for Word, Excel, PowerPoint, and OneNote. These Web and mobile applications provide lightweight viewing and editing capabilities built on top of (and integrated with) SharePoint. They are similar to how the Outlook Web Access application enables you to work with your Exchange mailbox with just a browser and Outlook mobile lets you work while on your mobile device.

Note While the Office 2010 clients add tighter integration with the latest SharePoint 2010 Server product, it is not required that you upgrade your clients and servers at the same time. Microsoft has created a "Business Productivity at Its Best" whitepaper that describes the integrated client and server capabilities and differences across versions of SharePoint and Office in more detail, which can be found at http://go.microsoft.com/?linkid= 9690494

Office Client Applications That Connect with SharePoint 2010

The user interface in SharePoint 2010 is great, and many people work directly in their Web browsers. But what if you're going to be offline or you prefer to do your SharePoint work right in the context of the document you are working on? Maybe you're somewhere with very low bandwidth and you're working with large files? Good news: Office 2010 has a few different options to help you out.

SharePoint 2010 has increased the integration with various 2010 Office clients. The SharePoint ribbon browser interface now directly links you with the following Office and Windows clients, which offer you the choice and flexibility to work with SharePoint in the context of the client tool that best supports the task you are performing:

- **Access**. Enables you to work with SharePoint list data offline in a read/write fashion. Also great for mashing up SharePoint data with other data sources (databases, spreadsheets, and so on) and creating queries and polished reports. This fits in great with the overall SharePoint composite application strategy and provides you with another alternative for migrating local Access databases to a shared and managed platform, including the new Access Services SharePoint capabilities. Access Services enable you to publish an Access database and have the data, forms, macros, queries, and reports usable via a Web browser.

- **Excel**. Continued support for browser-based Excel Services. New Office Web Application companion for browser-based viewing, editing, and coauthoring of spreadsheets. Continued integration of Excel with SharePoint for saving documents, adding metadata, checking-in/out, and workflow. Great for taking a list offline and performing advanced analysis using capabilities such as charts, graphs, slicers, and pivot tables.

- **InfoPath**. Tool for making advanced forms that can then be reused across SharePoint (via InfoPath forms services) and other Office applications (SharePoint Workspace, Access, Outlook). InfoPath 2010 now supports the creation of InfoPath forms services Web Part controls so you can now mash up InfoPath controls on the same page as other SharePoint data and Web Parts.

- **Office Upload Center**. Performs per-document level caching and central access to see all SharePoint files you have viewed recently and which items are pending check-in, regardless of which SharePoint site the content originally came from. Synchronizes changes only between the client and server applications across the Office suite.

- **OneNote**. Advanced wiki capabilities for collaborating, brainstorming, and sharing information. New Office Web Application companion for browser-based viewing and editing of information, including coauthoring support in both the browser and rich desktop client for concurrent editing.

- **Outlook**. Primarily used for Personal Information Management (PIM) and to show how team-based data in SharePoint relates to you. Examples include read/write access to SharePoint calendars, tasks, contacts, and discussion boards—even while offline. Outlook 2010 also adds the new Outlook Social Connector (OSC), which displays news and activity feeds for your contacts from SharePoint 2010 as well as other social systems (such as LinkedIn, Facebook, MySpace, and Windows Live) in a centralized view to help improve your collaboration experience.

- **PowerPoint**. Continued integration of PowerPoint with SharePoint for saving documents, adding metadata, checking-in/out, and workflow as well as slide libraries. New Office Web Application companion for browser-based viewing and editing of presentations. Client supports coauthoring so multiple people can edit the same presentation concurrently. New features to add videos directly from SharePoint and to edit the videos (for example, change display, trim, or resize). Also added the ability to broadcast a PowerPoint presentation by publishing it to SharePoint or Windows Live and then sending a link via e-mail for others to view the slide show via their Web browser where they can still see slide transitions, builds, and other advanced display features.
- **Project**. Supports exporting SharePoint task lists into Project for more sophisticated reporting on project tasks, milestones, dependencies, resources, and so on.
- **SharePoint Designer**. A free desktop application provided by Microsoft for advanced SharePoint site customization including HTML page design and creating and managing reusable Workflows and Business Connectivity Services.
- **SharePoint Workspace**. Used for taking SharePoint site content and data offline—either at the site or per-list level. Synchronizes changes only to efficiently use network bandwidth.
- **Visio**. With Visio 2010 you can now create workflows that can then be imported and used with SharePoint. You can also create browser-based Visio diagrams (using Visio Services as part of SharePoint 2010) and export SharePoint task lists to a graphical Visio diagram.
- **Windows Explorer**. SharePoint continues to have integration with Windows Explorer both for uploading and copying documents between SharePoint and another file storage location such as your local PC or a network fileshare.
- **Word**. Continued integration of Word with SharePoint for saving documents, adding metadata, checking-in/out, and workflow. New Office Web Application companion for browser-based viewing and editing of documents. Client supports coauthoring so multiple people can edit the same document concurrently.

Table 15-1 summarizes the level at which each client application can be used from directly within the SharePoint 2010 user interface:

Table 15-1 Office and Windows Client Integration with SharePoint Ribbon User Interface

Client Application	Site Level?	List Level?	Item Level?
Access	No	Yes	Yes
Excel	No	Yes	Yes
InfoPath	No	Yes	Yes
Office Upload Center	No	No	Yes
OneNote	No	No	Yes
Outlook	No	Yes*	No
PowerPoint	No	No	Yes
Project	No	Yes**	Yes
SharePoint Designer	Yes	Yes	No
SharePoint Workspace	Yes	Yes	Yes
Visio	No	Yes**	Yes
Windows Explorer	No	Yes	Yes
Word	No	No	Yes

* = Calendar, contact, task, document library, and discussion board lists only.
** = Task list types only.

SharePoint Workspace: Taking a SharePoint Site Offline

SharePoint Workspace (SPW) is the evolution of the product that was formerly known as Groove and supports working with SharePoint data offline. SPW has a number of key benefits for working with SharePoint data:

- **Extended offline capabilities**. It's more than just documents now! Prior to SPW, Groove only allowed you to take documents offline from SharePoint. You can now take documents and list data offline. While most SharePoint lists can be taken offline, calendars, wikis, blogs, and Web Parts cannot be taken offline with the initial release of SPW.
- **Business Connectivity Services (BCS)**. As mentioned earlier in this chapter, with BCS integration via SharePoint lists you can now use SPW to work with external data lists offline. Examples of this include working with CRM, ERP, or custom line-of-business systems. You make your updates, add new items, and delete items locally, and SPW will sync your changes back via the SharePoint server when you

reconnect, which will then update the back-end system that the data resides in.

- **Conflict resolution**. SPW manages conflicts (cases where more than one person updates the same thing at the same time) at the item level. This means that if two people edit the same row in a list at the same time, SPW will identify the conflict and allow the user to select which version to keep. This also allows multiple people to edit the same list concurrently without the need to have people serially check-in/out a spreadsheet.

- **InfoPath forms integration**. SPW uses InfoPath for its forms. This enables you to have very rich forms offline, including the ability to perform data validation. Using InfoPath enables you to learn a single forms designer technology regardless of how the form will be used to view or input data: SPW, SharePoint, Outlook, or Access.

- **Binary differentials**. When the SPW syncs data, it only syncs changes since the last sync. For example, if you have an 8MB PowerPoint file synced locally in SPW and someone makes a change to one slide, SPW will only sync the parts of that single slide that changed. This is great in general and especially when you're on a slower network, wireless, or mobile connection.

- **Desktop search**. SPW now enables you to use desktop search to locally search for and find content that has been taken offline within the tool.

- **Classic Groove workspaces**. These still exist in SPW and can be used for primarily non-SharePoint-based collaboration and information exchange both within the organization and externally with customers and partners. The classic Groove workspace continues to have the SharePoint Files Tool for synchronizing individual document libraries between the Groove workspace and SharePoint sites.

Taking a site offline with SPW is straightforward:

1. Click Site Actions in the ribbon of the SharePoint site that you want to take offline and select Sync to SharePoint Workspace from the menu (see Figure 15-1).

2. Click Configure to choose what content to synchronize (see Figure 15-2). Alternatively, clicking OK at this step uses the default choice, which is to synchronize all available content.

3. For each library or list that is available to sync, determine whether to download (see Figure 15-3) the following:

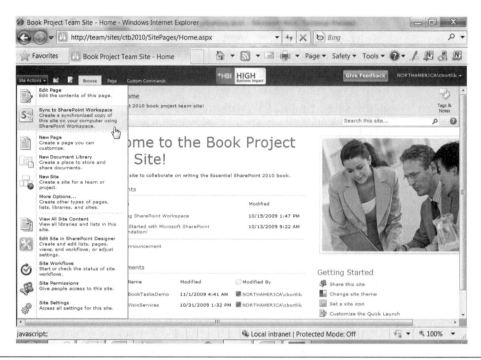

Figure 15-1 Synchronizing an entire site with SharePoint Workspace

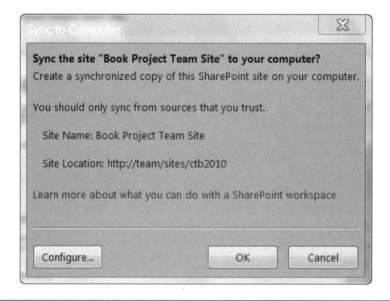

Figure 15-2 Optional ability to configure list level settings

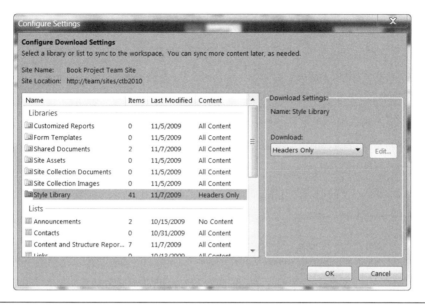

Figure 15-3 Determining what content to synchronize per list or library

- **All content**. Downloads the full contents of the selected library or list.
- **Headers only**. Only downloads the basic information for each item. For example, for document libraries it shows the basic file properties (name, modified date, and so on). You can later select to download the full library or just individual folders or files when you are online.
- **No content**. Does not bring the library or list offline. This can be brought offline later if desired.

4. Click OK to begin synchronizing the selected content (see Figure 15-4).
5. When synchronization is complete, you can view the status and see if any errors occurred (see Figure 15-5).
6. Clicking Open Workspace lets you access the new workspace that has been created (see Figure 15-6).

You can also selectively bring a list offline with SPW. To do so, navigate to the list using your Web browser, and then click the List tab under the List Tools section in the SharePoint ribbon and choose the Sync to SharePoint Workspace option (see Figure 15-7).

Figure 15-4 In-process synchronization with SharePoint Workspace

Figure 15-5 Summary of synchronization results within SharePoint Workspace

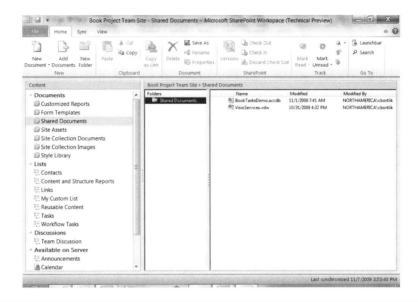

Figure 15-6 Viewing the site offline in SharePoint Workspace

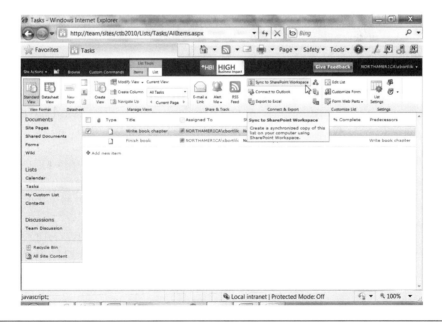

Figure 15-7 Selecting a single list to take offline in SharePoint Workspace

Documents and Data Caching

Office 2010 offers several different ways to handle document and data caching. Choosing the tool that is right for you will depend on what you need to do.

Documents

When working with documents, your primary tools are

- SharePoint Workspace
- Office Upload Center
- Outlook 2010
- Windows Explorer

SharePoint Workspace

SharePoint Workspace is the tool to use for those SharePoint sites that you frequently use and those where you want to make sure that you always have the latest copy of the site content synchronized and available—even when you are not connected to the corporate network. My Site and team collaboration sites are two examples of sites that are well-suited to use SPW to keep content up-to-date.

Office Upload Center

What if you only occasionally browse SharePoint sites and have a challenge remembering what sites you've checked out files from and have pending check-ins? Or maybe you're in a remote location and have a low bandwidth connection? Good news. Office 2010 now includes a new client application named the Office Upload Center. Now by just visiting the Office Upload Center you can see what documents you have most recently opened from SharePoint, manage your locally cached copies, and review and check-in documents (see Figure 15-8).

You can also customize how the Office Upload Center works and how you get notified of changes that are pending or failed to upload and the amount of disk space allocated to the file cache (see Figure 15-9).

Using the Office Upload Center is the default option in Office 2010 for caching Office files on your PC. It is not required. If you want to

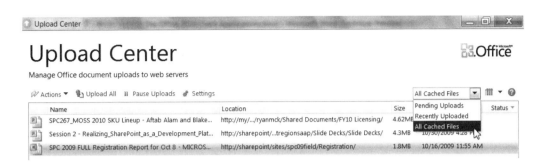

Figure 15-8 The Office Upload Center is a central location for caching all SharePoint files and providing a consolidated view of all files checked out and pending upload back to SharePoint

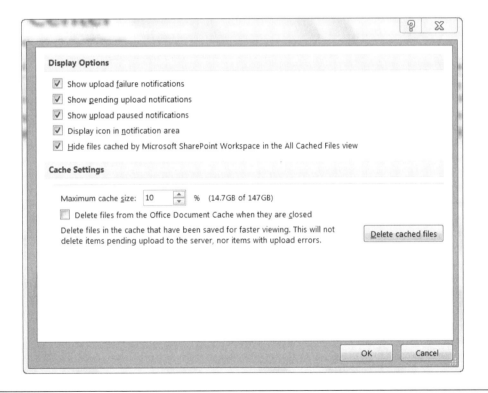

Figure 15-9 The Office Upload Center provides a variety of settings that you can set, including how much disk space to use for caching files, whether to show notifications, and whether files that are cached offline by the SharePoint Workspace should be displayed in this application

change Office to instead use a "local server drafts folder" on your computer and have this work as it did in Office 2007, you can change that option under the Offline Editing Options for Document Management Server Files setting within the Save options in any Office client product (see Figure 15-10).

Outlook 2010

As in Office 2007, Outlook 2010 also offers you the ability to take documents offline. We typically discourage the use of this feature for a few reasons. First, Outlook document synchronization with SharePoint is read-only. Second, do you really want your e-mail client to be synchronizing documents

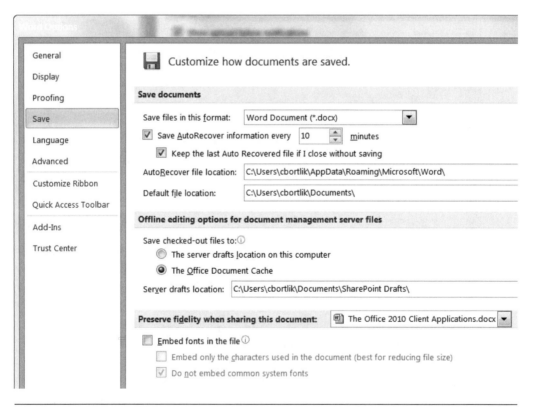

Figure 15-10 Setting Office 2010 to use Office Document Cache or local server drafts location

as well as what it already does around your e-mails, tasks, calendars, RSS feeds, and so on? Finally, it appears that Microsoft is starting to move away from Outlook as a rich offline client for SharePoint. The roadmap appears to be that Outlook will focus on being the client for Exchange Server while SharePoint Workspace is evolving into the client for SharePoint server. There will continue to be exceptions to this general rule considering that it does make a lot of sense to have your team calendars, tasks, and contacts from SharePoint integrated in Outlook. This is described further in the following section.

Windows Explorer

Use Windows Explorer to quickly move files between SharePoint and other file systems (such as a network fileshare or your local PC storage) if you are not concerned about applying new SharePoint metadata (inbound transfer) or preserving existing SharePoint metadata (outbound transfer). If you use Windows Explorer to perform an initial upload of files, you can use the SharePoint interface or edit in datasheet function to apply metadata. If, however, you use this function to reupload documents, you may overwrite your metadata. Furthermore, documents stored down to local and shared drives do retain their document property metadata but not SharePoint-specific metadata.

SharePoint Workspace and the Office Upload Center offer richer capabilities than Windows Explorer for working with SharePoint files offline. In addition, for Office-based documents, the new Backstage feature (described further later in this chapter) provides extensive capabilities for working with SharePoint while authoring the documents, which makes it easier for people to perform tasks such as tag documents with metadata, view other authors, and interact with workflows.

Other Considerations: Synchronization of Office Document Changes and Branch Cache

Office 2010 and SharePoint 2010 have made significant improvements under the covers in terms of how document changes are managed and synchronized between the server and your offline copy. For these scenarios, only the changes are synchronized between your PC and the server when updates are made. For example, take a scenario where you have a copy of a Word document on your PC that is 5MB and has been opened from SharePoint 2010. When someone adds a new table and saves the changes to SharePoint, the next time you open the file from the server, only what has changed will be sent to your PC. This is a major improvement, and it improves end-user performance and minimizes network traffic and impact.

Windows Server 2008 R2 and Windows 7 added a new capability known as Windows Branch Office Cache. If you have enabled this in your environment, SharePoint 2010 can take advantage of this. Branch Cache aids geographically distributed offices in how they access SharePoint documents over a Wide Area Network (WAN). With Branch Cache, the first time a person in a remote office accesses a file from the remote SharePoint server, a cached copy of that file gets stored on a server located in the remote (branch) office. Subsequent requests for that document within the office get fulfilled from the local branch copy of the file, saving what is often a slower call over the WAN. Branch Cache and SharePoint work together to manage changes and to make sure that security continues to be enforced so that only people authorized in SharePoint can access a certain version of the document.

Data

Like documents, Office 2010 offers you a number of choices on how to work with taking your data offline. These choices include

- SharePoint Workspace
- Outlook
- Access
- Excel

SharePoint Workspace

SPW is typically going to be your first choice for working with most SharePoint data. Why? It is the only Office client that allows you to bring most standard and custom lists offline while also allowing you to work with document libraries in the same workspace. SharePoint Workspace also integrates with InfoPath forms, so you can add more structure and data validation around the information that you are capturing. As described earlier, using the integrated Business Connectivity Services (BCS) you now have the ability to work offline with your linked data that ties SharePoint to back-end systems (such as CRM, ERP systems or custom databases based on SQL Server, Oracle, and so on) and be able to perform create, read, update, and delete operations on that data.

Outlook

As noted earlier, unfortunately there are a few areas that SharePoint Workspace does not yet integrate with SharePoint. The most obvious one is calendars. In this release, Outlook remains your only real option for easily taking a SharePoint calendar offline (see Figure 15-11). One benefit of doing this in Outlook is that you can then easily compare, overlay, and update both your personal and shared calendar in the same client tool.

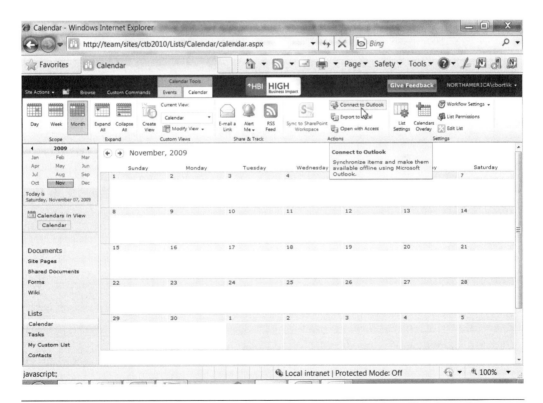

Figure 15-11 Outlook continues to be the best tool for taking a calendar offline from SharePoint and having read/write access. To take a calendar offline, select the Connect to Outlook option from the Calendar tab in the Calendar Tools section within the SharePoint ribbon.

Access and Excel

Both of these applications continue to offer the ability to work with SharePoint offline (see Figure 15-12). Typically, the cases where you want to consider either tool are for specific point solutions and scenarios. For example, maybe you want to quickly integrate and join SharePoint data with other data sources so you can run some complex queries and reports. In this case, Access is likely your best choice. What if you want to take your SharePoint list data into a rich client where you can do advanced graphing and charting, or add conditional formatting and maybe a pivot table to slice and dice all of that data? Excel is probably the tool you want to use here.

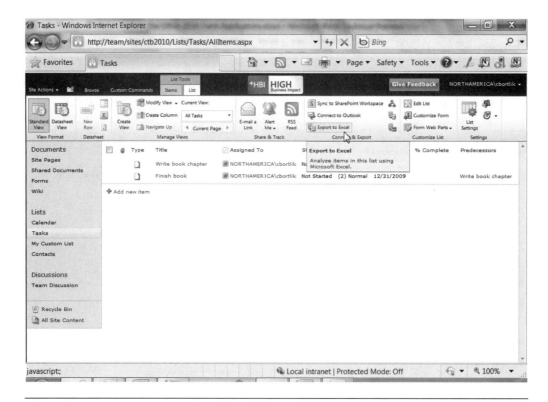

Figure 15-12 The ability to take list data offline in Excel, Access, and other Office clients can be located in the Connect and Export section of the List Tools command group within the SharePoint ribbon

Recommendations

Office and SharePoint 2010 offer a few different choices for working with documents and data. In summary:

- SharePoint Workspace should be used for sites that you use often, such as collaborative team sites or your My Site, or those sites that you need to have offline access to your SharePoint lists and documents.
- Use the Office Upload Center as a one-stop shop for information and usage for all of the SharePoint files that you have viewed and checked out—regardless of which site the files originated from. This is especially useful for those sites that you access infrequently.
- Outlook should only be used for working with SharePoint team data that intersects with your personal information management. Calendars are one example. Tasks, contacts, and discussion boards make sense in some scenarios. In general, using Outlook to synchronize document libraries is strongly discouraged.
- Windows Explorer should be used as a last resort if you find that working through SharePoint Workspace, the Office Upload Center, or via the browser is not appropriate for a specific document management scenario.
- Branch Cache in Windows Server 2008 R2 and Windows 7 is an option for helping to speed up SharePoint file access for remote branch offices.
- Excel and Access are great solutions for creating composite mash-up applications, rich data reporting, and integration with the server-side capabilities provided by Excel Services and Access Services.

Backstage

Users familiar with Office 2007 have by now grown accustomed to the "ribbon" fluent user interface that was introduced in Word, Excel, PowerPoint, Access, and parts of Outlook (those that used Word as the editor and viewer). The ribbon was designed to address usability issues that occurred over the past 25 years as more features were added to the menus in the Office suite. Past attempts at addressing these issues included toolbars, task panes, and the character that everyone loved to hate: Clippy.

The ribbon was Microsoft's attempt to press the reset button on the Office user interface and implement a design that addresses how we work and collaborate today. Office 2007 was designed to make features more accessible and discoverable. The ribbon was so successful that in 2010 it has been extended to other Office system applications including SharePoint, the rest of Outlook, SharePoint Workspace, OneNote, InfoPath, Visio, and Project.

The Office 2007 ribbon has addressed the usability issues for operations that you do within a document such as bold, tables, charts, and Smart Art. In Office 2010, Microsoft sought to address things that happen outside of the document and have been a challenge to work with. For example, it would be great if you could easily have context on the document:

- What document library is this document from?
- What is the workflow status?
- Who are my coauthors, and what is their status?
- What are my rights to perform updates and print this document?

To help answer these and many other common questions, enter the latest Office UI innovation: the Backstage.

The Backstage replaces the old file menu and the Office "pearl" that was introduced in 2007 as the icon in the top-left corner of each Office product. The Backstage is launched when you click the File menu tab in any Office 2010 client application (see Figure 15-13).

In the Backstage area, you find all of the features of things that you can do to the document as a whole. You can:

- Put the document under information rights management.
- Review the document for accessibility for those with disabilities.
- Start or see the workflow status of the document (see Figure 15-14).
- Publish the document to a SharePoint site.
- Check the version history of the document.

Like other parts of Office 2010, the Backstage is open and customizable. Using Visual Studio .NET, your company and partners can create extensible applications that plug information into the Backstage from other systems, databases, and processes.

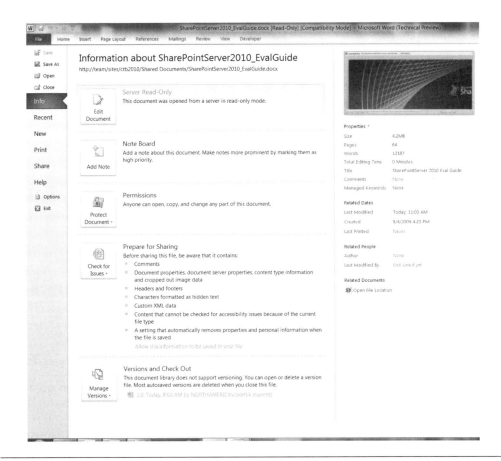

Figure 15-13 Using the Backstage view to review document information, properties, related authors, version history, metadata, and notes

Other Clients: Office Web Applications and Office Mobile Applications

One of the main themes across the Microsoft Office System in 2010 is the idea of choice and flexibility for how you work with SharePoint content. In 2010, new Web and mobile companion applications have been released for

- Word
- Excel

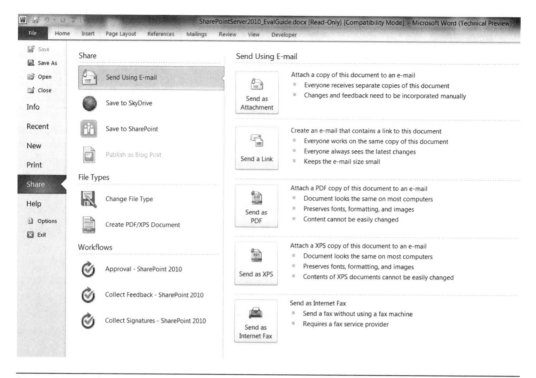

Figure 15-14 Sharing documents from the Backstage. From this section, you can access SharePoint sites to save to and activate related SharePoint workflows.

- PowerPoint
- OneNote

The vision for these four applications is just like how you can currently access your Exchange-based e-mail across three different devices: Outlook on the PC, Outlook Web Access in the browser, and Outlook mobile (or some other e-mail client) on your phone.

One of the fundamental design tenets for Office 2010 is that documents should seamlessly travel from the PC to the browser to the phone and round-trip without concern for loss of data or formatting. This is very important because you want to be confident that whatever changes you make to a document maintains the integrity of the document regardless of which application or device was used for the edits. By leveraging the Office Open XML document file formats, SharePoint is the foundation and glue behind the scenes that makes this all happen.

While going in-depth on each of these applications is outside of the scope for this book, you should be aware of them and factor them into your plans.

Office Web Applications

The Office Web Applications are not intended to replace the Office products that you use on your desktop today just like how Outlook Web Access is not a replacement for the rich functionality that Outlook provides. Rather, the Office Web Applications are intended to offer you the essential viewing and editing capabilities so you can work with documents stored in SharePoint wherever you are (see Figure 15-15)—for example, lightweight editing in Word, modifying slides in PowerPoint, and editing formulas and spreadsheet values in Excel. The Office Web Applications, like SharePoint 2010, leverage open standards and work across different

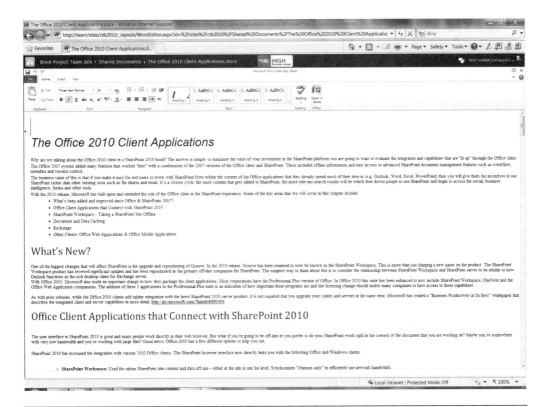

Figure 15-15 Editing a Word document in the Word Web application companion

browsers: Internet Explorer, Safari, and Firefox. In general, you will want to use these applications in cases such as when you're on someone else's PC, using a kiosk at a conference, or working in a hotel lobby and the Office client application is unavailable.

Office Mobile Applications

The new Office Mobile Applications for Word, Excel, PowerPoint, and OneNote enable you to read and edit documents on a Windows Mobile device. There is also a new SharePoint Mobile client that allows you to take SharePoint content on your phone and participate in some key tasks such as approving a document as part of a workflow.

What if you are not using a Windows Mobile device and are using something like a BlackBerry or iPhone? Good news. SharePoint and the Office Web Applications also have micro browser support for the most popular operating systems and browsers that run on other mobile device platforms.

Key Points

In this chapter, we covered the key concepts around working with SharePoint using the Office 2010 client applications and touched on the new Office Web and Mobile applications for working with SharePoint and Office when you don't have your PC.

- SharePoint Workspace (formerly Groove) is the best way for taking SharePoint documents and lists offline and synchronizing changes.
- The new Office Upload Center manages the SharePoint documents that you access via the Office clients. It caches a local copy of the documents, synchronizes changes only when you access the file again, and provides a central place to review all files pending check-in regardless of which site you accessed the files from.
- Outlook remains the tool to use for viewing and integrating your personal calendar with shared calendars on SharePoint.
- Access and Excel continue to provide rich advanced support for charting, graphing, filtering, and reporting on data. Improvements have been made around Excel Services integration, and a new

Access Services component has been added with SharePoint 2010 as an option for publishing Access data, forms, and reports for centralized browser-based access.

- The Backstage is new to the Office 2010 client applications and can be launched from the File button. This is where you can clearly view the context of your document as part of SharePoint libraries, workflows, and authoring permissions and to apply metadata and tagging.
- The new Office Web Applications for Word, Excel, PowerPoint, and OneNote are integrated with SharePoint and provide read and edit access to documents using the Internet Explorer, Firefox, or Safari Web browsers.
- Office Mobile Applications for SharePoint, Word, Excel, PowerPoint, and OneNote provide access to your content on-the-go while using Windows Mobile devices. Microbrowsers are also supported on many other non-Windows Mobile device platforms such as BlackBerry and iPhone.

CHAPTER 16

PLANNING FOR DISASTER RECOVERY: BACKING UP AND RESTORING

When you think of the information that you store in SharePoint, you need to ask yourself, "What would happen if SharePoint suddenly became unavailable?" In other words, does your SharePoint environment provide a mission-critical service to the business? In most cases, the answer is yes.

SharePoint can store a broad range of corporate information including unstructured content (like wikis, blog entries, and discussion threads), semi-structured content (like documents and images), and even structured content (list items with fixed columns). Information within SharePoint is delivered in one place, and by default, it is stored in one place. This "single storage" model (actually a collection of databases) makes business-side functionality like collaboration, communication, and data consistency easier to implement. The challenge, however, is that this puts pressure on IT staff to make SharePoint, now a business-critical application, highly available. Users will want reliable access to content, and they'll want comfort around plans to restore some portions of a site, a complete site, or a collection of sites.

The feature set contained within SharePoint Backup and Restore constitutes only one component of an overall disaster recovery plan. This chapter provides an overview of the native SharePoint Backup and Restore capabilities to recover or re-create entire Site Collections or individual sites. In addition, this chapter describes the components of your farm, Site Collection, or sites that are *not* covered with SharePoint's native backup and restore tools. The chapter's key sections include

- Disaster Recovery Planning
- Backup and Restore Options
- What's Not Covered in a SharePoint Backup

Disaster Recovery Planning

When creating a disaster recovery (DR) plan, you need to determine what you are trying to recover from. In other words, think of your disaster recovery plan like "taking out insurance" for your SharePoint environment. There are various levels of protection you may wish to set in place. You may be using a DR plan to create a replica copy of your environment to recover specific content (like the deletion of a site), or you may wish to create a plan to create a new environment from scratch (in the event of an actual disaster) that will quickly and effectively replicate the current environment.

For example, on one end of the spectrum, you could make things easy on your IT team and back up your data once every six months or so, but then you run the risk of losing a lot of data if something were to happen (a hard drive crashes, administrator or user error, and so on). On the other end of the spectrum, you can do a full backup of everything daily (or even more frequently—say hourly) to ensure that you always have the latest of everything—but does that make sense for your environment? You might ask, "Why would we *not* do that?" The challenge with effective disaster recovery planning is balancing the cost (actual dollars as well as resource time) against the protection required that makes the most sense (in the short and long term).

To properly capture these types of decisions, we recommend creating a disaster recovery operations document.

Creating a Disaster Recovery (DR) Operations Document

The following is a framework for a SharePoint disaster recovery operations document. It is important to note that a DR plan is only effective if it is both complete and accurate.

An effective SharePoint disaster recovery plan should contain full documentation on how to re-create an entire SharePoint environment *from scratch*. This requires a process (and discipline) that is accurate and well-maintained. Each and every time a SharePoint element (for example, a Web Part, xml file, configuration setting, and so on) is altered or added, the disaster recovery inventory document *must* be updated.

Here's an example of information that should be captured:

1. Overview
   a. Explanation of when to use this plan
   b. History of any updates
   c. Permissions required for executing the plan
2. SharePoint Backup/Restore
   a. Step-by-step execution plan for your environment
3. Adding Web Parts
   a. Location of all Web Part CAB or install files
   b. Instructions for installation
   c. Location of the latest Web.config file
4. Adding Additional Components (Features, Event Handlers, Workflows, and so on)
   a. Location of all files
   b. Instructions for file movement and/or installation
5. Testing
   a. Instructions on how to test new portal environment
      i. Smoke test (that is, a quick examination of the environment to inspect stability)
      ii. Validation of Web Part execution
      iii. Validation of security model
6. Miscellaneous
   a. Comments collected from previous restorations

When you've got a document underway, you'll want to start filling in your company-specific recovery steps, including your SharePoint backup and restore steps. To determine your specific steps, you'll need to decide on which SharePoint backup/restore option best suits your needs. Let's take a look at the various SharePoint options.

Backup and Restore Options

There are several backup and restore options in SharePoint Server 2010, including:

- SharePoint Central Administration backup and restore
- PowerShell cmdlets command-line backup and restore

- Two-stage Recycle Bin restore
- SQL Server database backup and restore

The first two options (SharePoint Central Administration and PowerShare cmdlets) provide out-of-the-box tools to back up a full farm.

The two-stage Recycle Bin is a tool used to recover individual files. It is not designed to support full-site or Site Collection recovery.

The SQL Server's backup and restore utilities are available only if you have a full version of SQL Server. SQL Express does not include a GUI for backup, but you can write a script to automate the backup.

Each of these options provides a different level of recoverability and usability—we discuss the options in the following sections, including when to use each.

Note   As powerful as the SharePoint Backup options appear, they do not contain all the elements necessary to re-create your SharePoint environment. Be sure to read the "What's Not Covered in a SharePoint Backup" section at the end of this chapter, which describes other important items that you will need to back up.

Central Administration Backup and Restore Tool

For those familiar with the backup/restore functionality in SharePoint Office Server 2007, one of the first things you will notice is that the Data Backup and Restore interface in SharePoint Server 2010 is much more robust in terms of the granularity of backup that can be enacted.

The Backup and Restore tools are still contained within SharePoint Central Administration. In the interface (see Figure 16-1), there is a link on the left for Backup and Restore.

The main features of the Backup and Restore tool within SharePoint Central Administration include

- **The ability to select specific farm components for backup**. This includes the selection of an entire farm or specific components within a farm such as the configuration database, Web application setup, content databases, service applications, and user profiles.

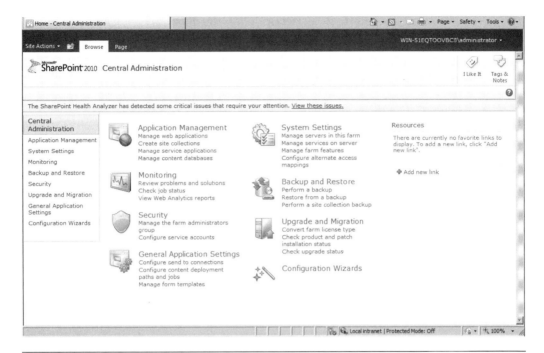

Figure 16-1 The Backup and Restore link, located on the left-side navigation within Central Administration, enables you to perform full and differential backups of your SharePoint farm

- **An improved interface for managing backups and restores**. The interface is well-organized with clear instructions on expected parameters and intended outcome.
- **The ability to do full or differential backups**. Full backup backs up the selected content with full history. A differential backup backs up all changes to the selected content since the last full backup.
- **The ability to restore a site or list**.
- **Backup process statistics**.

The Backup and Restore tool also provides information about overall disk space usage, status, and errors.

Using the Backup Utility

One of the great improvements of the SharePoint Backup utility is the increased flexibility offered in what can be backed up (from a farm down to a site). To complete a backup, click the Perform a backup link in the Backup and Restore screen within Central Administration. Figure 16-2 shows the interface for selecting the SharePoint components you wish to back up. Each component is associated with a SharePoint database (and ultimately, specific SharePoint content). *It is possible to select an entire farm for backup or individual components.*

Note To perform a backup, you must be an administrator on the farm. To run a restore, you must be a farm administrator and a server administrator on the front-end machines.

Another interesting feature of the SharePoint backup utility is the storage of backup history. SharePoint actually catalogs full and differential backups. This is done by examining the backup files on the file system (discussed later in this chapter) and identifying new content.

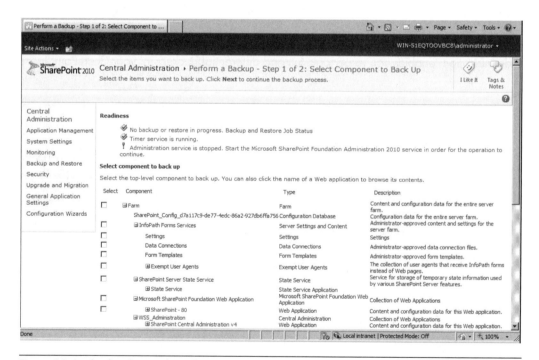

Figure 16-2 The backup utility allows you to be selective about which farm components to backup

- A **full backup** backs up the selected content with all the history. Specifically, a full backup backs up the entire database, including all file groups and data files, providing a high degree of data integrity. The downside is that full backups can take a long time for large data stores. We recommend keeping your content databases to a reasonable size (under 100GB) so that backups (and restores) can be completed in a reasonable amount of time.
- A **differential backup** backs up all changes to the selected content since the last backup (either full or differential). This option allows IT administrators to better manage disk space associated with SharePoint backup files. In addition, the backups are faster. The key issue with differential backups is that a restore requires the administrator to restore the last full backup in addition to the differential backups that have taken place.

Given the choice, which should you use? The idea is to use a combination of the two as follows: Start with a full backup of your data. Then perform a daily differential backup of all databases during offline hours. Next, perform a full backup of all databases on a weekly basis. Finally, perform a full restore (to an offline data source such as a mirror server or disk) of your backup set roughly once per month. This lets you to validate that your backup procedures are working correctly.

Figure 16-3 shows the Start Backup page for backing up a Site Collection. Enter a backup file path to set the location where SharePoint backup files will be stored. The Backup utility only accepts UNC file paths, and permissions on the folder must be sufficient to allow SharePoint Backup (running under the credentials of the logged in user) to write files to that folder, and there must be sufficient space to hold the resulting backup file.

Once the backup is completed, the Backup tool provides diagnostic details on the backup files created and any errors that may have occurred. As expected, the elapsed time associated with the backup process is proportional to the amount of data being backed up. A standard backup can take a few minutes (when content is light) to several minutes (when the amount of content stored is large) to create all associated files. Figure 16-4 shows a completed backup process. Diagnostic data includes status, elapsed time, file directory path, and associated error messages.

Examining the Backup Files

After the SharePoint backup completes, the corresponding backup files are placed on the file system in the designated path. For those familiar

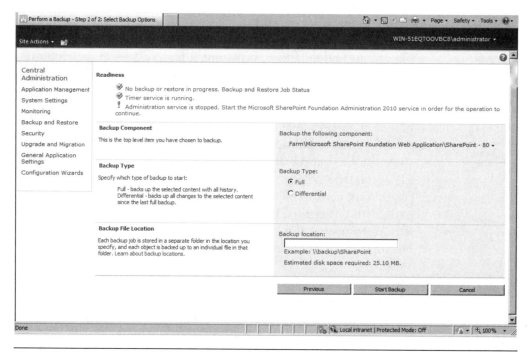

Figure 16-3 To start a backup, enter a UNC path to a location where the backup utility should write the files

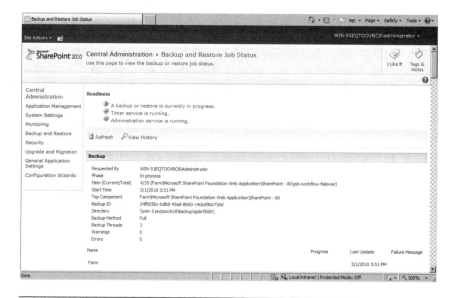

Figure 16-4 The status of a running backup or restore (or the result of the backup or restore) is reported in real-time

with SharePoint Backup and Restore, you'll notice that the collection of files is very similar to MOSS 2007. Figure 16-5 shows an example of the files associated with a farm backup.

Let's take a closer look at how SharePoint is managing the backup data. First, Figure 16-6 shows the contents of the spbrtoc.xml file. You'll notice that the information maps very closely to the diagnostics shown at the conclusion of the backup process.

Let's examine the actual contents of the backup folder. Figure 16-7 shows the files associated with a full farm backup. The backup files (file extension .bak) are segmented across a collection of files. A log file, spbackup.log, gives details on the executed backup process. All of this is managed by another .xml file, spbackup.xml.

The spbackup.xml file contains all the parameters and attributes needed to perform SharePoint backup and restore actions. Figure 16-8 shows a sample .xml file. The top section SPGlobalInformation contains data on the executed backup. It maps very closely to the data stored in

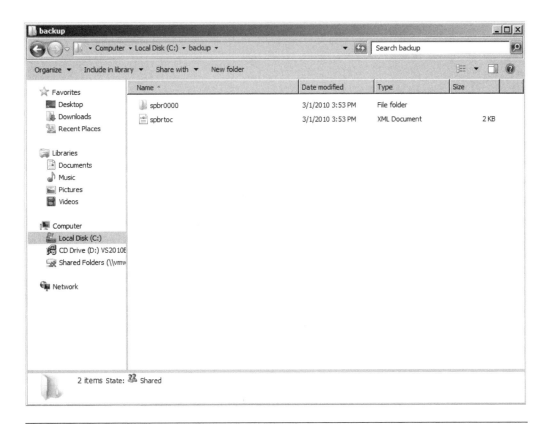

Figure 16-5 The SharePoint backups are placed in the appropriate location on the file system

```xml
<?xml version="1.0" encoding="utf-8"?>
<SPBackupRestoreHistory>
    <SPHistoryObject>
        <SPId>24f005bc-bdb8-45a8-8660-14cbd9b073dd</SPId>
        <SPRequestedBy>WIN-51EQTOOVBC8\Administrator
</SPRequestedBy>
        <SPBackupMethod>Full</SPBackupMethod>
        <SPRestoreMethod>None</SPRestoreMethod>
        <SPStartTime>03/01/2010 20:51:37</SPStartTime>
        <SPFinishTime>03/01/2010 20:53:49</SPFinishTime>
        <SPIsBackup>True</SPIsBackup>
        <SPConfigurationOnly>False</SPConfigurationOnly>
        <SPBackupDirectory>\\win-51eqtoovbc8\backup\spbr0000
\</SPBackupDirectory>
        <SPDirectoryName>spbr0000</SPDirectoryName>
        <SPDirectoryNumber>0</SPDirectoryNumber>
        <SPTopComponent>Farm\Microsoft SharePoint Foundation Web
Application\SharePoint - 80</SPTopComponent>
        <SPTopComponentId>7ebd371d-528d-432a-b6b5-4ec017129a03
</SPTopComponentId>
        <SPWarningCount>0</SPWarningCount>
        <SPErrorCount>0</SPErrorCount>
    </SPHistoryObject>
</SPBackupRestoreHistory>
```

Figure 16-6 The spbrtoc.xml file contains information about each backup that has taken place

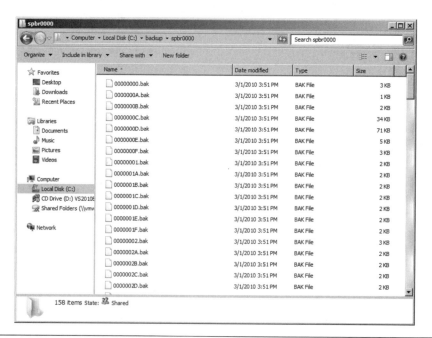

Figure 16-7 SharePoint spreads its backup information across a collection of .bak, .xml, and .log files

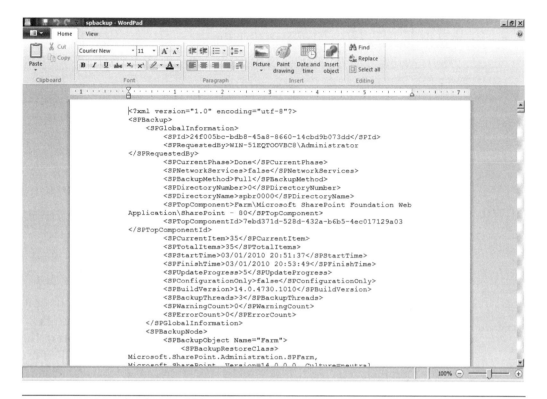

Figure 16-8 The spbackup.xml file contains the parameters and attributes needed to perform a restore

the top-level .xml file. The subsequent nodes under SPBackupNode map to specific components selected using the Backup interface. This file provides a roadmap for the potential restore of SharePoint data. Notice that unlike the manifest file used in the previous version of SharePoint Portal Server, this .xml file contains no specific references to portal URLs or database servers. This makes it easier to use these files, unaltered, to restore SharePoint on different servers.

Note Do not modify the spbackup.xml file. Doing so can corrupt your backup and/or your restored farm in an unrecoverable manner.

Using the Restore Utility

Before delving into the restoration process, it is important to note that there is one underlying requirement when performing SharePoint restores: The authentication source (Active Directory or another LDAP source, for example) must be the same. This is less critical for restorations on an existing SharePoint environment but may impact the re-creation on new servers.

Note   SharePoint maintains its security model (users, roles, access) in its databases. Therefore, this security model is maintained in the restoration. If, however, you restore the portal to a machine that does not have access to the same authentication engine (a specific Active Directory domain, for example) the security rules previously defined will no longer be valid. This scenario is most commonly seen in the restoration of a SharePoint environment onto a development server. It is important to ensure that the restoration environment has access to the same authentication engine as the backup environment.

As previously mentioned, SharePoint maintains version history associated with backup activity. This offers two immediate benefits: 1) more flexibility for the IT staff in terms of controlling what components of SharePoint to restore and 2) better management of disk storage space in terms of the amount of space used. Figure 16-9 shows a sample Backup and Restore History screen.

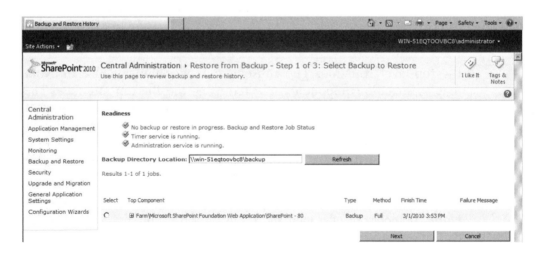

Figure 16-9 Central Administration provides a Backup and Restore History screen, which shows the contents of the history logs

---

Note The information contained in the .xml files previously discussed is shown on the interface to clearly identify the type of backups registered and the associated attributes. SharePoint will manage a complete collection of historical files associated with backups. This feature allows for the on-demand restoration of potentially corrupt or disabled components (a requirement for any plan for high availability).

As mentioned previously, to successfully execute a SharePoint restore, the user must have administrator privileges within SharePoint and have access to the files on the file system.

The restoration process is very straightforward. There are three steps associated with the SharePoint restore: the first, shown in Figure 16-10, is to select the location of the SharePoint backup files; the second, shown in Figure 16-11, is to select a specific SharePoint backup from the collection in history; finally; the third step is shown in Figure 16-12. Once a backup collection is selected, the restoration starts the moment you click Start Restore Process. The duration of the restoration is directly related to the elapsed time during the backup process. Expect a typical full-farm restore to take about the same amount of time it took to create the backup. Once complete, the restoration will have updated the appropriate SharePoint components with the specific content selected.

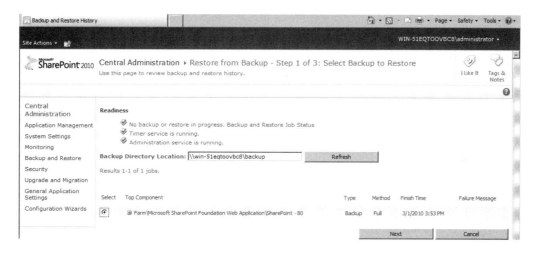

Figure 16-10 Restore Step 1

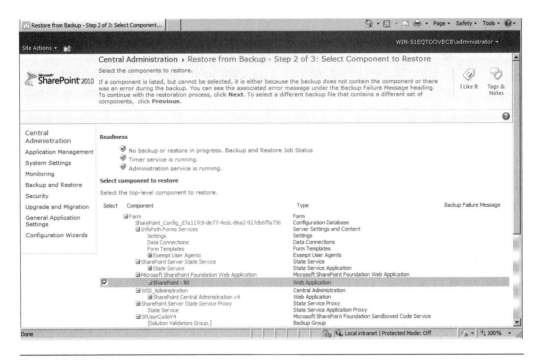

Figure 16-11 Restore Step 2

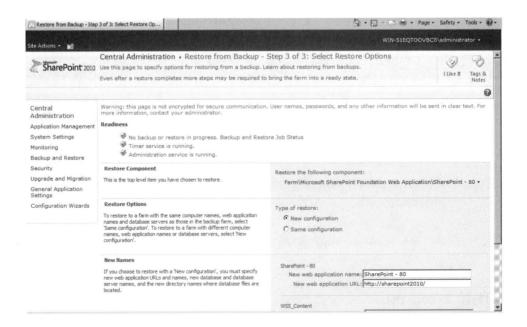

Figure 16-12 Restore Step 3

Note What's the difference between New and Overwrite on the restore page? Use New when migrating to a different farm or restoring such that you want to refer to a new machine or new database. Use Overwrite when you are restoring on the machines and databases that the original farm backup refers to. Use Overwrite for the catastrophic restore scenario; it does not give you the option to use a different machine or database name.

Note If a backup or restore fails, you can get details on why the operation failed in spbackup.log (for a backup) or sprestore.log (for a restore) in the backup location. If you have errors during the backup/restore process, you have to delete the failed Backup/Restore Timer Job before you can run the next backup/restore process.

Command-line Backup Tools

The stsadm.exe utility was used to perform command line operations with SharePoint 2007. It enabled SharePoint administrators to back up site collections using the command line. This made it easy to restore a Site Collection (or a single site) if necessary.

SharePoint 2010 introduces the use of Windows PowerShell cmdlets, which offer command-line execution of many SharePoint functions, including backup and restore. PowerShell offers over 300 new cmdlets that allow a more granular set of functions for execution than stsadm. Specifically, it allows administrators more flexibility on what gets backed up or restored. To see a list of available options for backup, type

```
backup-spfarm -?
```

Using the PowerShell cmdlets is very useful for regular backups because you can use the Windows Task Scheduler to create a recurring backup job. This can be done by creating a PowerShell script then using the Windows Task Scheduler to execute this script every day (off-hours).

The backup cmdlet also lets you do a full SharePoint backup as you would with the Central Administration page. The syntax looks like this:

```
Backup-spfarm -directory \\myserver\backuplocation -backupmethod
full
```

This command performs a full backup on a SharePoint farm and writes to the Backup and Restore History on the Central Administration page. You can then use either the Central Administration interface to restore from this backup or another command-line command. Backup and restore actions done via the Central Administration Web interface or the command line are indistinguishable.

Scheduling a SharePoint Backup

Like MOSS 2007, one of the things you'll notice on the Backup and Restore pages is that there is no tool for scheduling backups. This presents a problem for IT staff interested in ensuring that SharePoint backups are regularly obtained. As in the previous version, the best alternative is to use a simple batch file that executes the SharePoint backup from the command line. This batch file can then be scheduled using the native Windows Task Scheduler. We discuss the command-line backup options in the following section.

Two-level Recycle Bin

The SharePoint Recycle Bin is a convenience for users who accidentally delete a file or other item. Needing to recover a single item is a much more common situation than having to recover from a full-fledged disaster. The Recycle Bin provides an "undelete" feature to allow end users to recover accidentally deleted files, documents, list items, lists, and document libraries without running a content database-level backup and restore. This saves the SharePoint administrator(s) time and hassle because they can easily recover files for end users without having to initiate a full-fledged backup and restore process. In fact, in most cases, users will simply recover things themselves.

Note   The Recycle Bin captures deleted events. If items go missing due to errors, data corruption, or other problems, they will not be recoverable via the Recycle Bin. This is why a full backup process must also be in place.

When a user deletes an item, it moves to the first-stage Recycle Bin. Users with contributor rights can recover their items from the first-stage Recycle Bin. When the item is deleted from the first-stage Recycle Bin, the deleted item moves to a second-stage Recycle Bin. SharePoint

Administrators can recover items from the second-stage Recycle Bin if the items have not been purged.

Configuring the Recycle Bin

The SharePoint Recycle Bin is a Web application setting, which means that it can only be enabled or disabled for all of the Site Collections served by the Web application. If you turn it on, it's available on *all sites in all Site Collections* for that Web application.

The global settings for the Recycle Bin are part of the Web application General Settings. These settings are accessed through the Central Administration by using the ribbon to access general settings for a specific Web application (see Figure 16-13). The Recycle Bin settings are at the bottom of the General Settings page (see Figure 16-14).

We recommend that you configure the Recycle Bin to a size that is a percentage of the overall site quota and set an "auto-clean" schedule (the default is 30 days) for permanent file removal that fits your business needs. Again, these settings will apply to all Site Collections within the Web application.

Restoring Items from the Recycle Bin

The first level of the Recycle Bin is the user-level Recycle Bin (see Figure 16-15). It is accessible by any user with contribution rights associated with the deleted item and provides a site-level view of deleted content; it contains all items deleted from a particular site.

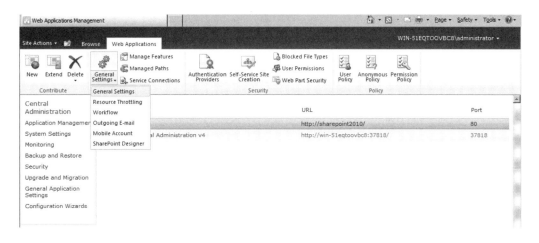

Figure 16-13 Accessing General Settings page through Central Administration

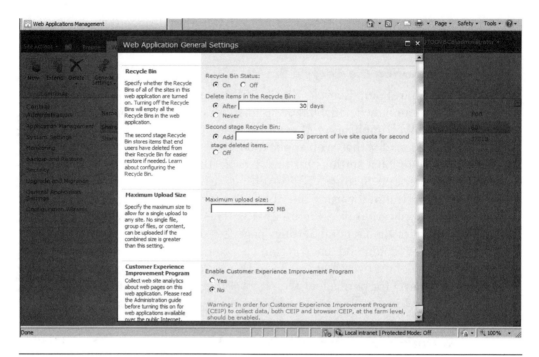

Figure 16-14 Managing the Recycle Bin settings through Central Administration

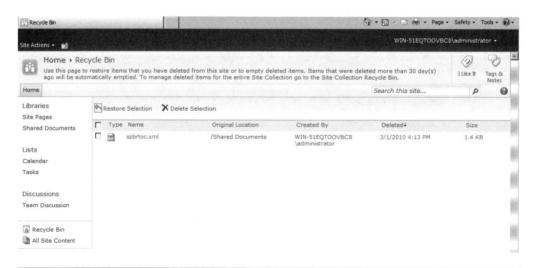

Figure 16-15 End-user settings for the Recycle Bin

Note The first-level Recycle Bin counts toward the site's maximum quota.

The second level of the Recycle Bin is the administrative Recycle Bin (see Figure 16-16). It is accessible by Site Collection administrators, provides a Site Collection-level view of deleted content, and contains all items deleted from a particular Site Collection.

In effect, SharePoint administrators no longer need to maintain replica environments for item-level restores. In addition, inadvertent site deletions can be managed through the use of custom event handlers that automatically back up a site prior to deletion. Both offer significant support time reductions.

SQL Server Backup

Microsoft SQL Server Backup and Restore is typically used by large organizations given that they already have SQL Server Tools or offsite data centers. It's also because the person/group responsible for the databases is a DBA, rather than the SharePoint Server administrator. If you are in a large organization where this situation is likely, then we recommend this option. We'll leave the steps to back up SQL Server to the DBA.

SQL Enterprise Manager has the capability to schedule backup tasks, which enables the DBA to automate the backup process. We recommend that the DBA(s) responsible for the SharePoint databases get proper training on the structure of the SharePoint databases.

It is important to note, however, that only the configuration and content databases get backed up. The "What's Not Covered in a SharePoint

Figure 16-16 Administrator settings for the Recycle Bin

Backup" section that follows describes other important items that you will need to also back up.

What's Not Covered in a SharePoint Backup

As powerful as the SharePoint Backup tool appears, it does not contain all the elements necessary to re-create your SharePoint environment. While SharePoint stores all of its content in SQL Server (documents, images, text, security, site metadata, and so on), there are a collection of files on the file system that are not in the database. These files do not get properly captured in a backup.

The following items play a pivotal role in the generation of SharePoint pages but are not covered in the SharePoint backup:

- Third-party or custom Web Parts
- SharePoint site definitions and XML files
- SharePoint .aspx template pages
- SharePoint script files

The first step in a successful recovery process is the restoration of the environment using the Backup and Restore tool. The subsequent steps involve restoring any elements that were not captured in the SharePoint backup. In many environments, the biggest concern is making sure non-native SharePoint Web Parts are part of the backup and restore plan. Whether purchased from a vendor, acquired online, or custom built, Web Parts must be registered in a specific way for SharePoint to consider them "safe." While this is not a chapter on deploying SharePoint Web Parts, let's touch quickly on the two main requirements for a successful Web Part deployment.

First, the associated .dlls need to be placed on the file system, either in the underlying BIN directory of the Virtual Server or in the Global Assembly Cache (GAC). Second, the Web Part must be placed in the list of Safe Controls. This is done in the SharePoint Web.config file. If you examine this file, you'll notice a collection of Web Part registrations under the SafeControls node. All Web Parts, even native SharePoint Web Parts, must be registered here. The challenge from a DR perspective is that this file, Web.config, and the associated Web Part .dlls are not captured in a SharePoint backup.

If these requirements are not executed in a restoration process, the SharePoint pages that contain the respective Web Parts will not properly generate (they may not generate at all, redirecting you to a generic error page). Therefore, it is important to inventory all non-native Web Parts used and to store the associated CAB or install files for future restoration. You may even do this in a SharePoint document library to ensure that they do get captured in the SharePoint backup process.

In addition to Web Parts, there are other system files that may be altered through standard or advanced SharePoint customization. These files include underlying .xml, .aspx, and script files. All SharePoint file system files reside in the following directory (called the SharePoint root):

```
C:\program files\common files\microsoft shared\Web server
extensions\14
```

It is important to note any changes made to files in this directory and take appropriate measures to document the alterations in your DR plan. Here's an example of a section that you should include in your disaster recovery plan so that you may track these changes:

Date	Description	Location	Made By	Approved By
4/20	Updated ows.js to accommodate customization	\14\TEMPLATE\ LAYOUTS\portal.js	mcardarelli	sjamison
5/18	Added logo.jpg file	\14\TEMPLATE\ IMAGES\logo.jpg	mcardarelli	sjamison

Outside the bounds of the SharePoint-related files necessary for full portal restoration, but equally important, is the need to have a plan to ensure that any replica environment stays consistent with the software, patches, and third-party Web Parts deployed in the original environment. A disaster recovery plan should always denote the current state of the SharePoint servers and should be updated as changes are made. This includes logging software version numbers (which change with the application of service packs and hot fixes).

As has always been the case with SharePoint, you can only restore a backup that was made with the same version of the software (version number matching exactly!) as is currently in place.

Key Points

Remember:

- SharePoint Disaster Recovery requires a well-maintained, documented plan.
- IT Administrators now have greater control over what components within SharePoint can be restored.
- SharePoint 2010 introduces PowerShell cmdlets that offer more granular backup/restore options than stsadm did.
- As your SharePoint environment matures, it will be increasingly more complicated to restore SharePoint and all its connected elements.

PART III

MIGRATING

CHAPTER 17

PLANNING YOUR MOVE FROM SHAREPOINT 2007 TO 2010

This chapter contains the following key sections:

- You're Ready to Deploy SharePoint 2010: Now What?
- Planning Your Upgrade
- Upgrade and Migration Options
- What Plan Is Best for You?
- Upgrade Considerations

You're Ready to Deploy SharePoint 2010: Now What?

The last version of SharePoint, SharePoint 2007, introduced so many compelling features that many organizations took full advantage of enabling business users to take more ownership and be more collaborative. Perhaps your SharePoint growth was incremental and highly regimented. Or maybe it grew virally across many instances within your organization. Your challenge in planning your move to SharePoint 2010 is to decide what to do with the content (and organization of that content) that is currently in SharePoint 2007. In this chapter, we help you decide how best to prepare for the move of your current SharePoint environment(s) to SharePoint 2010. Then we cover three options for upgrading to SharePoint Server 2010: an In-place Upgrade, a Content Database Move (sometimes called a Database Attach), and a complete rebuild with content migration.

With SharePoint 2007, Microsoft introduced the third version of their SharePoint Server product. Since that time, SharePoint has been widely accepted and deployed across many organizations of all sizes and vertical markets. The success of SharePoint has primarily been centered on the ease of use and administration around building collaboration and communication forums for employees, partners, and clients. With SharePoint 2010, Microsoft looks to extend the success of its SharePoint technologies by introducing new features like enhanced social computing. Additionally, improved search and advanced content management tools make the argument for upgrading to the newest version very compelling. What do you do if you already have an intranet or extranet or virtual team space using SharePoint Portal Server 2007 or Windows SharePoint Services 3.0 and you want to move to SharePoint 2010? Should you upgrade some of your existing environments or all of them? Or should you build an entirely new infrastructure and move your data, which could enable you to take better advantage of some of the new functionality offered—and perhaps reorganize and consolidate some of your content? In this chapter, we take a look at these questions and help you plan your upgrade.

Before we begin, however, it is important to emphasize that this chapter is exclusively focused on migrating from SharePoint 2007. For those users who are still using SharePoint 2003 and considering a jump right into SharePoint 2010, there are two options: 1) upgrade to SharePoint 2007, as an interim step, and follow the guidelines offered in this chapter or 2) use third-party tools (AvePoint, Metalogix, or Quest, for example) to migrate your SharePoint 2003 content directly into a new SharePoint 2010 environment. In either case, the appropriate planning is critical to a seamless and smooth transition.

Planning Your Upgrade

With the release of Microsoft SharePoint Server 2010 and SharePoint Foundation, Microsoft has provided tools to execute an in-place upgrade of current SharePoint 2007 environments. These tools are designed to take existing SharePoint environments and upgrade the database schema, the presentation tier, and the middle tier application layer to either SharePoint Foundation 2010 or SharePoint Server 2010. In the end, current SharePoint applications will be fully functional, all existing capabilities will be enabled, and all existing custom and third-party Web Parts will continue to execute. Sounds simple, right? Well, it's not.

The reality is that upgrading to the new version, if done right, will be very hard. This statement is not meant to scare or deter, but rather inspire and motivate. Really. The most critical task in this upgrade is *planning*. One possible scenario is to upgrade the software and leave the content and associated taxonomy alone; another choice might be that you choose not to upgrade but rather build from scratch. Technology can update the available functionality and introduce new database tables, but it cannot fix poorly designed taxonomies or appease overwhelmed system users. SharePoint 2010 planning involves investigation of new technology features, validation of the usefulness of those features in your environment, and integration of those features into your existing SharePoint framework. It will take time to do these steps properly, but it will pay off in the long run.

Upgrades are also a good time for some level of introspection and analysis. How has your current environment evolved since initial deployment, and where are things going strategically? There are lots of things to think about. Take a look at your organization's use of SharePoint and consider the following questions. For those questions that you answer with a yes, think about how functionality, processes, and support will change in SharePoint 2010. For those questions answered with a no, will you introduce this functionality with SharePoint 2010 or continue to avoid it? Your answers will influence the means of your upgrade. And as we show you later, your answers also impact the timing of your upgrade.

- Do you have business processes that are driven by (or enabled within) SharePoint?
- Are you currently taking advantage of SharePoint-based or custom workflow?
- Do you have a culture of e-mailing documents as a means of workflow, review, and collaboration?
- Do users require offline access?
- Are your content contributors responsible for tagging your documents? Are they diligent in this effort?
- Are your portal, search, and collaboration taxonomies in good shape? Do your users agree?
- Do you have a well-defined list that is driving your decision to upgrade to SharePoint 2010?
- Are users ready for the move to Office 2010 and the new features of SharePoint 2010? Will you need to train them?
- Did you heavily customize your SharePoint 2007 environment? Are you invested in third-party or custom solutions?
- Does your current infrastructure comply with the SharePoint 2010 technical requirements (this includes 64-bit technology, increased RAM requirements, operating systems, and so on)?

- After your upgrade, will you present the new interface with the SharePoint 2010 ribbon, or will you wait to alter your user interface in a subsequent phase?
- Are you using Internet Explorer 7 or later?

As this list shows, there is a lot to think about when moving a well-established environment to the next version of the associated technology. Many of these are connected directly with business users and processes. Let's look at some of these in more detail in the next sections.

Governance

As mentioned, one of the biggest challenges with this (or any) upgrade is executing on a well thought-out plan. You'll need a plan not just for the technical component of applying new software, but more importantly, the details on what you will (or won't) do with the software product after it is enabled. That's where governance comes in. As mentioned in Chapter 4, "Planning for Governance," governance implies having a documented strategy for managing content (among other things). If you have a governance strategy in place for a current MOSS 2007 environment, modifying or adapting it to SharePoint 2010 is evolutionary. If you don't have a governance policy today, consider developing one prior to the upgrade. This will establish clear rules on the use of native or customized SharePoint functionality. With this control in place, you can feel more comfortable in having some of the social computing components in SharePoint 2010 more widely used in a consistent manner. A governance plan is not a requirement for the upgrade but is critical to the ultimate success associated with post-upgrade usage.

SharePoint–Driven Business Processes

SharePoint Foundation 2010 and SharePoint Server 2010 are great tools that you can use to build more efficient business processes. With WSS 3.0 and MOSS 2007, many of these business processes (organizational workflow, e-mail-driven discussion threads, and lightweight project management, for example) were available but used sparingly.

SharePoint 2010 not only builds on previous business process capabilities, it integrates business processes deeper into the SharePoint environment by supporting additional features through the use of enhanced forms, workflow, Excel, Visio, and Access-based business applications and by incorporating line-of-business data into your portal with greater simplicity, resulting in an enhanced user experience. In addition, by introducing stronger social computing capabilities (tagging, for instance), SharePoint users can be consumers, producers, *and* influencers of content.

When planning for SharePoint 2010, it is important to identify and resolve barriers to business process adoption. Consider the following questions and associated recommendations:

- **Is your organization ready to embrace potential changes to your business processes?** User adoption and education are critical to introducing and leveraging change. Make sure everyone understands when the upgrade is happening and why.
- **Does your current portal content organization support an upgrade to this new technology, or does it limit it?** If users currently complain about the "findability" of content or the overall organization of intranet sites, an upgrade is a good time to make the necessary changes to increase ease of use.
- **Are there technology limitations that would prevent adoption?** Are you still using Office 2003? If yes, you should consider moving to Office 2010 (or at least Office 2007) before upgrading to SharePoint 2010.
- **Is there sufficient end-user training available?** Especially in an organization new to the ribbon user interface, end-user training (for content owners and administrators) is critical in advance of an interface change.
- **Are the end user and administrator comfortable with the change?** Communicate the changes and associated features of SharePoint 2010 well in advance of an upgrade so end users can process and embrace these changes.
- **Is there adequate IT support?** Ensure IT staff is properly trained and prepared for supporting the new features in SharePoint 2010; this includes direct (SharePoint administrators) and indirect (infrastructure personnel) resources.

Electronic Forms and Document Workflow

Does your organization still use paper-based forms? If so, are you looking to move to an electronic forms-based tool like InfoPath? Or can you take advantage of new flexibility with designing and customizing SharePoint list forms? Have you invested in data collection capabilities in SharePoint 2007, and how can these be enhanced?

How is workflow managed in your current SharePoint environment? Are rules in place to control the movement of data before it gets to SharePoint? One of the challenges of enabling the workflow capabilities in SharePoint 2007 (and this is still true with SharePoint 2010) was to have the discipline to enforce the rules around how the stages of the workflow are executed. Because the workflow is system-based, it needs to be well-defined. Typically, organizations use e-mail as the primary vehicle for workflow-based approval and validation. A number of e-mails are exchanged, decisions are made, and the workflow plan is ultimately executed, but the record of the decision is not typically stored with the document.

Planning for enabling electronic forms and/or automated workflow involves investigating the current forms and workflow processes within your organization and then defining how SharePoint will manage them. Define your users and document the decision points and time constraints of the various stages. This will help validate the usefulness of SharePoint's forms and workflow tools and help define if and where it should be implemented.

Another thing to consider is that SharePoint 2010 takes electronic forms capabilities to the next level by enhancing the native workflow capabilities by integrating Visio services to allow a visual element to workflow design. Also, you can now use SharePoint Designer to edit and customize native SharePoint list forms. Why does this matter? If you've invested in workflow with SharePoint 2007, whether through custom application development and/or third-party product, you should investigate how these processes might be simplified or enhanced by using new native functionality.

It is also important to note that new features like Web-based forms and document workflow should be part of a broader functional upgrade and should only be used to meet specific business requirements. There is a danger in using new features of SharePoint 2010 for the sole purpose of building a stronger perception associated with Return on Investment (ROI) without clear ties to the business needs. If that happens, users are more discouraged than excited.

Your upgrade can be impacted based on your ability and willingness to alter existing data collection and workflow processes in SharePoint 2007. This may include simple edits to data entry forms or more advanced initiatives like migrating away from a third-party workflow or business process tool.

Preparing for Social Computing

Even with the introduction of various new technologies, the most likely place that organizational information exists, aside from inside people's heads, is in their e-mail mailboxes. And we're not talking about letters to grandma—we're talking about important corporate knowledge like domain expertise, business intelligence, and key decisions that have been made. Most of this is information that can't be accessed by other users and may walk out the door when an employee leaves, leaving the company without some important organizational knowledge.

How much corporate knowledge is lost in your organizational e-mail mailboxes? Does your company have a formal process in place to capture, catalog, and store information gathered through e-mail communications with peers, clients, and partners? One of the challenges in solving this problem with SharePoint 2007 was that while it was very good at storing structured content (such as documents), it was not heavily used for unstructured content (like discussions and tips and tricks). Nor did SharePoint 2007 encourage social contribution through ratings, comments, or tagging.

That said, SharePoint 2007 did offer a number of new alternatives to help in the storage and retrieval of unstructured knowledge. As an example, discussion threads were e-mail-enabled. That meant users no longer had to cut and paste to post questions or answers within a community of expertise. SharePoint 2007 site templates like blogs and wikis allow users and teams to publish information not captured in formal documents. The challenge, however, was that these types of social tools were used sparsely, mainly because organizations were concerned with giving "too much freedom" to users. This has changed as the world itself has changed. Now, with Internet applications like LinkedIn, Facebook, and Twitter, organizations see the value in capturing real-time, unstructured information.

Is your organization ready to embrace changes in the way people communicate using things like wikis and blogs? Are you willing to give employees the freedom to publish content in small, unformatted bits (think of Twitter)? Does your current SharePoint taxonomy support the inclusion of this new type of information? The promise of capturing "lost" corporate knowledge, buried in various employee e-mails, is very exciting. It does, however, come with some cost and cultural change. This is an important point. Often times (and especially true with SharePoint 2010), functional upgrades require one part technology and two part business process. Users must clearly understand the benefits of altered approaches to their activities. This is a requirement for general user adoption.

Will you look to take advantage of social computing capabilities in SharePoint 2010? If yes, do you have a formal plan for managing and monitoring these features? More importantly, does the content organization and/or security model you are using in SharePoint 2007 prevent or limit any part of your vision?

There are a couple of challenges here for existing SharePoint 2007 organizations. First, if you have "dabbled" in social computing capabilities (with native functionality or third-party add-ons), then you need to consider whether these will be left alone or redone with native SharePoint 2010. The impact on your upgrade is that these steps will happen after the physical upgrade and may or may not be addressed before the new launch. Second, if you have not formalized a social computing strategy but would like to with SharePoint 2010, then you will want to begin the education and design pieces before the upgrade so users are well-prepared when this functionality is made available to them.

Working with SharePoint Content Offline

How often are your SharePoint users, publishers, or readers disconnected from your corporate environment? Are your remote users forced to check out or download a collection of documents before getting on a plane? Are you concerned that document versions fall out of sync because of your remote users? SharePoint 2010, with the integration of SharePoint Workspace 2010, offers a vastly improved story around offline access to document library content. Users can easily retrieve, alter, and synchronize much of the data in SharePoint easily and automatically.

While this may sound like a wonderful thing, there are configuration issues. There are also levels of functionality that go from simple (copy files for offline access) to advanced (using SharePoint Workspace and letting users collaborate with peers or external parties). Are you currently using an offline solution? Would you like to introduce this capability with your upgrade? How many users will be impacted, and how will your organization be rewarded with the use of offline capabilities?

One goal of offline-enabled tools is to provide users with a strong sense that they are part of the larger organizational community. One way to achieve this is to provide things like Web-based meetings, Web cams, and instant messaging. In SharePoint terms, enabling users to always access the current version of a given document helps maintain synchronization across the user community because people will always be on the same page. For more information on working offline, see Chapter 15, "Office 2010 Client Applications."

Getting Your Timing Right: When Should You Upgrade?

SharePoint 2007 offered a great way to easily store information. That information, mostly in document form, was probably a mixture of content that was highly vetted and placed in SharePoint for storage and content that was iteratively managed through various major and minor versions.

With this, SharePoint 2007 introduced two important themes:

1. As described in a previous section, SharePoint 2007 made it easier to store unstructured content through things like wikis, blogs, and discussion threads. This, by default, is typically done in real time as the information is conceived.
2. SharePoint 2007 provided the ability to empower business users to contribute content, manage security, tag content, and enable workflows, thus decentralizing the burden of delivering quality content.

Have you taken advantage of these features in your current deployment? If you have and are looking to get to the next level, then an upgrade in the short term makes sense. If you have not but would like to, then include them in your post-upgrade strategy—but spend some time planning this before you push through an upgrade process. If you have not and are not likely to for some time, then you might want to consider deferring your upgrade until you have greater momentum within the current deployment.

Remember the list of questions associated with your current SharePoint 2007 environment asked at the beginning of this chapter. Let's take a look at how the answers might impact your readiness for an upgrade to SharePoint 2010. Table 17-1 highlights the questions and recommended action and timing.

Table 17-1 Recommendations on Timing Your Upgrade Based on Attributes of Your Current Environment

	Answered Yes	Answered No
Do you have business processes that are driven by (or enabled within) SharePoint?	Analysis recommended. Understand how these might change in SharePoint 2010.	Analysis suggested. Identify two or three ways you might introduce this in SharePoint 2010.
Are you currently taking advantage of SharePoint-based or custom workflow?	Analysis recommended. Understand how you might eliminate or consolidate your workflow solutions.	Analysis suggested. Identify two or three ways you might introduce this in SharePoint 2010.
Do you have a culture of e-mailing documents as a means of workflow, review, and collaboration?	Analysis suggested. Identify ways to streamline document creation and revision directly in SharePoint.	Analysis recommended. Talk to business users about how new features might enhance current processes.
Do users require offline access?	Analysis recommended. Investigate SharePoint Workspace and how it might be leveraged for offline access.	Analysis suggested. Determine if offline access may be needed in future phases.
Are your content contributors responsible for tagging your documents? Are they diligent in this effort?	Analysis recommended. Investigate how current tagging processes can be or will be affected by the new SharePoint term store.	Analysis suggested. Identify ways to better leverage metadata by having a central term store for key business terms.
Are your portal, search, and collaboration taxonomies in good shape? Do your users agree?	Analysis suggested. Ensure that you have planned for proper search configuration post-upgrade (don't assume that it will just work).	Analysis recommended. Take a step back and determine if changes should be made in content organization as part of the upgrade process.
Do you have a well-defined list that is driving your decision to upgrade to SharePoint 2010?	Analysis suggested. Ensure that IT and business users agree on the priority and timing.	Analysis recommended. Take a step back and develop a strategy for implementation of new features.

	Answered Yes	Answered No
Are users ready for the move to Office 2010 and the new features of SharePoint 2010? Will you need to train them?	Analysis suggested. Ensure that training is offered in advance of upgrade deployment.	Analysis recommended. Understand how the SharePoint experience will be impacted by the version of Office in use.
Did you heavily customize your SharePoint 2007 environment? Are you invested in third-party or custom solutions?	Analysis recommended. Ensure that all custom components will work and be supported in SharePoint 2010.	Analysis suggested. Verify that no additional customization will be required post-upgrade.
Does your current infrastructure comply with the SharePoint 2010 technical requirements (this includes 64-bit technology, increased RAM requirements, operating systems, and so on)?	Analysis suggested. Ensure that this is true for your other environments (development, staging, and so on) and you have a good story around availability and uptime.	Analysis recommended. Perform the necessary analysis to prepare your environment and support staff on the requirements associated with SharePoint farms.
After your upgrade, will you present the new interface with the SharePoint 2010 ribbon, or will you wait to alter your user interface in a subsequent phase?	Analysis recommended. Ensure your contributors are well-trained on how to manage content in the new interface.	Analysis recommended. Consider putting the SharePoint 2007 interface in use until users can be transitioned to comfort with the ribbon.
Are you using Internet Explorer 7 or later?	Analysis suggested. Have a pilot team in place prior to upgrade to ensure a quality user experience.	Analysis recommended. Consider upgrading all users to IE7 before conducting the SharePoint 2010 upgrade.

Fixing Your SharePoint Structure

Does your current SharePoint navigation taxonomy (the structure and hierarchy of your site) make sense to users? What content do employees use on the portal? What content is missing or misplaced? Has your business changed, or will it change so that the current portal structure does not map to that vision? These are tough questions but ones that will ultimately have a significant influence on your upgrade path. SharePoint 2010 has some incredible new features, but they alone cannot make your portal "better." It's also hard to think about some of the items above (and how you might place and organize them) without having an appreciation for the stability of the current environment. Is an upgrade to SharePoint 2010 the right time to reorganize your portal content and better align it with what users want or the business demands? Or is your page and content organization stable and successful with less of a need for radical change? Can new functionality be included in these specific sections or added as additional pages without a major disruption to page organization? Your best tool in this piece of the planning will be a whiteboard. Draw your current portal structure. Think about where new functionality might be introduced. Change your marker color and start to make changes. In the end, which color dominates? This will help decide if an upgrade or migration is best.

Chapter 5, "Planning Your Information Architecture" walks you through defining your taxonomy and metadata SharePoint in more detail. Chapter 10, "Making Search Work: Content, People, Data," helps you define your search structure, which is a very important means of helping users find enterprise information.

Addressing New Features in SharePoint 2010

As you plan your SharePoint 2010 rollout, what are the two or three features in SharePoint 2010 that are organizational "killer applications" (that is, they draw your users to higher levels of adoption)? Will social computing functionality like content tagging draw people to participate more? Will more flexible content management give users a greater sense of empowerment? Will enhanced search help users find the "right" content faster? How do these new features fit into your existing portal taxonomy? The challenge is to sift through the long list of features of SharePoint 2010 and identify those that will be used and are useful to your organization. This list will help in your planning and will also excite users about the new system. Think about how these capabilities change what information is being stored in SharePoint and, more importantly, how users (readers, contributors, administrators) will be affected. With that list, decide how implementation may be impacted by changes to the existing site taxonomy, security model, or governance plan.

User Comfort, Skill Level, and Training

This is the big question: How ready are your users for SharePoint (and Office) 2010? What will the impact be on productivity and portal adoption if you chose to change the portal radically? How will you prepare employees for SharePoint 2010 and major changes for how business processes and content creation are managed? How can you do all of this within a timeline that works for the business units and IT? This is the piece most SharePoint implementers will forget. Even if Microsoft did have a "magic button" to seamlessly upgrade your current SharePoint environment to 2010 ... and all the features you really need are enabled ... and everything just worked ... would users be thrilled or terrified? The biggest disadvantage of having an existing SharePoint environment is that an upgrade means change—and change is scary. You'll need to manage that fear by not overwhelming users, providing them with proper instructions, and giving them a clear roadmap around how to use the new features (and associated benefits). A SharePoint upgrade cannot happen in a vacuum. Users need to be informed and prepared. Manage risk by managing change. Only deviate from your existing framework if there are recognizable benefits to the user community in getting there.

Another important change with SharePoint 2010 is the introduction of the ribbon interface (first seen in Office 2007) for content administration. For those familiar with Office 2007, this interface change will require some basic training but will be somewhat transitional given the exposure to the ribbon in Office. For those who have not seen the ribbon, primarily because their organization is currently using Office 2003, the change in interface may be dramatic. You will need to decide whether to train users, possibly as part of an Office 2007 or 2010 launch, or defer the presentation by setting SharePoint 2010 to maintain the same user interface shown in SharePoint 2007. Obviously, the decision will impact the timing and process associated with your upgrade.

SharePoint 2007 Customizations

Finally, how much have you altered your existing SharePoint environment? Have you created site definitions? Have you unghosted pages (that is, have you detached from the standard template so that the page is now stored in the database)? Have you stayed with native functionality or created a highly customized environment? These items could have a major impact on the usefulness (and success) of Microsoft's upgrade tools. If you have created a SharePoint environment with little to no customization, an automated upgrade may be more likely to succeed (but even the simplest In-place Upgrades have trouble sometimes). If you have customized SharePoint, you will need to identify those customization points and validate that each will successfully upgrade. Are you using third-party Web Parts? Have you created your own custom Web Parts? Will they work? Have you altered the underlying JavaScript or XML or ASPX pages? Take an inventory of changes you have made to SharePoint since you installed the software and use this list as a gauge for how hard an automated upgrade will be. Also, as a first step, run the native upgrade assessment tool that comes with SharePoint 2007 SP2 (STSADM.EXE -o preupgradecheck) to assess the likely success of your upgrade.

In addition, don't forget to assess whether any custom tools or add-ons you are using are 1) still needed with SharePoint 2010 (that is, do native components now provide the custom functionality?) and 2) operational in a SharePoint 2010 environment (that is, does the vendor support the new platform, or does the custom code still work?). You will need to determine this for all non-native components that you currently manage.

Upgrade and Migration Options

Now that we've identified some of the key items that you need to consider before you move to SharePoint 2010, let's cover the ways in which you'll get there. Microsoft tools support two strategies to move from 2007 to 2010: an In-place Upgrade and a Content Database Migration. A third option is to rebuild your environment completely from the ground up, migrating content as needed. Table 17-2 highlights some of the details associated with each choice.

Table 17-2 Some Pros and Cons Associated with the Various Upgrade Options

Upgrade Approach	Description	Pros	Cons	Comments
In-place Upgrade	Upgrades everything in one attempt	Simple; updates existing environment on current hardware	Everything is offline while it runs; no ability to revert back to an original site	Best option for single server or small farm; must meet infrastructure requirements of SharePoint 2010
Content Database Migration (Database Attach)	Creates new farm and then manually migrates the old databases to the new servers	New farm, minimal downtime as the existing 2007 environment is available	Complex; many manual steps; search scopes must be recreated; additional hardware is required	Best when moving to new hardware
Rebuild and Selectively Migrate	Creates a new farm and then manually migrates the content from the old servers or purchases third-party migration tools	New farm, selective data migration; allows for a fresh start with taxonomy and security model; new functionality is available at the start and does not need to be retrofitted	Complex; requires many manual steps and custom code or third-party tools; requires business and technology resources to properly design and implement a new portal	Best option when redesigning your portal and collaboration environment from the ground up; especially true if the current environment is dated or heavily customized

In-place Upgrade

The In-place Upgrade requires that you take the server farm offline and run the SharePoint 2010 installer. This process updates existing databases and servers in a single step. This is by far the simplest approach, given that it is an automated process with minimal manual intervention. The challenge with an In-place Upgrade is that it requires that your existing infrastructure complies with the requirements of SharePoint 2010. As an example, that means increased RAM and 64-bit hardware on all servers as well as specific requirements on the operating system version (Windows Server 2008 SP2+). If you have not kept your infrastructure to current Microsoft recommended patching levels, or you have a large farm, or you have made customizations, an In-place Upgrade may not be an option.

Note that just because an In-place Upgrade is not viable for a production upgrade doesn't mean you can't use this approach in a test environment to gauge the viability of the upgrade. In fact, we highly encourage it. With the wider adoption of virtual server technology, creating a test environment that meets the infrastructure requirements of SharePoint 2010 and allows for an In-place Upgrade test is very straightforward. The biggest value this approach offers is that it allows you to see where potential upgrade hurdles exist and, as needed, test the fixes.

Note   No matter how small or simple your SharePoint 2007 environment is, you should always test an In-place Upgrade with a copy of your data first. This will also validate that you are working with the appropriate and sufficient hardware.

Content Database Migration

A Content Database Migration requires that you build a brand new server farm for the new environment. Once MOSS 2010 is installed in the new farm, you then attach the WSS 3.0/MOSS 2007 content database to the SharePoint Foundation 2010/SharePoint Server 2010 farm. At that point, the content upgrade will run automatically for that content database. The Windows SharePoint Services 3.0/MOSS 2007 farm stays available and untouched by upgrade, which allows you to keep the old farm up and running. This is a good option for large and complex deployments or where you are deploying new hardware. In fact, we suspect that this will be the most common upgrade approach.

This is also another example of a process that can be tested (and retested) in a virtual test environment. If your upgrade fails during initial testing, you have the ability to troubleshoot and resolve these issues before going live.

Note   Content Database Migration is also known as a Database Attach.

Rebuild: Create a Separate Farm and Selectively Migrate Content

Rebuilding is a good option if you want to completely redesign your SharePoint 2010 environment from the ground up. Like the Content Database Migration, you build a new SharePoint 2010 server farm. But rather than letting SharePoint upgrade your content databases automatically, you create a new set of content databases and then selectively migrate content. This process is more manual and time-consuming, but has the advantage of creating the "cleanest" outcome because it gives you the opportunity to upgrade your content and infrastructure at the same time.

What Plan Is Best for You?

Because every SharePoint environment is different, every upgrade effort is different. So which upgrade option should you choose? In some ways it depends on both the state of your current SharePoint environment as well as your strategic vision for how you will use the new features in the next version. Table 17-3 offers some real business cases and the associated recommended upgrade strategy. The table presents a very general recommendation for simple scenarios but offers general guidelines on where to begin planning efforts. It is important to note that regardless of upgrade choice, the effort associated with planning and testing is significant. The actual technical upgrade is only one piece of the total upgrade effort.

Table 17-3 Some Guidance about Selecting the Appropriate Upgrade Strategy Based on Relevant Business Cases

Business Case	Recommended Upgrade	Comments
■ Relatively simple SharePoint Server 2007 environment ■ Few customizations or third-party Web Parts ■ Simple taxonomy that still is consistent with business needs	In-place Upgrade (same hardware) Database Attach (new hardware)	Because the environment is consistent with native capabilities and because no dramatic changes are required, an In-place Upgrade will provide the quickest path to an operational SharePoint environment.
■ Multiple organizational and team sites ■ Team sites are being heavily used and members need the Recycle Bin and workflow ■ Corporate content in portal areas is small and not heavily used	Separate content into different Site Collections; then perform In-place Upgrade on each Site Collection separately	Team site users will recognize immediate benefits from using SharePoint Foundation 2010. There is less of an urgency of upgrading the portal. Moving to SharePoint Foundation 2010 first will allow team members to leverage new features while the portal content is reviewed and eventually upgraded to SharePoint 2010.
■ Very mature SharePoint Portal Server 2007 environment ■ Site taxonomy is dated and does not reflect current business vision ■ Lots of customization and unghosted pages	Database Attach or Rebuild and Migrate	Going to SharePoint 2010 can be a good time to evaluate your current portal environment and do any necessary course corrections. The advantage of starting from scratch (and migrating content) is that it allows you to leverage new tools as they were intended (without having to retrofit changes).

Business Case	Recommended Upgrade	Comments
■ WSS 3.0-based intranet that started as team sites and grew to become a corporate intranet ■ Lots of pages with no easy way of navigating between pages ■ Search is not effective and has become a major user enhancement request	Double In-place Upgrade or Rebuild and Migrate	You cannot go directly from WSS 3.0 to SharePoint Server 2010, but you can go from WSS 3.0 to SharePoint Foundation 2010 and then upgrade again to SharePoint Server 2010. This will maintain the current site taxonomy but will offer better navigation and search (in addition to all the other native SharePoint features). You could also build a SharePoint portal from scratch and migrate content. Again, the advantage is that you can build a new taxonomy with a more enhanced security model.

Upgrade Considerations

No matter which process you select, there are several issues you may run into due to the customizations made in your WSS 3.0/MOSS 2007 environment.

The following customizations could complicate your upgrade from WSS 3.0 to SharePoint Foundation 2010 or from MOSS 2007 to SharePoint 2010:

- Styles, graphics, and branding for WSS 3.0 & MOSS 2007: You will need to re-create your branding using the new ASP.NET master pages associated with SharePoint 2010.
- Sites based on a custom site definition: You will have to re-create the site definition to include SharePoint Foundation 2010/SharePoint Server 2010 elements as needed and then add your definitions to the mapping file.

- Custom and third-party Web Parts: You will have to redeploy these Web Parts and ensure they still work.
- Web Part connections: You may have to re-create the connections.
- Data view Web Part connected to a line-of-business database: You may need to either re-create the Web Part or consider using the Business Connectivity Services instead.
- Customized JavaScript (for example, OWS.JS) as well as jscript. You will need to test these to ensure they still function properly.
- Document libraries with large numbers of and/or many subfolders: You may want to alter the list design based on SharePoint 2010's ability to handle many more than the 2000-item limit of SharePoint 2007.
- Profile database: You will need to reimport your profiles, which takes roughly an hour for every 200 profiles. Make sure you budget this time.
- Audiences: You will need to re-create the audiences in the new environment.
- Hardcoded URL references. If you change the underlying site topology, the URLs associated with sites and/or documents may change, causing references to break. Try to identify these early in your analysis.
- Custom search scopes, content sources, and best bets: You will need to recrawl your content and re-establish any search settings you created in SharePoint 2007.
- Custom security applied to portal, sites, subsites, and document libraries: You will likely need to revisit the permissions.

For a complete upgrade guide, check out http://msdn.microsoft.com/en-us/sharepoint/ee514557.aspx.

The following are some things you absolutely must do before your upgrade:

- Run the preupgrade scan tool that comes with SharePoint 2007 SP2.
- Do a full backup of your databases.
- Ensure you meet all infrastructure requirements associated with SharePoint 2010.
- Inventory all custom Web Parts and custom coding in your SharePoint 2007 environment.

- Install all prerequisites.
- Create custom elements (site definitions and so on) for things you've customized.
- For gradual upgrades, you'll need DNS names for the new environment, which may take time to propagate across your network.
- Create a communication plan (for details on this see Chapter 9, "Getting Ready to Launch: Planning for Training and Communications") to let users know when SharePoint will be down, when things will be ready, and what to expect.

After your upgrade, you should

- Review the sites: Did SharePoint migrate the sites correctly? Are they using the right template? Is the look and feel acceptable?
- Validate that the security model is correct.
- Test search and ensure that any custom scopes or managed properties are enabled.
- Look for errors in the SharePoint log or event logs. Ensure all services are running properly.

Additional Considerations

So far, we've outlined several questions to review in advance of your decision to upgrade your existing SharePoint 2007 environment or migrate content to a new SharePoint 2010 environment. The goal is to give you food for thought and, hopefully, convince you that a move to SharePoint 2010 requires careful planning and consideration. The decision to upgrade or migrate will be different for each organization. It will depend on the items already discussed, your users, and your ability to effectively deliver on the value proposition of SharePoint 2010 technologies. So what's your plan? Here is an outline of some steps to help you get ready:

1. Educate yourself on SharePoint 2010 features. Read, see demo, find training materials that will help you appreciate the new functionality in SharePoint 2010 and how it maps to your business.
2. Educate yourself on how SharePoint 2010 will work in your environment. Will the features you need really be available in the configuration you have?
3. Decide on the proper version of SharePoint 2010? Will you use SharePoint Foundation 2010 only? Or SharePoint Server 2010

Standard? Or, do you need extended business intelligence capabilities, Excel Services, business connectivity services, or a forms server offered by SharePoint Server 2010 Enterprise?

4. Identify the new features that you would like to implement (workflow, offline, and so on) and think about how they will integrate with the existing information architecture.

5. Document all the customizations made in your current environment. These include templates, Web Parts, and styles. This will serve as your checklist for functional validation as you go into Step 6.

6. Create a test environment with a copy of your existing SharePoint portal. Test the upgrade. Whether or not you have already made your decision, it is best to validate the upgrade process and identify any potential problem areas. Perform either an In-place Upgrade (or a partial upgrade if you have a lot of Site Collections) and get your portal up and running.

7. Next, verify that you can get all items that you documented in Step 5 to work successfully. Does the portal meet your needs? Will the downtime of an In-place Upgrade be acceptable to users?

8. Conduct focus group testing with representative users. Show them the upgraded portal. Demonstrate some of the new features. Talk to them about the positives and negatives of the existing environments. Identify your "killer applications."

9. Do a whiteboard session with portal team representatives. Lay out your current taxonomy. Talk about some of the feedback from the focus groups. Identify how the features identified in Step 4 will be integrated. Devise a proposed new portal taxonomy.

10. Take a step back. Reflect. After going through the process, how do you feel? Will an In-place Upgrade suffice? Or do you need to do a gradual upgrade? Or is this an opportunity to build something new (and better) and introduce significant business value? How will you get there? How long will it take? Do you need help?

11. Be sure to visit the Microsoft TechNet site for detailed upgrade information at http://msdn.microsoft.com/en-us/sharepoint/ee514 557.aspx.

Key Points

Remember:

- Plan your upgrade. Don't run an In-place Upgrade and assume everything will be fine. In-place Upgrades are great for testing the process, but they don't often get the job done.
- Test your upgrade in another environment before you upgrade production. Even the simplest upgrade process could fail, leaving your environment unstable or unavailable.
- Use your upgrade as an opportunity to improve business processes or collaboration practices. For example, you may decide to introduce a new feature (such as social computing or business intelligence capabilities) into your rollout so that users see immediate benefit, rather than just downtime. This will enable you to more easily justify any downtime users experience.
- You don't have to upgrade everything at once. You may decide, for example, that you can leave your existing team sites alone (for now) and stand up another server farm for blogs and wikis. Then you can slowly migrate existing team sites to SharePoint 2010. You can also use SharePoint 2010's option to upgrade the databases only, upgrading the UI at another time. This phased approach is a very important consideration.
- Consider your needs: Are you best suited for SharePoint Foundation 2010, SharePoint 2010 Standard, or SharePoint 2010 Enterprise?

SharePoint User Tasks

Many of the chapters of this book get into some detail regarding key end-user features, administrative considerations, and solution development tasks. The trouble is, you'll probably read through a chapter exactly once but might need a reminder of "how to do X" more than once. As such, we thought it would be useful to call out the most common things that users in any role will need to perform. Whether you're an experienced SharePoint user or are new to the toolset, this chapter should help with key tasks.

We've ordered the list below by which product or technology you'll need to have installed to accomplish the task. Items 1–16 are SharePoint Foundation-specific features and can be used whether you have SharePoint Foundation, SharePoint Standard, or SharePoint Enterprise. Items 17–20 require at least SharePoint Standard, and items 21–24 require SharePoint Enterprise. These items provide instructions on how to implement some of the core features of SharePoint—things like document management, business intelligence, site provisioning, security application, and other basic site administrative tasks. These items are focused on the SharePoint Power User (versus IT administrator) and are, for the most part, tasks that you can complete as a basic SharePoint Contributor, with a few exceptions where you need to be a Site Administrator.

This appendix contains the following key sections:

Tasks That Require SharePoint Foundation (at Minimum)

1. Creating a new team site or workspace
2. Creating a list or document library
3. Applying security to a site or workspace
4. Applying security to a list or document library
5. Creating a view
6. Adding and editing Web Parts
7. Uploading files
8. Saving files directly from Office

9. Adding metadata to files
10. Recovering a document from the Recycle Bin
11. Building and contributing to a blog
12. Building and contributing to a wiki
13. Subscribing from and publishing to an RSS feed
14. Signing in as a different user
15. Enhancing a site's navigation
16. Working offline

Tasks That Require SharePoint Standard (at Minimum)

17. Document routing
18. Targeting content by using an audience
19. Making use of advanced search
20. Managing My Site

Tasks That Require SharePoint Enterprise

21. Creating Key Performance Indicators (KPIs)
22. Making use of business data
23. Publishing an Excel file for Web-based rendering
24. Publishing an InfoPath form for Web-based rendering

1. Create a New Team Site or Workspace

One of the most fundamental tasks a user might need to perform is to create a site. All sites are created by using a simple wizard and are always based on a template. Templates are a great way to not only jumpstart site creation, but to also enforce some level of consistency across sites. The basic collaboration templates include team sites, blank sites, and workspaces. SharePoint Foundation also has a number of out-of the-box site templates, including a couple that we mention later in this list: wiki and blog.

To create a new site (which will always be created underneath an existing site), click Site Actions → New Site (see Figure A-1). On the Create page, browse the template categories. Complete the wizard by entering a title and selecting a template (see Figure A-2). The More Options button enables you to provide a description for the site and select other advanced items (see Figure A-3).

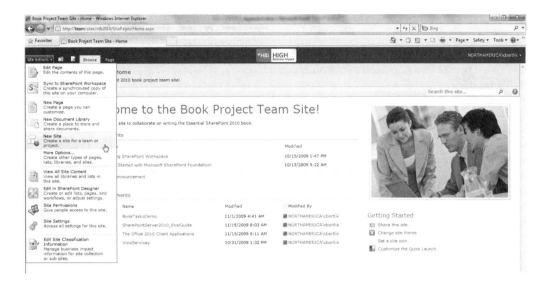

Figure A-1 The easiest way to create a new site is from a site's Actions menu

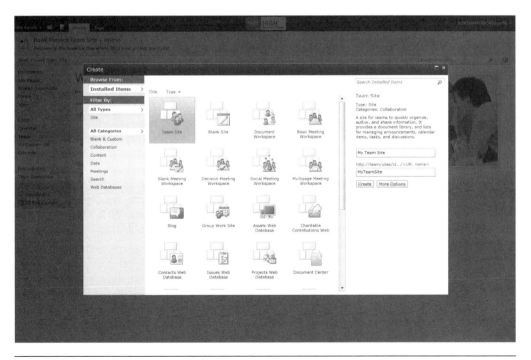

Figure A-2 Browse the site template categories to select the type of site that best meets your needs

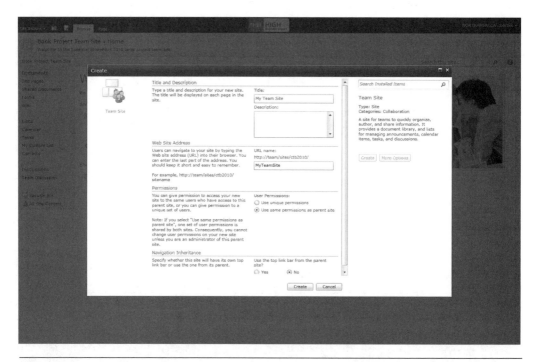

Figure A-3 More advanced options are available for setting site permission and navigation inheritance

Note   If you aren't able to create a site or you don't see the Site Actions menu, you may not have the correct permissions. Check with your administrator or the owner of the site.

Note   To create a new top-level site (otherwise known as a Site Collection), a SharePoint administrator must use SharePoint Central Administration → Application Management → Create Site Collections.

2. Create a List or Document Library

Once you've got a site created, you'll want to create a list. Using the Site Actions menu, click More Options. This will provide a variety of list templates that you can use—things like contact lists, document libraries, and

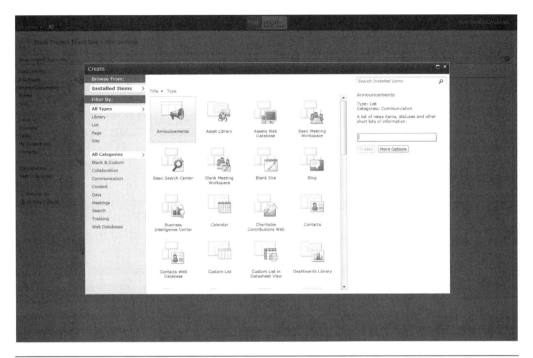

Figure A-4 The easiest way to create a new list or document library is from the Site Actions menu. The out-of-the-box templates include a large selection of list types

discussion boards (see Figure A-4). In effect, creating a list does two things: It creates a place in the SharePoint database where your list data can be stored, and it creates a user interface for your list in the form of a Web Part.

Note If you don't see the list type you want (for example, you're trying to create a slide library or KPI status list and the option isn't there), make sure you have those features enabled. You can enable features at the site level under Site Actions → Site Settings → Manage Site Features.

Once your list is created, you can change list options by using the List Settings button in the SharePoint ribbon List menu. This enables you to add/remove Columns, set permissions, add workflow, and set several other options.

3. Apply Security to a Site or Workspace

Once you have a site, you will likely need to enable additional users to use the site. In many cases, you'll simply inherit permissions from the parent site. However, you may find that you need to set permissions directly.

If you need to apply specific permissions, you'll want to use the Site Permissions options under Site Actions. This option takes you to a page to manage groups, permissions, and access requests (see Figure A-5).

The Grant section in the ribbon enables you to add and remove users from SharePoint groups within the site and to create new groups. The Modify section enables you to edit permissions for existing site users or groups and to remove user permissions completely. On the lower right section of the screen, you must select the group or individual that you want to make changes to. Clicking a group name in this section also enables you to add or remove members from existing groups. On this screen, you can also Check Permissions for Users, Manage Access Requests, and set Permission Levels (see Figure A-6).

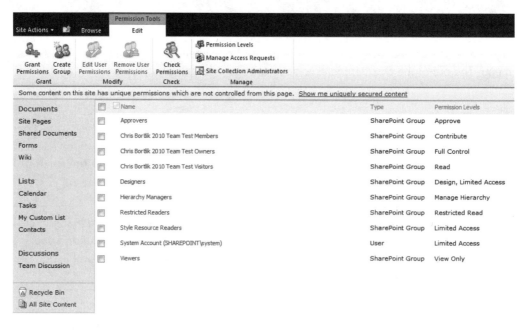

Figure A-5 Use the Site Permissions option under Site Actions to add or remove members of site-level SharePoint groups

Figure A-6 Use the Permission Levels option under Site Permissions to add, delete, and assign permissions (that is, List Permissions, Site Permissions, and Personal Permissions) to permission levels (like Full Control, Contribute, or Read) to users and groups

SharePoint only shows action links that a user can execute (this is called *security trimming*). Actions are hidden from users who do not have the proper permissions. To demonstrate this, execute the following steps:

1. Be sure you have Administrator privileges. Click Site Actions in the upper left and select Site Permissions.
2. Click Grant Permissions.
3. Select a user and give him or her Read permission only (either directly or via an existing group).
4. Click OK.
5. Go to the Welcome message in the top navigation and select Sign in as Different User. Enter the credentials for that user.
6. The Site Actions box will be missing. That user can only view content on the site and will not see any Administration links.

4. Apply Security to Lists or Document Libraries

One of the challenges of using a document library (or any document collection) is that it always seems that there are one or two documents that should have different security settings. From a business perspective, they fit logically in the grouping; from a security perspective, access should be limited to a subset of the major team. SharePoint addresses this problem with the ability to apply list-item security. This feature is not limited to documents; SharePoint permits the application of enhanced security on any list item, including images, links, and custom list items. To set item-level security, execute the following steps:

1. Click Site Actions → New Document Library to create a new document library.
2. Upload a few documents to the document library.
3. On one of your documents, select Manage Permissions from the context menu (see Figure A-7).
4. You will see a Permissions page detailing all security settings for the document. In general, a document will inherit permissions from its parent folder or library. To manage permissions directly, click Stop Inheriting Permissions from the Inheritance section in the ribbon (see Figure A-8). You will be warned that you are disassociating this document's security from the parent page and the document library. Click OK.

Note   It is important to be careful with item-level security, as it increases the complexity of security privileges within a list or document library. We recommend that you use item-level security only when absolutely necessary.

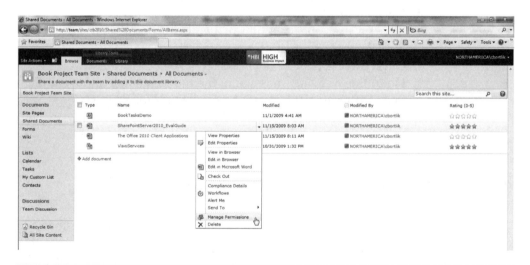

Figure A-7 To configure item-level security, select Manage Permissions from the item's context menu

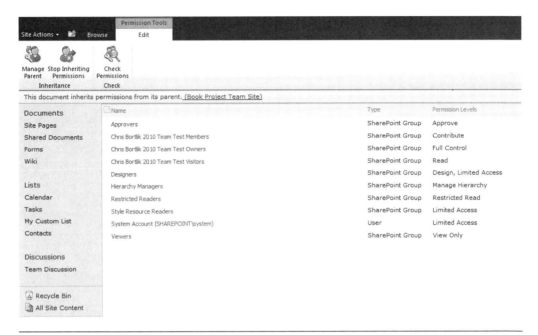

Figure A-8 The Stop Inheriting Permissions menu option enables you to set unique permissions on a single item

5. Click Grant Permissions. You will be able to set security for the document/list item by selecting the user or group and the associated security access. SharePoint will also allow you to send an e-mail to the associated users with a message about this document (see Figure A-9).

5. Create a View

Being able to render a collection of data from a SharePoint list in a variety of ways is a key strength of SharePoint. To create a new view on a list, select Create View from the List section of the ribbon menu (see Figure A-10). Select Standard View from the choices on the Create View page (see Figure A-11).

You then have a variety of ways to configure your view. You can sort, filter, group, and total the information on the view.

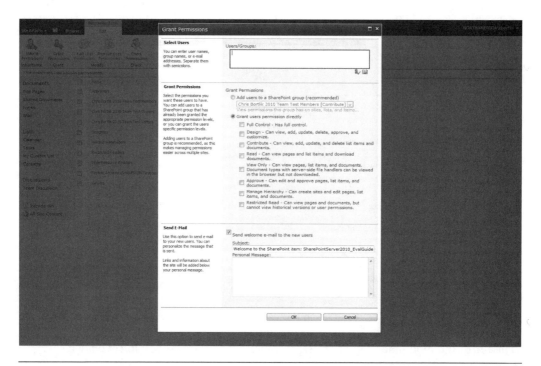

Figure A-9 The Grant Permissions page lets you apply specific permission levels such as Read or Contribute to an item

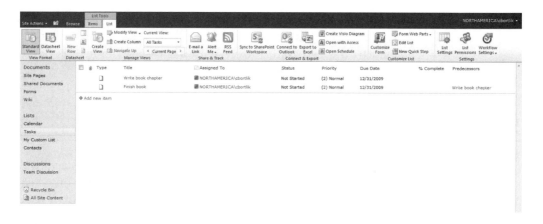

Figure A-10 To create a view, select the Create View option from the List section of the ribbon menu

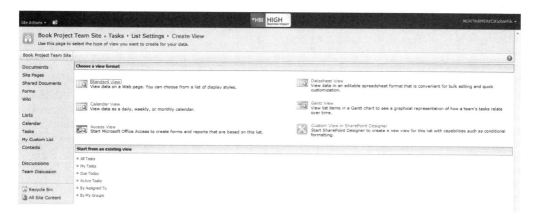

Figure A-11 SharePoint provides a variety of view types. The Standard View is the one you'll use most often.

Note   Never use view filtering to hide information that a user shouldn't be able to see. You're only obscuring the data; you're not actually securing it. You should apply item-level security to hide access to those items. Only use view filtering to hide items that the user should have access to but that may be convenient to hide in a given scenario—for example, showing items for a certain customer so that it's easier for the user to find the item he needs.

6. Add Web Parts to a Page

Once you've got a list created with a view you like, you can then drop a Web Part from the Web Part gallery so that all users can start interacting with your list and its view. To begin, click Site Actions → Edit Page. The Web page will change to Edit Mode, which means that the Web Part zones are visible, along with the Editing Tools menu in the ribbon (see Figure A-12). Click Web Part from the Insert menu in the ribbon to show the Web Part gallery (see Figure A-13).

Once you've added your Web Part, you can change a Web Part's options by clicking Options → Web Part Properties. The right-hand pane will enable you to change the view that the Web Part uses, change the toolbar type, and several other properties.

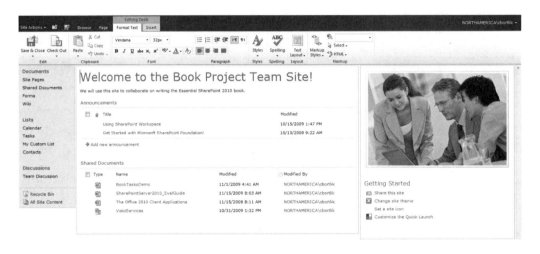

Figure A-12 Edit mode enables you to add and remove Web Parts on a SharePoint site

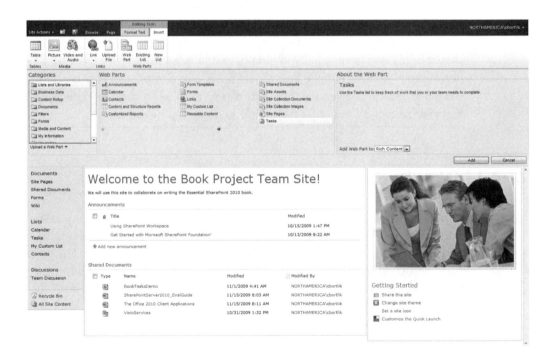

Figure A-13 The Lists and Libraries category of the Web Part gallery shows the available Web Parts for the lists in the site

7. Add Files to a Document Library

There are several ways to add files to SharePoint: You can upload them via the Web interface, e-mail them into SharePoint, drag them in using the Windows Explorer, or even save them directly from Office. We cover two ways in this tip: uploading and using Windows Explorer.

Using the SharePoint Web UI to Add Files to SharePoint

The easiest way to add a document to a document library is to use the Add document link on the SharePoint list. From this screen, you can either upload a single document or multiple documents at once (see Figure A-14).

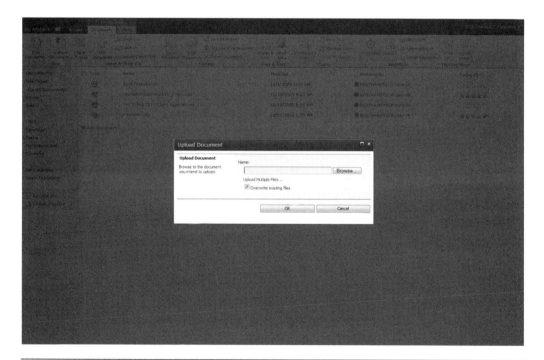

Figure A-14 The Add document link enables a user to upload a single document or multiple documents

Note   When adding files by uploading multiple documents or when using the Web folders view, not all documents may be immediately visible to other users if the library requires metadata. This is because you can't add metadata via these methods, and SharePoint will keep the documents checked out to the person who uploaded the files until all required metadata is provided.

Another way to add files to SharePoint is to use the Windows Explorer.

Using Windows Explorer to Add Files to SharePoint

To use the Windows Explorer, you need to map a network location to the SharePoint document library. Then you can simply drag and drop (or copy and paste) the files (see Figure A-15) using the Windows Explorer.

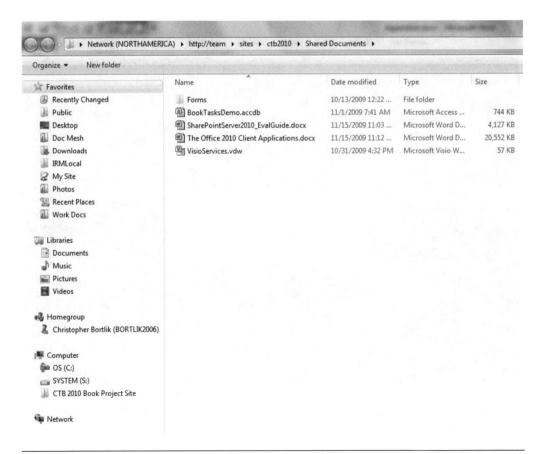

Figure A-15 A Web folder enables you to view SharePoint documents through the standard Windows explorer

To create a Web folder in Windows XP, open My Network Places. Click Add Network Place. Type in the URL of the document library (for example, http://myserver/sites/projectsite/shared documents).

To create a Web folder in Windows Vista or Windows 7, click Map Network Drive on the Windows Explorer toolbar. Then, click the Connect to a Web site that you can use to store your documents and pictures link (see Figure A-16). This launches the Add Network Location Wizard. Click Next. Click Choose a custom network location and click Next. Type in the URL of the document library (for example, http://myserver/sites/project-site/ shared documents). The network location then becomes available in Windows Explorer and in the Open/Save dialog (see Figure A-17).

8. Save a File from Office to SharePoint

Another way to add a file to SharePoint is to save the file from within Office. For this example, we assume you have Office 2003, 2007, or 2010. For these

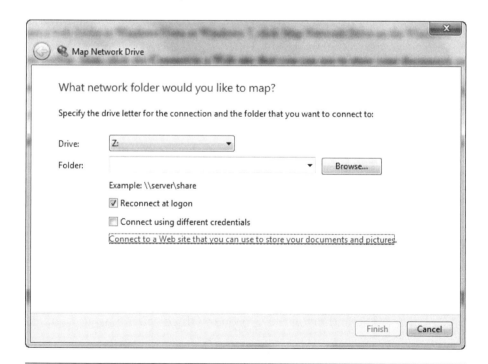

Figure A-16 The Add Network Location Wizard is hard to find in Vista and Windows 7. It exists as an option from the Map Network Drive option.

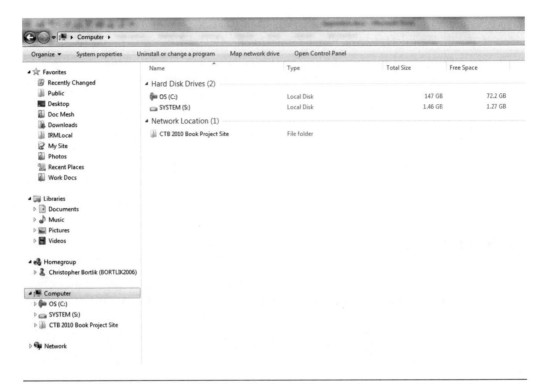

Figure A-17 SharePoint sites added through the Add Network Location Wizard show up in Vista and Window 7's Windows Explorer as Network Locations

versions of Office, if you opened the document directly from SharePoint, you simply need to click Save and the document is saved back directly to SharePoint. If you're saving the document to SharePoint for the first time, you have one option in Office 2003 and two options in 2007 or 2010.

Note For a list of what works and what doesn't for SharePoint 2010, depending on Office version, check out the "Business Productivity at Its Best" whitepaper from Microsoft at http://go.microsoft.com/?linkid=9690494

Depending on the version of Office you are using, you can

- Office 2010: Select the File tab → Save As
- Office 2007: Office Button → Save As
- Office 2003: File menu → Save As

These actions will get you to a dialog that enables you to save the document to your SharePoint locations. You can simply type http://yourintranet.yourcompany.com/sitename/ in the file location, and use the Network Places; or, create a shortcut that will remain in the list of shortcuts. In Windows XP, you will see SharePoint sites in three places in Windows Explorer (My SharePoint Sites, My Network Places, and My Site). In Windows Vista and Windows 7, mapped SharePoint sites show up in Network Locations (see #7).

Chapter 15, "The Office 2010 Client Applications," has additional details on how to add documents to SharePoint using a new product: SharePoint Workspace. This chapter also explains the new Office 2010 Backstage feature, which provides more functionality for saving and working with documents in SharePoint 2010.

9. Add Metadata and Standardized Document Templates to a Document Library for Better Content Tagging

One of the items on this list is "improved search." One key way to improve search results (as well as information presentation) is to provide better tagging around your content. This is not limited to just documents; you could use this technique on any list item. SharePoint 2010 offers a number of data types for list field definitions. They range from the very simple, like text or date, to the more complex, like calculated or business data.

For a simple example, let's use one of the more interesting data types in SharePoint: the Person or Group type. This allows you to associate a person or group with an item, complete with presence information and a hyperlink to the user's profile. This is a great way to assign task owners or identify item owners. To demonstrate this, execute the following steps:

1. Click Site Actions → More Options.
2. Click Custom List under the List section.
3. Name it **MyOwnerList** and click Create.
4. On the List ribbon menu, click Create Column.
5. Set the Column name to Owner and select Person or Group from the list of data types (see Figure A-18). Click OK.
6. Add a value to the list. Notice that the Owner field has a button labeled Browse (see Figure A-19). This will allow you to pick a specific person to place in this field (see Figure A-20).

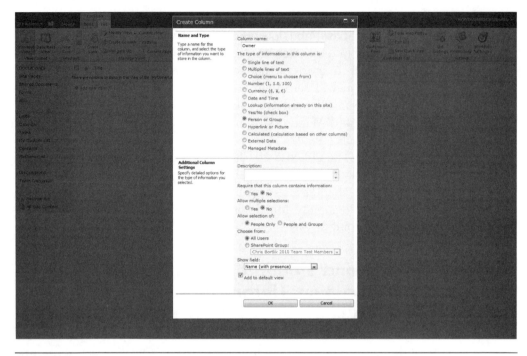

Figure A-18 Adding metadata column to a SharePoint list

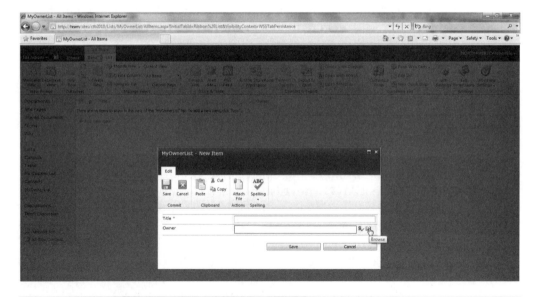

Figure A-19 Adding a new item to the MyOwnerList SharePoint list

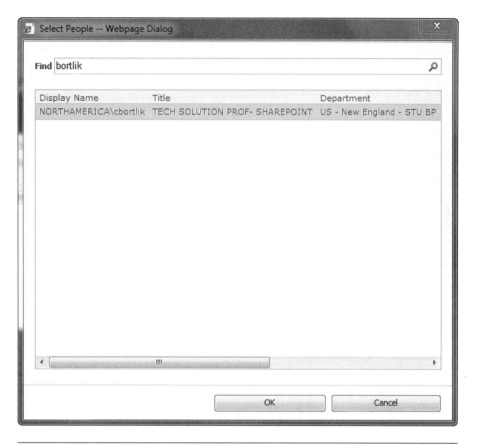

Figure A-20 Selecting a person from the browse option

10. Recover a Document from the Recycle Bin

If you inadvertently delete a document from your document library, you are able to restore it easily. SharePoint 2010 offers a Recycle Bin to allow user-controlled restoration of files, folders, and list items. The Recycle Bin is designed to provide a buffer between cleaning SharePoint content and losing important organizational data without having to involve an administrator to restore a file. To restore a file, execute the following steps:

1. In a document library, select a document.
2. Click the document and select Delete from its context menu. SharePoint asks "Are you sure you want to send this item to the site Recycle Bin?" Click OK to delete the file.

Figure A-21 Restoring a file from the Recycle Bin is very straightforward

3. Click Recycle Bin on the left-side navigation pane.
4. Your document is in the Recycle Bin. To restore, select the item(s) you want to undelete and click Restore Selection (see Figure A-21).

Note Clicking Delete Selection will move the item(s) into the second-stage Recycle Bin and can then only be restored by a Site Collection Administrator.

5. Your item(s) are now restored. All history and metadata have been maintained for the item(s).

11. Building and Contributing to a Blog

A blog is a great way to share information with an audience. On the Internet, blogs have become a popular means to share lessons learned, convey best practices, and provide personal insight. Corporations are starting to see the value of capturing this type of information inside of their firewalls. Employee blogs enable users to share information about project work, training classes, and other information that might be of value to peers and coworkers. All of this information can be made accessible to other employees by using a SharePoint blog, which can then be browsed and searched. Other employees can respond to blog entries with comments, facilitating captured dialog around a specific business problem.

To create a blog, execute the following steps:

1. Click New Site under Site Actions.
2. Provide a name and URL and select the Blog template. It may take a few minutes to generate the blog site.

The blog site is now created. Under the Blog Tools links, you are able to post new blog entries, manage posts and comments, and launch a blog editing program (such as Word) to publish more advanced posts to your blog. See Figure A-22 for a sample blog.

To update the categories that you can assign blog entries to, simply click Categories in the quick launch box on the left-hand side of the page. This lets you manage a SharePoint list that stores the categories for your blog.

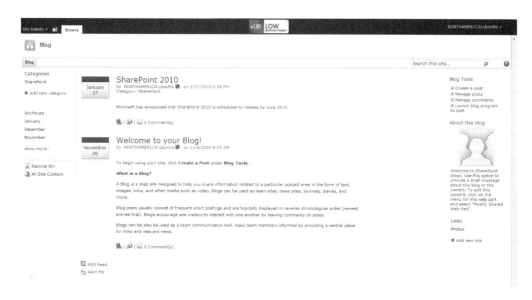

Figure A-22 You can create a blog using the SharePoint blog template

12. Build a Wiki

A wiki is a very popular means of unstructured collaboration among members of a virtual team. It offers all participants flexibility to add and alter the content within the wiki and effectively collaborate in building content with a group of colleagues. SharePoint supports the notion of a wiki; in fact, you can create wikis through the SharePoint interface because a wiki is simply another type of SharePoint site template.

SharePoint 2010 has improved the wiki experience beyond what was available in WSS 3.0 and SharePoint 2007. By default all SharePoint Web pages being edited in the browser now use a wiki-like editing experience. The wiki editor leverages the new ribbon interface to offer an environment for authoring that is like Word—including one-click access to add images or videos.

To create a new Wiki site, execute the following steps:

1. Click New Site under Site Actions.
2. Provide a name and URL and select the Wiki Site template. It may take a few minutes to generate the wiki site.

The wiki site is now created. There are instructions on how to use a wiki as well as standard information about recent changes made by the wiki community (see Figure A-23). Pages from the wiki show up on the quick launch bar.

Figure A-23 Creating a wiki site enables you to create editable Web pages easily with auto-linking, page history, search, and navigation

A wiki page provides WYSIWYG editing. To edit a page, click Edit this page at the top. You can insert tables, videos, and pictures or spell check the page, just as if you were using Word. Clicking Save updates the page. You can link to another page in this wiki site by enclosing the name of the page in double brackets on the edit form. For example, [[Office]] will create a link to a page called Office. Clicking a link to a page that doesn't exist will automatically create that page.

SharePoint 2010 adds intellisense to the wiki experience. As you start typing inside of the [[ ]] tags, SharePoint shows you available lists, libraries, and documents to make it easy to link to them.

Note To create a link to a page but then have the link display different text than the page name, type a vertical bar (I) after the page name and then the text you want displayed. For example, type [[Office | Office 2010]] to create the link labeled Office 2010 Page that points to the page named Office.

---

13. Expose List Data as an RSS Feed

Another useful feature in SharePoint is the capability to share list data (any list) as an RSS feed. This gives you the capability to publish SharePoint content outside of SharePoint. Any application that can consume RSS XML can read the data presented by the SharePoint RSS feeder and display that content. This is a great way to share collected information outside the bounds of a standard HTML page without code.

To use a list-based RSS feed, execute the following steps:

1. Navigate to an existing list.
2. Click List → List Settings.
3. Click RSS Settings (under Communications).
4. Select the Yes option next to Allow RSS for this list. Select the columns you wish to expose in the RSS feed (see Figure A-24). Click OK.
5. Click RSS Feed in the Share & Track section of the List ribbon menu. This brings you to the RSS content for your list.

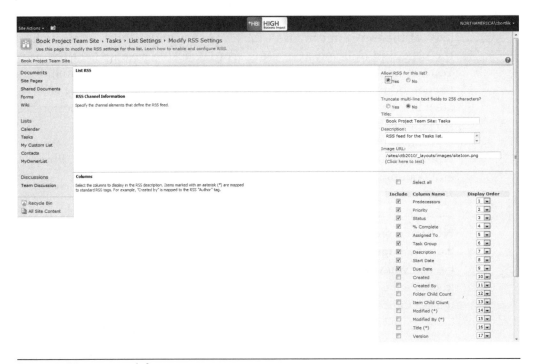

Figure A-24 List RSS definition

14. Sign In as a Different User

One of the challenges in building sites and solutions in SharePoint is testing the presentation for different types of users, especially when a security application is involved. It also poses difficulties for help desk and IT support staff when they are faced with the inevitable struggle with "It looks fine on my machine." However, SharePoint offers a feature that allows users to log out and sign in as a different person. This allows page designers and support staff to quickly replicate the experience of a specific user or role. It also allows an administrative user to sign into a site on another user's machine to fix an issue as needed.

To sign in as a different user, execute the following steps:

1. Go to a SharePoint page.
2. In the very top navigation bar, you'll notice a Welcome message showing the name of the person currently logged into SharePoint. Click the down arrow associated with it.

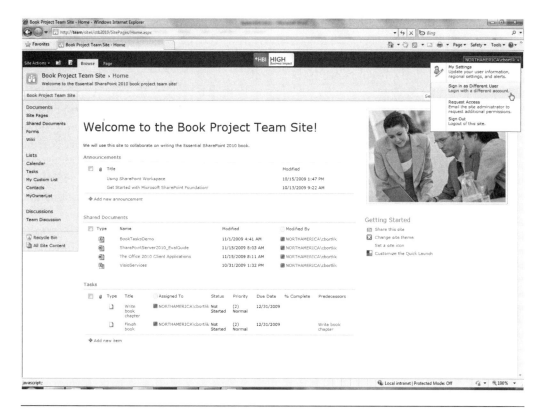

Figure A-25 SharePoint enables a user to sign in as a different user

3. Click Sign in as Different User (see Figure A-25).
4. You will get prompted for a username/password. Enter new credentials, and you will now be logged into SharePoint as that person.

15. Enhance a Site's Navigation

SharePoint 2010 has an improved user interface for navigating within and among pages. This is done primarily with several types of navigation tools:

- In general, the left-side navigation is both consistent and customizable on every page. For example, you will always be able to access the Recycle Bin and other key action tasks (provided the Site Administrator didn't override them).

- Breadcrumb-style navigation is used on every page. The top portion of the page will always show how to work back through the site hierarchy from the current page to the home page. You also have hyperlinks to all pages in between.
- Navigation can be set at a very granular level by the Site Administrator. To set navigation options for a site, go to Site Actions → Site Settings. Under Look and Feel, select Navigation. One of the interesting things you can do is update the quick launch, otherwise known as current navigation. You can also add global navigation, which appears as tabs across the top of your site, while local navigation shows up as links to the left of the page. See Figure A-26 for the navigation options and Figure A-27 for how the settings change the site.
- The new context-sensitive ribbon options that appear at the top of SharePoint 2010 pages only show the features that are relevant to the task you are performing and help surface commands that may have been buried and hard to find in prior SharePoint releases.

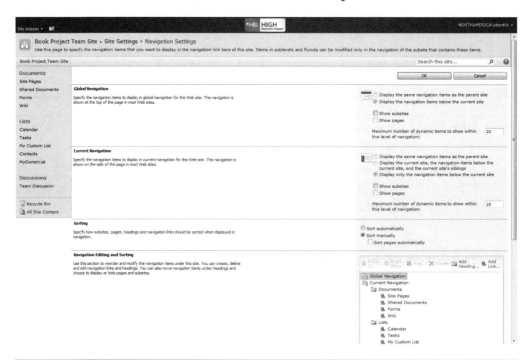

Figure A-26 Global navigation settings show up at the top of the page, typically as tabs or links, while current navigation typically shows lists and sites within the current site and can show any content you desire (simply add the new item as a link in the navigation page)

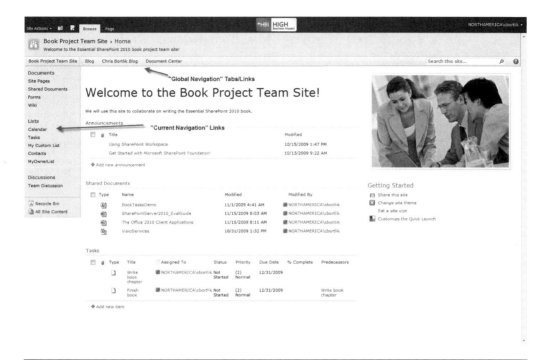

Figure A-27 The navigation options change the global and local navigation links on a site's pages

16. Work with a Document Offline

Offline access to critical business documents is important to all employees, especially those that are often disconnected from the corporate environment. While VPN and Direct Access in Windows 7 solve some of these challenges, they are not always the best or most reliable alternative for an employee sitting in a hotel room. SharePoint 2010 supports this need by enabling offline access to SharePoint content. This gives users the capability to download a local copy of a specific document (or collection of documents) and work disconnected from SharePoint. SharePoint will then allow that user, once reconnected, to synchronize the versions of the same document (local versus SharePoint-based) to aggregate the changes.

There are five ways to take SharePoint documents offline:

- The standard file system check-out (for a single document)
- Outlook 2007/2010 document libraries (one-way, read-only)

- Office 2010 Upload Center (two-way synchronization)
- Groove 2007 SharePoint Files Tool (two-way synchronization)
- SharePoint Workspace 2010 client application (two-way synchronization)

There are four ways to take SharePoint data offline:

- Outlook 2007/2010 (for team PIM-like data such as calendar or contacts)
- Excel 2007/2010 (for graphing and charting information)
- Access 2007/2010 (for tracking and updating information)
- SharePoint Workspace 2010 (for working with custom SharePoint list data offline)

For a rundown on when to use each of the various offline options for SharePoint, see Chapter 16, "Planning for Disaster Recovery: Backing Up and Restoring."

17. Document Routing

Workflow, especially around documents, is an integral part of most business processes. SharePoint 2010 integrates workflow into its core along with some out-of-the-box templates. SharePoint 2010 supports several workflow scenarios out-of-the-box, including: Approval, Collect Feedback, Collect Signatures, Disposition Approval, Three-State, Group Approval, and Translation Management.

To initiate workflow on a document or list item, execute the following steps:

1. Navigate to a list or document library.
2. Go into (List or Library) Settings.
3. Click Workflow settings under Permissions and Management.
4. You will see a collection of workflow templates. Choose Approval and give the workflow a name. You can configure the workflow to begin automatically when a document is added or modified, or you can configure the workflow to begin when a user manually initiates it. For this example, leave the default (manual). (see Figure A-28). Click Next.

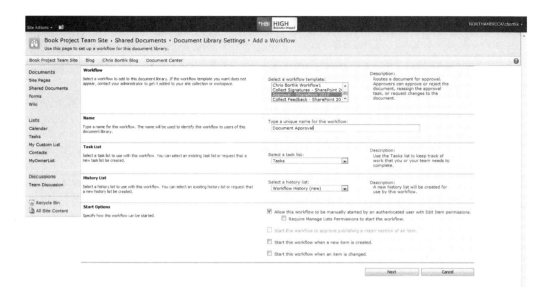

Figure A-28 The out-of-box workflows enable an end user to configure workflow on a list or document library. This is page one of the Approval workflow configuration wizard.

5. Define your rules and list of Approvers for the workflow (see Figure A-29). Click Save.
6. The workflow is now created. Users can initiate this workflow on an item by using the item's context menu.

To edit or remove an existing workflow, go to the Workflow settings. To edit a workflow, click the workflow name, which will relaunch the Workflow Configuration page. To remove a workflow, click Remove a Workflow. This page enables you to stop new instances of a workflow from running, which lets you wait until all existing workflows to complete before deleting the workflow (see Figure A-30).

Note When updating an existing workflow, you run the risk of changing business rules on older, existing workflows that are in mid-process. For this reason, you may want to suspend new instances on the existing workflow and then create a new workflow to handle the processing on newly created items.

Figure A-29 Step two of the Approval workflow template enables the user to assign a list of default start values, completion criteria, and other values

Figure A-30 Site administration enables you to delete a workflow or simply stop new instances of a workflow. This is useful because you will want to let the existing running workflows finish before deleting the workflow.

18. Filter and Target List Content Using an Audience

SharePoint Portal Server 2003 introduced the concept of audience-based targeting. This feature enables administrators to control visibility of Web Parts and SharePoint content. The most popular advantage of such an approach is that it offers the ability to put many Web Parts on a single page and then control visibility of those Web Parts by assigning audiences to the Web Parts based on the intended user(s). For example, a Site Administrator might put a reporting Web Part on a site but only target it at managers.

Note Audiences are created and maintained by a SharePoint administrator by using SharePoint Central Administration. Target audiences can also be set based on security and SharePoint Groups.

To configure an audience on a Web Part, execute the following steps:

1. Edit a SharePoint page (Site Actions → Edit Page).
2. Go into settings for a Web Part (Web Part Tools → Options → Web Part Properties).
3. Under the Advanced settings in the Web Part Configuration pane (right-hand side), the last option is called Target Audiences. Enter the name of the audience or look it up via the lookup icon (see Figure A-31).

Figure A-31 Audiences enable you to target Web Parts (and content) for specific groups of users

19. Find Content by Using Search

Content stored in SharePoint (or anywhere else for that matter) is only useful if you can actually find it. That's a very simple statement but a very hard objective to meet. SharePoint 2010 has greatly improved its underlying search engine to allow users to find content (documents, links, people, and so on) more easily. Three of the top features are

- Stronger relevancy ranking
- Wildcard searches
- Better search results presentation

Stronger relevancy means better results. The search engine associated with SharePoint 2010 now has a more complex relevancy ranking algorithm to better sort search results "in the right order." It takes better advantage of end user metadata tagging to leverage more information known about a single piece of content. It also adds phonetic searching to help find related content based on different spelling of names (example, Kaufman and Coughman) and nicknames (example, Jim and James).

One of the most frequently requested features in SharePoint 2007 search was wildcards. SharePoint 2010 adds this capability so you can now search for **"discuss*"** and find all results that contains words beginning with the phrase **"discuss"** (see Figure A-32).

If you execute the search on the term **"discuss*,"** you'll notice a very simple and clean user interface for search results. SharePoint presents the default search results view in relevancy ranking order but allows you to select from a list of other ways to sort the results. SharePoint 2010 now also displays search result refiners on the left-hand side, document thumbnail previews, and integration with the new Office Web Applications to review and edit Office documents within the browser.

Advanced Search also allows you to further filter the results by either altering the search query with Boolean conditions or specifying a specific content type to look for. Chapter 10, "Making Search Work: Content, People, Data," provides more information on search improvements and options.

20. Manage "My" Information

Much like SharePoint Portal Server 2003 and SharePoint 2007, SharePoint 2010 offers a personalized page called a My Site. Specifically,

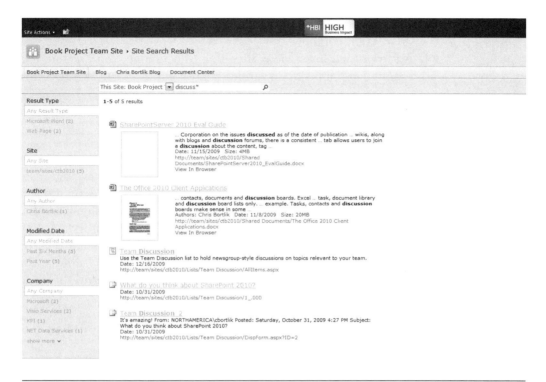

Figure A-32 SharePoint search provides the ability to perform wildcard searches

a My Site is a page dedicated to the content associated with the currently logged in user. Information contained on this page includes sites, documents, and tasks associated with the user. There are some interesting features that really allow a SharePoint user to better organize SharePoint content. As an example, you can create a shortcut to a colleague's profile page. This gives you access to his or her contact information and also includes the presence awareness indicator. You also have control over the look and feel of your My Site, including addition of Web Parts. The My Site page includes a list of all documents created by that user and a list of memberships (with hyperlinks) to SharePoint sites.

To demonstrate the My Site concept, execute the following steps:

1. Click My Profile in the top navigation bar.
2. If this is the first time you are accessing My Site, it may take a few minutes to create your site.

3. Once created, the site offers access to a personalized view of SharePoint content.

4. Add personal links, view SharePoint documents you created, and examine membership in various SharePoint sites (see Figure A-33).

21. Create a List of Key Performance Indicators

Business intelligence continues to be a very popular business initiative. Microsoft has responded to this demand by providing the average user with a set of BI tools for managing the creation and presentation of corporate metrics. One of the main pieces of a business intelligence initiative is the presentation of KPIs (Key Performance Indicators). A KPI offers a simple, graphical presentation of a measured business metric. The utilization of KPI data with SharePoint is done by defining a list item as a KPI. This allows you to set and measure a BI value and control the presentation of that data to users.

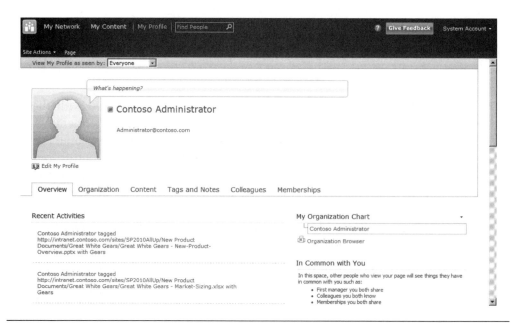

Figure A-33 A My Site provides a user with both a private site that can be configured as needed, plus a public profile that any user can view

Chapter 13, "Making Business Intelligence Work," provides a complete rundown of all of the BI-related capabilities in SharePoint 2010.

To create a KPI list item, execute the following steps:

1. Click View All Site Content from the Site Actions menu.
2. Click Create.
3. Click Status List under the List category.
4. Name it **MyBIData** and click Create.
5. On the New menu, click Fixed Value based Status Indicator. Notice that you can also use SharePoint, Excel, and SQL Analysis Services as other data sources.
6. Give the KPI a name of **Revenue**. Set the value to 100,000. Set the green goal to 120,000 and the yellow goal to 50,000. Click OK (see Figure A-34).
7. You will notice that this new KPI shows a yellow triangle in the Status column (see Figure A-35). Items above the goal would display as green circles, while items below the warning threshold would appear as red diamonds.

22. Make Use of Business Data

There are three key ways that users can make use of external business data: searching external data, using external data as metadata in a column, and simply displaying external data in a Web Part. This section shows you how to do all three.

Note External data connections and External Content Types are created and maintained by a SharePoint administrator by using SharePoint Designer 2010. If you don't have permissions to use external data within SharePoint, contact your SharePoint administrator.

Searching External Data

The business connectivity services can be crawled by SharePoint, which means that SharePoint search will provide search results from the structured data. For more information on searching and working with business data, see Chapter 14, "Mashups and Composite Applications."

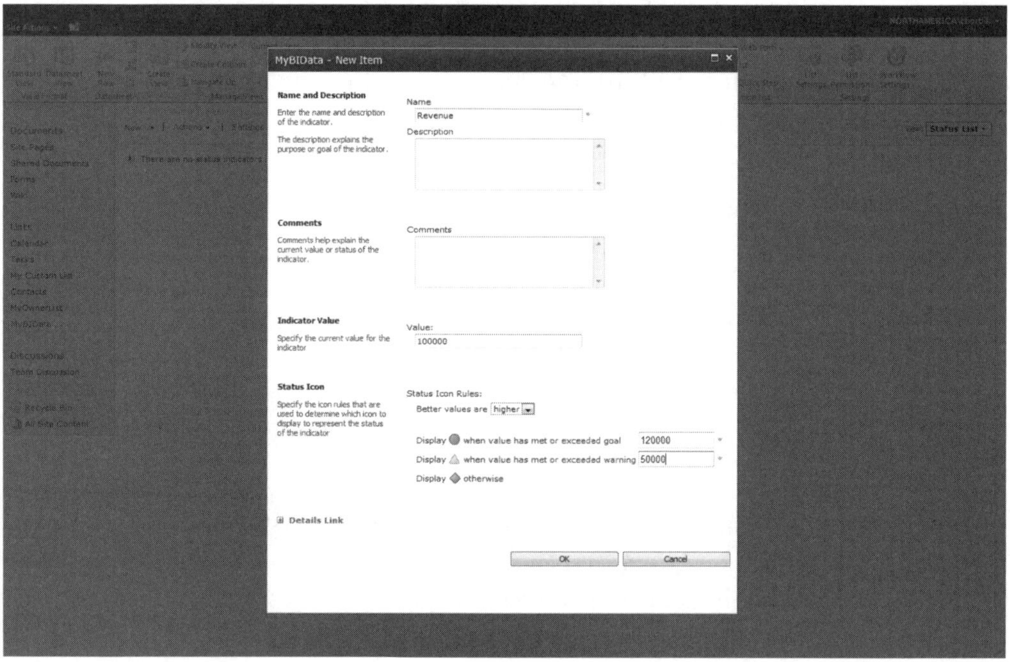

Figure A-34 Adding a KPI definition is as simple as creating a new list item

Figure A-35 KPIs automatically display real-time indicators based on the source data

Using External Data as Metadata in a Document Library

SharePoint 2010 Enterprise offers the ability to use external data entries in a metadata column.

To demonstrate this, execute the following steps (this example assumes you've already set up the External Content Type data connection):

1. Click Site Actions → More Options.
2. Click Custom List under the List section.
3. Name it **MyBusinessDataList** and click Create.
4. On the List ribbon menu, click Create Column.
5. Set the Column name to Address and select External Data from the list of data types. In the Type field, select external data type and additional fields that you want to promote into the SharePoint list (see Figure A-36). Click OK.
6. Add a value to the list. Notice that the Address field has a button that enables you to browse for external data. This will allow you to pick a specific item (in this case, a customer address from the database) for this field (see Figure A-37).

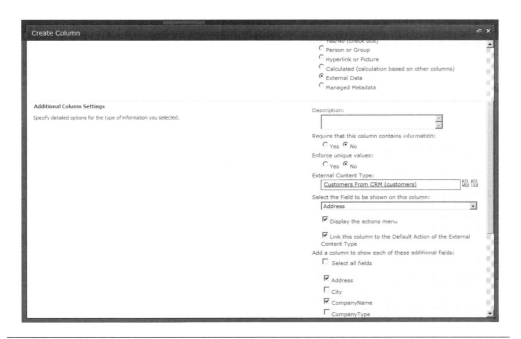

Figure A-36 Select the external Content Type to add a business data metadata column to a SharePoint list

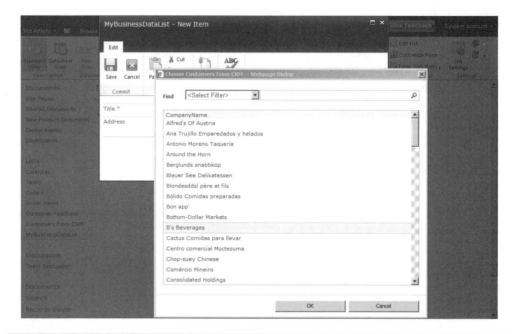

Figure A-37 Adding an external data metadata column to a SharePoint list enables a user to select data directly from a back-end database or application to use in a metadata column

Showing External Data in a Web Part

The final thing we'd like to mention is the out-of-the-box business data Web Parts that are available. To use the business data Web Parts, simply open the Web Part gallery (see Figure A-38). When the Web Part is available on the site, open its property page to select the external data entity you want to display. Then users can filter and display business information (see Figure A-39).

23. Publish an Excel Workbook for Web Rendering

From a user perspective, it's fairly simple to publish an Excel 2010 workbook to the server so that Excel Services can render it. You simply use the File Menu → Share → Publish to Excel Services option from within Excel 2010 (see Figure A-40). There are a number of things you need to be careful of, however—see Chapter 13 for more information on using Excel Services.

Figure A-38 The Business Data Web Parts enable you to display data from structured data sources

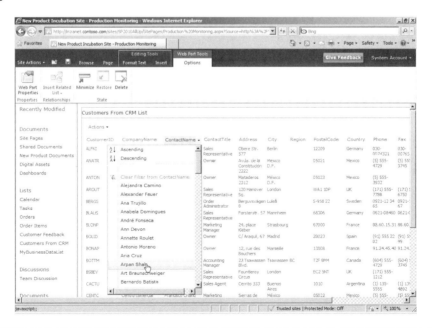

Figure A-39 Selecting the Customers entity makes it easy to allow users to filter and display the list of customers

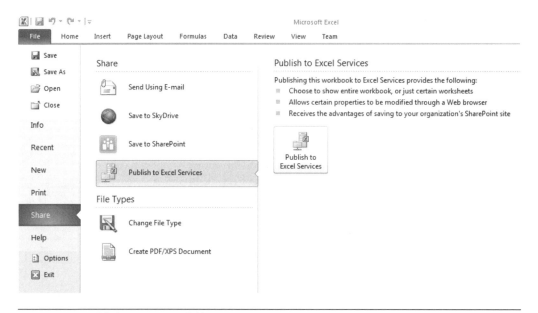

Figure A-40 Publishing an Excel file to Excel Services can be done by end users, provided the target is a trusted location

24. Publish an InfoPath Form for Web Rendering

A user can publish an InfoPath form for rendering on a Web server, but there are a number of key steps that you must complete. See Chapter 11, "Making Business Processes Work: Forms and Workflow," for a complete step-by-step walkthrough of publishing an InfoPath form or Web control on the server.

Key Points

This appendix provides the top 24 tasks that end users will likely need to perform, along with key tips and tricks.

Tasks That Require SharePoint Foundation (at Minimum)

1. Creating a new team site or workspace
2. Creating a list or document library

3. Applying security to a site or workspace
4. Applying security to a list or document library
5. Creating a view
6. Adding and editing Web Parts
7. Uploading files
8. Saving files directly from Office
9. Adding metadata to files
10. Recovering a document from the recycle bin
11. Building and contributing to a blog
12. Building and contributing to a wiki
13. Subscribing from and publishing to an RSS feed
14. Signing in as a different user
15. Enhancing a site's navigation
16. Working offline

Tasks That Require SharePoint 2010 Standard (at Minimum)

17. Document routing
18. Targeting content by using an audience
19. Making use of advanced search
20. Managing My Site

Tasks That Require SharePoint 2010 Enterprise

21. Creating Key Performance Indicators (KPIs)
22. Making use of business data
23. Publishing an Excel file for Web-based rendering
24. Publishing an InfoPath form for Web-based rendering

INDEX

SYMBOLS

- (minus) sign, for exclusions in searches, 297
+ (plus) sign, for inclusions in searches, 297
= (equals) sign, searching for numeric values, 297
< (less than) sign, searching for numeric values, 297
> (greater than) sign, searching for numeric-values, 297

A

About Us sections, in planning
    site architecture, 131
Access
    client applications that connect with
        SharePoint 2010, 441–442
    client-side information worker components,
        21–22
    composite applications and, 420
    Connect and Export for taking data offline, 456
    features in SharePoint Server 2010
        Enterprise Edition, 35
    recommendations for working with documents
        and data offline, 457
    SharePoint as replacement for, 45–46
    working with data offline, 540
access control
    authorization and authentication and, 266
    listing/describing access needs in security
        model, 257–258
    roles and responsibilities, 103
accessibility
    compliance, 414
    standards for, 382
actions
    adding custom actions to external list, 430–432
    workflow options, 343–346
Active Directory Groups, 246

activity feeds, My Sites, 219–220
activity groupings, in planning site
    architecture, 132
Add a Workflow page, 330
Add document link, 525–526
administration
    Central Administration. see Central
        Administration
    checking for administration rights, 267
    new features for searches, 320
    overview of, 84–85
    Site Collection settings, 86–87
    site settings, 87–89
    of sites, 134–135
Administrative Report Library, 319
administrators
    access to audit reports, 189–190
    benefits of SharePoint for, 4
    controlling Recycle Bin settings, 483
    Farm Administrators compared with, 248
    performing backups, 470
    supporting adoption of business processes, 493
advanced searches, 298–299, 544
advanced training topics, 282
alerts
    subscribing to search set results, 298
    updating reports based on, 401
AND, Boolean expressions used in searches, 297
announcements, guidelines and policies for, 119
application features, in SharePoint Server 2010,
    63–64
Application Management section, of Central
    Administration, 86–87
application servers
    deployment options and, 90–92
    file server scenarios, 42–43
    server roles in SharePoint, 90

Approval workflow, 328
Approve permission, for publishing sites, 251
architecture. *see also* IA (Information architecture)
   adding functionality to sites with service
      applications, 83–84
   administration, 84–85
   application features, 63–64
   Central Administration, 85–86
   considering changes to during upgrade
      process, 500
   creating new sites, 69–72
   database services, 62
   deployment options, 90–94
   fundamental concepts, 65–66
   lists, libraries, and items, 78–79
   navigation, 81–82
   operating system, 62
   overview of, 61
   pages, 80
   reviewing key points regarding, 94–95
   server roles in SharePoint, 89–90
   service applications, 64–65
   SharePoint Foundation 2010, 62–63
   Site Collections, 67–69, 86–87
   site settings, 87–89
   site templates, 74–78
   site values at three levels, 66–67
   subsites, 74
archives
   file server scenarios for handling, 41–43
   records management and, 186
Ask Me About section, of My Site, 211–212
ASP.NET, as Web page service, 29
associations, workflow
   with lists, 330–331
   options for, 343
   overview of, 328
audiences
   communication plans focusing on, 285–289
   features in Standard Edition, 34
   filtering/targeting list content based on, 543
   security exceptions, 244
   tailoring communications plan to, 283
   targeting with dashboards, 417
   training plan targeting, 273–274
audio, file server scenarios for handling, 41–42

auditing
   content policies and standards, 115
   records management and, 189–190
authentication
   access denied and, 266
   restores and, 476
authoring and production farms, 382
authoring, staging, and production farms, 382
authorization, 266
automated workflows, 494
authoritative pages, planning searches and, 316

B
Backstage
   features for working with documents
      as a whole, 458–459
   sharing documents from, 460
Backup utility, 469–471
backups
   Backup utility, 469–471
   Central Administration backup and
      restore tool, 468–469
   command-line, 479–480
   examining backup files, 471–475
   file server scenarios, 40–41
   limitations of SharePoint backup, 484–486
   options, 467–468
   reviewing key points regarding, 486
   scheduling, 480
   SQL Server Backup and Restore, 483–484
Balsamiq, for designing page architecture,
      137–138
Basic Information area, My Site, 209–212
Basic Search Center, 302
batches (.bat), 42
BCS (Business Connectivity Services)
   adding custom actions to external list, 430–432
   components of, 421–422
   creating External Content Type, 424–427
   creating external lists, 427–430
   features in Standard Edition, 35
   getting started with, 423–424
   introduction to, 420–421
   reviewing key points regarding, 436–437
   solutions, 422–423
   using External Data Column, 432

what's new in Office 2010, 440
working with external data lists offline, 444–445
BDC (Business Data Catalog), 420
best bets, searches, 318
best practices
Columns, 147–150
permissions, 252
standards describing, 112
BI (business intelligence)
application features in SharePoint Server 2010, 64
charts, 402
dashboards, 402–403
Excel Services and. *see* Excel Services
getting started with, 400
insights, 4–5, 30
KPIs (Key Performance Indicators), 404–405
new features in SharePoint 2010, 33
overview of, 399–400
PerformancePoint Services, 411–414
presentation tool options, 405–406
reports, 400–402
reviewing key points regarding, 417–418
scorecards, 403–404
strategy for, 415–417
Visio Services, 414–415
binary differentials, in SPW (SharePoint Workspace), 445
Bing, as search tool, 294
BizTalk Server 2008, 31
blogs
building/contributing to, 532–533
guidelines and policies for, 118–119
knowledge sharing and, 204
policies regarding, 215–216
preparing for social computing during upgrade process, 495–496
as structure for collaborative conversations, 229–232
Boolean expressions, in searches, 297, 544
brainstorming, in planning site architecture, 130
branding
guidelines and policies for, 120–121
master pages and, 390–392
page layouts and, 392–394
user experience and, 389–390

breadcrumb navigation, 538
browse
organization browsers, 219–221
site architecture supporting, 129
business analysis, designing searches and, 304
business capability, search functionality as, 293–294
"The Business Collaboration Platform for the Enterprise and the Web," 4
Business Connectivity Services. *see* BCS (Business Connectivity Services)
Business Data Catalog (BDC), 420
Business Data Web Parts, 434
business intelligence. *see* BI (business intelligence)
business objectives
associating with collaboration technologies, 203–205
clearly defining, 9–10
dashboards showing performance against goals, 402–403
documenting and using to guide decision-making, 11–12
identifying and implementing key objectives, 12
mapping objectives to SharePoint features, 13–14
organization-specific and other business drivers, 10–11
scorecards showing performance against goals, 403–404
business owners
as primary audience of governance plan, 101
roles and responsibilities, 104
business processes
application features for, 64
building efficient processes when upgrading, 492–493
Excel Services and, 409
identifying/resolving barriers to adoption of, 493
lifecycle of, 326
business representatives, analysis and design of searches and, 303–304
business requirements document, 304–305
business users, as stakeholders, 8

C

cache
    Office Upload Center for caching files, 450–452
    synchronization of branch cache, 453–454
calendars, working with offline, 455
capacity planning, searches and, 311
center of excellence
    roles and responsibilities, 105
    training and, 276–277
Central Administration
    backup and restore tool, 468–469
    Backup utility, 469–471
    configuring Recycle Bin, 481–482
    configuring searches, 312–313
    dedicated site for, 83
    managing content sources, 313–314
    overview of, 85–86, 88
CEWP (Content Editor Web Part), 384
charts, in BI (business intelligence), 402
check-out
    version management and, 174–175
    working with documents offline, 539
Check Permissions action, 265–266
clients, Office 2010
    client applications that connect with
        SharePoint 2010, 441–443
    client-side information worker
        components, 21–22
    integration with ribbon interface, 444
    overview of, 439
    starting workflows from, 335
    what's new in Office 2010, 440–441
    working with data offline, 454–457
    working with documents offline, 450–454
cloud computing, SharePoint Online, 27
cmdlets, PowerShell, 479–480
coaches, roles and responsibilities, 105
collaboration. see also communities
    associating business objectives with collaboration
        technologies, 203–205
    collaborative conversations, 229
    features in SharePoint 2010, 3, 32
collaborative application, building in
        SharePoint Server
    adding lists to site, 47–51
    adding status indicators for threshold
        reports, 52–54

adding Web Parts to site, 54–56
arranging Web Parts and adding data, 56–57
creating blank site, 47
overview of, 46–47
Collect Feedback workflow, 329
Collect Signatures workflow, 329
Columns
    best practices, 147–150
    configuring automatic Column indexing for
        lists, 181, 183
    Content Types inheriting column values, 145
    defining at site, Site Collection, or
        enterprise level, 143
    defining metadata using Site Columns, 192
    External Data Column, 432–433
    managed keywords, 150–151
    Managed Metadata. see Managed Metadata
    managing, 146
    in metadata architecture, 139
    names and types, 146
    planning, 147
    security exceptions, 244
command-line backup tools, 479–480
command scripts, file server scenarios, 42
communication plans
    activities for promoting new solutions, 286–288
    considerations in, 283–285
    focusing on method, message, and audience,
        285–289
    overview of, 271–272
    reviewing key points regarding, 289–290
    SharePoint launch and, 282
communication skills, information literacy,
        278–279
Communicator information worker component,
        21–22
communities
    associating business objectives with collaboration
        technologies, 203–205
    blogs, 215–216, 229–232
    collaborative conversations on, 229
    Content section of user profile, 221–222
    engaging users in social networking, 217
    enterprise wikis, 234–237
    features in SharePoint Server 2010, 4–5, 30
    governance plan for, 209
    Memberships section of user profile, 222–223

My Sites Basic Information, 209–212
My Sites Contact Information and
    Details area, 212–213
My Sites Preferences area, 213
My Sites status update area, 214
notes, 224–227
organization browsers, 219–221
overview of, 201–202
pilot project for, 216
preparing a launch and communications plan,
    216–217
ratings, 215, 227–229
responding to resistance and barriers to, 205–209
reviewing key points regarding, 237–238
status updates and activity feeds, 219
strategy for using, 202–203
tags, 215, 224–227
team sites, 233–234
training plans and, 278
use cases for, 205
user contributed content adding value to, 223
user profiles, 217–218
wikis, 215–216, 232–233
company directory, viewing, 219–221
compliance
    accessibility issues and, 414
    auditing and, 189
    document management and, 401
    information architecture reducing compliance
        risks, 125
composite applications
    building, 432–436
    features in SharePoint 2010, 4–5, 30–31, 33, 64
    overview of, 419
    what they are, 420
configuring document and records management
    adding Content Types to document
        libraries, 195
    defining Content Types that use Site
        Columns, 192–195
    defining metadata using Site Columns, 192
    enabling in-place records management,
        195–199
    overview of, 192
configuring searches, 312–313
conflict resolution, SPW (SharePoint Workspace)
    and, 445

Connect and Export, Excel and Access feature
    for taking data offline, 456
consistency
    in page design, 116, 136
    ribbon interface for, 271
Contact Information area, My Sites, 212–213
content
    deployment, 380–382
    features of SharePoint 2010, 4–5
    guidelines and policies, 118–121
    guiding principles, 110–111
    leveraging list data for content
        presentation, 374
    managing rich, 384
    organizing on pages, 135
    ownership, 134
    policies and standards, 113–115
    providing high value content as part of
        communications plan, 285
    repurposing, 374
    routing via workflows, 326
    user experience and, 389
content approval
    document version settings, 169–170
    Draft Item Security and, 173
Content area, of user profile, 221–222
Content by Query Web Part, 69
content database migration
    overview of, 504–505
    pros/cons, 503
Content Deployment Job, 381
Content Deployment Path, 381
Content Editor Web Part (CEWP), 384
content management
    application features in SharePoint
        Server 2010, 63
    ECM (enterprise content management), 30
    enterprise level. see ECM (enterprise content
        management)
    Web level. see WCM (Web content
        management)
content organization
    foundational elements in building information
        architecture, 126–127
    in planning site architecture, 131–132
    preparing for social computing during upgrade
        process, 496

content organizer
   overview of, 386–387
   processing content based on rules, 166
content pages, 80
Content section, of user profile, 221–222
content sources
   adding and configuring for searches, 313–315
   configuring for searches, 307, 310
   crawl schedule for, 308, 310
   supported in SharePoint, 303
Content Stewards, 282
Content Types
   adding to document libraries, 195
   associating workflows with, 343
   creating External Content Type, 424–427
   defining at site, Site Collection, or
      enterprise level, 143–144
   defining Content Types that use
      Site Columns, 192–195
   document sets and, 166, 175
   elements contained in, 142–143
   hierarchical organization of, 143
   inheriting metadata values from parents, 145
   list of types used by other organizations, 145
   in metadata architecture, 139
   planning, 144
   policies and standards, 117
   Site Collections and, 68
   syndication of, 166
context menus, workflows and, 334
Contribute permissions
   assigning permission levels, 259
   default permissions for users/groups, 250
   Members having, 278
contribution rights, to libraries, 267
corporate branding. *see* branding
Corporate Communications department, 120–121
Crawler Impact Rules, 315–316
Create Lists & Form, SharePoint Designer, 427
Create Page option, 80
CRM, linking SharePoint to back-end
      systems, 455
Current Navigation, site navigation options, 82
Custom Groups, 246, 249
custom page layouts, 393–394
custom user experience (UX), 389–390

custom workflows
   action options, 343–346
   adding Content Types to workflow tasks, 349
   adding send e-mail action to workflows,
      347–349
   association options, 343
   capturing workflow history log, 349–351
   creating site workflow, 343
   designing with Visio 2010, 355–357
   developing with SharePoint Designer, 340–341
   importing from Visio into SharePoint
      Designer, 357–360
   testing, 351–354
   Visio template for, 354–355
customization, dealing with during upgrade, 502

D
dashboards
   agility in, 417
   BI (business intelligence) and, 402–403
   deciding which presentation tool to use,
      405–406
   development in PerformancePoint
      Services, 414
   integration of PerformancePoint Services with
      SharePoint, 413
   scorecards compared with, 404
   strategic use of, 416
data
   quality and timeliness of, 399
   representing enterprise data. *see* BCS
      (Business Connectivity Services)
   representing local data. *see* composite
      applications
   working with offline. *see* SPW (SharePoint
      Workspace)
data caching, in Office 2010 suite, 450–453
data types, for list field definitions, 529
database administration, factors in planning site
      architecture, 134–135
database servers
   deployment options and, 90–92
   server roles in SharePoint, 90
databases
   file server scenarios for storing, 41
   migration of content database, 504–505

selecting values from external sources, 433
SQL Server as database service, 28–29, 62
Decomposition Tree, in PerformancePoint
    Services, 414
Default Groups, 246–248
default workflows
    associating workflows with lists, 330–331
    checking status of, 335–338
    start-up options, 331–332
    starting from Office 2010 client, 335
    starting manually, 332–335
    testing, 331–332
default.master, working with master pages, 391
demoted sites, planning searches and, 316
departmental solution, in n-server deployment, 92
deploying content. *see* content deployment
deploying SharePoint 2010
    content database migration, 504–505
    dealing with customization during
        upgrades, 502
    determining best plan for, 505–507
    electronic forms and document workflow and,
        493–494
    governance and, 492
    new features in SharePoint 2010 and, 500–501
    overview of, 489–490
    in-place upgrades, 504
    planning upgrade, 490–492
    rebuild migrations, 505
    reviewing key points regarding, 511
    SharePoint-driven business processes and,
        492–493
    site structure and hierarchy and, 500
    social computing, preparing for, 495–496
    timing upgrade, 497–499
    upgrade and migration options, 502–503
    upgrade considerations, 507–510
    user comfort, skill levels, and training, 501
    working with content offline, 496–497
deployment options, in SharePoint
    architecture, 90–94
design
    metadata architecture, 139–140
    page, 116–117
    policies and standards for, 115
    principles for page architecture, 136–137

roles and responsibilities in, 103
search, 303–304
site, 115–116
design document, creating, 305–307
Design permissions
    default permissions for users/groups, 250
    Owners having, 278
desktop search, in SPW (SharePoint Workspace),
    445
Destination Site Collection, 380
Details area, My Sites, 212–213
developers
    benefits of SharePoint for, 4
    new features in SharePoint for, 33
    source control and, 42
diagramming techniques, applying to site archi-
    tecture, 133–134
differential backups
    cataloging, 470
    features of Central Administration
        backup and restore tool, 469
    overview of, 471
digital asset management, 383
DIP (Document Information Panel), 184–185
disaster recovery. *see* DR (disaster recovery)
discussion boards, guidelines and
    policies for, 119
disk storage, cost and space issues, 44
Disposition Approval workflow, 329
DM (Document Management)
    check-out required, 174–175
    configuring, 192–199
    Content Approval, 169–170
    defined, 164
    DIP (Document Information Panel), 184–185
    Document Center, 185–186
    document IDs, 178–180
    document libraries, 167–168
    document sets, 175–178
    document version history, 170–172
    Draft Item Security, 172–173
    item-level security, 168
    managed metadata, 180–182
    overview of, 167
    version management, 168–169
    workflows and, 182–184

Document Center, 185–186
document IDs
   new ECM features in SharePoint, 165–166
   overview of, 178–180
Document Information Panel (DIP), 184–185
document libraries
   adding Content Types to, 195
   adding document sets to, 176
   adding files to, 525–527
   applying security to, 519–521
   check-out required, 174
   content tagging and, 529–531
   creating, 516–517
   Document Center and, 185–186
   external data as metadata in, 549–550
   guidelines and policies for, 119–120
   overview of, 167–168
   storing reports in, 401
   viewing available workflows in, 330
Document Management. *see* DM (Document
   Management)
document sets, 165, 175–178
document templates
   adding to document libraries, 529–531
   contained in Content Types, 143
documentation
   for disaster recovery, 466–467
   of governance plan. *see* governance plan
   of training plans, 275–276
documents
   document workflow in SharePoint
      deployment, 493–494
   folder limitations for organizing, 140–142
   initiating workflows, 540–542
   metadata as classification framework for, 138
   Office 2010, 450–453
   recovering from Recycle Bin, 531–532
   synchronizing changes with branch cache,
      453–454
   version history, 170–172
   working with offline, 450–453, 539–540
Domain Groups, 245–246
domain knowledge, building information
   architecture and, 126
DR (disaster recovery)
   backup and restore options, 467–468
   command-line backup tools, 479–480

creating operations document for, 466–467
   examining backup files, 471–475
   features of Central Administration backup and
      restore tool, 468–469
   limitations of SharePoint backup, 484–486
   overview of, 465
   planning for, 466
   reviewing key points regarding, 486
   scheduling backups, 480
   SQL Server Backup and Restore, 483–484
   two stage restore from Recycle Bin, 480–483
   using Backup utility, 469–471
   using Restore utility, 475–479
Draft Item Security, 172–173
Drop-off library, 166
dumps, file server scenarios for handling, 43
dynamic reports, in BI (business intelligence),
   401

E
e-mail
   corporate knowledge lost in, 495
   workflows as alternative to, 325
ECM (enterprise content management)
   auditing, 189–190
   check-out required, 174–175
   configuring document and records
      management, 192–199
   Content Approval, 169–170
   DIP (Document Information Panel), 184–185
   Document Center, 185–186
   document IDs, 178–180
   document libraries, 167–168
   document management, 167
   document sets, 175–178
   document version history, 170–172
   Draft Item Security, 172–173
   getting started with, 164–165
   Information Management Policies, 190–191
   item-level security in, 168
   managed metadata and, 180–182
   new features in SharePoint 2010, 33, 165–167
   overview of, 163
   record declaration, 186–188
   records management, 186
   reviewing key points regarding, 199
   in SharePoint Server 2010, 30

version management, 168–169
WCM (Web content management) and, 373
workflows and, 182–184
Edit Memberships, 222–223
Edit mode, adding/removing Web Parts
    on sites, 524
Editor, custom permissions and, 251
electronic forms
    creating, 360–361
    as option when deploying SharePoint 2010,
        493–494
employees
    recruiting, 204–205
    training, 277
end users. *see* users
Enterprise Edition
    Business Data Web Parts, 434
    Excel Services in, 407
    features in, 34–35
    form services, 35, 369–371
    PerformancePoint Services in, 411
    Standard Edition compared with, 26–27
    user tasks requiring, 514, 553
    Visio Graphics Services in, 359–360
enterprise level
    content management. *see* ECM (enterprise
        content management)
    data management. *see* BCS (Business
        Connectivity Services)
    defining Content Types and Columns at, 143–144
    search portal, 294
    wikis, 233–237
Enterprise Search Center, 301
equals (=) sign, searching for numeric
    values, 297
ERP, linking SharePoint to back-end systems, 455
evaluation skills, information literacy and, 278
Excel
    charts in, 402
    client applications that connect with
        SharePoint 2010, 442
    client-side information worker components,
        21–22
    Connect and Export for taking data offline, 456
    DIP (Document Information Panel) and,
        184–185
    Enterprise Edition and, 35

publishing workbook for Web rendering,
    550–552
recommendations for working with documents
    and data offline, 457
SharePoint as replacement for, 45–46
Web and mobile applications for, 459
working with data offline, 540
Excel Calculation Engine, 408
Excel Services
    business benefits of, 416
    charts in, 402
    composite applications and, 420
    getting started with, 408
    how it works, 408–410
    overview of, 406–407
    publishing Excel file to, 552
    support for, 442
    what's new in SharePoint 2010, 410–411
Excel Web Access, 408
Excel Web Services, 408
Exchange Server 2010
    as collaboration platform, 23
    in Microsoft's information worker platform,
        21–22, 31
exclusions/inclusions, in searches, 297
executables, file server scenarios, 42
executive sponsor, 104
executives
    getting participation in communications
        plan, 284
    getting sponsorship of communication plan, 283
    stakeholders in SharePoint strategy, 8
experts
    improving access to internal, 203
    leveraging existing, 283
expiration policies, documents, 190–191
External Content Type
    creating, 424–427
    external list creation, 427–430
    overview of, 421–422
    searching external data, 547–548
    showing external data in Web Parts, 550
    using external data as metadata in
        document libraries, 549–550
External Data Column
    selecting values from external sources, 433
    using, 432

external lists
    adding custom actions to, 430–432
    creating, 427–430
    External Data Columns and, 422
    working with offline, 444–445
extranets, 29

F
Farm Administrators, 248
Fast Search Center, 302
federated locations, searches and, 315–316
field controls, for media, 394–395
file server scenarios, 40–41
file shares
    reasons why file storage is still needed, 38–45
    SharePoint as replacement for, 35–38
files
    adding to document libraries, 525–527
    caching, 450–452
    restoring from Recycle Bin, 531–532
    saving Office files to SharePoint, 527–529
    working with offline, 453
filtering
    configuring key filters for indexing, 181–183
    list content based on audience, 543
    property filters in searches, 296
five-server deployment, 91
folders, limitations for document organization,
        140–142
formats
    content policies and standards, 114
    ribbon interface as formatting tool, 384–385
forms, defining for use with Content Types, 143
forms, InfoPath
    creating, 362–366
    electronic forms, 360–361
    form services in SharePoint, 35, 369–371
    introduction to, 361–362
    publishing for Web rendering, 552
    publishing to SharePoint libraries, 366–367
    reviewing key points regarding, 371
    SPW (SharePoint Workspace) and, 445
    testing, 367–369
four-server deployment, 91
FrontPage, as predecessor of SharePoint
        Designer, 338

FrontPage Server Extensions. *see also* Office
        Server Extensions, 24
full backups, 470–471
Full Control permissions
    assigning, 259
    default permissions for users/groups, 250
    security elements for groups, 241
functional groupings, in planning site architecture,
        131–132
functionality, user experience and, 389

G
getting started
    business objectives in SharePoint strategy, 9–14
    key feature areas, 4–5
    key stakeholders in SharePoint strategy, 7–9
    overview of, 3
    planning SharePoint strategy, 5–7
    reviewing key points regarding, 19
    success metrics, 15–18
global features, in SharePoint 2010, 3
Global Navigation, 82
goals. *see* business objectives
Google, as search tool, 294
governance board/steering committee, 104
governance plan
    blogs and wikis, 215–216
    community features, 209
    content policies and standards in, 113–115
    content-specific guidelines and
        policies, 118–121
    Content Types and metadata and, 117
    creating, 100
    design, 115
    guiding principles in, 106–112
    importance of, 97–100
    My Sites, 209–214
    new features in, 98–99
    overview of, 97
    page design, 116–117
    policies and standards in, 112–113
    ratings and tags, 215
    reviewing key points regarding, 121
    roles and responsibilities in, 103–106
    site design, 115–116
    social tags and ratings, 117–118

upgrades, 492
vision statement for, 102
what is included in, 100–102
Groove. *see also* SPW (SharePoint Workspace)
    classic Groove workspaces in SPW, 445
    upgrade for, 440
    working with documents offline, 540
Group Work Site, 234
groups
    checking group permissions, 263–264, 266
    controlling access to drafts, 173
    custom, 249
    default, 247–248
    list of groups needed in security model,
        257–260
    security elements for, 241
    security model and, 244–246
guidelines, content-specific, 118–121
guiding principles
    content, 110–111
    general, 107
    governance, 106–112
    security, 108
    site design, 108–109

H

hardware configuration, for searches, 311–312
help centers, 276
Help Desk role, 281
hierarchical diagram, in planning site
        architecture, 133–134
hierarchical organization
    of Content Types, 143
    of sites, 500
history log, workflows, 349–351
home page
    communication function of, 256
    posting content to, 114–115
HTML content, managing, 375

I

i-Filters, configuring searches and, 312
"I like it" tags, 224
IA (Information architecture)
    Columns, 146–151
    Content Types, 142–145

foundational elements in, 126–127
maintaining, 160–161
Managed Metadata and. *see* Managed
        Metadata
metadata. *see* metadata architecture
overview of, 123–125
pages. *see* page architecture
reviewing key points regarding, 161–162
sites. *see* site architecture
types of information needed to develop, 127–128
what's new, 125–126
identifiers, document. *see* document IDs
images
    managing Web content, 375
    in page architecture design, 137
Import from Visio icon, on ribbon interface, 357
importing workflows, from Visio into SharePoint
        Designer, 357–360
in-place records management
    declaring records in-place, 186–188
    enabling, 195–199
    vs. central management, 167
In-place Upgrade
    overview of, 504
    pros/cons, 503
    tools for, 490
inclusions/exclusions, in searches, 297
indexing
    configuring automatic Column indexing for
        lists, 181, 183
    search component for, 302–303
InfoPath 2010
    client applications that connect with
        SharePoint 2010, 442
    client-side information worker components,
        21–22
    creating forms, 362–366
    creating forms as alternative to lists, 427
    forms services, 35, 369–371
    introduction to, 361–362
    overview of, 360–361
    publishing forms for Web rendering, 552
    publishing forms to SharePoint libraries,
        366–367
    SPW (SharePoint Workspace) and, 445
    testing forms, 367–369

information
   business intelligence and, 399
   gathering for defining search requirements,
      306
   information architecture reducing information
      overload, 124–125
   literacy skills, 278–279
   routing via workflows, 326
Information architecture. *see* IA (Information
      architecture)
information management policies
   elements contained in Content Types, 143
   records management and, 190–191
information management, Site Collections
      and, 69
Information Rights Management (IRM), 243–244
information stores, allowing users to add content
      to, 204
information technology. *see* IT (information
      technology)
information worker products, Microsoft, 31
inheritance
   navigation and, 516
   of permissions, 242
   planning security and, 256
insights. *see also* BI (business intelligence),
      4–5, 30
instances, workflow, 328
Internet
   branding standards for presence on, 120
   reasons for using SharePoint for Internet-facing
      sites, 374–375
   site management and, 29
   user ratings and, 388
Internet mode, of SharePoint Server, 27
Internet solution, n-server deployment, 92–94
interviews, in planning site architecture, 130
intranet solution, n-server deployment, 92
intranets
   branding standards for presence on, 120
   managing, 29
   searches and, 294
IRM (Information Rights Management), 243–244
IT (information technology)
   information architecture reducing costs of, 124
   IT Pro, 4, 33

   stakeholders in SharePoint strategy, 7–8
   support for, 493
item-level auditing, 189
item-level security
   in document management, 168
   setting, 520–521
items
   lists containing, 78–79
   overview of, 65

K
key filters, configuring, 181–183
Key Performance Indicators. *see* KPIs (Key
      Performance Indicators)
keywords
   managed keywords, 150–152
   in searches, 296, 318
KPIs (Key Performance Indicators)
   creating, 546–548
   KPI Details report, 414
   overview of, 404–405

L
launch and communications plan, 216–217, 282
layout, of pages, 116–117
LCS (Live Communications Server), 23–24
learning skills, in information literacy, 279
libraries
   compared with lists, 167
   contribution rights to, 267
   document libraries. *see* document libraries
   document version history, 170
   IRM (Information Rights Management),
      243–244
   populating sites with, 78–79
   publishing InfoPath forms to libraries, 366–367
Limited Access permissions, 250
line-of-business (LOB), application features in
      SharePoint Server 2010, 64
Linked Web Parts, in PerformancePoint
      Services, 414
links
   content policies and standards, 114
   guidelines and policies for, 119
list actions, workflows, 345
list item menu, 430–432

List Template Gallery, 79
List Workflows, 341–342
lists
    adding custom actions to external, 430–432
    applying security to, 519–521
    associating workflows with, 330–331, 343
    backing up/restoring, 469
    compared with libraries, 167
    configuring automatic Column indexing for
        lists, 181, 183
    creating, 516–517
    creating external, 427–430
    creating KPI list item, 546–548
    creating new view on, 521–522
    document version history, 170
    exposing as RSS feeds, 535–536
    filtering/targeting content based on
        audience, 543
    fundamental concepts in SharePoint, 65
    initiating workflows on, 540–542
    IRM (Information Rights Management) and,
        243–244
    leveraging for content presentation, 374
    populating sites with, 78–79
    Visio Services supporting, 415
    working with offline, 447, 449
Lists & Forms group, SharePoint Designer, 427
Live Communications Server (LCS), 23–24
LOB (line-of-business), application features in
        SharePoint Server 2010, 64
logging document or list activity, 327
Lotus Notes, 23

M
maintenance
    Excel Services and, 409
    of security model, 263
major versions, in document version
        management, 169–172
Manage Hierarchy permissions, 250
Manage Permissions, 241, 251–252
Manage section, of ribbon interface, 357
managed keywords, 150–152
Managed Metadata
    managing terms and term sets, 153–159
    in metadata architecture, 139

new ECM features in SharePoint, 166
    overview of, 152, 180–182
    searching for Web content, 387–388
    sharing values and, 146, 152–153
managed terms
    benefits of, 158–159
    defining, 157–158
    types of Managed Metadata, 152
manual workflows, 332–335
master pages, 390–392
media
    field controls, 394–395
    file server scenarios, 41–42
Meet the Portal phase, in page architecture
        design, 137
meetings, for recurrent training, 276
Members
    Read and Contribute permissions, 278
    training requirements, 279–281
    user roles, 277
Memberships section, of user profile, 222–223
mentoring, benefits of collaboration
        technologies, 204
menu-based navigation, 82
messages, of communication plans, 285–289
metadata
    adding to document libraries for
        content tagging, 529–531
    Content Types inheriting, 145
    defining Content Types that use
        Site Columns, 192
    as document classification framework, 138
    elements contained in Content Types, 142–143
    managing. see Managed Metadata
    policies and standards, 117
    roles and responsibilities, 103
    sharing across Site Collections, 99
    using external data as in document libraries,
        549–550
metadata architecture
    document classification and, 138
    elements used in designing, 139–140
    IA (Information architecture) and, 138–142
    levels or taxonomies in, 129
    limitations of folders for document
        organization, 140–142

metadata properties, in searches, 309, 316–317
metadata steering committee, 105
metrics
    keeping it simple, 416–417
    for measuring success of strategies, 15–18
    in PerformancePoint Services, 412
    showing performance against goals, 402–403
Microsoft
    Access. *see* Access
    evolution of collaboration in Microsoft
        technologies, 23–26
    Excel. *see* Excel
    information worker products, 31
    Office 2010. *see* Office 2010 suite
    OneNote. *see* OneNote
    Outlook. *see* Outlook 2010
    PerformancePoint Server 2007, 411
    PowerPoint. *see* PowerPoint
    Project, 443
    Project Server 2010, 22
    Publisher, 21–22
    Visio 2010. *see* Visio 2010
    Visual Studio 2010, 26, 327
    Word. *see* Word
Microsoft Office SharePoint Server. *see* MOSS
    (Microsoft Office SharePoint Server)
migration
    of content database, 504–505
    options, 502–503
    SharePoint 2007 to SharePoint 2010. *see*
        deploying SharePoint 2010
    visual upgrade strategy, 271
mind mapping tools, for documenting site
    architecture, 133
MindManager, 133
minimal.master, working with master pages, 391
minor versions, in document version management,
    169–172
minus (-) sign, for exclusions in searches, 297
mobile applications, Office 2010, 441, 459–462
monitoring searches, 319
MOSS (Microsoft Office SharePoint Server)
    ECM and, 373
    evolution of collaboration in Microsoft
        technologies, 26
    SharePoint Server 2010 successor to, 27

SSPs (Shared Service Providers), 83–84
    upgrading to SharePoint 2010, 507–508
multilingual support, in SharePoint 2010, 383
multiuser collaboration, in Excel Services, 410
My Sites
    Basic Information, 209–212
    Contact Information and Details areas, 212–213
    introduced in SharePoint Portal Server
        2003, 30
    managing information on, 544–546
    Memberships tab, 222–223
    Preferences area, 213
    status update area, 214
    user profiles, 217–218

N

n-server deployment
    departmental solution, 92
    Internet solution, 92–94
    intranet solution, 92
    overview of, 91–92
names, content policies and standards, 114
navigation
    enhancing site's navigation, 537–539
    factors in planning site architecture, 134–135
    inheritance and, 516
    metadata managing, 181–183
    new features in SharePoint 2010, 32
    planning security and, 256
    ribbon interface for, 81–82
    structure or taxonomy of, 500
.NET Framework
    providing Web Part Framework for
        SharePoint Server, 27
    SharePoint built on, 62
newsletters, 283
notes, 224–227
numeric values, in searches, 297–298

O

objectives. *see* business objectives
objects
    displaying permissions levels of, 264–266
    securable, 240–243
    security at object level, 256
    security trimming and, 243

ODBC data sources, Visio Services supporting, 415

Office 2010 suite
Backstage and, 458–459
BCS (Business Connectivity Services) and, 422–423
clients. *see* clients, Office 2010
DIP (Document Information Panel) and, 184–185
documents and data caching, 450–453
information worker products, 31
introduction to, 28–31
Office Server Extensions, 24
saving files to SharePoint, 527–529
searches from within, 299–300
synchronization of document changes and branch cache, 453–454
usability issues addressed by ribbon interface, 457–458
Web applications and mobile applications, 459–462
working with data offline, 454–457

Office Communications Server 2010, 21–22, 31
Office Communicator (client), 31
Office Server Extensions, 24
Office Upload Center
caching SharePoint files, 450–452
client applications that connect with SharePoint 2010, 442
recommendations for working with documents and data offline, 457
working with documents offline, 540

offline
SPW (SharePoint Workspace) extending capabilities for working, 444
working documents offline, 539–540

offline content, deploying SharePoint 2010 and, 496–497

OneNote
client applications that connect with SharePoint 2010, 442
client-side information worker components, 21–22
improvements to, 440
Web and mobile applications for, 460

online training, 275

ontologies. *see also* IA (Information architecture), 123

operating systems (OSs)
providing core server and workflow services for SharePoint Server, 27
Windows Server 2008 as, 62

Operation Designer, 424, 426
operations document, for disaster recovery, 466–467
OR, Boolean expressions used in searches, 297
Oracle, linking SharePoint to back-end systems, 455
organization browsers, 219–221
organizational structure, site architecture not based on, 130–131
OSC (Outlook Social Connector), 442
OSs (operating systems)
providing core server and workflow services for SharePoint Server, 27
Windows Server 2008 as, 62

Outlook 2010
BCS solutions and, 422–423
client applications that connect with SharePoint 2010, 442
client-side information worker components, 21–22
document synchronization with SharePoint is read-only, 452–453
recommendations for working with documents and data offline, 457
working with calendars offline, 455
working with data offline, 540
working with documents offline, 539

Outlook 97, collaboration in, 23
Outlook Social Connector (OSC), 442
Owners
Design permissions, 278
training requirements by role, 279–281
user roles, 277

P

page architecture
design principles for, 136–137
levels or taxonomies in, 128
organizing content on pages, 135
stakeholder review of, 137

page architecture (*contd.*)
wire framing tools for creating iterations, 137–138
page layouts
creating custom, 393–394
including rich media in, 395
organization in, 116–117
overview of, 392–393
working with, 392–394
pages
adding Web Parts to, 523–524
design, 116–117
overview of, 80
roles and responsibilities, 103
vs. sites, 72
people searches, 320
people (users or groups). *see also* groups; users
security elements for, 241
security model and, 244–246
PerformancePoint Server 2007, 411
PerformancePoint Services
business benefits of, 416
Enterprise Edition and, 35
how it works, 412
overview of, 411
reasons for using, 412–413
what's new in SharePoint 2010, 413–414
permissions
applying, 260–262
applying to sites or workspaces, 518–519
assigning to securable objects, 240–243
best practices, 252
checking group, 263–264, 266
content approval and, 173
displaying permissions levels of objects, 264–266
inheritance of, 242
item-level security and, 520–522
listing/describing permissions levels in security model, 257, 259
managing security at site-level, 256
in security model, 249–252
setting site permissions, 516
for team sites, 247–248
Personal Documents library, 221
Personal Information Management (PIM)
Exchange and, 23
Outlook 2010 used for, 442

picture libraries, guidelines and policies for, 119
pilot project, for communities, 216
PIM (Personal Information Management)
Exchange and, 23
Outlook 2010 used for, 442
planning
Columns, 147
Content Types, 144
for disaster recovery, 466
electronic forms and/or automated workflows, 494
governance plan. *see* governance plan
security model. *see* security model
SharePoint strategy, 5–7
upgrades, 490–492
planning searches
components needed in search topology, 311
configuration options, 307
content source configuration options, 307, 310
content source crawl schedules, 308
documenting service account credentials, 308, 310–311
hardware configuration, 311–312
metadata property mappings in, 309
scopes and, 309
storage estimates for capacity planning, 311
topology scale and, 312
plus (+) sign, for inclusions in searches, 297
policies
content, 113–115, 118–121
in governance plan, 112–113
Information Management Policies, 190–191
portals
activities that promote, 284
definition of, 84
features in SharePoint 2010, 34, 63
searches and, 294
for SharePoint Server 2010, 29
supporting adoption of business processes, 493
upgrade process and, 500
Power Users
advanced training for, 282
roles and responsibilities, 105
training and, 276–277
PowerPoint
client applications that connect with SharePoint 2010, 443

client-side information worker components, 21–22
DIP (Document Information Panel) and, 184–185
for documenting site architecture, 133
Web and mobile applications for, 460
PowerShell. *see* Windows PowerShell
Preferences area, My Sites, 213
prefix matching, in searches, 297
prefixes, document IDs and, 179
presentation
    choosing best tools for, 405–406
    Excel Services and, 409
presentation tier, for business intelligence data, 399
product distribution, with Windows file servers, 40
productivity
    benefit of information architecture, 124
    impact of upgrade on, 501
    searches enhancing, 293–294
Project, client applications that connect with SharePoint 2010, 443
Project Server 2010, in Microsoft's information worker platform, 22
property filters, in searches, 296
Publisher, client-side information worker components, 21–22
publishing
    forms to SharePoint libraries, 366–367
    site templates, 378
Publishing Approval workflow, 329
publishing sites
    default permissions for, 250–251
    WCM (Web content management) and, 377–380

Q
qualitative metrics, 15–18
quantitative metrics, 15–18
query components, searches, 302–303
quotas, Site Collections and, 69

R
RAID 5, for SharePoint Data drives, 44
ratings
    policies, 117–118, 215
    for sites, 388

standards, 117–118
upgrade process and, 495
user contributed content adding value, 227–229
Read permissions
    assigning, 259–260
    default permissions for users/groups, 250
    Members having, 278
    Visitors having, 277
rebuild migration
    overview of, 505
    pros/cons, 503
records management
    auditing, 189–190
    configuring, 192–199
    defined, 164
    features in SharePoint Server 2010 Standard Edition, 34
    governance plan and, 99
    Information Management Policies, 190–191
    overview of, 186
    in-place management vs. central management, 167
    record declaration, 186–188
    records retention, 115
recruitment, as benefit of collaboration technologies, 204–205
Recycle Bin
    configuring, 481
    overview of, 480–481
    recovering documents from, 531–532
    restoring items from, 481–483
regulatory compliance, 189
relational actions, workflows, 345
relational database, SQL Server, 62
relationship capital, building via collaboration technologies, 203
relevancy, in searches, 301, 544
reports
    BI (business intelligence), 400–402
    deciding which presentation tool to use, 405–406
    KPI Details report, 414
    in PerformancePoint Services, 414
resource governor, controlling number of items viewed, 79
responsibilities. *see* roles and responsibilities
Restore utility, 475–479

restores
    features of Central Administration backup and
        restore tool, 468–469
    New vs. Overwrite, 479
    options, 467–468
    reviewing key points regarding, 486
    SQL Server Backup and Restore, 483–484
    two stage restore from Recycle Bin, 480–483
    using Restore utility, 475–478
Restricted Read permissions, 251
retention policies
    documents, 191
    Site Collections and, 69
Reusable Workflows, 341–342
reviewing
    content policies and standards, 115
    page architecture with stakeholders, 137
    site architecture with stakeholders, 133
ribbon interface
    adding custom actions to, 430–432
    consistency of look and feel with, 271
    content administration and, 501
    context-sensitive options, 538
    as formatting tool, 384–385
    Manage section, 357
    navigation with, 81
    Office and Windows client
        integration with, 444
    rich media control on, 395
    usability issues addressed by, 457–458
    Workflows icon on, 334
rich media, 394–395
richer user experience, 383–385
roles and responsibilities
    in governance plan, 103–106
    Help Desk role, 281
    training plans by role, 277–281
    training requirements by role, 279–281
RSS feeds, exposing list data as, 535–536
rules-based logic, organizing content with, 166, 386

S
sandbox solutions, 99
scope
    planning searches and, 309
    of searches, 317–318

scorecards
    agility in, 417
    BI (business intelligence), 403–404
    deciding which presentation tool to use,
        405–406
    KPIs (Key Performance Indicators), 404–405
    in PerformancePoint Services, 413
    strategic use of, 416
scrolling, page design and, 116, 136
Search Service Application page, 315–316
searches
    advanced, 298–299
    alerts and, 298
    analysis and design of, 303–304
    application features in SharePoint
        Server 2010, 63
    authoritative pages and demoted sites, 316
    benefits of SharePoint for Internet-facing
        sites, 374
    Boolean expressions used in, 297
    business analysis, 304
    as business capability, 293–294
    configuring, 312–313
    for content, 544
    content sources and, 313–315
    content tags improving, 529–531
    creating business requirements document,
        304–305
    creating design document, 305–307
    for external data, 547–548
    features in SharePoint 2010, 4–5, 33, 319–320
    features in SharePoint Server 2010, 30, 34
    federated locations and, 315–316
    how they work, 300
    improvements to, 383
    inclusions/exclusions, 297
    index and query components, 302–303
    keywords in, 296, 318
    limitations in SharePoint 2010, 320
    metadata architecture supporting, 129
    metadata properties and, 316–317
    monitoring and enhancing, 319
    for numeric values, 297–298
    from within Office, 299–300
    overview of, 293
    planning, 307–312

prefix matching, 297
property filters in, 296
reports and, 401
research skills and, 278
reviewing key points regarding, 322
scope of, 317–318
selecting right search option, 320–322
site templates used for, 301–302
URL searches, 298
user experience of, 300–301
user interface for, 318
using, 294–295
securable objects, 240–243
security
    applying to lists and document libraries,
        519–521
    applying to sites or workspaces, 517
    Draft Item Security, 172–173
    Excel Services and, 409
    exceptions, 243–244
    factors in planning site architecture, 134
    guidelines and policies for, 120
    guiding principles for, 108
    item-level, 168
security model
    applying permissions, 260–262
    checking group permissions, 263–264, 266
    custom groups, 249
    default groups, 247–248
    displaying permissions levels of objects,
        264–266
    example of complete model, 262
    listing/describing access needs, 257–258
    listing/describing groups needed, 257–260
    listing/describing permissions levels, 257, 259
    listing/describing unique security needs,
        253–256
    maintaining, 263
    overview of, 239–240
    people and groups and, 244–246
    permissions in, 249–252
    preparing for social computing during
        upgrade process, 496
    restores and, 476
    reviewing key points regarding, 268–269
    securable objects, 240–243

security exceptions, 243–244
security trimming, 243
    steps in defining and documenting, 252–253
    troubleshooting, 266–267
security table
    access defined in, 258
    sample of, 255
security trimming, 243, 519
send e-mail action, adding to site workflow,
    347–349
server farms
    architecture options for content
        deployment, 381
    governance plan and, 99
    selecting farm components for backup, 468
server roles, in SharePoint, 89–90
service accounts
    documenting credentials for, 308, 310–311
    unattended service accounts in
        Excel Services, 411
service applications
    adding functionality to sites with, 83–84
    features provided by, 64–65
    fundamental concepts in SharePoint, 66
service level agreements (SLAs), 103
sessions, recurrent training, 276
shapes, SharePoint workflows, 357
Shared Documents library, 221–222
Shared Service Providers (SSPs), 83–84
SharePoint 2003, migrating to
    SharePoint 2010, 490
SharePoint 2007, migrating to SharePoint 2010.
    see deploying SharePoint 2010
SharePoint 2010 platform, introduction to
    Access and Excel and, 45–46
    building example collaborative application.
        see collaborative application, building
        in SharePoint Server
    comparing SharePoint Foundation with
        SharePoint Server, 34–37
    evolution of collaboration in Microsoft
        technologies, 23–26
    as file share replacement, 35–38
    Office 2010 suite and, 28–31
    overview of, 21–23
    reasons why file storage is still needed, 38–45

SharePoint 2010 platform, introduction to (*contd.*)
  reviewing key points regarding, 57–59
  versions, 26–27
  what's new, 32–33
SharePoint Designer
  adding custom actions to list item menu and
    ribbon, 430–432
  building custom workflows, 327
  client applications that connect with
    SharePoint 2010, 443
  composite applications and, 420
  creating workflows with, 29, 340–341
  development options for SharePoint
    platform, 26
  importing workflows from Visio into, 357–360
  Lists & Forms group, 427
  Workflow Information page, 342
  workflow type options, 341–342
SharePoint Foundation 2010
  BCS (Business Connectivity Services) and,
    422–423
  comparing SharePoint Server 2010 with, 34–37
  database service used by, 28–29
  information worker products, 31
  in Microsoft's information worker platform, 21
  platform capabilities added to
    SharePoint Server, 63
  service applications hosted within, 83
  user tasks requiring, 513–514, 552–553
  as version of SharePoint platform, 26
  workflow capability in, 327
  WSS 3.0 upgrade to, 507–508
SharePoint Groups
  listing/describing groups needed in security
    model, 257–260
  types of groups in SharePoint, 245–246
SharePoint Online, 27
SharePoint Portal Server 2003, 30
SharePoint Portal Server (SPS), 24–25
SharePoint Server 2010
  application features, 63–64
  BCS (Business Connectivity Services) and,
    422–423
  comparing SharePoint Foundation with, 34–37
  editions of, 26–27
  Enterprise Edition. *see* Enterprise Edition

  features, 34–35
  information worker products, 31
  in Microsoft's information worker platform,
    21–22
  Office 2010 suite and, 27–31
  server roles, 90
  service applications, 64–65
  Standard Edition. *see* Standard Edition
  workflow capability in, 327
SharePoint Server 2010 for Internet Sites, 27
SharePoint Team Services (STS), 23
SharePoint Web-based solution, 422–423
SharePoint Workspace. *see* SPW (SharePoint
    Workspace)
simple.master, working with master pages, 391
single-server deployment, 90
Site Actions menu
  creating new list or document library
    from, 517
  creating new site from, 515
site architecture
  approaches to organizing sites, 131–133
  brainstorming with stakeholders as planning
    technique, 130
  diagramming, 133–134
  evolving to meet user needs, 129–130
  levels or taxonomies of, 128
  not basing on organizational structure, 130–131
  reviewing with stakeholders, 133
  site administration and, 134–135
Site Collection Administrators, 247–248
Site Collections
  assigning unique IDs to documents in, 178–179
  configuring searches, 313
  Content Types and metadata and, 117
  creating Columns as, 146
  defining Content Types and Columns at,
    143–144
  document sets and, 166
  enabling Recycle Bin, 481
  fundamental concepts in SharePoint, 65
  overview of, 67–69
  recovering, 465
  search services, 301
  settings, 86–87
  turning on Publishing feature in, 378–379

Site Columns. *see also* metadata, 192
site designer role, 106
Site Pages library, 80
Site Settings, 380
site sponsor/owner role, 106
site steward role, 106
site templates
    creating new site from, 515
    fundamental concepts in SharePoint,
        65–66
    out-of-the-box, 75–76
    overview of, 74
    saving customizations as templates, 76–77
    searches using, 301–302
    selecting with Silverlight-based menu, 71
    storing, 78
    types of, 377
site workflows
    capturing workflow history log, 349–351
    creating, 343, 346–347
    send e-mail action added to, 347–349
    task added to, 349
    testing, 351–354
    workflow type options, 341–342
sites
    adding functionality to, 83–84
    adding users to, 73
    administering, 134–135
    applying security to, 517
    backing up/restoring, 469
    creating new, 69–72
    creating site workflow, 343, 346–347
    defining Content Types and Columns at site
        level, 143–144
    deploying SharePoint 2010 and, 500
    designing, 115–116
    enhancing navigation of, 537–539
    fundamental concepts in SharePoint, 65
    guiding principles for, 108–109
    key feature areas of SharePoint 2010, 4–5
    managing security at site-level, 253–254
    organizing, 131–133
    permission levels for, 259
    populating with lists and libraries, 78–79
    posting content to, 113–115
    publishing. *see* publishing sites

reasons for using SharePoint for Internet-
        facing sites, 374–375
    recovering, 465
    roles and responsibilities, 103
    settings, 87–89
    subsites, 74
    synchronizing using SPW, 446–448
    themes, 99
    usage analysis, 389
    user ratings and, 388
    values at three levels, 66–67
    vs. pages, 72
    working with offline, 445–449
skill levels, deploying SharePoint 2010
        and, 501
SLAs (service level agreements), 103
Slicer feature, in Excel Services, 410–411
SMS, file distribution points, 40
social computing. *see also* communities
    features in SharePoint 2010, 3
    features in SharePoint Server 2010 Standard
        Edition, 34
    new features in SharePoint 2010, 32–33
    new features Office 2010, 442
    training plans and, 278
    upgrade process and, 495–496
social networking
    engaging users in, 217
    WCM (Web content management) and, 389
social tags. *see also* tags
    Managed Keywords and, 151
    new features for searches, 320
    policies and standards, 117–118
solution administrator role, 104
sorting options, new features for searches, 320
source control, file server scenarios, 42
Source Site Collection, 380
speed, in page architecture design, 136
SPS (SharePoint Portal Server), 24–25
SPW (SharePoint Workspace)
    BCS solutions and, 422
    benefits of, 444–445
    client applications that connect with
        SharePoint 2010, 443
    client-side information worker
        components, 21–22

SPW (SharePoint Workspace) (*contd.*)
  deploying SharePoint 2010 and, 496
  keeping document content synchronized and available, 450
  recommendations for working with documents and data offline, 457
  taking sites offline, 445–449
  working with data offline, 454–455, 540
  working with documents offline, 540
SQL Enterprise Manager, 483
SQL Server
  Backup and Restore, 483–484
  as database service, 28–29
  linking SharePoint to back-end systems, 455
  PerformancePoint Services supporting, 413
  providing database service for SharePoint Server, 27, 62
  Visio Services supporting, 415
SSPs (Shared Service Providers), 83–84
stakeholders
  brainstorming in planning site architecture, 130
  reviewing page architecture with, 137
  reviewing site architecture with, 133
  in SharePoint strategy, 7–9
Standard Edition
  Enterprise Edition compared with, 26–27
  features in, 34–35
  user tasks requiring, 514, 553
standards. *see also* policies
  accessibility and, 382
  branding, 120
  content, 113–115, 117
  design, 115
  metadata, 117
  ratings, 117–118
start-up options, workflows, 331–332
static reports, BI (business intelligence), 401
statistics, backup, 469
status indicators. *see* KPIs (Key Performance Indicators)
status updates, My Sites, 214, 219
status, workflows, 335–338
streaming media, 41–42
STS (SharePoint Team Services), 23
stsadm.exe, 479
subsites, 74, 115

success metrics, 15–18
System Settings section, of Central Administration, 86

T
Tag Cloud Web Part, 226–227
tags
  content, 529–531
  new features for searches, 320
  policies, 215
  upgrade process and, 495
  user contributed content adding value, 224–227
  users creating metadata tags for use in searches, 388
task actions, workflows, 345
task lists, Document Center and, 185–186
tasks, workflow, 349
taxonomies. *see also* IA (Information architecture), 123, 180
team sites
  creating, 514–516
  organizing content and people around specific objective, 73–74
  permissions, 247–248
  value of, 66
  as wiki, 233–234
  workspaces compared with, 71
team wikis, 233
technical management role, 103
technology. *see also* IT (information technology), 493
technology support team, 104
templates
  creating blogs with, 533
  page architecture and, 135
  page layouts and, 392–393
  saving list or libraries as, 79
  site templates, 377, 515
  viewing available workflows, 330
  Visio 2010 workflow template, 354–355
  workflow, 327–328
Term Set Planning Worksheet, 154
term sets
  creating, 156
  managing, 153–159
  planning, 155

term store
  for managing metadata, 166
  types of Managed Metadata, 152
Term Store Management Tool, 153
terms, managing, 153–159
testing
  InfoPath forms, 367–369
  workflows, 331–332, 351–354
themes, customizing sites with, 99
three-server deployment, 91
Three-State workflow, 329
time intelligence, in PerformancePoint
    Services, 414
timing, of training plans, 274–277
top-level sites
  creating, 69–70
  Site Collections and, 67
topology
  components needed in search, 311
  scale in planning searches, 312
  SharePoint deployment options and, 89
training plans
  advanced topics, 282
  approaches to, 277
  audience of, 273–274
  deploying SharePoint 2010 and, 501
  overview of, 271–273
  reviewing key points regarding, 289–290
  by SharePoint roles, 277–281
  supporting adoption of business processes,
    493
  timing of, 274–277
troubleshooting security model, 266–267
trusted locations, Excel Services and, 409, 410
two-server deployment, 90–91

U
UI (user interface). *see also* ribbon interface, 32,
  81, 318
upgrades. *see also* deploying SharePoint 2010
  considerations regarding, 507–510
  developing governance strategy prior to
    upgrade, 492
  options, 502–503
  in-place upgrade, 504
  planning, 490–492

selecting strategy based on relevant business
  cases, 506–507
timing, 497–499
WSS 3.0 to SharePoint Foundation 2010,
  507–508
Upload Center. *see* Office Upload Center
upper left principle, in page design, 117, 136–137
URLs
  sending list items as value in URL queries,
    430–431
  URL searches, 298
usability, user experience and, 389
user interface (UI). *see also* ribbon interface,
  32, 81, 318
user profiles
  Basic Information, 210
  Contact Information and Details areas, 212–213
  features in SharePoint Server 2010
    Standard Edition, 34
  Memberships section of, 222–223
  overview of, 217–218
  preferences, 213
user ratings. *see* ratings
User Solutions Gallery, 78
user tasks
  adding files to document libraries, 525–527
  adding metadata for content tagging, 529–531
  adding Web Parts to page, 523–524
  applying security to lists or document
    libraries, 519–521
  applying security to sites or workspaces, 517
  building/contributing to blogs, 532–533
  building wikis, 534–535
  creating KPIs, 546–548
  creating lists or document libraries, 516–517
  creating team sites or workspaces, 514–516
  creating views, 521–523
  enhancing site's navigation, 537–539
  exposing list data as RSS feeds, 535–536
  filtering/targeting list content based on
    audience, 543
  initiating workflow on document or list item,
    540–542
  managing information on My Sites, 544–546
  publishing Excel workbook for Web rendering,
    550–552

user tasks (*contd.*)
  publishing InfoPath forms for Web rendering, 552
  recovering documents from Recycle Bin, 531–532
  saving Office files to SharePoint, 527–529
  searching external data, 547–548
  searching for content, 544
  showing external data in Web Parts, 550
  signing in as different user, 536–537
  using external data as metadata in document libraries, 549–550
  working with document offline, 539–540
users
  adding content to information stores, 204
  adding value by contributing content, 223
  benefits of information architecture to, 124
  building information architecture and, 127
  creating activities that support training and communications plans, 283–284
  customizing user experience (UX), 389–390
  deploying SharePoint 2010 and, 501
  engaging in social networking, 217
  focus on end users, 6
  just-in-time training, 275–276
  leveraging team sites, 66
  managing expectations regarding SharePoint, 285
  richer user experience, 383–385
  roles and responsibilities, 106
  searches and, 300–301
  security elements for, 241
  security model and, 244–246
  site architecture evolving to meet needs of, 129–130
  stakeholders in SharePoint strategy, 8–9
utility actions, workflows, 346
UX (user experience)
  customizing, 389–390
  richness of, 383–385

V
v4.master, working with master pages, 390
version management
  backups and, 476

check-out requirements and, 174–175
in document management, 168–169
document version history, 170–172
Draft Item Security, 172–173
reports, 401
versions, in SharePoint 2010 platform, 26–27
video
  file server scenarios for handling, 41–42
  guidelines and policies for video libraries, 119
  media field controls, 394–395
View permissions, 251
views
  creating, 521–523
  of items in lists, 78
  options for, 523
  security exceptions, 244
Visio 2010
  client applications that connect with SharePoint 2010, 443
  creating workflows with, 29
  designing page architecture, 137
  designing workflows, 355–357
  documenting site architecture, 133
  features in SharePoint Server 2010 Enterprise Edition, 35
  graphical view of workflows with, 336
  importing workflows from Visio into SharePoint Designer, 357–360
  shape stencils for workflows, 356
  template for workflows, 354–355
Visio Graphics Services, 359–360
Visio Services
  business benefits of, 416
  composite applications and, 420
  overview of, 414–415
vision statement
  articulating long term vision, 12
  for governance plan, 102
  guiding principles supporting, 106
Visitors role
  Read permissions for, 277
  training requirements by role, 279–281
Visual Studio 2010
  building custom workflows, 327
  development options for SharePoint platform, 26

W

WCM (Web content management)
architecture of content deployment, 381–382
basic capabilities of, 375–377
content organizer in, 386–387
creating strategy for, 395–397
customizing user experience (UX), 389–390
features in Standard Edition, 34
improvements to, 382–383
managed metadata, 387–388
media field controls, 394–395
overview of, 373–374
publishing sites, 377–380
reasons for using SharePoint for
Internet-facing sites, 374–375
reviewing key points regarding, 397
richer user experience and, 383–385
social networking and, 389
terminology of content deployment, 380–381
user ratings, 388
Web Reporting and Analytics, 389
working with master pages, 390–392
working with page layouts, 392–394
Web 2.0. *see* communities
Web analytics, improvements in SharePoint
2010, 383
Web Analytics Reports, 319–320
Web applications
fundamental concepts in SharePoint, 65
Office 2010 and, 441, 459–462
Web-based forms, deploying SharePoint 2010
and, 494
Web-based meetings, 496
Web cams, 496
Web content management. *see* WCM
(Web content management)
Web front end (WFE), 90–92
Web page services, ASP.NET used by
SharePoint, 29
Web pages
document libraries holding, 168
ease of editing, 376
managing content on. *see* WCM (Web content
management)
Web Part Framework, in ASP.NET, 29
Web Part pages, 80

Web Parts
adding to pages, 523–524
building composite applications, 432–436
configuring audience on, 543
InfoPath 2010 and, 442
Linked Web Parts in PerformancePoint
Services, 414
search box of, 300–301
security exceptions, 244
showing external data in, 550
Web portals, 294
Web Reporting and Analytics, 389
Web Store database technology, 24
WFE (Web front end), 90–92
wikis
building, 534–535
guidelines and policies for, 118–119
knowledge sharing and, 204
policies, 215–216
as structure for collaborative conversations,
232–233
upgrade process and, 495–496
wildcards, in searches, 544
Windows 2003 R2, 38–40
Windows Branch Office Cache, 454, 457
Windows clients, integration with
ribbon interface, 444
Windows Explorer
adding files to SharePoint, 526
client applications that connect with
SharePoint 2010, 443
moving files between SharePoint
and other file systems, 453
recommendations for working with documents
and data offline, 457
Windows OS
providing core server and workflow services
for SharePoint Server, 27
Windows Server 2008 as, 62
Windows PowerShell
backup and restore cmdlets, 467, 479–480
in Excel Services, 411
Windows Server 2008
as base operating system for SharePoint Server
2010, 28
in Microsoft's information worker platform, 22

Windows Server 2008 (*contd.*)
  SharePoint built on, 62
  Windows Branch Office Cache, 454, 457
Windows SharePoint Services, 24–25
Windows Task Scheduler, 479–480
Windows Workflow Foundation, 29, 327
wire framing tools
  designing page architecture, 137–138
  page architecture and, 137–138
Word 2010
  client applications that connect with
    SharePoint 2010, 443
  client-side information worker components,
    21–22
  DIP (Document Information Panel) and,
    184–185
  features in SharePoint Server 2010 Enterprise
    Edition, 35
  searches from, 299
  Web and mobile applications for, 459
workbooks, Excel
  publishing for Web rendering, 550–552
  Visio Services supporting, 415
Workflow Information page, SharePoint
  Designer, 342
workflow services, Windows Workflow
  Foundation, 29, 327
workflows
  action options, 343–346
  adding tasks to site workflow, 349
  associating with lists, 330–331
  association options, 343
  capturing history log, 349–351
  checking status of, 335–338

  creating custom, 338–339
  creating site, 343, 346–347
  default, 328–329
  deploying SharePoint 2010 and, 494
  designing with Visio 2010, 355–357
  elements contained in Content Types, 143
  getting started with, 325–327
  importing from Visio into SharePoint
    Designer, 357–360
  improvements to, 382–383
  initiating on document or list item, 540–542
  overview of, 182–184, 325
  reviewing key points regarding, 371
  send e–mail action added to, 347–349
  SharePoint Designer for developing,
    340–341
  Site Collections and, 69
  start-up options, 331
  starting from Office 2010 client, 335
  starting manually, 332–335
  templates, associations, and instances, 327–328
  terminology, 327
  testing, 331–332, 351–354
  types of, 341–342
  Visio 2010 template for, 354–355
workshops, in planning site architecture, 130
workspaces
  applying security to, 517
  creating, 514–516
  team sites compared with, 71
WSS 3.0
  item-level security introduced in, 168
  upgrading to SharePoint Foundation 2010,
    507–508

Thinking SharePoint? Think Jornata.

Guiding People and Technology to Exceptional Performance

Jornata is a services provider that helps companies achieve exceptional performance by using Microsoft SharePoint and Microsoft Online Services.

Types of services we provide:

- **Vision and Strategy**: Working with executive team representatives, we offer assessment and recommendations for the effective use collaboration and social computing tools.

- **Implementation**: We can design and deploy a well-implemented SharePoint solution, delivering results with real-time knowledge transfer.

- **Development**: We love to build high-quality solutions. Our top-tier consulting team can guide a customer from whiteboard through deployment, offering prototypes via rapid application development and final delivery of well-documented custom code.

- **Training**: Our top-notch consultants and experts love to teach. We provide high-end training for IT Pros, Developers, and End-Users.

- **Support:** We believe in the long-term success of our customers. That's why we offer pre- and post-deployment support options so we can act as an escalation point for business critical application issues.

Microsoft
GOLD CERTIFIED
Partner

Business Intelligence
Custom Development Solutions
Portals and Collaboration
Search

For more information:

http://www.jornata.com

info@jornata.com

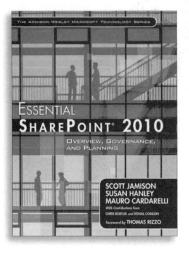

FREE Online Edition

Your purchase of *Essential SharePoint® 2010* includes access to a free online edition for 45 days through the Safari Books Online subscription service. Nearly every Addison-Wesley Professional book is available online through Safari Books Online, along with more than 5,000 other technical books and videos from publishers such as Cisco Press, Exam Cram, IBM Press, O'Reilly, Prentice Hall, Que, and Sams.

SAFARI BOOKS ONLINE allows you to search for a specific answer, cut and paste code, download chapters, and stay current with emerging technologies.

Activate your FREE Online Edition at
www.informit.com/safarifree

> **STEP 1:** Enter the coupon code: NCHXZAA.

> **STEP 2:** New Safari users, complete the brief registration form.
> Safari subscribers, just log in.

If you have difficulty registering on Safari or accessing the online edition, please e-mail customer-service@safaribooksonline.com